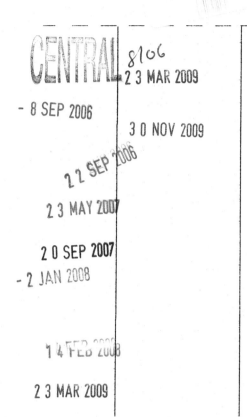

BRITAIN AND EMPIRE

Adjusting to a Post-Imperial World

L.J. BUTLER

I.B.Tauris *Publishers*
LONDON ● NEW YORK

Published in 2002 by I.B.Tauris & Co. Ltd
6 Salem Road, London W2 4BU
175 Fifth Avenue, New York, NY 10010
www.ibtauris.com

In the United States of America and Canada distributed by
St Martin's Press, 175 Fifth Avenue, New York, NY 10010

ISBN 1-86064-448-1

A full CIP record for this book is available from the British Library
A full CIP record for this book is available from the Library of Congress

Library of Congress catalog card: available

Typeset in Garamond by A. & D. Worthington, Newmarket
Printed and bound in Great Britain by MPG Books Ltd, Bodmin

CONTENTS

ILLUSTRATIONS

1   The empire mobilized: General Archibald Wavell, commander in chief
    of British forces in the Middle East, inspecting Indian troops serving in
    Egypt, early in the Second World War
    [Imperial War Museum, K3402]

2   Counterinsurgency in Malaya: a resettlement village constructed under
    the Briggs Plan, c.1952
    [Imperial War Museum, K13796]

3   The Cyprus Emergency: a British aircraft, bombed by EOKA at Nicosia
    airport, March 1956
    [PRO INF 10/111]

4   The Gold Coast general election, 1956. Before recording his vote, Dr
    Kwame Nkrumah has his thumb inked by a polling assistant
    [PRO INF 10/129]

5   Defending Britain's post-Suez Middle Eastern foothold: a Scout car
    leaving the levy camp at Dhala, Aden Protectorate, for a patrol, 1957
    [PRO INF 10/3]

6   Labour-intensive development: land terracing in the Kiambu district of
    Kenya's Central Province, completed under the Swynnerton agricultural
    plan
    [PRO INF 10/164]

7   Capital-intensive development: American visitors being shown the
    prestige Kariba Dam project in the Central African Federation, 1960
    [PRO INF 14/424]

8   Negotiating decolonization: R.A. Butler, First Secretary of State with
    responsibility for Central African affairs, meets Kenneth Kaunda and
    other North Rhodesian nationalist leaders in Lusaka, January 1963
    [PRO INF 10/392]

MAPS

ACKNOWLEDGEMENTS

I have incurred numerous debts in the course of researching and writing this book. I am particularly grateful to Dr Lester Crook of I.B. Tauris, not only for initially suggesting that I write the book, but also for his enthusiasm for the project, and for his patience and encouragement during the various stages of its completion. Special thanks go to Andrew Porter, who offered many shrewd, incisive and constructive comments on the original proposal and helped me to clarify both the scope of the book and the relationships between the various themes it attempts to explore. A book of this sort inevitably draws heavily on the scholarship of others, and I hope that the historians whose work I have incorporated will feel that my debt to them is properly acknowledged, both in the chapter notes and in the suggestions for further reading. Among the scholars who have, in many ways, and over many years, helped to shape my thinking on the problem of Britain's retreat from empire are Stephen Ashton, John Darwin, Kent Fedorowich, David Fieldhouse, Anthony Gorst, Robert Holland, Denis Judd, David Killingray, Peter Marshall, Simon Smith, Anthony Stockwell, Sarah Stockwell, Martin Thomas and Nicholas White. While they can take substantial credit for any merits the book may have, they are in no way responsible for its shortcomings. My thanks, too, to Alison Worthington, who applied her meticulous editorial skills to my typescript, and helped unravel some of its more tortuous constructions. I would also like to record my gratitude to the staffs of the Public Record Office, Kew; the British Library; the Art and Photographic Departments of the Imperial War Museum, London; the University of London Library; the Institute of Historical Research, University of London; the Library of the School of Oriental and African Studies, University of London; and the Bodleian Library, Oxford.

ABBREVIATIONS

AFPFL	Anti-Fascist People's Freedom League
BDEE	British Documents on the End of Empire
CAB	Cabinet
CDAC	Colonial Development Advisory Committee
CD & W	Colonial Development and Welfare (Acts)
CDC	Colonial Development Corporation
CO	Colonial Office
CPP	Convention People's Party
DO	Dominions Office (Commonwealth Relations Office)
EEC	European Economic Community
EFTA	European Free Trade Area
EOKA	*Ethniki Organosis Kypriaku Agonos* (National Organization of Cypriot Fighters)
GATT	General Agreement on Tariffs and Trade
ILO	International Labour Organization
IMF	International Monetary Fund
INA	Indian National Army
JICH	*Journal of Imperial and Commonwealth History*
KADU	Kenyan African Democratic Union
KANU	Kenyan African National Union
MAFF	Ministry of Agriculture, Fisheries and Food
NATO	North Atlantic Treaty Organization
NKG	New Kenya Group
NLM	National Liberation Movement (Ghana)
OHBE	*Oxford History of the British Empire*
OMOV	One Man One Vote
PRO	Public Record Office, Kew
SEATO	South-East Asia Treaty Organization
TANU	Tanganyikan African National Union
TUC	Trades Union Congress
UDI	Unilateral Declaration of Independence
UGCC	United Gold Coast Convention
UMNO	United Malays National Organization

UN   United Nations
UNIP   United National Independence Party (Zambia)
UNSCOP   United Nations Special Committee on Palestine
US   United States

INTRODUCTION

One of the most dramatic indicators of Britain's changing status in the twentieth century was the contraction and eventual demise of the British Empire. The disintegration of the British imperial system was remarkably rapid. From being the largest empire in the history of the world in the 1930s, Britain's global system amounted, by the late 1960s, to little more than a few outposts or 'points', together with a set of relationships, whose significance was increasingly difficult to measure, embodied in the Commonwealth, successor body to the empire. Moreover, Britain's external relationships seemed, by the late 1960s, to have undergone a fundamental reorientation: from being a power with truly global interests, Britain was coming to be seen as one of a number of middle-ranking powers whose interests were bound up in continuing plans for the integration of Western Europe.

Tracing the origins of the dismantling of the imperial system in chronological terms has long been a contentious issue. To some, the impact of the First World War represented so great a drain on Britain's resources that the eventual unravelling of the imperial system seemed inevitable.[1] Certainly, major changes took place between the wars in the style of imperial control employed by Britain. The self-governing components of the empire, the old settler-colonies or 'Dominions', achieved technical independence in 1931, although they remained closely bound to Britain diplomatically, militarily and economically, as well as by strong, though more nebulous ties of kinship and sentiment. Elsewhere in the empire, India, for many in Britain still the centrepiece of the imperial system, its symbolic heart, was gradually evolving towards self-government, and seemed to be set on a course similar to that already followed by the Dominions. These inter-war developments underline one of the most important characteristics of the British imperial system throughout its life: its capacity for flexibility and pragmatic adjustment to changing circumstances. What might superficially appear to be a weakening of imperial resolve could, on closer examination, be seen as embodying a sustained effort to 'streamline' the empire, to equip it to respond to new conditions and to perform new functions, without losing its overall value to Britain. Arguably, this tradition of imperial adjustment, whose pedigree stretched back at least into the late eighteenth century, made it possible for policy-makers in London to contemplate seemingly radical departures, and yet for these to disguise a fundamental continuity in imperial purpose: the safeguarding of Britain's global interests, strategic and economic. It seems indisputable that until the Second World War, and arguably beyond it, the British Empire was to a great extent taken for granted by successive British governments, regarded as a 'natural' feature of Britain's complex of overseas relationships. Its affairs had to be managed with care, employing a variety of means, and the entire structure required an ingenious approach to problems of defence. Yet for the generation of politicians and policy-makers active during this period, the importance of the imperial system was unquestioned, offering as it seemed to do both a measure and a major source of Britain's international prestige and economic stature.

To stress this capacity to absorb change is not to diminish the significance of some of the changes which affected the imperial system. For instance, with the possible exception of India and one or two other territories, Britain's highly diverse 'dependent empire' was seen by few commentators before the Second World War as being ready for anything resembling 'self-government', still less 'independence' (a term unknown in administrators' everyday discourse). For most of these territories, serious thinking on the long-term purpose of British policy, or on the scope for political development, had scarcely begun. This makes the changes in their constitutional relationship with Britain, in the 20 or so years after 1945, all the more remarkable, and underlines the fact that they were largely unforeseen.

Immediately after the Second World War, Britain had been obliged to withdraw from its most prized imperial possession, India, in circumstances which suggested that the British authorities had lost control. Similarly, in 1948, Britain surrendered its mandate over Palestine, amid conditions verging on anarchy and civil war. Almost a decade later, the independence of Ghana was quickly followed by the beginning of the sustained wave of decolonization in Africa, later described as the 'wind of change', which, within a few short years brought British colonial rule in the continent to an end. Sandwiched between these two phases of relatively intense activity was a period, commencing shortly after the war's end and continuing well into the 1950s, during which the imperial government attached great significance to its colonial possessions, seeing in them the means to achieve faster metropolitan economic stabilization. During the so-called 'Second Colonial Occupation', an attempt was made, building on wartime experiences, to promote rapid colonial economic development, ostensibly in the colonies' own interests, but with the welcome additional consequence of strengthening Britain's own economic position and recovery. In international terms, too, continuing management of a global imperial system was a means to maintain Britain's status as the world's third leading power.

But close examination of the imperial system reveals that it was always more than the sum of its parts. As was suggested in one of the most important theoretical contributions to British imperial historiography, there was, in addition to those parts of the world formally bound to Britain, a substantial group of nominally independent countries whose ties to Britain were so strong, and in which Britain enjoyed *de facto* paramountcy, that they amounted to an 'informal empire'.[2] Thus, a country such as Egypt, under formal British control for a relatively short period, continued to be under effective British influence long after it had formally achieved independence in 1922. Although it had slipped out of the orbit of formal political control, Egypt became, in many ways, more important to Britain, and to the maintenance of the imperial system, than many other components of the empire, including the often sizeable swathes of territory which constituted Britain's African colonies. In Egypt's case, the country's value to Britain was intimately linked to the vital importance of the Suez Canal in linking the metropole to Asia and Australasia. Preserving British influence in Egypt therefore became associated with a wider network of strategic and commercial interests, accounting for the large military presence Britain maintained in the country, and for Egypt's growing importance in British strategic thinking. In the Middle East generally, a fundamental problem confronting imperial managers was how to preserve this influence, making it both effective and acceptable to countries under Britain's sway. In the inter-war years, the tactic of substituting informal influence for formal control appeared to have succeeded. However, as in the rest of the imperial system, the Second World War would throw into question Britain's ability to continue to protect its interests on terms which it found acceptable. Much would depend on the possibility of maintaining workable alliances with local elite groups, a partnership potentially beneficial to either side. This, in turn, raises fundamental questions about the nature of the power Britain exercised through its global system. It has become axiomatic that a small island nation such as Britain, often lacking significant military power, could not hope to exert its influence in the world, on any long-term basis, through the crude application of force. While coercion and repression were certainly deployed at various times, in a variety of contexts, subtler techniques were needed if the empire were not to become an impossible drain on metropolitan resources.[3]

Although the term has its critics, not least among writers working within post-colonial contexts, the phenomenon of British disengagement from its dependent empire has come to be known as decolonization. At a simple level, this refers to the 'transfer of power' to sovereign, independent nation states, for example in Asia and Africa. What is striking about the British experience of decolonization is that policy-makers in London appear to have interpreted the process as representing not the end of Britain's relationship with a variety of non-European territories, but rather the beginning of a new set of relationships based on continuing close links in the diplomatic, military and economic spheres. In this sense, the historical distinction between *intention* and *outcome* becomes crucial. The post-colonial order of the late 1960s and early 1970s was not necessarily the one envisaged by those who planned and implemented the retreat from formal empire. Of central importance here is the suggestion that 'independence', as it subsequently came to be understood, was not what London had originally planned, when it first began to think seriously about the colonies' future. Nevertheless, for a variety of reasons which will be examined in this book, and responding to a new set of international conditions and conflicting pressures, London did seek to put its colonial, and wider, imperial, relationships on a new footing after the Second World War. Thus although Britain, according to this view, chose to decolonize, and often initiated the processes involved, the consequences sometimes took British policy-makers off guard.

In many instances, British attempts to modernize the character of colonial rule involved the introduction not only of constitutional reform, but also of electoral politics. In one dependent territory after another, an essentially autocratic style of government was adapted to include features of the British political system. The often startlingly volatile consequences of these constitutional experiments in turn raise questions over the extent to which Britain was able to retain overall control over the forces it had unleashed or encouraged, however unwittingly.

Related to this issue is the problem of the extent to which Britain was forced to adjust its systems of control by political developments 'at the periphery', that is, within individual territories. Was it, as many contemporary and later writers asserted, the force of nationalism which expelled Britain from its colonies? Given that economic, social and political change had been features, to varying degrees, of most of Britain's colonial territories at different stages in their association with Britain, why was it in the mid-twentieth century that these apparently gave rise to a series of mass movements, coalitions, albeit sometimes temporary ones, brought together by the overriding aim of removing British control? Could it be that the British had invited their own expulsion through the increasingly intrusive colonial policies they introduced during and after the Second World War, violating the tradition of minimizing the impact of the West on 'traditional' societies? Yet, if the British imperial system had proven to be capable of flexibility and pragmatic responses to changing circumstances in the past, why should a similar course have been any less successful after 1945?

A further theme which no discussion of imperial disintegration can ignore is the radically changing geopolitical context in which attempts to manage Britain's empire were made. Beginning with the outcome of the First World War, long-term shifts were taking place in the pattern of international relations during the twentieth century. These gathered pace after the Second World War with the formalization of ideological hostility in the Cold War. This introduced a new set of global conditions to which, once again, the British imperial system was obliged to respond and adapt. Colonial rule threatened at times to become a major issue in the Cold War, projected through new international institutions such as the United Nations, the major forum for 'superpower' rivalry for allegiance in the developing world.

Related to the question of Britain's capacity to manage the process of decolonization was the problem (for British policy-makers) that territories could not be isolated from developments in neighbouring regions: concessions granted to one colony could seldom be withheld from others in the same region without antagonizing their populations. Thus, a momentum could develop, involving far-reaching changes not anticipated, still less planned, by London. Equally, it would be unsafe to reach broad-ranging conclusions about the causes of Britain's imperial retreat based only on the experience of withdrawal from a few select territories. While useful comparisons and patterns may emerge, the diversity of the empire's components means that the scope for very different approaches to decolonization always needs to be borne in mind. Given the sheer complexity of the relationships embodied in Britain's imperial system, and the wide variety of circumstances in its many components, it seems unlikely that decolonization can safely be attributed to a single cause, any more than the earlier, dramatic expansion of European overseas rule in the later nineteenth century can be explained solely in terms of changing economic, strategic, diplomatic or political requirements.[4] As this book will attempt to demonstrate, Britain's position as a major international power was buffeted by several important shifts in the second half of the twentieth century, which combined in such a way as to require the managers of Britain's imperial system to seek new means of defending Britain's fundamental global interests. Our task, then, will be to try to assess the relative significance of the various pressures acting on British policy-makers, especially in the decades after 1939, and to explain why the particular constellation of political, diplomatic and economic circumstances which they faced had such far-reaching consequences for Britain's relations with the developing world. Underlying these problems will be the need to establish not only why Britain disengaged from its imperial system, but also why this disengagement took place when it did.

CHAPTER 1

THE IMPERIAL SYSTEM BETWEEN THE WARS

When applied to Britain's complex array of overseas interests before the Second World War, the expression 'imperial system' would be misleading if it were taken to imply that its components formed a coherent or consistent bloc. During the inter-war period, Britain's formal empire was composed of a highly varied collection of territories. Their political, economic and social development, and their cultural characteristics, could be plotted along an extremely wide spectrum. In looking for some common experience linking them all, the connection with Britain is often all that exists. But this connection could also take a wide variety of forms. The most senior members of the empire, the 'Dominions' or 'settlement colonies' constituted a distinct group. Between the wars, their sometimes ambiguous relationship with London would be clarified and given statutory form. India, long considered the most valuable 'possession', was so important in the imperial schema that it technically constituted an empire in its own right. The remainder of the dependent empire defied the taxonomer's art, being composed of around 60 colonies, protectorates and other constitutional abstractions. Beyond these three broad classifications lay an uncharted and more subtle category representing Britain's 'informal' empire, consisting of countries which, although not formally bound to the British Empire, were under varying degrees of effective influence from London. Some parts of this informal empire were far more important to Britain, in practical terms, than many of its formal possessions. Above all, it avoided the expense of direct administration by Britain, and was thought, not necessarily correctly, to be more acceptable to local populations than a more overt, formal British presence.

For successive British governments between the wars and well beyond this period, the empire was a given. For most policy-makers, managing the empire involved a set of often unspoken assumptions about Britain's interests and status in the world. These did not have to be codified to have substance or importance. For a generation of ministers and senior civil servants brought up in late Victorian and Edwardian Britain, the empire, and much of what it represented, was simply taken for granted, and its absence or disintegration was unthinkable. This was reflected in the lack of interest shown either by politicians or most of the public in issues affecting the empire. Parliamentary debates on imperial topics, especially those affecting the largely unknown

1

colonial empire, could empty the Commons of all but a few enthusiasts. Occasionally, as over India's future, the old spark of imperial rhetoric could be rekindled. But generally speaking, those responsible for managing the imperial system were untroubled by the unwelcome attentions of a British public and governing elite increasingly preoccupied with domestic issues, or with preventing another great war.

Unlike many other imperial systems of the pre-1914 world, the British Empire not only survived the First World War intact, it also greatly increased its territorial extent. The peace settlement ushered in a new age of mandates, under which responsibility for administering former German and Ottoman territory was delegated by the League of Nations to the victorious powers, chiefly Britain and France. As a result, the British Empire came to occupy almost a quarter of the world's land area, the world's largest overseas empire, and by far the most valuable. During the First World War, it had been axiomatic in British government thinking that this expansion was necessary to safeguard the security of the empire as a whole. Yet, as the inter-war years were to illustrate, a bigger empire posed greater problems of imperial defence, with Britain standing to lose more than any other power in a major conflict, at a time when the international climate was becoming increasingly uncertain, and fundamental questions were being raised about the scale of resources Britain could safely commit to defending its global interests. Against the background of clear domestic pressure for an end to conscription, the British government was keen to limit the scope for possible complications abroad. In August 1919, the War Cabinet informed the armed services that their planning should be based on the assumption that 'the British Empire will not be engaged in any great war during the next ten years'. This 'Ten-Year Rule', which became the keystone of British defence thinking, was renewed for a further ten years in 1928.

Imperial defence and 'overstretch'

In the inter-war period, British politicians habitually saw the empire, particularly the Dominions and India, as a source of strength. Important lessons had been learned by British policy-makers in the period of imperial 'crisis' immediately following the First World War. Facing simultaneous explosions of nationalist opposition in Ireland, India and Iraq at a time when the metropolitan economy, and the numbing scale of Britain's war-related debts, demanded cuts in government spending, affecting defence commitments in particular, Britain had abandoned any thought of further imperial expansion, pruned some of its responsibilities, introduced new techniques of management and explored means of conciliating nationalism. In the Middle East, this would involve a quest for pliable local collaborators and the substitution, where feasible, of informal control for direct rule. In India, it would mean limited constitutional reform. In Ireland, it led to the Anglo-Irish Treaty of 1921 and partition, which, while not solving the Irish 'problem', muted its significance in Westminster for another half century. For the remainder of the 1920s, while the other leading powers were absorbed primarily in their own domestic concerns, the British Empire could legitimately be regarded as the world's sole 'superpower'.[1] Yet this situation was secure only so long as no hostile power emerged or major war threatened Britain's global interests. It was a basic desire to preserve stability, and hence to protect its international system, that reinforced the long British diplomatic tradition of appeasing potential challengers.

Very soon after the First World War, Britain was forced to recognize that it could no longer assume an identity of interests in foreign affairs between itself and the Dominions, nor were the Dominions themselves bound by a common outlook. The Dominions were keen to assert their autonomy in defence and diplomatic matters. An early indication of this came during the Imperial War Conference of 1918, when the Dominions successfully blocked an Admiralty proposal for an imperial naval force. Similarly, Canada unilaterally withdrew the troops it had contributed to the Allied expeditionary force to Russia. The peace-making process also revealed that among the Dominions, Australia, New Zealand and South Africa had developed their own 'sub-imperial' ambitions, seen in their bids to acquire former German colonial territory in the Pacific and Southern Africa respectively. More fateful, arguably, were the circumstances surrounding Britain's decision not to renew the Anglo-Japanese alliance of 1902, the cornerstone of Britain's Far Eastern defence calculations. While Australia and New Zealand, concerned for their own security, argued that the alliance should be renewed, Canada, responding to United States pressure, opposed this.[2]

The strength of imperial bonds in the defence sphere was tested by the Chanak Crisis of 1922. Turkey refused to accept the commitments it had made under the Treaty of Sèvres (1920), under whose terms Britain appeared to have gained control of the Straits of Constantinople, and attempted to force Greece out of Asia Minor. Encouraged by Britain, the Greeks resisted, but following their retreat, the Turks turned their attention to the British forces at Chanak. Lloyd George looked to the Dominions for military support in arresting the Turkish advance, but only New Zealand's response was immediate and positive. Australia was hesitant, Canada declared that only its parliament (then in recess) could sanction military action, and South Africa, whose prime minister was on holiday, was no more forthcoming. This was an abrupt and sobering warning to Britain that it could no longer take Dominion acquiescence in its foreign policy for granted, but it also illustrated that an isolationist mood was developing in Canada and South Africa.[3] This episode not only brought an end to Lloyd George's coalition, but led his successor, Bonar Law, to declare that Britain's role was not to be 'the policeman of the world'. At the Imperial Conference in 1923, Australia and New Zealand proposed a genuinely 'imperial' foreign policy, one which would reflect the views of the Dominions.[4] Unanimous Dominion hostility to becoming embroiled in the affairs of Europe was signalled in 1925 by their refusal to underwrite the Locarno Treaty, which guaranteed the existing frontiers of Western Europe.[5] This trend was accentuated by the outcome of the 1926 Imperial Conference, after which it was clear that the Dominions would determine their own defence priorities and decide

how far they should co-operate with Britain in any future war. Between the
wars, the Dominions' own military capacity was relatively slight. The most
important contribution they made to the imperial security system was the
cruiser squadron made available by Australia, but even this remained firmly
under the Australian government's control.[6] There would be no automatic
falling into line with priorities dictated by London.

Fortuitously, the Dominions' unwillingness to make defence commitments
to Europe reflected the thinking of British military chiefs, who, throughout the
1920s, took a global, imperial view in defence planning. The British Army, for
instance, saw its major role as being to protect the frontiers of the empire,
especially in Asia, where the longstanding fear of Russian/Soviet aggression
against India persisted, leading Britain to station around a third of the army
there, and in the Middle East, in order to defend the Suez Canal and Britain's
new regional interests. Beyond this, the army's role was to sustain imperial
garrisons and to be available to colonial authorities in a policing capacity.[7] In
making its defence arrangements, however, the British government increasingly
had to consider the constraints surrounding the use of Indian contingents
outside India.[8] As nationalist sentiment grew between the wars, the Government of India became unwilling to subsidize imperial defence by paying for the
use of its troops. In 1920 the viceroy declared that the continued use of the
Indian Army in the Middle East, at Indian taxpayers' expense, might lead to 'a
complete breakdown in the political situation'.[9]

Cost emerged as a major consideration in imperial defence planning in the
1920s. The indifferent performance of the British economy, combined with
government awareness that defence spending must not be allowed to obstruct
a more interventionist social policy, demanded by the new conditions of near
democracy in Britain, dictated a climate of retrenchment.[10] Where possible,
money was saved by introducing new technologies to perform old functions.
Thus the possibilities of air power were exploited to control restive populations
in the Middle East and elsewhere. Air bombing of insurrectionists, as practised
in Iraq and elsewhere, not only saved imperial manpower, but was a conveniently discrete expression of power, less visible to metropolitan and
international critics of colonial repression. Had it not been for this new role
eagerly taken up by the Royal Air Force, Britain might have had to withdraw
from some of its newly acquired territories, for instance in the Middle East.[11]

The greatest responsibility for imperial defence continued to be borne by
the Royal Navy. In 1926, the Chiefs of Staff defined the security of the sea-
lanes as the cardinal principle of imperial defence. They recognized, however,
that Britain could not aspire to maintain fleets capable of defending both
Britain and the entire empire. The compromise policy adhered to during the
1920s was to maintain a mobile main fleet, equal in size to that of any other
power. In practice, this 'one power standard' meant that the Royal Navy should
have a strength equivalent to that of the United States. At the Washington
Naval Conference of 1921–22, Britain formally accepted naval parity in capital
ships with the USA, which in effect meant pursuing a policy of disarmament.
But it was the accompanying decision to allow the alliance with Japan to lapse

which marked a critical turning point in British defence policy, one that would have enormous implications for the future. At the 1930 London Naval Conference, the concept of parity with the US was taken further and applied to cruisers, destroyers and other types of vessel. The Admiralty had argued that Britain's requirements for cruisers exceeded those of other powers, because so much of the empire's trade depended on the security of sea routes, but US attitudes, and Britain's own growing financial difficulties, combined to thwart this aim.[12]

Political evolution and the Commonwealth

Between the wars, Britain and the Dominions came to form an elite grouping within the British Empire. Increasingly referred to as the 'British Commonwealth of Nations', a term which came into use during the First World War encapsulating the aspirations of enthusiasts for imperial federation, this grouping enjoyed a generally close, even cosy, relationship, even though there was growing evidence that on some important issues their interests diverged.[13] In response to pressure from within the Commonwealth, particularly from South Africa and the Irish Free State, Britain sought to clarify the meaning of Dominion status. The philosophically inclined former prime minister, Arthur Balfour, presided over the official deliberations which eventually produced a splendidly flexible piece of studied ambiguity, in which Dominions were defined as:

> autonomous communities within the British Empire, equal in status, in no way subordinate to one another in any aspect of their domestic or external affairs, though united by a common allegiance to the Crown, and freely associated as members of the British Commonwealth of Nations.[14]

This Balfour Definition was seen by Britain not as representing a dilution of imperial bonds, but rather as a means of strengthening them by emphasizing the equality of Britain and the Dominions and the importance of the latters' acceptance of this arrangement. The emphasis on common allegiance to the British Crown had the incidental effect of enhancing the monarchy's value to metropolitan audiences. The British government appeared optimistic that the precise form in which the Commonwealth relationship was expressed would not in any significant way affect the substance of that relationship.[15] Nevertheless, this marked the end of pre-war dreams of achieving a truly integrated Imperial Federation, centred on London, in which responsibilities, especially for defence, would be shared.

Under the Statute of Westminster (1931), the independent status of the Dominions, defined at the Imperial Conference of 1926, was given formal recognition. Under this legislation, the relationship between the Dominion and imperial parliaments was resolved: the Dominions were now free to amend their own constitutions without reference to Westminster, and Britain surrendered its authority to interfere with Dominion legislation. Even more significant, arguably, was the fact that the Dominions gained autonomy in conducting their own foreign policies: henceforth, a declaration of war by Britain would not automatically apply to the Dominions.

These provisions promised to soothe the constitutional ripples prominent in domestic politics in the Dominions since the war. The position of the Irish Free State remained anomalous: the unthinkable was already being speculated upon – could a republic (which Ireland appeared set to become) remain a member of the Commonwealth, a conundrum which would assume major practical significance after the Second World War. It was the flexibility and ambiguity of Dominion status which made the concept so appealing to the politicians of some of the countries to which it applied. It made it possible for them to maintain an official position of support for the empire, through the common bond of loyalty to the Crown, while also enabling them to assert their political maturity and autonomous interests. This was particularly important in the more 'volatile' Dominions, South Africa and the Irish Free State. Else-where, for example in Australia and New Zealand, relatively little time was spent agonizing over the precise nuances and implications of the statements of 1926 and 1931.[16] In reality, during the inter-war period the Dominions were all well aware of the important practical features of their links with Britain, especially in the areas of economics, emphasized during the Depression, and defence, for which Britain remained at least nominally responsible. Added to these, in the cases of Canada and the Australasian Dominions, dependence on emigration from Britain was a further important cementing influence, even when it provoked objections from local trade unions fearful for their members' job security, or, in the case of South Africa, triggered Afrikaner suspicion of the potential for reinforced imperial influence.[17] Less easy to measure, but arguably equally significant, were the cohesive effects of 'race sentiment' on that part of the Dominions' population descended from British migrants. Replenished by continued inter-war migration, and strengthened by the empire's post-war expansion and inter-war anxieties about the future, this was founded chiefly on assumptions of racial superiority, and was a factor suffi-ciently important to demand the attention of government in all four 'senior' Dominions.[18]

For Britain, too, the cultivation of a distinctive 'imperial' culture was an important aim between the wars. The potential of wireless broadcasting for reinforcing intra-imperial ties was recognized at an early stage in the life of the new medium. Despite the general mood of retrenchment, funding was made available for the BBC to launch its Empire Service in 1932, the year George V made the first royal Christmas broadcast.[19] Sport, too, appeared to be another fruitful area for the consolidation of imperial bonds, with the first British Empire Games being held in Canada in 1930.

Imperial economic integration and its problems

For Britain, the inter-war years saw the beginnings of an important phase of economic readjustment. While the foundations were being laid for booming new economic sectors, often geared more to the metropolitan market, the traditional 'staple' industries which had been so important to nineteenth-century growth now faced structural crisis arising from technological backwardness, under-investment and the development of overseas competition in a contracting world market. These conditions provided fertile ground for enthusiasts for imperial solutions to Britain's economic problems. This period witnessed greater attempts than ever before to integrate the imperial economic system. Against the background of worldwide economic instability, economic nationalism and attempts by some countries to pursue policies of autarky, steps were taken to strengthen the cohesion of the British Empire as a global economic bloc. Particularly after the onset of the Depression in 1929, concerted attempts were made to use imperial economic policy to assist the metropolitan economy. The structures created during the 1930s especially, and reinforced during the Second World War, would survive well into the 1950s. Arguably, the metropolitan outlook which had brought them into being, and which was in turn bolstered by them, proved even more long-lasting.

One of the most important developments in imperial economic policy between the wars was the introduction of a discriminatory system of tariff protection, designed to promote increased trade within the empire at a time when the volume of world trade was shrinking. This policy of Imperial Preference had been central to Joseph Chamberlain's schemes of tariff reform and had finally been introduced in 1919, when preferences were introduced on some imports from the empire into Britain. In the following year, some 26 colonial governments had introduced reciprocal preferences favouring British exports.[20] During the 1920s, with Britain's competitive position slipping, the cause of tariff protection was championed by Leopold Amery, who linked it to the promotion of closer imperial economic bonds. But when calls for full Imperial Preference were tested at the general election of 1923, they cost the Conservatives the election and demonstrated that pre-war fears of more expensive food had not dissipated.

The erosion of traditional free trade was taken much further after the onset of the Depression in 1929. The National Government introduced import tariffs in 1931 as a temporary device pending the construction of more durable arrangements. In 1932 the Import Duties Act introduced a general tariff of 10 per cent, but the Dominions were given temporary, and the colonies permanent, exemption from this.

At the Imperial Economic Conference held in Ottawa during the summer of 1932, various reciprocal trade agreements were negotiated. Britain succeeded in obtaining increased preferences for itself, which helped to increase the volume of trade between Britain and the empire during the 1930s. Ottawa demonstrated, however, that there was no general taste among the Dominions for a fully fledged imperial trading system: what the conference achieved was, in effect, a series of bilateral agreements. Between 1930 and 1938, British exports to the empire rose by over 6 per cent, while imports from the empire grew rather more, almost 9 per cent between the late 1920s and the late 1930s, but these figures fell far short of what had been hoped for by British ministers. Arguably the deals struck at Ottawa were of greater benefit to the Dominions than to Britain, whose consumers were forced to pay higher prices for imported goods than would have obtained under a free market.[21] Nevertheless, all the Dominions, including Canada (despite its close commercial ties with its southern neighbour) depended heavily on British markets for their produce, and this pattern was only strengthened as the economic nationalism of other countries closed off alternative markets. Although the empire grew in importance to Britain as a market in the 1930s, an important contrast to the period before 1930 was that up to the outbreak of the Second World War, Britain maintained a balance of payments deficit on visible trade with the empire. This was necessary in order to allow member countries to meet their own debt obligations and pay for invisible exports. To profit from invisibles, Britain had to accept the visible trading deficit. Moreover, it could be argued that Britain had little option but to offer the Dominions preferential trading rights if it wanted the latter to earn sterling and so be able to pay their debts.[22] Although it probably contributed to the restoration of business confidence, which was vital to Britain's economic recovery in the later 1930s, Imperial Preference failed to fulfil the hopes of its traditional champions, and soon alternative strategies to secure a revival of trade were being discussed, including new bilateral trade agreements with countries outside the empire, and most importantly through negotiations with Washington, culminating in the Anglo-American Trade Agreement of 1938, though most of the preferences agreed in 1932 survived in one form or another into the 1960s.

However, for the British government, the Ottawa Conference had a political significance almost as great as its economic importance. Neville Chamberlain, the Chancellor of the Exchequer, believed that the conference had done much to convince the Dominions of the advantages of the Commonwealth connection, and to reinforce that connection. The danger, looming since the late nineteenth century, that Canada would be drawn inexorably into the United States' economic system, had, commented Stanley Baldwin, been averted.[23]

Yet Ottawa also demonstrated the Dominions' ability to extract concessions from Britain, raising questions about the 'complementarity' of British and Dominion economic interests. The Dominions were simply unwilling to play the role of permanent suppliers of food and raw materials to the mother country: rather, they were keen to build up their own secondary industries as a way of diversifying their economies. It is revealing that soon after the worst phase of the Depression had ebbed, the Dominions too were seeking to develop their trade links beyond the empire, although Britain remained their biggest market.[24] For its part, Britain, fearing the likely effects on its own farming industry, was reluctant to give the Dominions exclusive privileged access to the home agricultural market.[25]

Within Britain, the Ottawa Agreements had important political repercussions, splitting the government. The Samuelite Liberals, clinging to the abandoned orthodoxy of free trade, feared that Imperial Preference would ultimately damage Britain's trade with the rest of the world, an important consideration given that the greater part of Britain's overseas trade was with non-empire countries. A declining voice within government, the Liberals pinned their hopes on the World Economic Conference, due to convene in London in June 1933, at which it was hoped a general lowering of trade barriers could be achieved in the interests of reviving international trade. In the event, the conference revealed only that most governments were determined to cling on to the protective arrangements they had already constructed.[26] The attitude of the US government, anxious above all to restore domestic economic stability, proved decisive. Nevertheless, from Washington's point of view, the Ottawa Agreements remained as a barrier to the recovery of world trade, and their future would become a major issue in Anglo-American relations, especially during the Second World War.

One of the advantages of colonial rule was that Britain could, to a great extent, shape economic activity within the colonies in its own interests. This normally involved the maintenance of 'open' trading regimes, which barred the colonies from imposing tariffs on metropolitan exports. While helping to safeguard the market shares of British manufacturers, this also operated to block the diversification of the colonial economies into industrial production, although this was seen as part of the 'natural' complementarity of the British and colonial economies.[27] The Ottawa Agreements were applied by Britain to the colonial empire. The colonies received preferences in British and Dominion markets, and were obliged to provide preferences in return. However, since they were already exempted from protective tariffs under the Import Duties Act, the effects were not great. One important consequence of Imperial Preference for the colonies was to spur the development of manufacturing industry in some territories, particularly in the Far East. The introduction of tariffs shielded producers in Hong Kong and elsewhere from Japanese competition. This in turn raised concerns that 'artificially' stimulated colonial industries might displace British imports, not only in their home markets but also, conceivably, in Britain itself.[28]

Another device introduced by Britain in the early 1930s to limit Japanese and other foreign penetration of colonial markets was the quota system, applied particularly to textiles. Quotas on imports from a particular source did not breach the 'open-door' commercial treaties which applied to some colonies. They were useful to British exporters in colonies where Japan had already secured a significant foothold, but elsewhere, the scheme's impact was less noticeable.

Another Depression-related innovation followed Britain's departure from the Gold Standard in 1931, a move intended to achieve financial stability and help restore international confidence in sterling. The Dominions (except Canada), the colonies and several countries outside the empire pegged their currencies to the pound, thereby creating the Sterling Bloc, which served Britain's principal aim of regaining and developing financial influence. The bloc, which came to be the most important inter-war economic grouping, was composed of countries who depended heavily on the British market, conducted most of their trade in sterling, and held their currency reserves either partly or fully in sterling. In turn, the British government's concern to keep the voluntary members of the bloc loyal, by maintaining their confidence in sterling, influenced domestic economic policy in Britain during the 1930s, by underlining the importance of balanced budgets and financial restraint.[29] During the 1930s, the empire became increasingly attractive to British investors. This was partly because the Dominions and colonies had a good record of paying interest and sinking fund liabilities, at a time when numerous foreign governments had problems in this respect.[30] A growing proportion of Britain's overseas investments would be made in the empire. In turn, the empire relied ever more heavily on the London money markets when raising loans. This affected the Dominions above all, for whom Britain remained the most important source of development capital. The Sterling Bloc, even more perhaps than the system of Imperial Preference, was seen by British policy-makers as a substantial expression of Britain's continuing role as a global power, offering the means to reclaim at least some of the economic power lost to the United States as a result of the First World War. The depth of the US recession after 1929, coupled with the Sterling Bloc's relative success, reinforced this optimistic assessment of Britain's international financial prospects.[31]

In addition to introducing preferential tariff regimes, the British government sought to increase demand for imperial produce within Britain, chiefly through the Empire Marketing Board, established in 1926 to conduct market research and advertise imports from the empire. This experiment achieved only limited success, perhaps being better known for its patronage of poster artists and early documentary film-makers. The Board was, ironically, a victim of retrenchment during the Depression, being dissolved in 1932, although it was succeeded in 1937 by an equally unsuccessful version catering for the colonial empire.[32]

The inter-war period witnessed a transport revolution which had enormous implications for the cohesion of the empire. Above all, the development of air transport promised to shrink what were still formidably long, and potentially vulnerable, maritime arteries. The military possibilities of air power were soon to be realized, from Iraq to Afghanistan. Although still the preserve of the wealthy few, civilian air travel also offered huge savings in time. The British government appreciated its potential and determined to participate in its development, culminating in the creation of Imperial Airways.

A combination of concern about stubbornly high domestic unemployment levels after the First World War, and a broader dream of strengthening Britain's bonds with empire, led the British government to encourage emigration from Britain to the empire. The 1922 Empire Settlement Act offered financial help to those emigrating to the Dominions. With what proved to be unwarranted optimism, the British government continued, until the onset of the Depression, to see emigration as a panacea to metropolitan difficulties.[33] Although the 1922 Act was renewed in 1937, the government's emigration policy was a disappointment: during the worst years of the Depression, more people entered Britain than left it.

India and the challenge of nationalism

Britain's determination to consolidate the strength of the British Empire following the First World War involved an attempt to place relations with India on a new, secure footing. During 1917, in order to maintain Indian loyalty to the war effort and to pre-empt the growth of hostile nationalism at a time when British military resources were preoccupied, the Secretary of State for India, Edwin Montagu, had set out the goal of responsible government for India within the British Empire. Montagu later consulted the viceroy, Lord Chelmsford, and between them, in 1918, they produced a report on India's political future. This envisaged a lengthy preparatory period, during which Indians would be drawn into the administration of the country, in increasingly self-governing institutions. Britain was confident that it would remain in control over this evolutionary process. The 1919 Government of India Act, which embodied Britain's aims, introduced the principle of dyarchy, in which Indians were given a considerable role in government at a provincial level, leaving Britain responsible for central government, above all for those areas such as security and finance, which reinforced the existence of the Raj. Central to these reforms was the British belief that local, Indian affairs could safely be demarcated from larger, imperial issues, and that dyarchy would largely satisfy Indian aspirations, enabling Britain to concentrate on those matters pertaining to India's value to the imperial system.[34] Introduced at a time when nationalist sentiment was running high, aggravated by episodes of repression, particularly the Amritsar Massacre of April 1919, constitutional reform was partly an attempt to win Indian goodwill, since it was becoming increasingly clear to London that continued reliance on force to maintain rule in India was impracticable.

The 1919 'Montagu–Chelmsford' reforms had important consequences for the character of Indian politics. An ever-widening range of groups came to understand that the defence and maintenance of their interests hinged on successful participation in the new political structures created at provincial level. The seeds of a democratic system were sown, with approximately one-tenth of the adult male population being enfranchised. This promoted a political fabric in which winning elections became a major concern, and this in turn impacted on the nature of Indian political organizations. Most impressive of all was the reorganization after 1920 of Congress as a truly nationwide, mass-based party, with a structure shadowing that of the Raj at provincial, district and village level.[35] Under Gandhi's influence, Indian nationalism appeared to acquire a moral ascendancy over the Raj which the British found novel and perplexing, and which cast them in the role of oppressors devoid of legitimacy. By eschewing violence, though not always successfully, and by deploying weapons such as strikes, demonstrations and commercial boycotts, Congress won sympathy in the wider international arena.[36]

Although Indian nationalism suffered its own set-backs and crises between the wars, it obliged the British to revise some of their basic assumptions about India's future. Although increasingly anachronistic, long-held prejudices about the inherently fractured nature of Indian society persisted, reinforcing a British belief that Congress was an 'artificial' entity, and that communal and status divisions precluded the development of an authentic nationalist movement.[37] Although Britain was keen to avoid potentially expensive (and increasingly embarrassing) confrontations with Indian nationalism, it still harboured a profound reluctance to be seen to be making political concessions under duress. From the British point of view, a fundamental problem with the constitutional arrangements introduced in 1919 was that, instead of encouraging the growth of a class of 'responsible' elected Indian politicians, dyarchy had fostered a greater interest in working the new electoral machinery. The Simon Commission, created by Baldwin in 1927 to review the Montagu–Chelmsford reforms, concluded in its 1930 report that by trying to preserve a unitary Indian constitution, the Raj had undermined its own position by conjuring nationalist opposition at the all-India level. More useful, for Britain's purposes, would be to capitalize on provincial diversity, making the provinces the effective focus of Indian political activity. This, coupled with financial devolution to the provinces, would lay the foundations for a federal structure for India.

Meanwhile, in an attempt to forestall a potentially dangerous conflict with Congress, the viceroy, Lord Irwin, announced in 1929 that Britain's aim for India was Dominion status. This declaration seemed to reflect a strengthening bi-partisan consensus on India's future in Britain, a consensus that was not seriously challenged by the tirades of Conservative 'die-hards', coalescing around Winston Churchill, who found in resistance to concessions to Indian nationalism a useful theme on which to criticize the British government of which he was no longer part.[38]

Britain's last major initiative in handling Indian affairs before the outbreak of war came with the Government of India Act of 1935. This built upon the Montagu–Chelmsford reforms by extending dyarchy to full provincial self-government. A federation was also provided for, which would bring together the provinces of British India (approximately two-thirds of the sub-continent) and the princely states. This device, which failed to take shape because of the princes' own reluctance, was intended to preserve in British hands control over key policy issues such as defence and foreign affairs, and over a large portion of Indian public finances, while introducing a system of government which could plausibly be depicted as responsible.[39] By creating a federal legislature which included not only greater communal representation but also representatives of the Indian princes, the British hoped to prevent Congress securing control of the organs of central government, while encouraging groups naturally inclined towards conservatism as a corrective to any Congress drift towards radicalism.[40] It was thought in London that implementing the federal system would be a lengthy process, during which the Raj would continue to operate the most important levers of power, and retain responsibility for the rights of minorities, especially the Muslims, while nationalism would be distracted by the opportunities created by provincial self-government. In those provinces where Congress came to power, the exercise of governmental responsibility was expected to create tensions within the movement and detract from its 'all-India' pretensions.[41]

Although the 1935 Act could be seen as part of a long-term process of disengagement, it could also be interpreted as an attempt by Britain to reassert its fundamental interests by reinforcing India's role within the imperial system, especially in the diplomatic and defence spheres. The emphasis in the Act on provincial responsible government was in effect a device to ensure that, should Congress ever achieve control over India's central government, it would find its freedom to manoeuvre constrained by powerful countervailing forces operating at the local level. Consolidation, not retreat, appeared to be Britain's central purpose. Provided that nationalism could be 'tamed' in this way, there seemed every prospect that India's dependence on Britain for capital, security and administrative expertise, along with the more nebulous bonds inevitably arising from nearly two centuries of interaction, would enable Britain at some stage in the future to guide India towards Dominion status, without any fundamental British interests being jeopardized. Meanwhile, the transfer of responsibility for many day-to-day issues to Indian politicians would free the Raj from nationalist criticism, and allow the irritations generated by routine administration to be given a more diffuse focus.[42]

Beneath the day-to-day business of politics and the immediate implementation of British policy, the relationship between Britain and India was undergoing some fundamental changes throughout the inter-war period. The long-prized economic ties between the two countries shifted significantly after the First World War. Obliged for the sake of wartime and post-war political stability to grant India greater financial and economic autonomy, Britain soon found that indigenous Indian industry was developing and posing vigorous competition to British exporters, particularly of cotton textile goods (for which India had been the largest single market before 1914). The 1935 Act included a number of safeguards designed to protect British economic interests in India from possible discriminatory action by a future Congress-led central government. Between the wars, Congress had been espousing increasingly nationalistic economic policies, which would have reserved key industries to Indian control. Nevertheless, it seemed to many British businessmen that their interests were being sacrificed by the British authorities in the hope of assuaging Congress. Although Indian industrialization eroded British exporters' market share, it also created opportunities for exporters of more sophisticated products.[43] This argument would be deployed during the Second World War by those advocates of industrialization in the colonial empire. In the field of finance, however, Britain was determined to retain control. In practical terms, the ability to manage India's currency, in the interests of supporting the value of sterling, was arguably more important to Britain than trade as such, desirable though the latter continued to be to Britain's hard-pressed staple industries.

Similarly, it became evident from the 1920s onwards that India would no longer be able to provide Britain with a large and cheap army for deployment wherever imperial interests required. During the 1930s, the long-awaited modernization of the Indian Army began.[44] For the first time, Indian forces were to be equipped with their own air power and artillery, and their role was no longer to provide an imperial reserve. However, this process of re-equipping the army was expensive, and Indian political opinion, increasingly vocal in the legislature in Delhi, had to be deferred to by Britain. Accordingly, it was agreed that London would meet much of the cost of Indian rearmament, a decision which helped to reverse the financial relationship between Britain and India by the end of the Second World War.[45] Nevertheless, during the 1930s, British control over the Government of India's financial policies ensured that 'sound finance' prevailed, that the Home Charges (the military and administrative expenses of the Government of India in Britain) continued to be paid, and that the Indian economy continued to help stabilize sterling and Britain's balance of payments.[46] Therefore although the Indian economy had become much less complementary to that of Britain, compared to the 'High Noon' of the Raj before the First World War, it still served metropolitan interests in important ways. A fundamental aim of future British planning for India would be to ensure that, even if India's constitutional status changed, as many of the benefits of imperial rule (to Britain) as possible would be preserved. This helps to explain Britain's continuing robust attitude towards Indian nationalism on the eve of the Second World War.[47]

Although the federal system envisaged in 1935 was not implemented, provincial autonomy did proceed following the elections of 1937, fought under an enlarged franchise: this in itself could not have been predicted during the First World War.[48] These elections gave Congress control initially of seven provinces, and all the benefits and disadvantages accompanying responsibility for day-to-day government at a local level. But the elections also demonstrated that communal separatism was not yet a major factor in India's politics. The Muslim League managed to win only a quarter of the seats allocated to Muslims, although experience of life under Congress provincial ministries helped confirm many Muslims in their fears about a Hindu-dominated central government.[49] In this field, as in so many others, it would be the Second World War that created opportunities for decisive change.

In Britain, a vocal but unrepresentative section of the Conservative Party, led by Winston Churchill, regarded the 1935 Act as a betrayal of a cherished imperial vision and an unwarranted abdication of British responsibility in the face of nationalist agitation. In reality, Britain was attempting to repeat the strategy it had unveiled in 1919, creating openings for groups which it hoped would become useful political allies, and channelling the energies of political opponents, especially Congress, into the 'safer' and more containable arena of provincial politics. Although it has been tempting to discern a clear, uninterrupted progression from the Montagu Declaration to India's eventual independence 30 years later, closer examination reveals that Britain's inter-war initiatives were intended to reassert imperial control over India, to re-establish the Raj on the basis of new alliances with like-minded collaborators.[50] Precisely when India would achieve Dominion status under the 1935 constitution was a question shrouded in ambiguity as the 1930s drew to a close. Indian nationalism appeared to have been successfully blunted and there was little to suggest that, scarcely more than a decade after the 1935 Act, India would be rent by insurmountable communal tensions, leading to violence, partition and the collapse of Britain's long-term plans for the sub-continent. As in so many aspects of imperial life, it was the Second World War that transformed both the internal political situation in India and Britain's capacity to deal with that situation.

The Middle East

The new empire in the Middle East which Britain acquired after the First World War significantly increased Britain's overseas responsibilities. At the San Remo Conference of 1920, former Ottoman territory in the Middle East was distributed between Britain and France in the form of mandates of the League of Nations, generally against the wishes of the Arab populations affected. At last, the nineteenth-century vision of a continuous swathe of empire stretching from Suez to Singapore had been achieved, yet uppermost in the minds of policy-makers in London was the problem of how these new regional interests were to be paid for, and how the twin aims of protecting the security of imperial communications and supplies of oil, while preserving the goodwill of local populations, could be reconciled.[51]

In the early post-war period, there was a tendency among British policy-makers to assume that challenges to regional security, for example from heightened nationalism, could be dealt with by the effective application of military force ('War Imperialism'). But this view, in turn, was based on the mistaken assumption that the wartime pattern of imperial co-operation would continue, and that defending the enlarged empire would be a shared enterprise. According to one point of view, championed by the post-war Foreign Secretary, Lord Curzon, since territory in the Middle East had been acquired chiefly to strengthen the defence of India, then logically the Government of India should contribute to its upkeep.[52] However, this argument was difficult to sustain at a time when Britain was attempting to conciliate moderate nationalist opinion in India by introducing limited constitutional reform. The Dominions were no more willing than the Government of India to contribute more to imperial defence, and the British public, wearied by total war, seemed equally reluctant to subsidize artificially inflated defence budgets.[53]

The dangers inherent in seeking to impose in the Middle East the kind of highly centralized administration the British had developed in India were made startlingly clear by the rebellion which gripped Mesopotamia in 1920. This was eventually brought under control, but it brought into question the wisdom of 'war imperialism'. Practical considerations suggested that the sensible course would be to revert to earlier, indirect, styles of imperial control, and to form durable alliances with local rulers, thereby reducing the direct costs of administration borne by Britain to a minimum. It was for this reason that the Secretary of State for War, Winston Churchill, favoured deals with the Hashemite princes Feisal and Abdullah, and their installation as the rulers of Iraq and Transjordan respectively.

Palestine, valued by Britain as a defensive buffer for the Suez Canal Zone, in addition to being a key component of the overland route to India, was an important exception to the new preference for indirect control. Here, commitments made in the Balfour Declaration (1917), promising British support for the Zionist goal of a Jewish National Home, precluded government through an Arab ruler, and a 'colonial'-style administration was created, answerable to the slightly bemused Colonial Office in London. This more conventional form of direct administration would expose Britain to unwelcome pressures during the inter-war period, as communal tensions escalated and the British found themselves attempting to maintain peace between the Arab and Jewish populations of Palestine.[54]

Nevertheless, in its extensive new sphere of 'informal' empire, Britain was broadly successful between the wars in finding local rulers enthusiastic to collaborate, ranging from the monarchies of Egypt and Iraq to the tribal leaders of the Arabian Peninsula. Ruling 'indirectly' through them, Britain was able to run its Middle Eastern empire most economically.[55] Nevertheless, British policy-makers had to be aware of the growth of pan-Islamic ideas in the region in the wake of the First World War. Their response was to evince a moderate sympathy for Arab nationalism, on the assumption that it need not necessarily conflict with wider imperial interests.[56]

Between the Treaty of Lausanne (1923) and the later 1930s, when rivalry between the great powers was abeyant, Britain could enjoy a period of unchallenged regional hegemony.[57] Apart from its well-established strategic importance to the imperial system and the route to India and the Far East, the Middle East was increasingly prized by Britain as a potential source of oil. Before the Second World War, the region produced little more than one-twentieth of the world's supply, yet Britain proved to be particularly keen to maintain its influence in territories where oil had been discovered, or where reserves were thought likely to exist. In the face of strong US and French pressure, Britain had been obliged to give up any pretensions to solitary control over the Middle East's oil wealth, but the need to ensure the safety of production facilities and the vital pipelines to the Mediterranean were an additional reason for London to seek friendly relations with the Arab world.[58]

In 1930, Britain agreed that Iraq would become independent in 1932. This enabled Britain to reduce its military strength in the country in exchange for an alliance and a new military base. There was no question, in London's view, of allowing Iraq's changed status to have any substantive effect on British interests: rather, it was assumed that considerable informal influence over the country would remain.

But the core of Britain's Middle Eastern empire was Egypt. Occupied 'temporarily' by Britain in 1882, the country had been made a protectorate following the outbreak of war in 1914. Its critical importance to British policy-makers lay first in the Suez Canal, the vital link between the empire's eastern and western halves, and second in the deeply held (and longstanding) conviction that control of the region between the Nile and the Persian Gulf ensured the security of the western approaches to India. After the First World War, these assumptions were as firmly entrenched as ever. If anything, the strategic importance of Suez seemed even greater, especially once Japanese naval power increased the Royal Navy's need to be able to reinforce the Far East quickly via the Canal.[59] In 1919, however, local resentment at increased wartime British interference and the operations of the war economy, together with fears that Egypt might be subsumed under colonial rule, sparked serious local disorders and an intensification of nationalist feeling, symbolized by the growth of the mass Wafd movement.

The veteran empire-builder Lord Milner, sent to Egypt to investigate, recommended measures to reconcile British interests with Egyptian nationalism. If Britain could deny other powers influence over Egypt, he reasoned, there was no need to obstruct the country's autonomy, that is, 'the appearance of power could be conceded without its substance being lost'.[60] In 1922, under the Allenby Declaration, the country was awarded a limited degree of independence. But effective British control was ensured by the so-called 'reserved points', issues which Britain signalled were not negotiable. Among these were defence and foreign policy, and the Suez Canal.[61] Yet this policy required tact on the part of those responsible for its administration, if Egyptian sentiment were not to be further inflamed. Unfortunately, Britain's High Commissioner in Egypt in the later 1920s, Lord Lloyd, took a robust line on the importance of impressing the local population with the reality of British power. His highly 'imperial' style seemed at odds with London's preference for a more discreet expression of the reality of British influence.[62] Nevertheless, nominally independent Egypt was expected to maintain a very special relationship with Britain, shaping its foreign policy in accordance with London's 'advice', and enabling Britain to continue to use the country as a military base.

By the mid-1930s, as Mussolini's Italy strengthened its military presence in both Libya and East Africa, the need for Britain to enjoy security in the Suez Canal, and in the vast desert expanses to its west, was underlined. The Anglo-Egyptian Treaty of 1936 tied Egypt into Britain's regional system through an alliance. In return for withdrawing its advisers, replacing its High Commissioner with an ambassador and promising to withdraw its armed forces from Cairo and Alexandria once new facilities in the Canal Zone were ready, Britain secured a 20-year military pact with the Egyptian government.[63] Reinforcing these arrangements was the presence of a substantial British garrison.

The deteriorating international climate of the later 1930s had major implications for Britain's position in the Middle East. The failure of Britain and France to reach agreement with Mussolini's Italy over the latter's invasion of Ethiopia in 1935, and an apparent increase in Italian belligerence generally, forced Britain to look to its own security arrangements in the Middle East. Unfortunately, this coincided with events in Europe and the Far East which required a reappraisal of British strategic thinking and resulted in a contraction in the defence resources available for the Middle East. To complicate matters further, the worsening situation in Nazi Germany had triggered an increase in Jewish immigration into Palestine, aggravating the already heightened communal tension in the mandate.[64] The British had sought to maintain an uneasy balance by sanctioning the growth of distinct communal authorities in Palestine, the Jewish Agency and the Supreme Muslim Council. These arrangements could not survive the strains imposed by a 12-fold increase in Jewish immigration combined with the inability of the British authorities to create a workable legislature involving both communities.

In 1936, mounting Arab frustration erupted in a large-scale rebellion. Because Palestine was second in importance only to Egypt in British calculations, the Arab Rising, which continued until 1939, was profoundly dangerous to Britain's wider Middle Eastern interests. In the event of war with Italy, and aggression towards either the Eastern Mediterranean or the Red Sea, Palestine would become a major transit base for Indian troops. It was also vital because of the Haifa oil pipeline.[65] For the British, the revolt was serious not only because of the military strain it placed upon imperial resources, at its height tying down 18 battalions of the British Army. There was concern also that sympathy for the Palestinian Arabs might affect the attitudes of fellow Muslims in India and elsewhere. Britain responded to the Arab rebellion by creating a Royal Commission chaired by Lord Peel. In its 1937 report, this commission proposed that Palestine should be partitioned into autonomous Arab and Jewish regions, with Britain retaining its overall mandated responsibility for the territory. Although this appeared to represent official acceptance by Britain of the Zionist case, it was quickly eclipsed during 1939 by Britain's more pressing need to secure Arab goodwill in the event of war. In its 1939 White Paper on Palestine, Britain courted the Arab majority by explicitly rejecting a Jewish state in Palestine, and by clamping down on Jewish immigration.

Between 1936 and the outbreak of war, Britain attempted to safeguard its Middle Eastern position by seeking new allies, and by trying to identify co-operative 'moderates'. A further characteristic of British policy in these last years of peace was a willingness to transfer power to local rulers. Practical considerations underpinned a growing emphasis in London on securing whole-hearted Arab support for Britain, and removing any sources of Arab grievance which could be removed. During 1938 and 1939, it was an axiom of British strategic planning that in the event of war with the Axis powers, an attack would be made on Italian interests in the Eastern Mediterranean. Britain's willingness to conciliate Arab feeling was not unconditional, however. In the case of Palestine, not only was the local Arab leadership sent into exile, but it was emphasized by London that self-rule, scheduled to be achieved after a non-negotiable ten-year period, would be circumscribed by a treaty designed to safeguard British economic and strategic requirements.[66]

The colonial empire: 'trusteeship' and 'development'

The remainder of the 'dependent empire', the 60 or so territories constituting, in common parlance, 'the colonies', offered a bewildering range of sizes, political arrangements, cultural tradition and ethnic composition. In some cases, individual colonies embodied a similar degree of diversity. It has been fairly said that any unity which cemented this collection of polities was provided by the thin veneer of British administration.[67] During the 1920s, British colonial policy was characterized by an absence of any sense of urgency. Before the Second World War, there was nothing to suggest that Britain was keen to accelerate the progress of the colonies towards full self-government.[68] The fundamental assumption shaping British policy-makers' attitudes was that even though colonial rule would evolve and adapt over time, this was a process over which Britain would retain control, principally because in most colonies, unlike India, there was no force of nationalism yet capable of offering a serious challenge to British rule. As far as British colonial Africa was concerned, this certainly appeared to be the case. Yet, however much policy-makers might have been preoccupied by the problems posed by settler communities in East and Central Africa, an embryonic discussion on African political development was already emerging.

Just as imperial expansion continued in the early post-war years, so colonial rule was to become more effective and meaningful, in contrast to the pre-war period, when British rule was in many cases largely notional. In theory, each colony remained a distinct constitutional entity, and was supposed to adhere to a regime of financial self-sufficiency, avoiding subventions from the metropolitan Exchequer. Although the colonial state's activities were circumscribed by a lack of finance and personnel between the wars, its presence was increasingly felt by local populations. Financial considerations and the tiny numbers of administrators constituting colonial governments dictated that Britain's style of colonial rule would be cautious and dependent on the collaboration of local elites, whose goodwill was essential, and through whom Britain generally sought to rule 'indirectly'. Gathering taxes and maintaining 'law and order' represented the bulk of most administrators' work. According to the concept of the 'dual mandate', Britain, like the other colonial powers, had two major responsibilities arising from its rule over colonies. First, it had a duty to protect the interests of the colonial populations; secondly, it had a duty to the rest of the world to make sure that colonial economic resources were exploited for the world's benefit.[69]

Before the Second World War, there was a growing recognition among colonial administrators, drawing especially on experience in Africa, that many of the problems confronting particular colonies were broadly similar, and might be tackled in a co-ordinated way. One practical outcome of this was reorganization within the Colonial Office, with the creation of 'subject' departments, handling broad themes such as economic policy, and the appointment of specialist advisers on problems such as education, labour and health.[70] Nevertheless, the idea that each colonial government was autonomous and distinct remained very strong, especially with traditionalists in the Colonial Office.[71] A debate on whether the initiative in colonial policy should come from London or from the colonial governments would continue long into the Second World War. Following the publication of the Warren Fisher report on the Colonial Service in 1930, the first tentative steps were taken towards the creation of a unified colonial administrative service. Nevertheless, longstanding traditions of administrative particularism proved difficult to dislodge, and each colonial government remained a constitutionally separate entity.

One of the central concepts of inter-war British colonial rule, as it affected Africa, was indirect rule, a body of theory derived from the experiences of Lord Lugard as colonial governor in Northern Nigeria (1912–19). This was based on the notion of administering colonial populations through indigenous agencies ('chiefs' and 'Native Authorities'), enjoying legal and financial power. Not only did such a system obviate large, costly complements of expatriate administrators (fewer than 8,000 officials staffed the mainstream apparatus of British colonial Africa in the late 1930s), it also had a respectable imperial pedigree, having been employed in the Indian princely states and elsewhere.[72] Lugard's ideas, enshrined in *The Dual Mandate in British Tropical Africa* (1922), reflected a belief in Britain's self-appointed role as 'trustee' of the 'less developed' peoples, supervisor of the gradual process by which they would achieve a 'higher' stage of development. At a time when most African populations were still regarded as being 'primitive', caution seemed far preferable to an artificial acceleration of social and political development.[73] An important expression of this outlook came in 1923, when the Colonial Secretary, the Duke of Devonshire, famously declared that Kenya was primarily an African country, in which the interests of the African population were paramount. This infuriated the colony's white settler population, who felt that London had betrayed them. Over the next 30 years, Kenya's settlers would strive to consolidate their hold over the territory's administrative structures, but the Devonshire Declaration stood as a reminder of an earlier imperial commitment, one which could not easily be discarded. One practical reflection of racial assumptions at this time was the absence of Africans in senior posts in colonial civil services. In East and Central Africa, for example, no African occupied a position higher than that of a minor clerk.[74] A fundamental, and sometimes flawed, assumption in the system of indirect rule was that traditional chiefs existed through whom the British could rule. This outlook tended to ignore the practice of collective leadership characteristic of some African societies, and risked bestowing on collaborating chiefs an excessive degree of authority, enabling them to consolidate, and sometimes abuse, their political power.[75]

In Tanganyika in the later 1920s, Governor Sir Donald Cameron (1925–31) had applied similar ideas (known here as 'indirect administration'), aiming 'to develop the native on lines which will not Westernise him and turn him into a bad imitation of a European'. In this case, indirect rule had the further role of defending African interests against the claims of settlers who hoped, through 'closer union', to create a new East African Dominion controlled by them. Cameron saw indirect rule as a means both to shield Africans from predatory settlers, and to give them some political autonomy beyond settler interference. While giving Africans practical training in politics, Native Authorities were also thought to provide a conservative counterweight to the more radical ambitions of Westernized Africans.[76]

The weaknesses of indirect rule were underlined in the *African Survey*, published by the experienced Indian administrator Lord Hailey in 1938. His work, a vast systematic study of political, economic and social conditions in British Africa, became an important influence on Colonial Office thinking. According to Hailey, the static conception of administration enshrined in Lugard's philosophy was inconsistent with a growing recognition of the need to improve colonial living standards through the promotion of welfare services and economic development, a theme which would increasingly preoccupy the Colonial Office in the later 1930s. Native Authorities could hardly be expected to implement the kind of interventionist policies increasingly thought to be necessary to the survival of colonial rule. Nor did such sedate bodies offer much opportunity for the swelling ranks of Western-educated Africans.[77] Hailey identified the need to give this group a greater role in the technical branches of colonial government. More fundamental still was the question of how indirect rule could be reconciled with the development of parliamentary institutions (which, based on the experience of the Dominions, seemed to be the ultimate target). Hailey, while stressing the importance of this issue, was unable to offer a clear solution.[78]

In the inter-war period, London took on an increasing responsibility for the colonies' economic development. Symbolic of this was the British government's guarantee of a £10 million loan for East Africa in 1926. An important justification for such measures was their potential value in creating or preserving jobs within Britain itself.[79] Such a metropolitan-centred rationale for development naturally worried the Colonial Office, which feared that 'development' would become inseparable from schemes of short-term benefit to Britain in reducing unemployment. While the Colonial Secretary, Leopold Amery, hoped to create a general development fund on which the CO could draw, the Treasury, operating in a climate of tight budgetary restraint, found this idea unacceptable. The Colonial Development Act of 1929 created a fund of £1 million per year, to which colonial governments could apply for development assistance, the whole scheme to be administered by a Colonial Development Advisory Committee based in London. This assistance, taking the form either of grants or interest payments on colonial loans, could be given only to development schemes with a demonstrable economic benefit to Britain. As metropolitan unemployment remained high in the early 1930s, it soon became clear that the 1929 Act was of limited value, either to Britain or the colonies.[80] A fundamental weakness lay in the insistence that the initiative in development must come from the colonial governments themselves, not from the CDAC. Given their reduced size (the consequence of retrenchment) and lack of experience in economic policy, these administrations were generally ill equipped to assume so dynamic a role. Yet the 1930s exposed the fundamental weakness of many colonial economies in the face of fluctuations in international trade. The collapse in commodity prices severely affected the primary-producing colonies, underlining their dangerous dependence on a narrow export base.

Prolonged economic disruption gave rise to social unrest in several colonies during the 1930s, most notably the West Indies and West Africa. The West Indian disturbances (1935–38), triggered by the disastrous fortunes of the sugar industry, were particularly worrying to London, and secured the most damaging publicity. For the Colonial Office, this episode underlined the need to embark on a new approach towards development, with a new emphasis on the colonies' needs, particularly in the welfare sphere, rather than the economic interests of Britain. It also seemed vital to introduce reform in the West Indies in order to pre-empt any escalation of American anti-colonial sentiment.[81] The British government's response was to appoint a Royal Commission, chaired by Lord Moyne, to investigate social and economic conditions in the West Indies and to make recommendations. By the time the Commission reported, after a 15-month sojourn in the region, war had broken out and the context of metropolitan policy-making had been given a radically enhanced significance. Independently, the respected academic W.M. Macmillan criticized previous colonial policy for its failure to promote development.[82] Lord Hailey, too, was a vocal champion of increased metropolitan spending on the kind of research needed to achieve development in Africa. From within the administrative system, Sir Bernard Bourdillon, governor of Nigeria, won sympathy from the Colonial Office with his assertion that the colonies urgently required metropolitan financial aid in order to develop welfare services.

Such thinking dovetailed with the ideas of Britain's reforming pre-war Colonial Secretary, Malcolm MacDonald, son of Ramsay. Convinced that unprecedented levels of Treasury expenditure were needed to tackle the problem of colonial poverty, MacDonald couched his argument in *political* terms, emphasizing Britain's need to demonstrate its good faith as a colonial power at a time when colonial rule was increasingly becoming an international issue.[83] Soon after becoming Colonial Secretary in 1938, MacDonald set up a committee within the Colonial Office to examine the question of revising the Colonial Development Act. Although the Munich Crisis and the work of the Moyne Commission delayed the preparation of legislation, by the end of the year MacDonald's ambitions had broadened to include not only more aid for colonial economic development, but also social service provision, an area he regarded as being even more pressing.[84] As more prescient officials were aware, these two questions were closely connected: the likelihood of raising colonial welfare standards in the long term depended on improving the economic condition of the colonies. By the summer of 1939, the Colonial Office felt ready to propose new colonial development legislation.

Official discussions on colonial social welfare inevitably raised more fundamental questions about the wider purpose of colonial rule and involved exposing the philosophy of trusteeship to more searching scrutiny. The problem of education illustrates this point very well. Partly in response to the developing debate on trusteeship, and partly as a result of pressure from the missionary lobby, the Colonial Office had established an Advisory Committee on Native Education in Tropical Africa in 1923. The committee's report, published in 1925, marked the first clear statement of British educational policy in Africa, and echoed some of the attitudes common to earlier American philanthropic investigations, such as those funded by the Phelps-Stokes Fund.[85] Central to the report was the belief that educational provision in Africa should be tailored to local needs, and that an imported Western system would be inappropriate. According to this view, a traditional British-style education was relevant only to that minority of Africans who would eventually assume administrative roles in commerce and within the colonial state. In this sense, in its capacity to minimize social disruption in African societies, education was the 'ideological embodiment' of indirect rule.[86] Although even basic educational provision was still in its infancy before the war, there was already some discussion of the future need for higher education in Africa. The Currie Report (1933) warned that ignoring the aspirations of educated Africans for university education might become a source of political friction, although some colonial governors, concerned more about promoting secondary education, and aware of the financial constraints, thought these views were exaggerated.[87] Revealing, however, was the fear expressed by a number of governors that 'errors' previously made in India, in cultivating an unrepresentative educated elite, should not be repeated in Africa. More prosaic was the Treasury's mounting concern at the financial implications of the Colonial Office's strengthening argument that London was morally obliged to share in the cost of providing colonial education. This fundamental fear, that the development initiative might involve Britain in open-ended commitments, became a recurring theme as Colonial Office plans, and definitions of development, became more ambitious.

The entire field of colonial labour policy was one which increasingly preoccupied the Colonial Office in the 1930s. Here, the impetus to examine policy came from the interest being shown by external groups, above all the International Labour Organization (established in 1919 as an agency of the League of Nations), and from specific instances of labour unrest, notably the strike of African workers on the Copperbelt of Northern Rhodesia in 1935. The ILO became interested from an early stage in setting minimum standards for labour legislation, and expected member states to apply these to their colonies. To the Colonial Office, which tended on principle to resent outside 'interference' in its responsibilities, the kind of standards laid down by the ILO often seemed more appropriate to industrial societies than to most colonial territories. Restating a traditional refrain in discussions of colonial matters, and still under the spell of the orthodoxy which asserted that colonial governments should be allowed free rein to determine what was applicable to their colonies, the Office claimed that it would be impracticable to construct a labour policy which could be applied to the whole colonial empire. As in so many other fields, however, the impact of the Depression served to undermine this parochialism. Incidents such as unrest on the Northern Rhodesian Copperbelt persuaded the Colonial Office to adopt a more interventionist stance, and to issue guidelines to colonial governments on the need to ensure adequate machinery to supervise labour conditions (1935) and recommending the appointment of labour officers in colonies where sufficient people were in paid employment (1937). Malcolm MacDonald reminded colonial governments in 1938 of the need for labour departments to be adequately staffed.[88] Finally, early in 1938, the Colonial Office appointed its first Labour Adviser, Major Granville Orde Browne.

Meanwhile, the Trades Union Congress, increasingly interested between the wars in overseas labour conditions and the development of trade unions in the colonies (in part from a desire to stem the competitive threat posed by cheap, unorganized labour), itself produced 'model' regulations to aid new labour organizations.[89]

Whatever the problems of extracting a greater metropolitan commitment to raised colonial living standards, by the end of the inter-war period, the Colonial Office had become convinced of the need to present the colonial empire in the best possible light, to opinion both in Britain and abroad. Partly in response to growing international interest in colonial affairs, officials recognized that colonial policy had to be depicted as being energetic and purposeful, with London and the colonial governments collaborating fruitfully in the interests of local populations' welfare.[90]

The growing threat to imperial security

During the early 1930s, there emerged a new set of international circumstances which eroded the relative security that the British imperial system had enjoyed since the end of the First World War and tested Britain's capacity to maintain the integrity of its global system. Growing evidence of the intentions of a group of 'aggressor' nations, Japan, Germany and Italy, highlighted tensions within the imperial system, and different strategic priorities emanating from London and the Dominion capitals, reminding policy-makers that defence was the empire's Achilles' Heel. This, of course, unfolded against (and was fed by) the conditions of global economic depression which imposed severe constraints on the ability of a country like Britain to prioritize rearmament. Like Britain itself, the Dominions struggled to digest the unpalatable risk that their collective interests might be challenged by a combination of three hostile powers. The British and Dominion governments varied in their interpretations of which of these posed the greatest threat, and how exactly they might combine in the future. What was certainly common to all the Dominion governments' assessments was the conviction, carried over from the 1920s, that Britain should avoid any firm commitment to the defence of mainland Europe.[91]

It was in the Far East that the spectre of aggression first manifested itself. One of the gravest errors of twentieth-century British diplomacy had, arguably, been the decision to allow the Anglo-Japanese alliance to lapse, leaving Britain exposed in the Far East. This had inspired the Admiralty to propose the construction of a major new naval base in the region, which would be capable of holding out until a fleet could arrive to relieve it. On the grounds that Japan was now the likeliest threat to Britain in the Far East, the Admiralty suggested building the base at Singapore. A metropolitan mood in favour of retrenchment in defence spending meant, however, that work on the base was fitful and sporadic, even though the Chiefs of Staff concluded in 1926 that its completion was the most urgent priority for defence spending.[92] It took clear evidence of the potential threat from Japan, in the form of the latter's invasion of

Manchuria in 1931 and attack on Shanghai in 1932, to convince the British government to speed up the construction of the Singapore base.[93] From summer 1932, with imperial Japan determined on its policy of expansion into China, Australia understandably sought assurances about British plans to defend its Far Eastern interests. The Chiefs of Staff responded that so long as the Singapore base was in good order, and a Royal Navy fleet could be despatched in time, Australia need not be concerned.[94]

Given the importance attached to the supposedly impregnable Singapore base in British strategic thinking, it was perhaps easy to overlook the simple fact that the base's role assumed that Britain would be in a position to reinforce it in time of emergency by sending a fleet to the Far East. This in turn was based on the assumption that the Royal Navy would not be facing a simultaneous threat closer to home in European waters (or, for that matter, anywhere else within its normal sphere of operations). It was German rearmament and the growing appreciation of Hitler's expansionism which called this thinking into question. The British government's arguably fateful decision not to resist Hitler's remilitarization of the Rhineland in 1936 was partly the result of the Dominions' opposition to such intervention in continental Europe. Subsequently, during the Sudeten Crisis of 1938, alarming rifts emerged within the Commonwealth. Both South Africa and Canada made it clear that they were not prepared to go to war on this issue, and their stance may have reinforced Chamberlain's commitment to appeasement.[95] However, it seems unlikely that the Dominions were shaping British foreign policy in any decisive way. More likely, Dominion attitudes only served to confirm Chamberlain in a course of action to which he was already committed, though he had no wish to add to strains within the Commonwealth. Looming over the 1930s was the simple question of whether Britain was in any condition, militarily, to countenance another war, and what the economic and financial effects of such a war might be, given that the First World War had brought the country perilously close to bankruptcy. For Chamberlain, policy towards Nazi Germany was partly a reflection of what was taken to be British popular reluctance to face war over the fate of Eastern or Central Europe, but also of the strong strategic argument that a European war might endanger the security of the British Empire.[96] Nevertheless, in the wake of Munich, as conditions in Europe worsened and as the British government's attitudes towards Hitler hardened, Dominion opinion was of declining influence in London.[97] The policy of appeasing Nazi Germany, although based on a long tradition of diplomacy, ultimately failed: it proved impossible to deter Hitler through rearmament, or to ensure good behaviour by Germany in Europe by an offer to re-open the question of Germany's colonial ambitions.[98]

Meanwhile, Italy emerged as a potential threat to British interests following its invasion of Ethiopia in October 1935. This not only endangered the British Empire's communications links through the Mediterranean but also revealed the fragility of Britain's position in the Middle East.[99] Shortly after this incident, a sub-committee of the Committee of Imperial Defence identified the key problem facing British strategic planners: the need to avoid becoming embroiled in conflicts simultaneously with Japan in the Far East, Germany in Europe and with any other power along the main line of communication between the two.[100] Both Australia and New Zealand were acutely aware that the deteriorating situation in Europe would have implications for their own security, and, given the rise of Italian ambitions in the Mediterranean, made plain to London their fears that Britain might be unable to meet its defence commitments to them in the event of a crisis. In February 1937 the Chiefs of Staff listed in order of importance the Commonwealth's strategic commitments. These were: the security of the global imperial communications system; Britain's own defences against German aggression; the security of imperial interests in the Far East against Japanese incursions; the security of the Mediterranean and the Middle East; and finally, safeguarding India against Soviet aggression.[101]

At the Imperial Conference held in London in the summer of 1937, Britain sought both to reassure the Australians and to clarify Dominion attitudes towards the developing international climate. The British government promised its partners that, if war came, the twin pillars of imperial security would be the defence of Britain and of the Singapore base. In turn the Dominions asked for firm commitments that whatever might occur in the Mediterranean, a fleet would be sent to the Far East.[102] Although there were growing strains and anxieties, the Commonwealth relationship was holding firm. This was symbolized by the statement by the Canadian prime minister, Mackenzie King, at the 1937 conference, that if Britain were ever to be attacked by Germany, all the Dominions would come to its assistance.[103] However, in Washington circles, Canada's own ability to defend itself was causing anxiety, and fears emerged that Japan might attack the Dominion as the first stage of a bid to invade the United States itself. This led Roosevelt in August 1938 to underwrite Canadian security against foreign aggression, a painful reminder of Britain's inability to perform this role and an expression of the evolving close relationship between Canada and the United States.[104] Prior to this, at the end of 1937, the Cabinet had endorsed the recommendations of Sir Thomas Inskip, Minister for the Co-ordination of Defence, on how Britain's defence commitments might better be matched to its available resources. In the new schema, preparing an expeditionary force for despatch to the Continent in the event of war became the lowest priority, precedence being given first to the defence of Britain itself and second to the defence of the empire and overseas trade. This was a logical position to adopt, given the Treasury's insistence that the economic resources of the empire, a key asset which Germany lacked, would be decisive in a future protracted war. Yet as Inskip himself warned the Cabinet only two months later, it was impossible for Britain realistically to plan the defence of the empire against three major aggressors operating in three different parts of the world.[105]

Over the ensuing two years, Britain was obliged to revise drastically its thinking on imperial security priorities. Increasingly the Mediterranean and the Middle East eclipsed other potential theatres of action, yet safeguarding British interests in the region was becoming more difficult. In the wake of Italy's actions in Ethiopia, it became essential to guarantee the security of nominally independent Egypt, with which a new treaty was signed in 1936, but nationalist tensions here continued to simmer. Communal unrest in Palestine was another problem. As the situation in Europe continued to deteriorate, the Middle East grew in importance to British planners. In October 1938, the Chiefs of Staff, responding to the worsening situation in Palestine and the European crisis over Czechoslovakia, and concerned about the danger of unrest in the region, urged that after the defence of Britain itself, the priority for British forces should be the security of Egypt and the Middle East generally.[106]

Early in 1939, the Chiefs sketched their ideas on the conduct of a European war. Assuming that the war would be one of attrition, and that the only scope for offensive action would be in the Mediterranean, they stressed that Britain's military strength in Egypt would have to be increased, providing a base from which attacks could be made on Italian interests. But this growing concentration on securing the Mediterranean had important ramifications for wider imperial strategy, calling into question Britain's ability to supply reinforcements for the Far East. The Chiefs of Staff did not doubt that in the event of Japanese aggression, a fleet should be sent to Singapore, but they were uncomfortably aware that the outcome of a second global war would depend largely on Britain's capacity to hold on to its vital positions and on the willingness of other powers, especially the United States, to provide assistance.[107] Nevertheless, in March 1939 Chamberlain assured the Australian government that if war broke out in Europe, and if Japan were to enter on the side of Germany and Italy, it was still Britain's intention to keep its promise to send a fleet to Singapore. If it transpired that Britain found itself locked in a struggle with an unanticipated constellation of enemies, then the size of the fleet Britain would despatch would depend on the timing of Japan's entry, and on the scale of the losses sustained by that time by both Britain and its enemies. This remained, in theory, the core of Britain's commitment until previous calculations were overturned by Japan's stunning military successes early in 1942. It was also on the basis of this pledge that the Australasian Dominions supplied forces to the European and Middle Eastern theatres.[108] In the months immediately preceding the outbreak of war in September 1939, a stiffening of Dominion resolve to resist aggression, matching that now espoused by London, became evident. With the exception of the Irish Free State (Eire), keen to trumpet its autonomy by remaining neutral, the Dominions had achieved a degree of consensus on support for Britain which would have been inconceivable at the time of Munich. But the plight of the Australasian Dominions in the face of Japanese expansionism, and the need for clear geopolitical perspectives, was captured with devastating simplicity by the Australian premier Robert Menzies' comment in 1939 that 'what Britain calls the Far East is to us the near north'.[109]

CHAPTER 2

THE IMPACT OF THE
SECOND WORLD WAR

The Second World War had a profound effect on the British imperial system. While every aspect of that system was tested by the conflict, the outcome seemed to be a revival and strengthening of Britain's imperial commitment. This was symbolized by the appointment of Winston Churchill as prime minister in 1940, and the resulting definition of the war in imperial terms.[1] By the end of the war, not only was the empire intact, with all lost British territory being recovered, but Britain also appeared to have acquired a new sense of imperial purpose, a commitment to guiding its dependent empire to eventual self-government, and, meanwhile, to raising colonial living standards through a programme of economic and social development. The war's impact on the imperial system was seen, perhaps, most clearly in the dependent empire. Crucially, during the war, Britain had been led to adopt styles of administration and interventionist policies which threatened to upset the delicate pre-war balance of local power, creating conditions in which a new political climate could develop, and making old-style British rule untenable.[2] This was seen most clearly in the case of India, where wartime developments led Britain to concede the principle of post-war independence. Yet the same was arguably equally true in those parts of the world where Britain had traditionally relied on an 'informal' presence to project its influence.

Defending the empire

The war illustrated the problems facing Britain in attempting to defend a genuinely global imperial system, and its inability to prosecute a war unaided in two hemispheres simultaneously. The lesson of the entire period since the mid-1920s, that imperial defence would require the assistance of at least one powerful ally, prompted London increasingly to seek to appease the United States, and involve the Americans in security arrangements. Once war had broken out in Europe, Britain found itself, as expected, seeking US support. During the so-called ABC talks, held early in 1941, the initiative rested with the still neutral United States, where unease about the threat to US interests from Germany and Japan was coalescing, but which, for domestic political reasons, was still reluctant to undertake firm commitments. At the talks, to which Canada, Australia and New Zealand sent observers, Britain and the US reached agreement that the defeat of Germany and Italy was the priority, and that they needed to deter Japanese aggression. Less congenial were Anglo-US exchanges on Britain's prioritization of the Middle Eastern and Mediterranean theatres (where Washington thought Britain was concentrating too great a proportion of its resources), and especially its Far Eastern strategy.[3] Although British naval planners considered it vital that the Singapore base should be bolstered by an American fleet, Washington hesitated. Meanwhile, Churchill, who was not yet convinced of the threat posed by Japan, and whose priority was to bring the United States into the war, urged the Admiralty not to pursue this point. A compromise was reached in which it was agreed that the Atlantic and the Pacific should primarily be the Americans' responsibility, while Britain would concentrate on defending South-East Asia.[4] To deter Japan, the main US fleet was to be stationed at Pearl Harbor, though the American presence in the Atlantic would be reinforced, allowing Britain to despatch more ships to Singapore.

Mobilizing imperial resources

As in the First World War, Britain looked to the Dominions and the dependent empire to provide military and economic assistance to the war effort. As in the earlier conflict, the empire responded magnificently, providing forces which played a key role in all the major theatres of war. However, the process of mobilizing imperial resources involved strains which, in the long term, served to undermine the conditions on which pre-war British calculations and policies had been based, and ultimately, to weaken the entire system. There was no attempt to revive the Imperial War Cabinet which had functioned during the First World War: much improved communications technology made this unnecessary, and on political grounds, it would have been difficult to reconcile this retrograde step with the greater independence the Dominions had achieved between the wars. Nevertheless, the Dominion governments were closely consulted by London throughout the war, and the volume of communication between London and the Indian and colonial governments expanded dramatically. One important departure was the attempt to co-ordinate the imperial war effort on a regional basis, for example in the East African Governors' Conference, the West African War Council and the Eastern Group Supply Council, established under the umbrella of the Government of India and with satellites in East Africa and the Middle East. Occasionally, ministers of Cabinet rank were appointed to oversee the activities of particular regions. Lord Swinton, a former Colonial Secretary, became Resident Minister in West Africa in 1942, creating an important co-ordinating link between London and the region's existing machinery.

The colonial territories in particular felt the effects of government regulation to an extent unknown in peacetime.[5] At the outbreak of war, the Colonial Office had introduced a range of emergency controls, similar to those applied in wartime Britain. Individual colonial governments had been advised of the steps that would be necessary to control their economies, especially by regulating trade and conserving precious foreign exchange. Initially, a major concern was to prevent colonial raw material exports falling into enemy hands, and to maximize the production of these items for metropolitan consumption. Because British shipping space rapidly became scarce, and because British industry was increasingly geared to war, not export production, measures were introduced to limit colonial imports, through a system of quotas, leading inevitably to local shortages, inflation and rising living costs. Tight controls over colonial imports would survive the war years, becoming an important post-war tool designed to limit purchases of goods from dollar sources. However, it was not until the marked deterioration in Britain's fortunes in summer 1940, following the collapse of France and Italy's entry into the war, that the full panoply of government controls was introduced. With the end of the Phoney War, the colonies faced a new phase of marked austerity. As Britain's limited dollar reserves were depleted, Indian and colonial production assumed a growing significance for the war effort. With the fall of Singapore in February 1942, greater constraints were imposed on colonial imports and the colonies were urged to make good the production of vital commodities, such as rubber and tin, no longer available from South-East Asia.

India's contribution to the war effort, in terms of men, munitions and supplies, was particularly impressive. By the end of the war, around two and a quarter million men were serving in the armed forces, and the sub-continent had developed into an enormous supply base for Allied operations in Asia and the Middle East. One important concession had been made to India soon after the outbreak of war: Britain had agreed to pay for defence expenditure incurred by the Government of India for use outside India. What this meant in practice was that London would underwrite the expansion of the Indian armed forces in addition to military costs arising outside the country. This was the necessary price of attempting to preserve Britain's collaborative arrangements in India.[6] In India, as in the colonies, the demands of recruitment and supplying the armed forces, along with general economic mobilization, led the British authorities to intervene in daily life to an unprecedented degree.[7] India's economy, particularly its industrial sector, received an important stimulus during the war, leading some British manufacturing exporters to fear for their future share of the Indian market. Like many other parts of the dependent empire, India experienced severe inflation during the war, due to an increase in money supply used to help subsidize the war effort, and to the effect of import controls. Until 1943, when rationing and price control schemes were imposed, the cost of ordinary consumer goods rose sharply, seen most dramatically in the cost of food. The sub-continent experienced serious problems with food shortages, aggravated by hoarding and distribution difficulties, leading eventually to one of the war's worst civilian crises, the Bengal famine of 1943, in which between three and four million Indians died. This disaster inevitably focused Indian resentment even more clearly on the British authorities.

As the war progressed, the resources of Britain's African empire similarly grew in importance to the Allied war effort. In March 1942, the Colonial Secretary, Viscount Cranborne, declared that African produce was urgently required, and that the continent's minerals and food had become a 'vast armoury' for the Allies.[8] The need to increase colonial commodity production led to the conscription of civilian labour on a large scale, in addition to more than a third of a million Africans recruited into the armed forces, many in supporting, non-combatant roles. In some colonies, such as Nigeria and Tanganyika, the authorities resorted to imposing forced labour on civilians, for example in the tin mines around the Jos Plateau, where grim working conditions were encountered. The diversion of so much African labour into war-related activities prompted fears that food production for local requirements might suffer.[9] One consequence of this production drive was to strengthen the hand of East and Central Africa's white settler community, which took the opportunity of wartime pressure to penetrate more deeply into the apparatus of the colonial state with a view to placing settler interests on a more secure footing than had existed between the wars.

One of the most important results of wartime imperial economic mobilization was the consolidation of the Sterling Area into a tightly bound financial unit, building on the arrangements introduced after the financial crisis of 1931, and operating common exchange controls which survived the war by over 20 years. Before the war, this had been an open system, in which members of the bloc were free to withdraw their sterling holdings or convert them into other currencies as necessary. After the outbreak of war the bloc, minus some of its non-empire members, developed into a mechanism through which Britain could manipulate members' financial resources for the benefit of the war effort (and, subsequently, to finance post-war metropolitan reconstruction). Members' hard currency earnings, especially dollars, were pooled in an Exchange Equalization Account maintained by the Bank of England, which in turn made issues of funds when members required them. In practice, access to these earnings was restricted during and after the war, and came to depend on a particular member's political clout: of all the Sterling Area members, the colonies found that their needs cut the least ice with the system's managers. During the war the advantage of the Sterling Area was that Britain could absorb members' exports without immediate payment and draw freely on their earnings to finance war-related activities without matching this expenditure with exports: in other words, London could finance a considerable portion of the war's costs on credit. Around £2,348 million was provided in this way by members, who were credited with 'sterling balances'. These arrangements, which, as the economist John Maynard Keynes observed,[10] amounted to the jettisoning of inter-war maxims of good financial housekeeping, brought about a revolution in the relationship between Britain and the components of its imperial system: having been their principal creditor in the 1930s, Britain emerged from the war massively in debt to them: by 1945, of total sterling debts of £3,355 million, £2,723 million was owed to Sterling Area countries. The rapid accumulation of sizeable sterling balances threatened to have important political ramifications. For example, in the case of India, to which Britain owed £1,321 million by the end of the war, the Treasury suggested in 1942 that the Government of India should make a larger contribution to the war effort by cancelling part of its sterling balances. This position reflected the influence of Keynes, who argued that as it would not be possible to make the sterling balances freely convertible, they should be frozen and released to creditors gradually, as circumstances permitted. This evoked vigorous protests from the Secretary of State for India, Leopold Amery, who saw the balances not as a problem, but as an asset which would help British exporters rebuild their markets after the war.

A further financial shift arising directly from the war was the widespread introduction of more progressive taxation regimes, including income tax. This important departure, in part the consequence of a need to curb the inflationary spiral arising from import shortages, offered the longer-term promise of freeing colonial governments from some of their dangerous dependence on revenue from imports and exports. This encouraged some optimism during the war that future colonial economic development might be financed to an increased extent from local resources.

Although import controls led to a slight softening of metropolitan attitudes towards colonial industrialization, especially where this might assist the war effort,[11] and some colonies did achieve a greater degree of self-sufficiency than before the war, the most important economic change affecting many colonies was direct government intervention in the purchase and marketing of their major commodities. Early in the war, the dislocation of international trade, shortages of merchant shipping and the resulting loss of the colonies' traditional markets exposed the problem of what was to be done with colonial surpluses of crops such as cocoa in West Africa. Political considerations, above all the desire to avoid colonial unrest in wartime, and fears about the effects disrupted exports might have on colonial government revenues, led Britain to introduce bulk-purchasing schemes for many colonial commodities. Improvised in 1939 to meet the immediate problem of West African cocoa, this involved crops being bought at fixed prices on behalf of the Ministry of Food in London, with the established trading firms (such as the United Africa Company) acting as the colonial state's agents. In 1940, these ad hoc arrangements were regularized, and a West African Cocoa Control Board established.[12] Two years later, the system was extended with the creation of a West African Produce Control Board, with responsibility for marketing a wider range of the region's produce. State marketing proved to be so successful, and lucrative to Britain, that in 1944 London published plans to extend the system into the post-war period. Despite the protests of big expatriate firms who had lost their pre-war oligopolistic control over West Africa's trade, the British government was unmoved. The war had, accordingly, led to a revolution in the organization of West Africa's export trade, one which would persist not only into the post-war period, but would be retained with enthusiasm by post-colonial regimes as a useful source of state income. However, the wartime need for collaboration between big business and the colonial state (which many officials, harbouring a spirit of 'romantic anti-capitalism', saw as politically dangerous), fuelled African suspicions that the interests of local entrepreneurs were being subordinated to those of powerful British firms, intensifying the hostility to the latter which would become increasingly evident after the war, eventually contributing to the disturbances which erupted in the Gold Coast so startlingly in 1948. Moreover, it was difficult to disguise the fact that whereas bulk-purchasing arrangements with the Dominions or other independent countries were negotiated, the colonies, lacking this bargaining power, were normally paid considerably less than world market prices for their commodities, the profits accruing to the British government.[13]

Tapping into the vast resources of the dependent empire tested the entire imperial machine to its political and administrative limits. Growing wartime intervention gave the colonial state considerable experience in the economic sphere, which accordingly lost some of the terrors which had haunted administrators during the Depression, and set the foundations for a more 'managerial' style of colonial rule after the war. Although it ultimately enhanced official confidence, arguably giving the colonial state a new sense of purpose after the apparent 'aimlessness and drift' of the 1930s, wartime economic mobilization, and its justification to sometimes unreceptive colonial audiences, initially placed enormous strains on inexperienced colonial governments already overworked and depleted by the departure of officials for military service. Their new responsibilities, especially in the economic sphere, frequently forced administrators to introduce unpopular measures which threatened to erode the delicate political balance which was maintained in many parts of the dependent empire between the wars. Nevertheless, the growth in the colonial state's range of activities during the war would set an important precedent for *dirigiste* post-war colonial, and post-independence, government attitudes and policies.

One important consequence of the mobilization of the colonies for war was the tendency for unprecedented centralization in colonial policy-making. Increasingly, it was the Colonial Office, rather than individual colonial governments, which took the initiative as new policy areas surfaced to rival the customary concerns of law and order, tax-gathering and so on. In this respect the war was accentuating a trend already visible before the war, for the Colonial Office to seek to deal thematically with problems common to a number of colonies, rather than organizing its work almost totally on 'territorial' lines. This trend worried some traditionalists, who feared for the sacrosanct status of the 'man on the spot'. Nevertheless, at least until the late 1940s, the Colonial Office cast off its habitually reactive stance and gained, from the war, a new willingness to intervene and direct.[14]

The social consequences of heightened economic activity were often disruptive and unsettling. Increased opportunities for employment and inclusion in the cash economy were accompanied by urbanization and greater awareness of the growing intrusiveness of the colonial state, creating conditions fertile for the development of anti-colonial criticism. The effects of wartime military service for colonial populations are less clear. While these might involve the acquisition of new technical skills, overseas travel, encounters with non-colonial personnel and a general broadening of horizons, and even the development of political aspirations, it seems that for many returning Africans the priority was to take up the threads of pre-war life as quickly as possible, and that those who had remained at home during the war were more likely to be active in post-war politics. On the other hand, in some cases, such as the Gold Coast, the post-war frustration of demobilized soldiers' expectations seems to have been important in crystallizing local unrest.[15] Uncertainty about the likely long-term effects of the war on colonial populations coloured speculation both in London and among colonial administrators. Some more far-sighted administrators recognized at an early stage, however, that their ability to devise and implement policy from the high ground of bureaucratic autonomy was likely to be eroded.[16]

Mobilization of colonial resources had its ideological as well as administrative aspects. Populations had to be convinced of the importance of their contribution to the war effort. Significantly, the Colonial Office had taken steps during summer 1939 to create a public relations department. In tandem with the Ministry of Information, this body tried, during 1940, to depict the colonies as being content under British rule and willing to join in the common struggle. Propaganda methods, however, did not always come easily to the Colonial Office, and its critics attacked its apparent complacency early in the war.[17]

Colonial development and welfare

It was in this context that a demonstration of Britain's commitment to colonial development and welfare appeared to the Colonial Office to be necessary and timely. Malcolm MacDonald, who had done so much before the war to modernize the flavour of colonial policy, was reluctant to lose the momentum his exploration of development policy had already gained. He understood the propaganda value of a wartime pledge to raised living standards, seeing this in terms of Britain's overall defence policy.[18] At the outbreak of war, a complete suspension of development activity seemed inevitable, in view of the Treasury's insistence that Britain's immediate needs must take priority. Accordingly, the Colonial Development Advisory Committee's activities were suspended. However, the Moyne Commission, which reported late in 1939, underlined the scope for political unrest arising from poverty in the West Indies, which in turn strengthened the Colonial Office's arguments for sympathetic treatment of development questions more generally. The Commission's report was felt to be too critical of Britain's past record to permit publication in full in wartime: Neville Chamberlain feared that it would give too much comfort to German propagandists, and might damage the war effort. Instead a summary was published, the full report not appearing until after the war. Skilfully deploying political arguments, and in the least auspicious of circumstances, MacDonald capitalized on the impact of the Moyne Commission's report to push through the proposals for development on which the Colonial Office had been working since summer 1938, persuading his colleagues in Cabinet that it was essential for Britain's colonial policy to appear in the best possible light, and that a gesture by London at this stage would help secure colonial loyalty.[19] What was distinctive about the Colonial Development and Welfare Bill introduced by MacDonald in May 1940 was that it promised metropolitan funding for colonial welfare provision. Nevertheless, the Treasury remained sceptical about the entire initiative (especially its apparently open-ended commitment to colonial welfare), and, as the war entered what was for Britain its most critical phase, the Colonial Office soon encountered problems in securing the funds promised when the conflict had still appeared 'phoney'.

Given their proximity to the then still neutral United States, which was about to take up leases on bases in the area, the West Indies were considered to be candidates for special treatment, in which it was vital for Britain to be able to impress Washington that it was addressing its colonial obligations seriously. London therefore decided to establish a separate Development and Welfare organization for the region, under a comptroller, Sir Frank Stockdale, responsible for disbursing development funding.

Development policy was an early casualty of the general deterioration of the war situation in summer 1940. In June, a 'blitzkrieg' telegram warned colonial governments that progress with development would not be possible in the foreseeable future: retrenchment, not expansion, was prescribed for welfare and other services in the colonies. A year later, Lord Moyne (by now himself Colonial Secretary) sought to reassure colonial administrators that Britain's commitment to development had not evaporated: he nevertheless appended to this a call for further reductions in colonial consumption in line with those being experienced in Britain. The resulting financial surpluses might, he suggested, be converted into interest-free loans to Britain and eventually become an important source of funding for colonial development projects.

Military reversals in the Far East

In September 1940, Japan began its offensive. By November, it had entered French Indo-China, and the following summer reached agreement with the Vichy regime giving it the use of airfields in the region. Late in 1941, feeling the economic effects of international blockade and facing dwindling oil supplies, Japan prepared for attacks on European territory in South-East Asia and US bases in the Pacific. On the night of 7 December 1941, the attack on Pearl Harbor began, along with action against the Philippines, Malaya and Hong Kong. It was Pearl Harbor which, by bringing the United States into the war, ultimately sealed the fate of Japanese expansionism. The attack on Malaya led to the fall of Singapore on 15 February 1942, and the loss of around 138,000 British and Commonwealth troops, in Churchill's words the 'worst disaster and largest capitulation in British history', and an event which shattered any remaining myth of white 'supremacy' and fatally undermined the prestige upon which European colonialism had depended. British strategists had not only failed to anticipate Japanese tactics, expecting an onslaught by sea not land, but they had consistently underestimated the military calibre of their opponents. This appalling military reversal triggered an outraged response in Britain, along with much soul-searching about the shortcomings of imperial rule which had

apparently made such a defeat possible, with leading colonial pundits contributing to a lively metropolitan press debate. The fall of Malaya stung British
sensibilities into accusations that its administrators had been negligent, ill
prepared and apathetic. The failure of the local population to respond more
actively to the invasion was also a source of deep embarrassment, signifying a
lack of empathy with colonial ambitions. The loss of Malaya deprived the Allies
of access to around half the world's supplies of strategically vital rubber and
tin, while easing Japan's entry into the Dutch East Indies and Burma. With
Australia and India exposed to the threat of Japanese invasion, the imperial
system appeared more vulnerable than ever before. Some Indian nationalists
took heart from this reversal for Britain. Australia and New Zealand, meanwhile, were forced to look to the United States for protection, underscoring the
hollow nature of Britain's pre-war guarantees to them, and weakening Britain's
bonds with its Pacific Dominions.

Ironically, this low point in imperial fortunes also marked the beginning of
a sustained attempt to resurrect a metropolitan sense of the empire's purpose.
Knowledge that the civilian population had offered relatively little resistance to
the invasion suggested that pre-war colonial propaganda had failed in its object
of inculcating a measure of identification with the British: new messages would
have to be developed, stressing the partnership between Britain and its colonial
subjects. The Japanese occupation of Malaya involved important changes for
the territory which it would be difficult for the returning British to undo: there
was no question that recovery of the South-East Asian territories was a priority
for Churchill and his colleagues, but this would involve not only a major
military campaign but a re-thinking of pre-war colonial assumptions. The
displacement of European rule by fellow Asians inevitably stimulated nationalist sentiments in the region. Japanese emphasis on the creation of a 'Greater
East Asian Co-Prosperity Sphere' from which European influence was
excluded was at least partially successful in disguising the colonial pretensions
of Tojo's regime. In political terms, the Japanese impact was often conservative, with Malay sultans retaining their positions and Malay administrators
holding on to office. Economically, the territory suffered from the severing of
traditional networks of trade, though physical damage was largely the consequence of the scorched-earth policy adopted by the British following the
Japanese invasion. The British found themselves supporting groups whose
fundamental outlook was anti-colonial. For example, the Special Operations
Executive offered Malayan Chinese Communists training in sabotage designed
to frustrate the Japanese, but these skills proved equally effective against the
British themselves after 1948 during the Communist insurgency. The shifting
alliances of war could also cause ideological confusion: South-East Asian
Communists sometimes proved resistant to Comintern blandishments about
the need to co-operate with European imperialists in their struggle with
'fascists'.[20]

Relations with the Dominions

As had been the case in the First World War, the Dominions made a large and important contribution to the imperial war effort, particularly in terms of manpower. Only Ireland remained technically neutral, but large numbers of Irish men served in the British armed forces. A number of factors ensured the Dominions' entry into the war alongside Britain, apart from the often-cited bonds of kinship and sentiment. Still dependent on Britain both economically and, theoretically, for their defence, the Dominions were still largely inclined to see Britain as the heart and clearing house of their relations with the wider world. In most cases, Dominion governments recognized the wisdom, in domestic political terms, of a prompt show of loyalty to London.[21] Especially important from Britain's point of view was the fact that the Dominions agreed at the start of the war that they would meet the costs of deploying their own forces. Canada's chief contribution was to provide naval protection for that most important sea route linking Britain with North America. By 1944, the duty of escorting the shipping convoys on which Britain depended had fallen largely on the Royal Canadian Navy.[22] The Canadian government also provided Britain with various loans and financial gifts which by the end of the war amounted to over $2 billion (Canadian). At the end of the war, as well as cancelling Britain's war debts, Ottawa provided a fresh loan of $1.25 billion (representing one-tenth of Canada's Gross Domestic Product for 1946). Canada would also become closely involved, along with the United States and Britain, in the arrangements for the production of uranium needed for the ultra-secret atomic bomb project.[23]

Developments after 1939 had important long-term consequences for Britain's relations with the self-governing members of the empire. Not only did the Dominions gain in autonomy during the war, and become more ambitious in developing diplomatic ties which suited their own needs, but even the idea of Dominion status arguably suffered a wound which proved mortal. The most dramatic expression of this shifting relationship was the response of the Dominions to the series of military reversals suffered by Britain between 1940 and 1942, and their attempts to establish new strategic ties with the United States, amounting to a 'strategic revolution' which it proved impossible for Britain to reverse after the war.[24] Canada, for example, relied largely on the Royal Navy for the defence of both its coast and its transatlantic links with Britain. Ottawa was understandably relieved, therefore, when, following the collapse of France, and the loss of French naval capacity, Washington proved willing to conclude the Ogdensburg Agreement, which guaranteed Canadian security. In 1941, this was reinforced by the Hyde Park Agreement, which led to the creation of a Permanent Joint Board on Defence. The US–Canadian border, the longest undefended frontier in the world, ceased to exist as far as production for the war effort was concerned. Although Canada's bonds with Britain remained firm, they were now less significant to Canada itself than the new alliance with the United States, a point not lost on Churchill.[25]

The fall of France similarly revealed the fragility of Britain's pre-war defence pledges to Australia and New Zealand, specifically the promise that any Japanese aggression would result in the despatch of naval contingents to the Far East. In August 1940, Churchill sought to reassure both Canberra and Wellington that if either Dominion suffered actual invasion by Japan, Britain would go to their assistance, 'sacrificing every interest except only the defence and feeding of this Island on which all depends'.[26] The unexpected speed of Japan's military advance late in 1941 made a nonsense of this rhetoric. At a time when much of the Australian army was in the Middle East, Australia was left especially vulnerable after Pearl Harbor, leading the Dominion's prime minister, John Curtin, to announce that his country now sought American help 'free from any pangs to our traditional links or kinship with the United Kingdom'. Once the full implications of Britain's Far Eastern disaster had become clear by February 1942, with the Royal Navy's hurried retreat to the coast of East Africa, Australia understandably felt abandoned, its confidence in British protection shattered. The relationship between Britain and Australia never entirely recovered from this episode, which resulted in much closer defence ties between Australia, New Zealand and the United States after the war, culminating in the ANZUS Pact of 1951.

Britain's relations with South Africa became a source of increasing concern to London during the war. As anti-British sentiment among the Afrikaner community developed, the continuation of imperial bonds seemed to hinge on the fate of the prime minister, General Jan Smuts. Yet South Africa seemed intent on expanding its own influence in Africa, bringing it into conflict with British interests. For example, in 1943 the Southern Rhodesian parliament voted for co-operation with South Africa in arranging a pan-African conference to map out the co-ordinated development of central-southern Africa. This was seen by officials in London as an unwelcome challenge to Britain's own evolving ideas on African development. Above all, Pretoria's brand of sub-imperialism focused on the incorporation of the High Commission Territories into South Africa, a fate which both Britain and the territories resisted. While this problem would persist into the post-war era, of more immediate concern was the danger that South African nationalism might become definitely anti-British in flavour, especially if Smuts lost power and was succeeded by nationalist hard-liners. A further consideration was the possibility that South African anti-imperial attitudes might migrate northwards, infecting settler communities in East and Central Africa. For Britain, reliant on South African wartime co-operation, maintaining good relations with Pretoria clearly posed particular difficulties.[27]

The Middle East

The Middle East witnessed a vigorous reassertion of imperial authority by Britain during the war. The region assumed growing importance in the war effort. At the outbreak of the war, the Chief of the Imperial General Staff, Sir Edmund Ironside, had described the Suez Canal as 'the centre of the British

Empire'. The war confirmed the canal's vital importance to imperial communications. Moreover, Middle Eastern oil supplies became essential. In 1941,
Churchill argued that the loss of the Middle East would be 'a disaster of the
first magnitude to Great Britain, second only to a successful invasion and final
conquest'.[28] Even allowing for possible Churchillian hyperbole, considerations
such as these account for Britain's robust handling of political developments in
the region, and its willingness to extract Arab co-operation through coercion if
necessary. For example, during 1941–42, Iraq's pro-German ruler was removed, Syria and Lebanon (previously under Vichy French control) were taken
under the British mantle and Iran was occupied jointly with the Soviet Union.
Most dramatically of all, in nominally independent Egypt, a prime minister
sympathetic to the Axis powers was replaced by the simple expedient of
surrounding the royal palace with British tanks. Cairo during this period
became, in effect, 'the military capital of the British Empire'.[29] However, *force
majeure*, even in wartime, was an unsatisfactory basis for projecting British
influence, and strong-arm tactics were tempered with conciliation. In his 1941
Mansion House speech, for example, the Foreign Secretary, Sir Anthony Eden,
aimed to soothe Arab sentiment by pledging Britain's 'full support for any
scheme of Arab unity which commands general approval', though in practice
this was as far as Britain was prepared to go.[30] Similarly, London held out the
promise of eventual independence for Syria. By 1943, following the decisive
second battle of El Alamein, Britain's position seemed secure, and the Middle
East's role stabilized as a supply zone for other theatres in the war. With this
greater security the immediate threat to India and East Africa was removed
and, more generally, Churchill felt confident in standing his ground in dealings
with Washington on the future of the British Empire, most famously in his
Commons speech of October 1942, when he declared that he had not become
prime minister 'in order to preside over the liquidation of the British Empire'.[31]
Although by the end of the war, Britain's paramountcy in the Middle East
appeared impressive, especially in its possession of a greatly expanded informal
empire, challenges to this position had been generated by the war and by
Britain's own wartime actions. The increased British presence, symbolized by
the Middle East Supply Centre, a huge administrative machine imposed on the
region to mobilize and manage its economy for the war effort, triggered fears
that it might survive the transition to peace: as in the dependent empire proper,
increased intervention by the British authorities, in contrast to pre-war policies
of caution, generated local friction in a cumulative manner, whose effects
would have to be faced after the war. At an international level, Britain's
position was complicated by the growing interest being shown in the Middle
East by the United States and the Soviet Union. The former assiduously
cultivated its influence in oil-rich Saudi Arabia, while the latter, with its
foothold in Iran already established, dreamed of extending its influence into
Turkey, and even of securing trusteeship over Italy's ex-colony, Libya, which
had been under British military rule since 1943.[32]

The continuing importance of the Middle East to Britain was underlined in
a series of government discussions during the last months of the war. Accord-

ing to one school of thought, championed by Sir Anthony Eden, Britain's strategic and political interests dictated that it must remain the predominant power in the region, and that it should assume responsibility for defending the Suez Canal on a permanent basis. The latter was a riposte to sympathy within the Labour Party for some form of international supervision of this critical artery. Echoing Churchill, Eden insisted that the Middle East was one of the most vital strategic areas in the world, describing its defence as 'a matter of life and death to the British Empire, since as the present war and the war of 1918 have both proved, it is there that the empire can be cut in half'.[33] His preference for British control of the Middle East, however, did not prevent Eden from seeing scope for greater international co-operation in maintaining security, though he considered it essential that this should be combined with acceptance that the great powers had particular defence responsibilities in their own areas of interest.[34]

Squaring this emphasis on the Middle East with the wider requirements of imperial defence presented British military planners with dilemmas similar to those they had faced in the 1930s. In June 1945, a sub-committee of the Chiefs of Staff committee assessed the entire question of the empire's security, attempting to predict conditions into the mid-1950s and beyond. Significantly, the Soviet Union was already identified as the major likely threat. The priorities in defence planning were seen as Britain itself, the Indian Ocean, because of its role in imperial communications, and finally the Middle East. Remarkably, given the imminence of dramatic political changes in the sub-continent, India was still regarded as being both an important base and a vital source of manpower and industrial production. It seemed likely that if war with the Soviet Union were to break out, the Middle East would be the first zone at risk, and that little could be done to protect the precious oil resources of Iraq and Persia. The explanation for this bleak assessment was that the communication routes which traversed the Middle East were simply judged to be less vital than those across the Indian Ocean, and might be affected by any military action within Europe. Above all, it was concluded that meeting the defence requirements in the Middle East should not involve a diminished presence either in India or in the Indian Ocean. In the event, the War Coalition took no firm decisions on Britain's presence in the region, bequeathing this conundrum to the incoming Labour government.[35]

India

The corrosive effects of the war on British assumptions and calculations were seen nowhere more clearly than in India. Here, the onset of war involved a crucial error of judgement by London which had lasting significance. In September 1939, Indians were simply informed by the viceroy, Lord Linlithgow, that they were at war, and their views on Indian participation were not sought. Stung by this evidence that, for all the pre-war intimations of near-Dominion status, India was, in reality considered by Britain to be firmly within the dependent empire, Congress demanded to be included in central government, and when this was denied, the Congress provincial ministries resigned in protest. While effective power therefore reverted to British administrators, convenient in wartime, lasting mistrust was sown between them and Indian nationalists. Viceroy Linlithgow's 'August Offer', made in 1940, proposed Dominion status for India after the war, and the inclusion of Indians in a larger Executive Council and a new War Advisory Council, and promised that minority views would be taken into account in future constitutional revision.[36] This was not enough to satisfy either Congress or the Muslim League, who both rejected the offer in September, and shortly afterwards Congress launched a fresh campaign of civil disobedience.

It was partly to appease Washington, to guarantee India's uninterrupted contribution to the war effort, and also to quell dissent from Labour members of the Coalition, that Churchill decided in March 1942 to send Sir Stafford Cripps, the deputy Labour leader, on a mission to India to secure a political breakthrough in relations with nationalist leaders. Attlee had urged Churchill to make a gesture towards Indian opinion, hoping that Cripps could achieve what Lord Durham had done in Canada over a century before.[37] Essentially the Cripps mission was empowered only to repeat the proposals already made in 1940, that is to offer India full Dominion status after the war (or the option to secede from the Empire-Commonwealth), in return for Indian co-operation during the war and a moratorium on further political advance for its duration. An important caveat to the offer, in keeping with the spirit of the 1935 Government of India Act, was that no part of India could be forced to accept membership of the post-war state, whatever form this took.[38] The Cripps initiative had a variety of consequences. It won some admiration within Washington, where the complexities of the sub-continent's political situation became better understood. Congress, however, was unimpressed, and held out for immediate inclusion in India's central government. When this was not forthcoming, Gandhi launched the 'Quit India' campaign, the most serious act of Indian resistance since the Rebellion of 1857, intended to force the British from India. This was a failure, repressed by the authorities and demonstrating that the Raj had not yet lost the will to resort to coercion when necessary. Perhaps more importantly, the campaign led to the banning of Congress and the detention of its leadership and many of its supporters, and for this reason was a serious tactical blunder: the absence of figures such as Gandhi and Nehru until their release in spring 1945 created a dangerous political vacuum, while creating new opportunities for groups willing to collaborate with the Raj.[39] Of these, the most important was the Muslim League, which under the skilful leadership of Mohammed Ali Jinnah secured recognition by Britain of its claim to represent all India's Muslims and engineered for itself a pivotal position in India's future and in the sub-continent's wartime government. Because of the all-important rider to the Cripps Offer, the Muslim League had been awarded an effective veto on the exact form a self-governing India would take. Since the Lahore Resolution of March 1940, the League had been committed to achieving 'Pakistan', a separate homeland for Muslims. Jinnah's achievement was to redefine what had been an internal, 'communal' problem as an international one: he argued that India's Muslims constituted a nation in their own right and were accordingly entitled to self-determination, and meanwhile to equal representation in India's government.[40] While the specific nature of a future Pakistan remained unclear, even to its chief advocate, Jinnah, its appeal to India's Muslims rapidly developed, providing the League with a powerful political weapon in its dealings with the British. A Muslim homeland did not necessarily have to be a separate, sovereign state, rather it might be composed of the predominantly Muslim northern area, perhaps within a loose federal structure. These were questions which would have to await the conclusion of the war. Meanwhile, Jinnah's success demonstrated the potential advantages of collaboration with the British. The British, in turn, arguably paid a very high political price for securing wartime Muslim co-operation. There were good, practical reasons for wishing to court the League's goodwill during the war, as around half of the Indian Army was Muslim. However, the apparently privileged position which this gave Muslims encouraged nationalist claims that Britain was cynically following a 'divide-and-rule' strategy, with fateful consequences for the post-war integrity of the Indian sub-continent.

The heightened Asian consciousness inspired by Japan's military successes in 1941–42 was felt in India, creating new opportunities for those who opposed British rule. For the majority, this took the form of support for Congress, but for others, the Japanese-supported Indian National Army provided a more direct vehicle for resistance. Led by renegade Congress leader Subhas Chandra Bose, the INA had some 11,000 members by 1943, with a further 20,000 in training. Yet the army achieved little military significance: its importance lay in demonstrating that Indian loyalty to the Allied war effort could not be assumed.[41] Overall, the effect of the war was to upset the precarious pre-war stability on which British policy and planning for India had been based. Britain lost both the initiative, and control over the timing of India's independence. By the end of the war, the question facing London was not whether, but when India would achieve Dominion status. The full implications of this, and the details of implementing it, would provide the post-war Labour government with one of its most pressing problems.

Relations with the United States

Reflecting on Japan's devastating attack on Pearl Harbor in December 1941, Churchill described it as a 'blessing': with the United States' entry into the war, the eventual defeat of the Axis Powers seemed assured. Although its alliance with the United States was of overwhelming importance to Britain during the war, that alliance was not without its difficulties. In addition to the inevitable differences over strategy and military priorities lay the more fundamental problem of traditional American anti-colonialism and the continuing scope for submerged economic rivalry.[42] Even with the combined resources of the empire, Britain desperately needed US assistance to sustain its war effort. In March 1941, the British government's long campaign to secure this finally paid off, and Washington began providing material help under the Lend-Lease scheme. By the time the United States entered the war, Britain was already heavily dependent on this help, but, in return, Washington was in a much stronger position to attempt to influence British policy on a range of subjects, including the future of the British Empire. Britain's evident vulnerability offered the Americans irresistible opportunities to try to secure economic footholds in regions such as the Caribbean, the Middle East and South and South-East Asia.[43]

In August 1941, Churchill and Roosevelt, meeting off the Newfoundland coast, signed the Atlantic Charter. Article 3 of this declared that *all* peoples had the right to choose how they were governed. Although Churchill subsequently claimed he understood this to refer to the populations of Nazi-occupied Europe, the article's wider significance for the populations of the dependent empire was clear. The War Cabinet agreed that Churchill should clarify the issue in Parliament.[44] In his speech of 9 September 1941, Churchill asserted that the Atlantic Charter applied to those parts of Europe currently occupied by Germany and did not extend to India and the colonies, policy towards which, he claimed had already been made clear in numerous earlier statements.[45] This was an embellishment of the truth: officials in the Colonial Office could produce no list of such declarations, and the question of Britain's imperial aims remained unresolved. For the remainder of the war, officials in Whitehall were involved in a protracted debate on how to clarify these aims, and to do so in such a way that American opinion would be satisfied.

At a practical level, US interest in the empire became apparent during 1940–41 with reference to the West Indies, focusing on Washington's desire to lease bases in the region and its suggestion that a joint US–British commission be created to supervise development policy. American criticism of colonialism seemed to have been vindicated by the collapse of the South-East Asian colonies by early 1942, a sequence of events which reinforced the conviction that colonial rule was inherently flawed. The key issue henceforward was whether the pre-war system could ever be restored.

Britain's growing dependence on Lend-Lease encouraged sustained US pressure on Britain to make compensating concessions by opening up the British Empire to US economic activity, by dismantling the Sterling Area and removing the system of Imperial Preference, against which American business had railed since its construction, and accepting in its place a new free trading international order. The war underlined the fact that the United States was now the world's predominant economic power and encouraged American policy-makers to discard their inter-war isolationism and accept a global post-war role.[46] This shift in thinking was fuelled not only by a desire to enhance US access to world markets (although concern to sustain post-war domestic employment made this an important consideration), but also by a growing belief that the political instability of the 1930s, and even the outbreak of war, were partly the result of economic conditions, especially the restrictions on trade arising from the dangerous spirit of economic nationalism. The American solution was to promote multilateralism in trade, supported by freer convertibility of currencies (based on more stable exchange rates). Given this new

emphasis on removing discriminatory trading practices, Washington saw
Britain's commitment to Imperial Preference as a particular problem. The
Atlantic Charter had included a promise to co-operate to achieve free access
for all nations to the raw materials and markets necessary for prosperity,
although the British side had succeeded in inserting the caveat that existing
obligations would be respected. Potentially more threatening to Britain were
the provisions of the Mutual Assistance Act of 1942, which formalized lend-
lease arrangements. In return for receiving the material it needed for the war
effort, but could no longer afford to pay for, Britain was obliged to accept
Article VII – a commitment to work towards the abolition of trade discrimination. Although the implications of this commitment for the system of Imperial
Preference were ambiguous, there was alarm in London at this apparent attack
on the empire. Voices were soon raised arguing that, given Britain's likely post-
war situation, it could not contemplate abandoning what might be an important economic lifeline. The Americans stressed that Article VII was not a *quid
pro quo*, but rather had to be seen as part of a wider initiative to reconstruct the
entire world economic order, and US officials assured their British counterparts
that Britain's economic circumstances would be taken into account when final
arrangements were made. Nevertheless, as the war progressed, there was a
tendency for British official attitudes to harden, partly in response to the
successful wartime exercise in imperial solidarity, and partly because of more
hard-headed calculations of the potential post-war value of the imperial system
to Britain. Contrasting British and US attitudes became more apparent when
discussions began in 1943 on future commercial policy. The British position
was that any abandonment of Imperial Preference would have to be compensated with sweeping reductions in US tariffs, which were likely to encounter
domestic political resistance in the United States. While initial exchanges in
Washington appeared hopeful, encompassing broad agreement on the desir-
ability of pursuing an international convention on trade liberalization, there
followed a long hiatus, with Anglo-American talks not being resumed until
Autumn 1945. Deepening pro-empire sentiment on the British side, coupled
with increasing resentment at US pressure, largely explains the sluggish
progress of discussions in the later years of the war. By the time serious
negotiations resumed, the question of commercial policy had, for the British
side, been eclipsed by the more pressing, though related, issue of securing a
substantial US loan.[47]

More progress was made during the war in securing agreement on a new
international monetary system, which Washington regarded as the essential
underpinnings of a multilateral trading order. At Bretton Woods in 1944,
Britain endorsed the creation of the International Monetary Fund, a stabilization fund to which member states would contribute, enabling them to purchase
the currency of other members to finance their trading requirements. The fund
was intended to promote exchange rate stability and so facilitate international
trade. From the outset, it was clear that because of its economic strength, the
United States, as largest single contributor, would effectively dominate the
IMF's operations. This worried the Bank of England, which feared that the

dollar's position as the world's major trading currency would be reinforced at the expense of sterling. British critics of the IMF also feared that it would erode national autonomy in economic policy-making, and that it would undermine the Sterling Area. Staunch defenders of the imperial system, such as Leopold Amery, were suspicious of US motives and believed that a renewed attack on Imperial Preference would shortly follow. Critics on the left in Britain saw a threat in the IMF to the policy goal of full employment, for which continuing controls on foreign exchange and bilateral trade agreements seemed necessary. Keynes, enjoying a wartime influence in Whitehall circles quite disproportionate to his official status, saw no alternative to British co-operation with the United States.

Meanwhile, within the British government, there were inevitably some who refused to accept the implied criticism of Britain's colonial record in the Far East. In August 1942, the Colonial Secretary, Lord Cranborne, wrote to the Foreign Secretary, Eden, offering a spirited defence of that record and emphasizing Washington's share of responsibility for the disaster of early 1942.[48] Publicly, however, Britain had to follow a more conciliatory path. Among the most worrying aspects of Washington's growing interest in colonial affairs, and of British wartime dependence on the US, was the emergence in 1942 of the question of placing the European colonial empires under international supervision, a notion which posed an obvious threat to Britain's imperial status. Responding to a proposal by the US Secretary of State, Cordell Hull, that London and Washington should make a joint statement on colonial policy, officials in Whitehall confronted the key question: how far could Britain accept a degree of international control over its colonial administration in the postwar world? Two possible responses emerged. First, Britain (and the other colonial powers) could hold on to responsibility for its colonies within a framework of international accountability yet to be established; secondly, control of the colonies could be transferred to a new international body.[49] Not surprisingly, opinions within the British government offered sharp contrasts. The Dominions Secretary, Labour leader Clement Attlee, was sympathetic to international supervision, arguing that this would lighten the burden of defending the colonies. At the other extreme, Leopold Amery and Lord Cranborne urged the retention of direct British responsibility for the colonies, for whose welfare they argued Britain had a moral responsibility, while accepting the case for some form of international supervisory framework.[50] Cranborne emphasized the difference between Britain's Far Eastern and African colonies. Since the US was less interested in the latter, it was not inevitable that they would be absorbed into a system designed for the former.

At the end of 1942, the War Cabinet discussed a memorandum prepared jointly by Attlee, Cranborne, Eden and the Colonial Secretary, Oliver Stanley, in an attempt to provide a coherent response to US pressure, and to overcome American suspicions, popular and official, that British colonial rule was outmoded. It was vital, ministers argued, to convince Washington not only to underwrite a programme of colonial defence, but also to accept the colonial powers' right to continued authority, even over those Asian colonies lost to

Japan.[51] The earlier differences among British ministers appeared to have been resolved in the interests of a united front: above all, Britain must take the initiative.

In response to Cordell Hull, Britain's four ministers suggested that regional commissions could be established to allow colonial powers, or 'parent states' as Hull had termed them, to act jointly in those parts of the world where they had common defence or economic interests. The Far East, Africa and the Western Atlantic were identified as areas where regional commissions might be appropriate. These points formed the substance of the draft declaration submitted to the State Department by the British government in February 1943. Its tone was paternalistic and evolutionary, and, while it accepted the case for regional machinery to promote international co-operation, and for United Nations involvement in regional defence, the draft was adamant on Britain's exclusive right to administer its territories, and to foster their economic, social and political development until they could administer themselves. No timetable for colonial political advance was suggested. Cordell Hull's draft, issued in March, conflicted with London's outlook in key respects. It not only reasserted the relevance of the Atlantic Charter to the colonies, but pointedly employed the term 'independence' (ironically *not* included in the Atlantic Charter, and deliberately avoided by London). To the horror of the Colonial Office, Washington seemed keen to establish target dates for colonial independence. Moreover, it proposed an International Trusteeship administration to protect the interests of colonial populations until this had been achieved. Given the divergence in aims between Britain and the United States, it proved impossible to compose a mutually acceptable declaration, and London hoped that in this atmosphere of stalemate, the entire idea would evaporate.[52]

Nevertheless, US enthusiasm for the principle of international accountability in colonial rule persisted, and Roosevelt continued to pursue the idea of an international trusteeship council, which would administer the former South-East Asian colonies. This proposal exposed divisions within the British government. Some, concerned above all to placate Washington, were willing to concede that this might be the price of maintaining the alliance. Others, especially the India Office and Colonial Office, were robust in defending their respective records and in resisting the idea of surrendering territory to international control. Here, during 1944, the Colonial Office took a proactive role, suggesting the alternative formula of 'partnership' between Britain and its colonies, leading eventually to self-government within the Commonwealth. Late in 1944, to pre-empt what might be unacceptable US proposals, and to retain the initiative in British hands, the Office circulated a memorandum on 'International aspects of colonial policy' to the War Cabinet. Developing the theme of 'partnership' within an acceptable international framework, officials sought the end of the mandate system and affirmed the right of the colonial powers to decide the rate at which political change in their colonies should be introduced. Meanwhile, their obligations to the international community, in relation to defence, commercial policy and other issues, were to be catered for by non-executive regional commissions and through the specialist agencies of the United Nations Organization. The supply of information on colonial affairs to a proposed International Colonial Centre would, it was hoped, take care of the question of accountability on colonial issues. Because of its overriding concern with maintaining good Anglo-American relations, the Foreign Office tended to look askance at the Colonial Office's suggestions. More importantly, the proposal to end the mandate system encountered opposition not only from the United States but also from the Dominions, some of which themselves operated their own 'sub-imperial' systems.[53]

As the Allies developed their own thinking, late in the war, on the shape of the post-war world, it became clear that these questions could not be evaded. Late in 1944, the Americans made it clear that the entire question of colonial trusteeship and the future of the mandates was bound to be addressed at the UN Security Conference, scheduled for April 1945 in San Francisco. To Churchill, this smacked of a fresh attempt to subvert British imperial interests. Meanwhile, at Yalta in February 1945, Churchill had, perhaps unwittingly, conceded that the UN's Trusteeship Council should have more powers than its League of Nations predecessor, including the right to visit trust territories. The Yalta Agreement, together with the determination of mandate-holding Dominions, such as Australia and New Zealand, ensured the frustration of the Colonial Office's strategy. When the UN conference eventually met in San Francisco, it was agreed that colonial populations would have the right to petition the Trusteeship Council. Although abhorrent to Britain, this channel of external interference was accepted in order to avoid alienating Washington and leaving Britain isolated at the UN.[54]

Although this episode clearly strained Anglo-American relations in the latter years of the war, longer-term considerations arguably operated to Britain's advantage. First, as the power of the Soviet Union became increasingly clear, the US government had no wish to act in any way which might prompt either the departure of Churchill or the collapse of his Coalition; still less did it want to provoke any general disintegration of its closest ally's power. Secondly, on strategic grounds, Washington (especially the military) came to see the post-war advantages of having access to island bases in the Pacific, and so general denunciations of 'colonialism' became significantly muted in the later phase of the war.[55]

Post-war planning and the aims of colonial policy

The failure to produce a satisfactory joint Anglo-American statement on colonial issues cleared the path for the Colonial Office to clarify its own thoughts and make a unilateral declaration on British policy. Since late 1942, with the war entering a new phase, and the prospect of victory now more realistic, officials had gained a new confidence about the possibilities for a radically modernized, progressive approach to colonial rule, an approach characterized by a distinctive sense of long-term mission. To some extent, the Colonial Office was resuming the initiative which had been interrupted by the hiatus of military set-backs, repeated ministerial changes and the distraction of justifying the colonial enterprise to Washington. By mid-1943, the momentum and direction first achieved by MacDonald before the war could be recovered.[56] This formed the background to the most important wartime statement of British colonial policy, delivered in the Commons by Oliver Stanley in July 1943, which was in effect a declaration of Britain's independence from Washington in the formulation of colonial policy. Many of the individual points made by Stanley had been made previously: the novelty of his speech lay in their grouping together in a forceful and confident declaration of Britain's long-term intentions. What had, for officials, been implicit or neglected now coalesced in a coherent agenda for liberal imperialism. Stanley declared that Britain's aim was to guide the colonial territories towards 'self-government within the framework of the British Empire'. No timetables for colonial political advance were disclosed: rather, in keeping with the Colonial Office's evolutionary assumptions, great emphasis was placed on the need for adequate economic and social development to serve as the foundations for constitutional progress.[57] Unstated, though implicit, was the assumption that this preparatory process would in most colonies be lengthy. In May 1943, a Cabinet Committee had privately noted that it would be 'many generations' before some colonies were ready for self-government. In those cases where 'plural communities' existed, it was judged impossible to predict how long the work of integrating them into viable units might take.[58]

A further important characteristic of British colonial policy by 1943 was that it seemed to be grounded in a secure bi-partisan consensus. Influenced by its small but active lobby group, the Fabian Colonial Bureau, the Labour Party had produced its own statement of colonial policy in March 1943. The pamphlet was welcomed as containing nothing fundamentally at odds with mainstream thinking within the Colonial Office. Accepting the doctrine of partnership, and sharing ministers' gradualist model for colonial development, the Labour leadership had shed the radical edge of some of its earlier policy pronouncements. The foundations of broad agreement between the two main parties had been laid, an agreement which would survive well into the 1950s, and which smoothed the transition between the Coalition and Attlee's government in 1945.

Armed with its declaration of policy aims, the Colonial Office could begin serious discussions on planning the post-war reconstruction of the colonies.[59] In this respect, the Office was ahead of many other departments in Whitehall. In its commitment to development and welfare, in the doctrine of partnership and the goal of eventual self-government, it had a package of complementary policies. Even before Stanley's speech, during 1941, the Colonial Office had made an abortive foray into reconstruction, creating a committee chaired by Lord Hailey to try to anticipate the kind of problems likely to emerge after the war. But it was not until 1943 that serious consideration could be given to reconstruction problems, and steps were taken to create the bureaucratic machinery needed to consider major policy questions and their implications. Given the emphasis now attaching to colonial material progress, one obvious area of concern was the acceleration of colonial development in its widest sense: only real economic growth in the colonies could provide secure foundations for the spectrum of social improvements, and ultimately political progress, to which London was now committed.

By 1943, there was growing unease in the Colonial Office that existing arrangements were producing disappointing results. US criticism of the slow progress achieved in the West Indies, voiced through the Anglo-American Caribbean Commission, only strengthened this concern.[60] While little actual progress could be expected in wartime, because of the scarcity of resources, more worrying was that colonial governments did not yet appear to have grasped the importance of coherent planning in development. Given their lack of training and personnel, this, perhaps, should not have been surprising. But it did raise the question of how far the initiative in promoting development could be left to individual colonial governments. In an important memorandum produced in August 1943, Sydney Caine, the Colonial Office official with overall responsibility for development policy, called for fundamental changes in the handling of development proposals, with the state taking a much more active role in economic planning.[61] Wartime mobilization had accelerated a pre-war trend for the work of the Colonial Office to be organized by broad subject, common to the colonial empire as a whole, rather than territorially. During the war, a further ten so-called 'subject' departments were created to tackle important themes arising from new concerns. There was also much discussion during the war of equipping the Colonial Service to undertake the new functions being envisaged for its members. The Resident Minister in West Africa, Lord Swinton, concluded that many colonial administrators were ill suited to the work of economic management, dismissing a large proportion of them as 'misfits'.[62] While this may have been a sweeping comment on staff struggling to perform their ever-widening range of duties, the Colonial Office was engaged throughout the war in a fundamental reappraisal of Colonial Service organization. To overcome the problem that all expatriate civil servants were technically responsible to the territorial government which employed them, one suggestion canvassed early in the war was for a 'general list' of specialist officers to be created, paid for by the British government and made available to any colony which needed them. An even more ambitious, and abortive, scheme, unpopular with officials in London, was to 'fuse' the Colonial Office staff and the Colonial Service. The Colonial Office's own favoured course was to concentrate on developing local civil services in the colonies, establishing minimum standards of services and competence to implement the colonial development and welfare (CD & W) policy, if necessary by injecting metropolitan funding. This proposal also foundered, partly through fears that Parliament would object to subsidizing colonial civil servants, and partly because the scheme already seemed to be out of step with the devolutionary thrust of colonial policy: such overt administrative centralization might, it was thought, smack of 'imperialism'. Although an official committee, chaired by the Duke of Devonshire, agreed that the training of colonial officials should be entrusted to the universities of Oxford, Cambridge and London, the question of creating a general list had not been resolved by the end of the war.[63] Discussions on the structure and role of the Colonial Service would continue into the 1950s, by when the careers of many officials were approaching an unexpectedly rapid conclusion.

The central importance attached to economic development as the basis for social and political progress is underlined by the fact that although by the mid-war years only a fraction of the available CD & W funds had been earmarked, officials were already concluding that the legislation of 1940 would have to be expanded in scope and given a longer duration: only in this way could successful, long-term development planning be realized. During 1944, discussions between the Colonial Office and the Treasury began, with the Colonial Office once again stressing the political importance of proving Britain's commitment to a reformed brand of colonialism in order to overcome the Treasury's misgivings about future funding commitments, given the likely post-war state of Britain's own finances. To drive home his case, Stanley reminded his Cabinet colleagues not only of the economic benefits likely to accrue to Britain from intensified colonial development, but also of the role development would play in strengthening the colonies' role in the imperial system which would be the key to Britain's influence in the post-war world. The War Coalition accepted this argument, and agreed to introduce a new CD & W Act, providing a total of £120 million for a ten-year period.[64] In itself an important propaganda coup for the Colonial Office, the 1945 CD & W Act inevitably fuelled unrealistic expectations of post-war progress in development. Realists, however, had never lost sight of the unpalatable truth that sustainable growth would have to be driven as far as possible from local, colonial resources: ultimate self-government, in any meaningful sense, had to be grounded in financial self-sufficiency.

Few officials in London pretended that the machinery established in 1940 to promote colonial development was really adequate: the dismal experience of colonial governments' preliminary attempts at 'planning' had only reinforced this view. This strengthened a growing tendency for the initiative in colonial policy formation to be assumed by the Colonial Office, introducing a degree of centralization and control from London quite alien to the inter-war pattern of devolved colonial administration.

In the face of criticism that the Colonial Office was itself ill equipped to perform some of these new functions, outside expertise was recruited onto a variety of new advisory committees. Of these, one of the most important, if ultimately abortive, experiments was the Colonial Economic Advisory Committee, established by Oliver Stanley late in 1943. The committee, which included authorities like Lord Hailey, along with representatives of business and academic economists, produced a variety of reports, some of which formed the basis of advice circulated to colonial governments. However, when it touched on controversial subjects, like colonial industrialization, or non-British sources of development funding, the committee found itself confronting bureaucratic resistance and a Colonial Office determined to retain control of the development agenda. Since development had become, in effect, the Office's *raison d'être*, it was perhaps inevitable that officials should seek to keep enthusiastic outsiders (unable to take a global view of policy) at arm's length. The question of Colonial Service reform is a good example, and a revealing one, of a component of the reconstruction agenda on which officials were not willing to involve lay opinion.

A further, recurring, problem associated with external contributions to the reconstruction debate was that advisory bodies were inclined to overlook the cost of the initiatives they proposed. This was symptomatic of a more fundamental weakness in the entire development strategy: the extravagant optimism about future possibilities which it was prone to inspire. An index of this optimism is the emphasis being placed by the later war years on the scope for 'mass education' (subsequently termed 'community development'). This involved a very catholic definition of education to embrace all those fields, such as health and improvements in agriculture which, taken together, would promote social progress in its widest sense, and draw on the initiative of the colonial peoples themselves to promote general improvement. While some in the Colonial Office remained cautious about the likely future constraints on colonial development, one consequence of wartime discussions was to raise expectations in the colonies that the cessation of hostilities would be followed relatively quickly by a demonstrable increase in living standards. It might be argued that one function of the entire development debate was to maintain colonial morale in wartime and ease Britain's task of extracting from the colonial empire those resources needed for the war effort. It remained to be seen at the end of the war whether Britain would be in any position to implement its ambitious development policy, or whether wartime commitments had been rhetorical, delivered primarily for propaganda and diplomatic reasons.

Political development in the colonies

Apart from Jamaica, which achieved internal self-government in 1944, and adjustments to the constitutions of the Gold Coast, Nigeria and British Guiana, little actual constitutional reform took place in the colonial empire during the war.[65] Political development was effectively suspended, and in some colonies, for example Kenya, the authorities clamped down on local political organizations and detained potentially troublesome activists. However, US pressure, and concern to avoid colonial unrest during the war made it necessary for Britain to think seriously for the first time about its long-term political objectives in the colonial empire, culminating in Stanley's watershed speech on self-government in July 1943. Crucially, wartime discussions on political development took place in an atmosphere in which there was little overt guidance from ministers, or much immediate sense of the aspirations of colonial populations. To this extent, they reflected the preoccupations of the administrative elite in the Colonial Office, and were inclined to be characterized by a high level of abstraction, however elegantly expressed in the many memoranda produced in these years. Inevitably, given the sheer diversity of the dependent empire, there could be no single, comprehensive plan. India's future had arguably been mapped out before the war: by the end of the war what remained to be decided was exactly when and in what form Indian independence would come, questions which Attlee's government had to address as a matter of urgency. The administrative structure of the empire precluded much close collaboration between the India Office and the Colonial Office, but officials in the latter did glean some broad lessons from Britain's experiences in the sub-continent. Above all, perhaps, they believed that 'errors' made in India should not be repeated in the colonies. Specifically, a conviction gained ground that concessions had been made precipitately to a vocal, but unrepresentative and even irresponsible intellectual elite, and that in Africa, for example, greater care would be needed to foster more durable alliances with traditional power structures. Translating such vague ideas into coherent policies, however, took time, and the general air of uncertainty hanging over the early war years, combined with the immediate task of achieving effective mobilization of colonial resources, delayed the clarification of political goals.

One colony where wartime developments proved crucial, and which bore some similarities to India, was Ceylon. By the outbreak of war, there was broad agreement within the British government on the direction of Ceylon's future. In 1939, the colony was awarded a quasi-Cabinet system of government, and it seemed that continuing progress towards full Cabinet government would result from the co-operative partnership between local ministers, representing the Sinhalese majority, and British officials. The outbreak of war, however, led the Colonial Office to place a moratorium on further change, but officials chose not to inform their Sinhalese collaborators until August 1941. Meanwhile, in stark contrast to India's nationalists, local politicians co-operated in the war effort.[66] As early as 1940, however, the island's recent record of communal tensions led the Permanent Under-Secretary at the Colonial Office, Sir Cosmo Parkinson, to conclude that Ceylon might pose Britain its most intractable colonial problem. During the war, Ceylon's importance grew, not least as the source of nearly two-thirds of the Allies' rubber following the loss of Malaya, raising the question whether wartime loyalty would lead to political concessions from Britain. Although often depicted as a 'model colony', Ceylon experienced a vigorous and at times bitter anti-colonial campaign producing a demand in 1942 for independence by the Sinhalese political leader, D.S. Senanayake. Associated with this heightened politicization was growing tension between the Sinhalese majority and the Tamil minority. Against the background of developments in India, it was clear that Ceylon's future would indeed be a major post-war problem for British policy-makers.[67] In 1943, Senanayake's persistence was rewarded with a British commitment to full responsible self-government, and in 1944 the Soulbury Commission was appointed to advise on Ceylon's future. Its report, published in 1945 as the war drew to a close, provided the framework for the colony's independence in 1948.

In relation to Britain's African empire, official thinking on future political development, at best sketchy before the war, entered a new phase, in which the fundamentals of policy were examined in what became an increasingly systematic manner. At the start of the war, Malcolm MacDonald recognized that the war was likely to awaken African political aspirations, and he believed that

Britain needed to decide what the purposes of colonial policy were, and what their outcome was expected to be. In particular, he sought an answer to the most difficult question – what would be the outcome of the policy of indirect rule? How was reliance on the native administrations, for example in West Africa, to be reconciled with the development, however gradual, of legislative councils? What were Britain's long-term intentions in those parts of Africa with mixed racial populations, such as Kenya, and what would the implications be for closer association of the territories in East and Central Africa? As the war progressed, these questions would be posed in relation to an overarching problem: how could nascent nationalism, for example in Africa, be co-opted and moulded into a partner in the work of reform now being envisaged by the Colonial Office? MacDonald summoned a meeting at Carlton House in London in October 1939, attended by some of the leading British authorities on Africa, including Lord Hailey, Margery Perham and Lord Lugard. Most agreed that it would be dangerous to give concessions to the African intelligentsia, which, like Congress in India, had its eyes firmly on securing control of the organs of central government and administration. MacDonald subsequently called for a 'seething of thought' among his officials in response to these fundamental problems, but the deterioration of the military situation during 1940 intervened. However, one practical consequence of this early initiative was the decision to despatch Lord Hailey once more to Africa, to undertake a comprehensive review of the political situation.[68]

Hailey's report, *Native Administration and Political Development in British Tropical Africa*, was submitted to the Colonial Office early in 1941, and quickly established itself as a key text in British official thinking on Africa. Hailey made clear that British policy could not carry on along its pre-war lines. Although he did not detect any significant force of nationalism emerging, he believed that economic and social development would swell the number of Western-educated Africans with political aspirations, and that these aspirations must be provided with a 'safe' outlet. A fundamental problem, according to Hailey, was that as the development initiative gathered pace, it would involve colonial governments becoming more interventionist and therefore the focus of local grievances and political controversy, which in turn might undermine the authority of the colonial state. Asking the awkward question how far Britain could take colonial acceptance of its rule for granted, Hailey emphasized the importance of being able to argue (not least to Washington) that the logical outcome of London's policy was eventual colonial self-government. One of Hailey's most important conclusions was that the existing Native Authorities of rural Africa were inadequate agencies for political advance, and that greater African political participation was needed through regional councils and involvement in administration. To help the colonial state to perform its new social and economic tasks, more reliance would have to be placed on educated Africans and less on traditional African representatives.[69]

Hailey was opposed, however, to what he called 'premature "constitution-mongering"', and offered no detailed proposals for constitutional change. Nevertheless, his belief in the need for new collaborators and new government structures marked a breakthrough in official thinking. Of crucial importance was his recognition that development, already the centrepiece of British colonial self-justification and the immediate priority, was inextricably bound to the need for political reform whose overall objective was self-government. Without suggesting practical solutions, he had shown the connection between the twin elements of colonial policy which might make it acceptable to international opinion.

Although the Colonial Office had taken the initiative in examining future policy on Africa's political development, some colonial governors volunteered their own opinions, occasionally running out of step with thinking in London. In Nigeria, for example, Sir Bernard Bourdillon, appointed in 1935, addressed much the same question that MacDonald had posed. While he was opposed to 'artificial' experiments, he was convinced that Nigerians had to be given a greater role in managing their own affairs, with the ultimate goal of responsible self-government. He had no fixed views about how this should be achieved, and he did not rule out simultaneous reforms of 'native' institutions and representative bodies. In view of the diversity of Nigeria, Bourdillon advocated a concentration on regional development, with the creation of regional councils for each of the territory's three provinces, and a central council in Lagos. Beyond this, he felt that employing Africans in senior administrative posts, broadening the responsibilities of native administrations and including some 'unofficial' African representatives to the executive councils would all help to promote a constructive political climate and pre-empt tensions between Westernized Africans and the relatively traditional and conservative majority of the population.[70]

In the Gold Coast, meanwhile, Sir Alan Burns, governor between 1941 and 1946, had anticipated the need for political reform by discussing the subject in London before assuming his new post. Among his proposals were the appointment of two Africans to the Executive Council, an increase in African elected representation in the Legislative Council and the recruitment of Africans as District Commissioners. The latter suggestion found favour in the Colonial Office. As Lord Cranborne commented (revealingly), on the assumption that British colonial rule was permanent, such a measure would be a practical move towards assimilation.[71] Officials were more cautious, however, on the question of involving Africans in the machinery of central government. These misgivings were supported by Lord Hailey, who thought that change should be introduced from the bottom of the administrative pyramid, not from the top. Burns, drawing support from Bourdillon, dismissed these objections, pointing out that he was being made increasingly aware of the extent of hostility towards Europeans in the Gold Coast and the colonial government. Confronted with this argument, the Colonial Office relented, and in September 1942 Africans were appointed to the executive councils in both Nigeria and the Gold Coast. This episode served to strengthen the Colonial Office's belief that there was a need to plan West Africa's political future in a co-ordinated way.

This was the background to an important contribution by O.G.R. Williams, head of the Colonial Office's West Africa Department. In a memorandum submitted in the summer of 1943, Williams took up Burns's warning that it would be hazardous if the political aspirations of the small Westernized elite were not satisfied, and argued that political development in the region should be closely related to material and social progress. In particular, constitutional change should be built upon secure educational foundations, and the opening of the administration to African entrants should be tied to the growth of educational facilities. Williams drew on Hailey's report to propose a highly tentative five-stage plan for West Africa's political development. This would begin with the granting of extended powers to municipal councils, an expansion in the number of elected members, a larger role for the Westernized elite in the Native Authorities, and the development of councils in rural areas. Significantly, it was assumed that these changes would be very gradual, possibly taking generations to complete, preparing the ground for the creation of unofficial majorities in the legislative councils, and finally self-government. Williams circumvented the key issue of reforming the composition of executive councils, where effective power lay.[72]

When Williams's ideas were discussed in the Colonial Office in July 1943, Lord Hailey adopted what seemed to be a more adventurous position. He suggested not only that London should declare its aim for West Africa to be responsible government, but also that Africans should be involved in the territories' executive councils with semi-ministerial roles. This was considered to be too radical a course, and Hailey was uncomfortable when both Burns and Bourdillon did include African unofficials in their executive councils (this anticipated the distinct unease he felt when both Nigeria and the Gold Coast introduced unofficial majorities in their legislative councils after the war).

If the Colonial Office had reached a stalemate in proposing acceptable stages of political development, there was, nevertheless, a parallel attempt during the war to identify potential sources of political opposition in the region, and to create a new set of workable alliances with likely future leaders of West African nationalism. In May 1943, for example, Stanley invited the African editors of leading West African newspapers to Britain, a strategy which has been described as 'managing nationalism'. Among these was the Nigerian Nnamdi Azikiwe, who submitted a plan ('The Atlantic Charter and British West Africa') which showed that the thinking of West African nationalists was not significantly different to that of the Colonial Office. In this respect it is ironic that in the same month, on the retirement of Sir Bernard Bourdillon, London appointed the conservative-minded Sir Arthur Richards to replace him. In retrospect an unfortunate choice, Richards, who remained governor until 1947, arguably undid much of Bourdillon's constructive work, seeing his role as being not to 'manage' nationalism, but to contain and disarm it.[73]

In other parts of British Africa, especially where there were significant white settler populations, there seemed little scope for constitutional speculation on the West African model. Britain's wartime dependence on the commodities produced in East and Central Africa, especially after the loss of South-East Asia, had not only enabled the settlers to entrench themselves among the colonial state's levers of power and attempt to seek redress for their economic difficulties during the Depression, but had also highlighted the divergence between settler aspirations for self-government and territorial amalgamation, and longstanding metropolitan pledges to uphold the interests of the African majority. In 1942, in response to strong settler pressure, the East African governments had created a Civil Defence and Supply Council, seen in London as part of a concerted bid for Dominion status under white rule. Observing these developments, the Colonial Office concluded privately that self-government would eventually be achieved on settler terms.[74]

When, in July 1942, the Colonial Office reviewed the situation in Kenya, for example, it was frankly acknowledged that fine talk between the wars of trusteeship had a distinctly hollow ring. Largely because of the success of settler spoiling tactics, London had failed to devise political arrangements capable either of reconciling the divergent interests of the territory's settlers and Asian business community, or of giving teeth to the Devonshire Declaration on the paramountcy of African interests. Similarly, discussions on closer association between the East African territories had been abortive, and the settlers had consequently become increasingly impatient with Colonial Office control. The danger, as noted by the head of the Colonial Office's Africa Division, Sir Arthur Dawe, was that the war might encourage the settlers to seize the initiative in forging a polity to their own tastes, or that they might fall under the influence of expansionist South Africa. To forestall this, Dawe proposed a federal structure for East Africa, composed of five provinces, one of which, the White Highlands, would become a largely autonomous settler enclave.[75] These discussions coincided with Harold Macmillan's tenure of the post of Parliamentary Under-Secretary at the Colonial Office. Macmillan rejected Dawe's assumptions and, in suggestions which reinforced his reputation as an unorthodox Tory, called for the large-scale nationalization of land in Kenya and its dedication to collective farming. (Ironically, part of the long-term 'solution' to Kenya's problems did indeed subsequently involve ambitious programmes of land transfer, designed to foster a stable and quiescent Kikuyu yeomanry).

During 1943, the governor of Kenya, Sir Henry Moore, introduced fresh proposals for the amalgamation of the three East African territories. This unitary arrangement, because it would focus real political power in settler hands, was unacceptable to the Colonial Office, which refused to yield on the principle of African paramountcy. Oliver Stanley then suggested another federal solution, in which the central legislature would have an official majority, with Kenya having an unofficial majority in its provincial legislature. The deputy prime minister, Clement Attlee, rejected this scheme, asserting that the Labour Party would not accept an unofficial majority in Kenya. Equally, the governors of Uganda and Tanganyika, fearing Kenyan predominance and committed to the tradition of trusteeship, resisted a representative form of closer association, and argued that each territory should remain free to evolve in its own way. Their paternalistic outlook gave them a preference for government shaped by 'official', not 'unofficial' (that is, settler) concerns. Following the appointment of Sir Philip Mitchell as governor of Kenya at the end of

1944, a way was found out of this impasse. An East African High Commission was unveiled in 1945, designed to foster closer *economic* not *political* links through the development of common services, but this did not eradicate concern about settler ambitions for the region.

Meanwhile, in Central Africa, the Bledisloe Commission recommended in 1939 that Britain should work towards the long-term goal of drawing Northern and Southern Rhodesia, and their impoverished neighbour Nyasaland, closer together, with the proviso that African interests must be protected. The commission was unable to suggest how this might be achieved in practical terms, partly because of the variety of 'native' policies currently in operation in the region, and it seemed that despite the potential economic gains, amalgamation was not yet practicable. This did not deter Central Africa's settlers, especially those in Southern Rhodesia, who, under the leadership of their premier, Sir Godfrey Huggins, dreamed of creating a new Dominion under effective Rhodesian control.[76] The settlers' longstanding desire for full amalgamation of the three territories evoked some sympathy from members of the War Coalition. As in the case of East Africa, the Colonial Office sought to devise arrangements which would safeguard the Africans of the two northern territories, while securing a better deal for those in the 'self-governing colony', Southern Rhodesia. In doing so, the Office's wider aims were to pre-empt criticism of British colonial rule (not least from metropolitan liberal opinion), and to draw the sting of South African northward expansion. More prosaically, officials in London doubted whether the settlers, numbering around 85,000, had the capacity to administer a new state containing a majority of five million Africans.[77] Should the new Dominion encounter problems in this respect, either Britain would face having to reassert direct control (which would be politically contentious) or, much worse, risk the region succumbing to the gravitational pull of Pretoria. Although the Southern Rhodesian settlers had opted in 1922 not to join South Africa, officials in London feared that if their regional ambitions were frustrated they might reconsider this decision. Following discussions at Cabinet level, the Colonial Secretary told Parliament in October 1944 that amalgamation in Central Africa was not feasible at that stage, but that instead a Central African Council would be created the following year, designed to promote greater regional co-operation, for example in technical matters. Nevertheless, this body was not seen by London as an intermediate stage on the road to full amalgamation: settler leaders greeted its formation with muted enthusiasm, and did not lose sight of their overarching aim.

The question of integrating colonial territories into larger, more viable groupings was relevant beyond Africa. In the West Indies, for example, the possibility of some sort of federation had been discussed fitfully for many years before being addressed squarely in the report of the Moyne Commission in 1940. This had suggested a preliminary experiment, bringing together the Leeward and the Windward Islands, in order to gauge the possible benefits of wider federation. Although its primary concern had been issues of development and welfare, the commission had also recommended far-reaching political reforms through the introduction of universal suffrage. However, following a visit to the West Indies in 1942–43, the Permanent Under-Secretary at the Colonial Office, Sir Cosmo Parkinson, had concluded that outside Jamaica, whose new constitution had already been agreed, there was no great need for such change. Instead, Parkinson advised that the views of the various colonial governors in the region should be sought on the question of federation.[78] London was aware of the need to tread carefully, as Washington took a particular interest in developments affecting what it regarded as its own 'backyard'. More immediately, the Colonial Office was confronted by the long particularist tradition of the West Indian islands, and the scope for tensions and rivalry between them. The fact that the islands were not at equivalent stages of constitutional development was a further complication. Within the islands, suspicions that this new British interest in federation betrayed covert US pressure, itself informed by American economic ambitions in the region, together with a fear that London might use federation as a pretext to delay progress towards self-government, clouded the issue. Ultimately, it was concern that the smaller islands could not stand alone as self-governing states, and that they needed to group together in order to be heard, that convinced the Colonial Office to pursue the federal option, and to seek governors' views in March 1945.[79] This problem would continue to exercise officials in London in the post-war period, merging with their wider discussions on the future of smaller colonial territories.

Given the depth of the humiliation experienced by Britain in South-East Asia, it is not surprising that planning for this region's post-war future should have been a major preoccupation for London during the war. For Churchill, bridling against American criticism of colonialism's record, it was inconceivable that Britain's territories in the region should not be recovered. To some extent, it was convenient that the US preoccupation with defeating Japan freed British Far Eastern forces to concentrate on this overriding strategic goal. The broad moral of the collapse of Malaya and Singapore was that there could be no return to the ramshackle political arrangements of the 1930s. Officials already intent on reform used the disaster as an opportunity to propose ambitious new schemes, basing renewed British claims to colonial legitimacy on the complementary ideas of 'nation-building' and 'partnership', while the region's likely post-war strategic importance and economic value to Britain provided convincing arguments for wholesale change.[80] Wartime planning for South-East Asia was conducted jointly, and in secret, by the Colonial Office and the War Office, on the grounds that the region would initially come under British military administration. As in other parts of the colonial empire, the Colonial Office was keen to explore the benefits of closer territorial association, but the consequences in South-East Asia were arguably more bold and ambitious than anywhere else. At the end of May 1944, the War Cabinet approved the Colonial Office's plan for a new Malayan Union to incorporate the previously diverse collection of Malay states under varying degrees of British rule. The creation of a modern, centralized colonial state in Malaya had two major rationales. First, drawing on the lessons of 1942, was the conviction that integration would produce a territory easier to defend and more amenable to rapid economic development, which would be very much in Britain's post-war interests. Secondly, planners hoped to give all Malaya's ethnic communities a stake in a new multiracial system, and so proposed to extend citizenship privileges to the Chinese and Indian populations. This would not only produce a state which in time could become self-governing, possibly as part of a larger South-East Asian Dominion, but it would also give the non-Malay population, especially Chinese entrepreneurs, a vested interest in co-operating in future economic growth, and in participating fully in the life of the territory. Furthermore, this new Malayan Union was to be under direct British control, Sarawak and North Borneo were also to be brought under Crown Colony government, and a governor-general appointed to co-ordinate government policy throughout the region.[81] Singapore would be maintained as a distinct colonial territory. What was intended ultimately to be a step towards regional devolution therefore involved a striking reassertion of imperialism by Britain, and a fundamental shift in relations between the British authorities and the traditionally privileged Malay elite. In effect, the Malayan Union scheme involved the re-negotiation of existing treaties between Britain and the Malay rulers under which the latter would retain their social status but lose their sovereignty and be obliged to share political rights with their Indian and Chinese neighbours. Inevitably, such a radical change would provoke Malay opposition, but Britain's enforced absence from the peninsula during the war precluded consultation and the full assessment of local grass-roots opinion. Of course, London's inability to embark on any meaningful consultation with the Malay sultans strengthened the hands of officials determined to achieve their radical policy objectives, though it also meant that dangerous political sentiments would be unleashed after the war when the Union scheme could finally be revealed.

One final theme emerging during the war straddled both political development and development in its broader, current sense. In the colonial context, the first signs of local political mobilization were often associated with the emergence of labour organizations. At an early stage in the war, the Colonial Office had recognized the potential challenge which colonial trade unions might pose to controlled and moderate constitutional development and political activity. It therefore sought to mould the development of these unions, to prevent them becoming radical or subversive. To do this, the Colonial Office enlisted the aid of the Trades Union Congress, which before long was sending advisers to many parts of the colonial empire, while colonial officials continued the work of gathering information on labour conditions in several regions. Metropolitan encouragement of trade union development was neither empty rhetoric nor the whim of reformers such as Malcolm MacDonald. Under the 1940 CD & W Act, to qualify for grant aid, colonial governments were expected to demonstrate that they were attempting to create a framework in which trade unionism could flourish (a message repeated by the Colonial Office in 1941).[82]

The impact of war on the metropolitan economy

If the First World War had placed enormous financial strains on Britain, the Second World War led to a state of near bankruptcy. Mobilizing the economy for war, and diverting the resources necessary to conduct the war, together with war-related damage, had cost Britain around one quarter of its national wealth. A large part of Britain's foreign assets, totalling £1,000 million, including many of its dollar investments, had been sold off to pay for vital imports. The war had eroded that vital income from overseas earnings which before the war had helped to support the balance of payments. In 1945, Britain's total foreign debts stood at around £3,700 million. The merchant navy, another valuable source of invisible earnings before the war, had been reduced in size by nearly a third. By 1943, British exports stood at less than one-third of their pre-war value, meaning that valuable overseas markets were lost. This had been aggravated by the conditions attaching to Lend-Lease, which had barred Britain from using US material in its export industries. Given the demands of war, export production had been allowed to shrink, and nearly half the total labour force was involved either in military service or in war-related production. It was estimated that British exports would have to be expanded by around 75 per cent of their 1938 value, a process which was likely to take at least three years, if it was achievable at all. Superimposed on these problems would be the additional burdens of making good the physical damage caused by the war, and fulfilling the coalition government's wartime promise to introduce a welfare state and to try to maintain full employment. The huge and difficult task of converting a wartime economy into a peacetime one would leave Britain still dependent on the United States for a wide range of essential imports. The problem was likely to become particularly acute when Washington terminated Lend-Lease, and Britain had to start paying for the goods it imported from the US. Significantly, much British wartime planning had been based on the assumption that Lend-Lease would continue until the end of the Pacific war, which was thought likely to come approximately 18 months after the defeat of Germany. During the so-called 'transition period', Britain would have a breathing space in which to begin converting its economy to a peacetime footing, tackle domestic reconstruction and start work on restoring its export trade. In these circumstances, it was not thought that further US financial assistance would be needed.[83] In practice, however, the Allied use of atomic weapons against Japan in August 1945 made British planners' calculations invalid, and Whitehall was soon forced to turn its energies to securing a massive injection of dollars to assist metropolitan recovery.

In March 1945, with the war in Europe entering its concluding phase, Keynes had sketched the economic options available to Britain. He had already, in September 1944, suggested that the country was facing a 'financial Dunkirk' in view of its depleted resources, its debts and its massively expanded overseas commitments. Given the country's post-war predicament, it could choose what Keynes termed 'starvation corner', which would involve the continuation of wartime austerity measures, tight controls over currency and imports and a rejection of the multilateralism favoured by the United States. To address the impending financial deficit, Britain would have to retrench not only in its domestic spending, but also with respect to its now inflated overseas responsibilities. As Keynes put it: 'We cannot police half the world at our own expense when we have already gone into pawn to the other half.'[84] The alternative course would be to seek some form of transitional financial help from Washington, taking the form either of a free gift, or, more probably a loan, preferably with as few 'strings' attached to it as possible. This US aid would ease the balance of payments problem, while allowing Britain to finance its reconstruction programme and maintain domestic living standards.[85] Keynes, like many of his Treasury colleagues, was inclined to believe that the United States would be willing to provide Britain with a large dollar loan on favourable terms, or perhaps even with a free gift of dollars. One of the most controversial prescriptions Keynes offered to avoid 'starvation corner' was the cancellation of part of the colonial sterling balances. Politically, however, this was a sensitive issue, given that the colonies had been encouraged to expect access to these potentially valuable sources of development capital. Meanwhile, the difficulties of converting these sums into hard exports were reinforced by the dislocation of British industry and post-war concentration on more desirable export markets, particularly in hard currency areas. Although official discussions continued, the future of the sterling balances was not settled until the early 1950s.[86] Meanwhile, the fact that the British government opted to avoid 'starvation corner' is, in retrospect, not surprising. It would have been very difficult for any post-war government to explain to the British electorate that their collective wartime sacrifices were now to be rewarded with yet more stringency and privation. Equally the sheer cost of the war, which was widely understood in Whitehall, and the accompanying balance of payments problems, seemed to indicate that external financial support was unavoidable. Another important consideration was that Britain simply could not abandon its overseas commitments and expect to remain one of the 'Big Three' world powers. However, maintaining those commitments also appeared to dictate some form of US assistance. Finally, if Britain were to attempt to consolidate its wartime apparatus of trade discrimination and currency restrictions, and so renege on its promises to Washington, it risked triggering an economic war with the United States. All of these considerations arguably made the British government's decision to seek American help unavoidable, although at the time it was seen by many as a controversial choice, heavy with implications both for British national autonomy and for the future of the imperial system.

By the end of the war, London could look with satisfaction at an imperial system which was, ostensibly, not merely intact but had also survived the strains and rigours imposed by the conflict, and appeared to have a new sense of purpose and direction. Much play had been made of the reformed style of colonial rule upon which Britain seemed intent. Economic and social development would be the precursors to planned political development leading ultimately to self-government within the British Commonwealth. These commitments had been the necessary price of securing the full mobilization of imperial resources and of appeasing a sometimes tiresome American ally. Yet these commitments inevitably encouraged expectations in the colonial empire which Britain was in no position to satisfy. Given Britain's own straitened circumstances after 1945, there seemed little prospect of implementing the wide-ranging social and other reforms which lay at the heart of the outlook nurtured within the Colonial Office since the days of MacDonald. Moreover, the impact of the war itself had unleashed forces and tensions within the imperial system, embracing the colonies, India, the Dominions, and the 'informal' empire which could not later be contained. Shifts had occurred which would prove irreversible. As one historian has commented: 'Paradoxically, the ultimate cost of defending the British Empire during the Second World War was the Empire itself.'[87] However, although the war had weakened Britain, brought forward the probable date of India's independence and set in train developments which would create problems for Britain in many colonies, it had also demonstrated to Britain the value of its colonial territories. It would be reasonable to argue that Britain's war-induced weakness gave rise not to a willingness to shed dependencies (except, as in the case of India, where there seemed to be no alternative), but to hold on to them with a renewed determination.

CHAPTER 3

ATTLEE AND POST-WAR
ADJUSTMENTS, 1945–51

For the Labour government of Clement Attlee which took office before the end of the Second World War, maintaining Britain's status as one of the 'Big Three' global powers was an unquestioned priority. In the government's world-view, the empire occupied a central role. However, imperial policy in the post-war years was affected by the new conditions in which Britain found itself. The country's economic situation was of overriding significance. Exhausted by the demands of war, the British economy faced a difficult period of readjustment, at a time when it was expected to support not only greatly extended overseas commitments, but also an ambitious programme of domestic social reform. The international climate, too, harboured many uncertainties: the disintegration of the wartime alliance with the Soviet Union and the onset of the Cold War lent added significance to fears that the United States might once again retreat into isolationism, leaving Britain to shoulder the burden of defending Western Europe from a Soviet Union whose ambitions were already beginning to seem threatening, and which seemed to include the dissolution of the British Empire. In the wider international arena, Britain faced the unwelcome interest shown in colonial affairs by members of the new United Nations. Economic problems and the developing Cold War convinced Attlee's Cabinet of the value of the empire: far from being intent on liquidating the empire, the government sought ways of strengthening it and maximizing its strategic and economic potential. Whether this would be possible would depend in part on US attitudes, and on the attitudes of colonial populations. Sensitized by their wartime experiences of Washington's anti-colonial stance, ministers also had to take into account the development of anti-colonial nationalism. Although the latter seemed as yet to be confined to Asia and the Middle East, the possibility of its spreading to Africa had to be borne in mind. Moreover, in the context of the Cold War, the colonies appeared ripe for Communist penetration.[1]

As John Darwin has argued, the decisions taken by Attlee's government in the period 1945–48 marked a historic turning point in Britain's development as an international power: these decisions, the retreat from South Asia and Palestine, the search for a new *modus vivendi* in the Middle East, the cultivation of the 'special relationship' with the United States, the re-definition of the nature of the British Commonwealth, and the adoption of new policies towards the political evolution of the dependent empire, especially in Africa, would effectively shape Britain's external policies for almost a generation.[2]

The economic context of external policy

A major determinant in policy during this period was Britain's economic position. Attlee's ministers were unfortunate in having to confront three major crises during their time in office: in 1947, in relation to sterling and the dollar shortage, in 1949 over devaluation, and in 1950–51, surrounding the financial implications of massive rearmament. All of these would have important repercussions for Britain's external policies, and especially the imperial connection. Forced to shed more than a billion pounds' worth of overseas assets during the war, Britain was now the world's largest debtor, to the tune of around £4.7 billion. Having depended for so long on invisible earnings, Britain's balance of payments position seemed bleak. Compounding this, in August 1945, was the shock of Washington's abrupt termination of Lend-Lease. As John Maynard Keynes famously observed, Britain faced a 'financial Dunkirk' unless it could secure substantial US assistance. Keynes and his team of negotiators failed to persuade Washington to provide the hoped-for interest-free grant (in recognition of Britain's wartime sacrifices). Instead, the American loan of $3.75 billion (at 2 per cent interest), and the writing-off of Lend-Lease debts of $21 billion for $650 million, came with unpalatable 'strings'. Among these, one of the most problematic for Britain was the promise to ratify the 1944 Bretton Woods Agreement by cancelling the sterling balances and making the pound fully convertible into dollars by the middle of July 1947. The sterling balances were funds held in the Bank of England by overseas governments, representing Britain's sterling debts to these countries, often arising from wartime expenditure. By the end of the war, they totalled £3,150 million, about a quarter of which was owed to the colonies, with other major sums owing to India and Egypt. Cancelling the balances was opposed by the Treasury and the Bank of England, which saw them as assets, enabling Britain to import goods on credit and reinforcing the position of sterling as a major world currency. In political terms, too, cancelling the balances would be difficult.[3]

It is generally agreed that the time was not right in summer 1947 to launch the convertibility operation, which involved removing the controls on exchanging sterling into dollars. While the Treasury and the Bank of England saw the attempt as a demonstration of sterling's strength, which would bolster overseas confidence in the pound, in reality, Britain simply lacked the dollar resources to make this practicable. The large dollar loan secured in 1946 was being used up at an alarming rate, Britain's dollar earnings had not yet recovered from their wartime decline, and some essential imports could only be obtained from the dollar area. To aggravate matters, Britain was already facing internal economic difficulties early in 1947, when a severe winter caused a fuel crisis and a consequent decline in industrial production.[4] Significantly, when the Chiefs of Staff concluded in 1947 that it was unlikely that Britain would face another major war within the next five years, they felt this was just as well, since the country's economy was unable to meet the demands involved.[5] During summer 1947, as the date of convertibility drew near, the drain on Britain's meagre exchange reserves accelerated. The crisis was eventually eased by the suspension of convertibility in August. Subsequently, a massive export drive was launched to try to restore the balance of payments position. This, together with the impact of Marshall Aid, which became effective in spring 1948, gave Attlee's government a brief respite.[6] The Marshall Plan, announced in June 1947, provided $12 billion to assist European recovery, of which Britain received the lion's share, $2.7 billion. Washington's motives were not entirely altruistic: as well as bolstering the Western European democracies against Communism, this aid was intended to help the construction of an 'open' world economy, benefiting US exporters. One unwelcome aspect of this for Britain was the implicit attack on the Sterling Area.[7] With the signing of the General Agreement on Tariffs and Trade (GATT) in October 1947, Britain committed itself to the phased dismantling of Imperial Preference. Yet the events of summer 1947 strengthened a metropolitan tendency to see the Sterling Area as the key to Britain's economic salvation. Britain in effect relied increasingly on an imperial economic system in which the Sterling Area members could trade with one another without restriction, but in which trade outside the area, especially with dollar countries, was highly regulated. As during the war, the Sterling Area became a mechanism through which the dollar resources of the empire and Commonwealth could be 'pooled' and rationed. The Sterling Area and Imperial Preference were given new life by Britain's post-war economic difficulties. An increasing proportion of Britain's trade was conducted within the empire, reaching its zenith in the early 1950s.

Not surprisingly, Britain's growing financial problems led to calls within the government for major reductions in Britain's overseas commitments, especially its military spending. Not only would this save dollar expenditure, but it could also free scarce labour for deployment in the export drive. Among the additional responsibilities currently being borne by Britain were support for the Greek regime in its civil war against Communists, justified on the grounds that such a sensitive region as the Mediterranean could not be left vulnerable to Soviet encroachment in the event of a Communist victory, and Germany, where occupation forces had to be maintained, and civilians in the British Zone supplied with food. At a time when US help to Britain and Western Europe was still limited, and Cold War tensions appeared to be worsening, it was clear that, given its already severe balance of payments problems, Britain's economy was being stretched too far. All of this coincided with the deteriorating situation in India and Palestine.[8] Evidently, cuts had to be made. There followed, during February 1947, a series of decisions which had far-reaching consequences for Britain's world role. Chief among these was Foreign Secretary Ernest Bevin's declaration that the question of the future of Palestine would be referred to the United Nations, that aid to Greece and Turkey would end almost immediately, and that Britain would withdraw from India by June 1948 at the latest. These decisions seemed to represent a watershed in Britain's world role, a recognition of national enfeeblement, and an acceptance that some tasks, such as the defence of Greece and Turkey, would have to be surrendered to the much more powerful United States. Yet this can also be seen as a process of pragmatic readjustment to realities, following the abnormal period of extended commitments during and immediately after the war. Although the decisions of 1947 were taken under duress, in an atmosphere of crisis, they did not signal any abdication of Britain's overall global role: there was no question, for instance, of withdrawing from the Middle East, or of abandoning plans to consolidate British influence in South-East Asia or Africa.[9] Moreover, there was a visceral belief among senior ministers that the process of adjusting overseas commitments in the face of financial constraint should not be allowed to escalate into a general retreat: as the Chiefs of Staff argued, this would be tantamount to a serious reversal in the Cold War.[10]

As a result of the failure of convertibility, the emphasis in British economic policy was to return balance to the trade between Britain and the Sterling Area and the dollar area. It was mainly in order to help the export programme that the government decided, in September 1949, to devalue the pound by over 30 per cent, to a new value of $2.80. The Chancellor, Sir Stafford Cripps, was especially anxious to make British (and Sterling Area) exports more competitive in dollar markets, to ease the Sterling Area's overall trade deficit with the dollar area, although, perhaps significantly, the Sterling Area's members were not consulted over devaluation. He also hoped to reinforce confidence in sterling and stop Britain's exchange reserves falling to dangerous levels.[11] Devaluation was followed by a marked increase in exports to dollar markets, reaching £2,254 million in value in 1950, compared with £920 million only four years previously. It seemed that the British economy had recovered and settled into a healthy rhythm, which was expected to achieve full viability by 1952 (by which time Marshall Aid would have expired). Sterling was still a major international currency, being the vehicle for about half of all international trade.[12] This optimistic trend was interrupted by the outbreak of the Korean War in June 1950, and by the accompanying rearmament programme, encouraged by Washington, on a scale unprecedented in peacetime, but justified by fears that events in Korea might be only the beginning of a more sustained campaign of Communist aggression. According to the War Office, a major conflict was 'probable' in 1952. Defence spending, which increased from 8 to 14 per cent of Britain's Gross National Product, created exceptional strains within the economy, fuelling inflation, and undoing many of the gains arising from devaluation.[13] By 1951, the British economy, still the leading economy in Europe, was again in crisis, resulting in a tailing-off of investment, a drop in exports and politically controversial cuts in welfare expenditure, as resources were targeted towards defence production. Not only was Britain unable to capitalize on the export boom then developing in Europe, but also the dollar surpluses which some Sterling Area members had managed to achieve were once again under threat.[14] Nevertheless, the devaluation of 1949 can be seen as the point at which US pressure to dismantle the Sterling Area evaporated, with Washington accepting Britain's distinctive, extra-European position in the world economy.[15] The economic disadvantages of rearmament were accepted by most ministers as the unavoidable cost of ensuring military protection from the United States, and demonstrating to Washington that Britain was a reliable and valuable ally.[16]

Labour and the Commonwealth

For Attlee and his colleagues, winning the Commonwealth's co-operation in the fields of defence, diplomacy and economic policy was the key to Britain's continuing great power status. Theirs was a vision of an expanding and multiracial grouping, closely bound to Britain politically, strategically and economically, yet flexible enough to become the vehicle for Britain's self-projection in the modern world. It was essential that existing ties with the 'old' Commonwealth members, the Dominions, be consolidated, but beyond this, the Commonwealth should be able to absorb former dependencies as they became independent.[17] It was a source of great satisfaction to Britain that most former colonies did join the Commonwealth in this period. The major exceptions, Palestine and Burma, were, given their special circumstances, perhaps understandable. The inclusion of India and Pakistan was a watershed, making multiracialism a reality. Equally important was the Commonwealth's ability to retain India as a member, even when it opted for a republican constitution. This dilemma exposed divided opinion in Whitehall. Some officials, and existing Commonwealth members, feared that the implied challenge to the Crown as the cement of the Commonwealth would weaken the ties between long-established members. Others, conversely, felt that the Commonwealth could exercise a wholesome influence on 'young' India. Crucially, the loss of India would affect British prestige and create difficulties at the UN and in South-East Asia, should India emerge as the focus of an anti-Western grouping.[18] On this question, Attlee, determined to retain Indian membership, eventually succeeded, having appealed personally to Nehru. In April 1949, the conference of Commonwealth prime ministers (the successor to the pre-war imperial conferences) agreed a new formula under which the king was recognized as 'head of the Commonwealth', although this was a development hardly likely to convince the Irish Free State to continue its membership after it formally became a republic in 1949.[19] The Commonwealth remained a body whose members had remarkably little in common, other than their connection with Britain. Significantly, it was London which occupied the pivotal position, effectively deciding who could or could not become a member.[20] However, Britain was increasingly sensitive to the susceptibilities of the Commonwealth's more senior members, quietly dropping the soubriquet 'British' from the association's title in 1948.[21] One potentially destabilizing factor was friction between Commonwealth members. In the 1940s, the most worrying case of this was the dispute between India and Pakistan over Kashmir, unresolved at the time of independence. A further difficulty, which would haunt successive British governments, was how to reconcile the inclusion of South Africa, committed after 1948 to frankly racist policies, within a multiracial community. Would Pretoria, for example, accept the acceleration of devolution in parts of

Black Africa after 1947? One solution was to create some form of junior membership for new entrants, an idea which came to nothing, but would be revived in the 1950s.[22] Anticipating difficulties which would surface later in the course of decolonization, the South African prime minister, Malan, argued in 1951 that the entry of a newly independent country into the Commonwealth would require the consent of existing members. Henceforward, London would have to take account of Pretoria's hostility to the development of a truly multiracial Commonwealth.[23] One consequence of the expansion of the Commonwealth was a loss of the close relationship which had existed between its members: there was reluctance among the British Chiefs of Staff to share military intelligence freely with the new members, especially if the source of that information was Washington. Unofficially, an 'inner club' of senior members emerged, with Britain and the 'old' Dominions maintaining their traditional intimacy through separate consultations.[24]

An important indicator of the Attlee government's commitment to the Commonwealth was its promotion of emigration from Britain to the Dominions and Southern Rhodesia, surprising at a time when Britain was facing a persistent labour shortage. London's measures, including the offer of free passages overseas to demobilized servicemen, was justified in terms of safeguarding the interests of settler societies and strengthening the Commonwealth. Significantly, practical counter-arguments to this policy, especially the fear that emigration would fuel the development of overseas economic rivals, were eclipsed by racially based assumptions, namely the notion that the British 'race', however dispersed globally, would retain its identity, and, by bolstering Commonwealth links, reinforce Britain's global influence.[25] Such mobility within the Commonwealth had important implications for the question of Commonwealth citizenship. At the 1947 Commonwealth conference, it was agreed that each Commonwealth member state should introduce its own citizenship, though all would still give preferential treatment to 'Commonwealth' citizens over 'foreigners', a factor which would facilitate mobility.

More immediately, the reliability of the Commonwealth as a source of military assistance was another major preoccupation for London. Britain's over-committed capacity, aggravated by the Cold War, which called for an ability to respond globally to possible Communist aggression, argued for an attempt to utilize and co-ordinate Commonwealth and colonial military resources. Specifically, this involved creating regions in which Britain and a Commonwealth partner would share defence responsibilities, and using colonial (especially African) manpower on a much greater scale than before in peacetime.[26] In practice, there were limits to an expanded Commonwealth role. While India and Pakistan had already made plain their non-aligned preference, disappointing the Chiefs of Staff's hopes for continuing post-independence military co-operation, the older Dominions were already looking beyond their immediate links with Britain to safeguard their own security: their developing ties with the United States inevitably affected their relations with Britain. Canada's premier, Mackenzie King, turned his face away from anything resembling centralized Commonwealth policy-making, preferring instead to increase co-operation with the US, and Canadian efforts were concentrated in a NATO role. Australia, understandably preoccupied with the Cold War in Asia, was reluctant to contribute to Middle Eastern defence, as was South Africa, whose primary interest was in Africa. By 1950, however, partly because each sought an enhanced role in world affairs, both Australia and New Zealand had become committed to co-operating in Commonwealth plans for Middle Eastern defence, to Britain's relief.[27] Since this might leave their own regional interests vulnerable, both countries were seeking a security guarantee from Washington, a legacy of Britain's humiliation in 1942. The growing strategic alignment between the United States, Australia and New Zealand led in 1951 to the conclusion of the ANZUS Pact, from which Britain was pointedly excluded, so as to avoid any 'colonialist stigma'.[28]

Securing an adequate supply of manpower continued to concern the Chiefs of Staff. They had successfully argued for the renewal of conscription in April 1947, but their worries heightened after Indian independence and the loss of the Indian Army. With Attlee's support, they turned to British Africa as a possible replacement, but concluded that the cost of training African troops and providing the necessary leadership, would be too high. Similarly, the idea of creating a major strategic base in East Africa was eventually abandoned, largely due to the intractable problem of developing an adequate transport infrastructure in African conditions.[29]

The results of attempts to achieve greater Commonwealth co-ordination could be disappointing. Following the Communist takeover of China in October 1949, the British government, although eventually willing to recognize Mao Zedong's new regime, looked to the Commonwealth to help reinforce the military presence in vulnerable Hong Kong. India was frankly hostile, in view of its anti-colonial stance, while other Commonwealth governments were cool, indifferent or willing to make only token contributions.[30] However, during the Korean War, in which Britain succumbed to US pressure and agreed to support UN military intervention, a Commonwealth contingent, including members from Britain, Canada, Australia, New Zealand and India, took part.[31]

London's 'globalist' perspective and attachment to the Commonwealth had important consequences for Britain's relationship with Europe. Although Attlee and his ministers had no doubt that Britain had a major role to play in Europe's post-war recovery, especially in organizing its defence against possible Soviet aggression, their faith in the Commonwealth as a barrier to Communist expansion, and their desire to preserve and enhance Commonwealth ties, made them reluctant to become involved in schemes to promote the political and economic integration of Europe.[32] Commitments to Europe which were not perceived as being compatible with Britain's wider Commonwealth interests were therefore to be avoided. These attitudes were reinforced by the British government's economic priorities at this time, grounded in the important role envisaged for the Commonwealth and the Sterling Area. The early success of the Sterling Area seemed to confirm the wisdom of this orientation: in the late 1940s, the Sterling Area absorbed about half of Britain's exports, twice as much as Britain sold to Western Europe.[33] In addition to this, Britain believed that its claims to be a world power, enjoying a 'special' relationship with the United States, required a distinctive position in relation to Europe, being at the same time the foremost European power (for example, orchestrating Western Europe's response to the Marshall Plan) without being absorbed into what still seemed to be an unstable continent. More immediately, there was concern that if European integration developed too rapidly, Washington's incentive to guarantee European security against the Soviet Union might be reduced. By 1948, realizing that, unaided, Western Europe could not resist the Soviet bloc, and aware that Britain's own atomic weapons project would not bear fruit for some years, Bevin was determined to ensure US (and Canadian) participation in the region's defence. This conviction was sharpened when, in August 1949, the first Soviet atom bomb was exploded, considerably in advance of Western analysts' predictions.[34]

To secure a US military guarantee, it was necessary first to demonstrate that Western Europe could help itself. This led Britain, France and the Benelux countries to conclude the Brussels Pact early in 1948, shortly after the Communist takeover in Czechoslovakia. Only three months later, the Soviets began a blockade of Berlin in response to attempts to integrate the western zones of occupied Germany, resulting in the joint British–US airlift of essential supplies to the beleaguered city. The most important consequence of this escalation of the Cold War was the speedy enlargement of the Brussels Pact into the North Atlantic Treaty of April 1949, which committed the United States to the defence of the other members, and Britain to the defence of Europe. However, the Berlin crisis also served as a useful pretext for the extension of conscription, compensating for the loss of Indian military manpower, and guaranteeing Britain adequate strength for a global, not merely a European, role. Again, conveniently, the deepening Cold War ensured broad domestic acquiescence in this move. In turn, the outbreak of the Korean War, widely seen in the West as inspired by Moscow, saw the North Atlantic Treaty Organization given teeth when American ground troops returned to Europe, relieving Britain of the major responsibility for the region's defence. The 'revolution' in American foreign policy, embodied in the Marshall Plan and the Truman Doctrine, offered a welcome breathing space for the Labour government and its successors, enabling Britain to devote more of its resources to safeguarding its imperial and Commonwealth interests, while simultaneously witnessing a marked decline in US anti-colonial rhetoric.[35]

For a combination of economic and strategic reasons, then, Britain's relations with the United States and the Commonwealth were seen as more important than ties with Europe.[36] This explains London's cool reaction to the Schuman Plan, unveiled in May 1950, to integrate the steel industries of France and West Germany. The scheme's supporters, especially Jean Monnet, had anticipated British resistance and had therefore given little advance warning of their proposals. Crucially, Paris laid ground-rules for negotiation which Britain could not accept, namely a prior commitment to the idea of 'supranationality', or the willingness to abdicate national sovereignty to a higher authority.

Britain's decision not to become involved in the Schuman Plan was partly a rejection of this principle, partly the result of London's preference for strengthening its links with the United States and the Commonwealth, and partly a reflection of the recently nationalized British steel industry's greater interest in world, rather than Western European, export markets.[37] The same kind of negative British response greeted the Pleven Plan of October 1950, a scheme, developing the supranationalist principle, to create an integrated European military force, answerable to a European defence minister and assembly. While the British government sought to be associated with broad movements towards European integration, it did not want to participate.[38]

South Asia

In the imperial sphere, the Labour government's most pressing problem in 1945 was the future of India. Here, the manner in which the 'transfer of power' unfolded was clearly at odds with what Britain had hoped to achieve, and suggests that a loss of control, caused by a worsening local situation, rather than considered planning, shaped London's decision to withdraw.[39] Attlee, one of the few senior British politicians to have visited India, and an architect of the 1935 Government of India Act, took a close interest in this question. While sympathetic to Indian demands for self-determination, he harboured doubts about the integrity of Indian nationalism, once describing it as 'the illegitimate offspring of patriotism out of inferiority complex', a view reinforced by the experience of the wartime 'Quit India' movement, whose suppression he had pragmatically endorsed. More immediately, Attlee needed to pre-empt accusations of 'scuttle' in India, which might strain relations within the Commonwealth and with the United States, damage Britain's prestige, and be politically embarrassing at home.[40] By the summer of 1945, Britain's effective control of India was rapidly dwindling. Having alienated Congress during the war, while cultivating the Muslim League, each of which feared losing face with its supporters by making compromises, Britain was inheriting the consequences of its earlier tactics, above all its promise in 1942 to grant independence at the end of the war, but still hoped that the constitutional framework set out in 1935, envisaging Dominion status for an Indian federation, might be achieved. The Cabinet Mission of spring 1946, an attempt to preserve Indian unity, produced a proposal for a federation in three tiers, with a central government keeping control of foreign affairs and defence, and maintaining the Indian armed forces intact.[41] But neither the viceroy, Wavell, nor the mission, could secure a settlement acceptable to both Congress and the League, while from London's point of view, neither partition nor a Congress ascendancy was acceptable, since either solution would aggravate the communal problem and make Britain's plans for post-independence defence co-operation less achievable.[42] Despite constitutional deadlock and spiralling communal violence, India was still regarded as valuable. For example, in spring 1946, the Chiefs of Staff agreed that Indian military manpower had actually increased in importance to Britain, and they saw in north-west India the potential for air bases from which the Soviet Union could be reached. Late in 1946, there were still over a quarter of a million Indian troops serving overseas, mainly in the Middle East and South-East Asia.[43] For these reasons, a friendly India, associated with Britain both by Commonwealth membership and a defence treaty, was deemed essential.[44]

British military planners' projections were based on the assumption of a 'stable and contented' India, yet this illusion was rapidly disintegrating as Congress stepped up its demands for immediate independence. Meanwhile, Muslim support for Jinnah intensified as it became clear that Britain might jettison the communal safeguards enshrined in the 1935 Government of India Act, in the interests of a rapid withdrawal. During August 1946, having failed to secure for Muslims half the seats in the new interim government under Nehru, Jinnah launched the campaign of Direct Action, which triggered rioting across northern India. Thousands died in the ensuing violence, which Britain could not contain. By the end of the year, Wavell was recommending a 'breakdown plan', involving a staged withdrawal of British personnel from India, which ensured its author's dismissal and cleared the way for a decisive metropolitan initiative.[45] After briefly considering the use of coercion, London realized by the middle of 1946 that it no longer had the resources to do this: not only was the necessary military manpower lacking, but also the reliability of the administration (more than half of which was already Indian), whose loyalties were increasingly under strain, was in question. The desire for continuing ties after independence was a further reason for eschewing force.[46] The Chiefs of Staff warned in 1946 that maintaining British rule in India, if the Indian Army were considered unreliable, would require the deployment of five British divisions, which in turn would require a completely unacceptable reduction of Britain's other global commitments.[47] After nearly two centuries of relying upon the ultimate sanction of force in India, Britain had been obliged to abandon coercion as an effective adjunct to political manoeuvring.[48] It remained vital, however, to portray Britain's departure from India as the result of deliberate policy, not as something forced on a reluctant London, still less the prelude to a general imperial collapse.[49]

The major decisions affecting India were taken late in December 1946 and early 1947, against the background of a harsh metropolitan winter, aggravated by fuel shortages and the resulting dislocations of industry and transport. Having already agreed that overstretched British forces must be withdrawn from Greece, and that the Palestine problem would be referred to the United Nations, Attlee accepted, despite Bevin's criticism, that withdrawal from India could take place no later than June 1948, a decision the Cabinet confirmed on 13 February 1947.

Hoping that an imposed deadline would force the antagonists to compromise with one another, Attlee announced in February 1947 the proposed date for British withdrawal. Lord Louis Mountbatten, chosen as a suitable successor to Wavell, had stipulated this as a condition of accepting his appointment.[50] Once in office, Mountbatten quickly became aware that if Britain were to avoid involvement in a civil war, which seemed increasingly likely, there was no alternative to partition and a hasty exit from India. Under his June Plan, power was to be transferred to separate states, India and a 'moth-eaten' Pakistan, physically divided by Indian territory, which left millions of Muslims in India. Congress achieved its goal of an independent, secular state. Forever described in British accounts as the 'transfer of power', the consequence of mutual agreement between Britain and India, South Asian decolonization was accompanied by much bloodshed, by an unprecedented migration of millions of panic-stricken refugees seeking sanctuary with their co-religionists, and by London's ultimate failure to shape post-independence India according to pre-war British calculations. Britain had not wanted partition: it came because Congress and the Muslim League could agree on nothing less. Among the victims were those collaborating Indian princes who had, for so long, been a vital buttress of British rule, but who were now abandoned and forced to seek some settlement with the new Dominions. The most important remaining problem, from Mountbatten's point of view, was to ensure that India did not leave the Commonwealth. This was resolved by Attlee's announcement in June 1947 that the two post-partition successor states would be free to determine this question for themselves.[51] In a manner reminiscent of London's attitude towards the Dominions in 1926, policy-makers had already concluded that to make India's membership of the Commonwealth voluntary offered the most promising safeguard against the risk of secession. For their part, Congress and the League accepted partition in order to avoid a descent into total chaos.

Britain escaped from India relatively unscathed, but at the cost of sacrificing the hoped-for defence treaty in the process.[52] More importantly, according to some historians, the manner of Britain's retreat appears to have precluded the kind of fundamental reassessment of Britain's real international stature which Indian independence ought to have encouraged.[53] After 1947, no longer able to draw on the enormous Indian Army, Britain would increasingly have to look to its *own* military resources to maintain its world power status. Moreover, India's independence raised a wider question: if Britain had been unwilling or unable to hold on to its most valuable possession, what did this suggest for the future of the rest of the dependent empire?

Once India and Pakistan had achieved independence, it was difficult to withhold similar concessions from Ceylon, which, in February 1948, became the first Colonial Office territory to become independent, in a manner far more to London's taste than had been the case in India. The Second World War had demonstrated Ceylon's strategic value, leading Britain in 1943 to promise the island self-government, with Britain retaining control over foreign policy, defence and currency questions. Initially, Attlee's government favoured a deceleration in Ceylon's constitutional development, fearing that precipitate independence, might provoke fresh cries of 'scuttle' from the Opposition. A further consideration was London's anxiety to avoid fomenting nationalism in Malaya. As in India, there was an important ethnic/communal dimension to the decolonization of Ceylon. Sinhalese politicians sought responsible government, and Dominion status, in order to pre-empt the introduction by London of a constitution which would secure the political rights of the Tamil community. The Soulbury Commission, which examined the Ceylon question in the last phase of the war, had concluded that it was preferable to make generous, early concessions than to grant 'too little, too late', an approach which would become a recurring theme in the history of British decolonization. To do this, as the Colonial Secretary Arthur Creech Jones put it, would demonstrate to colonial populations that Britain's commitment to eventual colonial self-government was not empty.[54] What had hitherto been a remote and largely theoretical proposition had now become a reality. An important advantage for Britain was that the Sinhalese political elite was conservative, and sought to avoid creating a populist challenge to British rule. As elsewhere in Asia, the war had encouraged the growth of the radical left, which after successes in the 1946 elections, joined forces with other opposition groups in demanding full independence outside the Commonwealth. If the conservative elite were to prevent the growth of radical nationalism, it was essential to achieve quick results and derive concessions from the British. This, and the background of rapid change in India, prompted the Sinhalese nationalist leader Don Stephen Senanayake to escalate his demands for immediate independence. The British government, having capitalized on Sinhalese fears of Indian regional domination to extract assurances of future co-operation in diplomacy and defence (specifically access to the important naval base at Trincomalee), and anxious to bolster the 'moderate' elite, represented by Senanayake, against its 'extreme' opponents, accepted the Sinhalese case.[55] In what would become the defining leitmotif in subsequent episodes of decolonization, Britain had identified an indigenous political class to which power could safely be transferred, with no apparent threat to fundamental British interests. In Ceylon, Britain had found a 'model for subsequent transfers of power'. But a reminder of the important Cold War dimension to post-war colonial questions was also raised by the case of Ceylon. Because of its defence agreements with Britain, Ceylon's independence was condemned by the Soviet Union as an illusion, and the ex-colony's entry into the UN was accordingly vetoed by Moscow for another seven years.[56]

The fate of Burma was similarly affected by developments elsewhere in South Asia. Unlike Ceylon, Burma's experience of the Second World War had been deeply disruptive, and decisively eroded Britain's power to construct and maintain a collaborative relationship. Conquered by the Japanese in 1942, the country enjoyed brief 'independence' until being reclaimed by the British in 1945. Like Ceylon, Burma had been promised self-government by Britain as soon as was practicable. Aung San, the Burmese leader whose Independence Army had temporarily supported the Japanese during the war, was viewed by some in London as a traitor who should be treated as such, but Attlee sought to include him and his Anti-Fascist People's Freedom League in the arrangements for a new assembly which would appoint an interim legislature. This accommodation was largely a reflection of Britain's dearth of resources to mount effective operations against armed Burmese nationalists, but was also based on the belief that only the AFPFL could keep ethnically diverse Burma both united and linked to Britain. When Britain's wartime promise was finally implemented in January 1948, Burma became a republic and left the Commonwealth. Unwilling to accept treatment less favourable than that accorded to India's nationalists, and reluctant to re-open the door to British and Indian business interests, Burma's leaders rejected continuing links with Britain. Burma's independence outside the Commonwealth could be looked upon by London with an unusual degree of equanimity, largely because most of the country's exports were bought by India, and so earned no dollars for the Sterling Area. The position would be very different in relation to major dollar-earning territories, such as Malaya and the Gold Coast.[57]

The Middle East

Even while India's future was being debated in London, the government's attention was occupied in a fundamental reappraisal of Britain's position in the Middle East, a region of longstanding formal and informal influence. Conventional wisdom had it that the Middle East was of enormous importance to Britain. Although it had long had a special significance, laying across one of the great imperial communication routes, giving access to the Far East, once India became independent, the region acquired a growing importance in its own right. Recognizing this, and keen to reinforce Britain's informal influence in the region in the face of growing Arab nationalism, stimulated by the war, Bevin proposed at an early stage that a new, constructive partnership should be sought with the Arab world, involving British aid to help raise living standards, dispensed through a new British Middle East Office, a strategy he called working through 'people not pashas'; wartime tactics of coercion were no longer feasible in view of the mounting constraints on British military spending. As would be the case with Britain's other overseas aid initiatives, what proved to be unrealistic initial expectations gave way to a more modest, but relatively successful development programme. Bevin's ambition to secure the support of a younger generation of politicians and technocrats was, however, ultimately obstructed by the unrelenting caution of the Treasury. By the end of the 1940s, Bevin's strategy was bankrupt.[58] Meanwhile, Bevin hoped that in return for promoting regional development, he would be able to secure a new clutch of treaties with Arab states, especially with Egypt, the core of Britain's Middle Eastern position, which would safeguard British interests.[59] In this, Bevin met only partial success. An agreement with Transjordan in 1946 (the year Britain's mandate ended), amended two years later, offered security to British bases, with Britain promising continued assistance to the Arab Legion, which would remain under British command. A similar agreement reached with Iraq in 1948 collapsed after local protests.[60] Yet Britain's confidence in its ability to mould the potent force of Arab nationalism into an acceptable form had, ironically, led London to attempt to control the development of its chief post-war vehicle, the Arab League. Founded in 1945 to co-ordinate the Arab states' interests, this included Egypt among its founder members. The British government hoped that Egypt's leading role would help guide the Arab League towards co-operation with Britain. Very quickly, such illusions were shattered as Egypt itself became increasingly reluctant to fall into line with Britain's regional aims.[61]

During 1946, Attlee was willing to 'think the unthinkable', questioning the rationale for a continued British presence in the Middle East, and triggering a lengthy debate on this subject in official circles. Attlee's thinking was shaped in part by a continuing hope to avoid confrontation with the Soviet Union, in part by the apparent strategic revolution arising from atomic weapons, the impact of air power and its possibilities, and in part by India's imminent independence. Attlee was pessimistic about the possibility of defending the Middle East and the Mediterranean sea route to the East (regarding the usual preoccupation with defending the sea-lanes as outdated), and particularly questioned the need for a British presence in the Eastern Mediterranean, including Greece and Palestine. His preference was for a large buffer zone, a 'wide glacis of desert and Arabs', separating British and Soviet interests, to minimize the risk of conflict. The Chiefs of Staff could not accept such thinking: for them, Britain's vulnerability to attack by atomic weapons emphasized the need to have air bases in the Middle East, within striking distance of sensitive targets in the Soviet Union.[62] Bevin, usually loyal to Attlee, sided with the Chiefs on this issue. Only when the Chiefs, led by Field-Marshal Montgomery, threatened to resign, did Attlee back down. Central to the Chiefs' case was the argument that withdrawal by the British would create a vacuum in the Mediterranean which the Soviets would be unable to resist exploiting.[63] To the Chiefs of Staff, the Middle East was the 'hub' of defence planning, one of the three 'pillars' in their strategic framework, the other two being the defence of Britain itself, and the defence of the sea-lanes: if one of these were to crumble, all would be lost. Reinforcing this strategic orthodoxy, it has been argued, was the psychological importance of the Middle East to the British Army as the site of its few major successes in the first half of the twentieth century.[64] At this time, the Chiefs were working on the assumption that from 1952 onwards, as the Soviet Union recovered from the Second World War, the risk of aggression would increase, and that, after Western Europe, the Middle East was the region in which the Soviets were most likely to intervene. This emphasis on the importance of the Middle East to Commonwealth strategy would increase as it became clear that East Africa could not become a viable alternative military base.[65] The Middle East, of course, had other important functions. As well as being a crucial communications centre, a protective shield to Africa from Communism, and potentially a valuable offensive air base, it was a region in which Britain had substantial economic and commercial interests. In the late 1940s it absorbed British exports worth around £150 million. Even more important, the region had become a major source of non-dollar oil since the 1930s. British companies were heavily involved in the oil industry, especially in Iran. Middle Eastern oil was not only vital for Britain's own needs but it was also a valuable revenue earner. This economic interest lent added weight to the strategic argument for maintaining a large British military presence in the region.[66] Whether Britain actually had the resources to defend the Middle East, however, remained debatable. The biggest concentration of British military power, and the largest

military base in the world, was in the Suez Canal Zone in Egypt, a vast complex of facilities which by 1951 sheltered around 40,000 troops. This made
Egypt by far Britain's most important Middle Eastern toehold.[67] After the war,
it was a British priority to establish the Suez Canal base on a new and more
secure footing, grounded in friendly co-operation with Egypt, rather than
relying on military occupation: as Attlee pointed out in 1946, Britain lacked the
resources to maintain an Egyptian presence by force, and to try to do so would
only sour Britain's relations with the Arab world. This would involve a re-
negotiation of the 1936 Anglo-Egyptian Treaty. To secure this, Britain was
willing to withdraw its forces, as the Cabinet agreed in May 1946, on condition
that in an emergency, it would have the right to re-enter Egypt. Attempts to
devise a new treaty, however, were unsuccessful, partly because Egypt linked
the question to its claims to sovereignty over the Sudan, theoretically an Anglo-
Egyptian Condominium, which Britain was unwilling to concede, and partly
because the Egyptian government, responding to local nationalist sentiment,
was anxious to see the British depart. An additional stumbling block was
Britain's desire to obtain Egyptian military co-operation, a suggestion which,
given local feelings, Cairo understandably resisted. Negotiations foundered
early in 1947, and London decided to remain in Egypt under the terms of the
1936 treaty, despite Egyptian protests and the increasing cost of defending
British facilities against attacks by local nationalists. A more modest attempt to
involve Egypt in Middle Eastern defence did not bear fruit until 1954.[68]

Meanwhile, during 1945 and 1946, the British position in the Middle East
was also being threatened by the deteriorating situation in Palestine, where
Britain faced problems not unlike those simultaneously coalescing in India. The
bitter consequences of Britain's irreconcilable promises to the Arab and Jewish
communities during the First World War, and those made to the Arab world in
1939, were to be inherited by Attlee's government, culminating in yet another
reversal for British policy. Although London still aimed to create a bi-national
state, comprising approximately two-thirds Arabs and one-third Jews, in which
the rights of each community would be guaranteed, a violent Jewish campaign
to achieve a Jewish state began late in 1945. In the immediate post-war period,
as in India, communal violence escalated to an extent which the British
administration seemed unable to control. Nevertheless, the Chiefs of Staff, led
by Montgomery, insisted that Palestine remained vital to Britain on strategic
grounds: its development as Britain's principal Middle Eastern base would
facilitate military withdrawal from Egypt, and so put Anglo-Egyptian relations
on a more amicable basis.

Complicating the situation was the intense international interest in the fate
of the Mandate, affected by widespread sympathy for Holocaust survivors and
for the Zionist cause. This was felt especially in the United States, where
President Truman, perhaps mindful of the sizeable domestic Jewish constituency, but more importantly anxious to obtain a more secure US presence in the
Middle East, urged Britain in October 1946 to implement a liberal immigration
policy to replace the restrictions imposed under the 1939 White Paper, and
supported the case for a Jewish state. He was not prepared, however, to

assume any responsibility for the situation within Palestine. Britain, still involved in negotiating the terms of the enormous US loan, could not afford to antagonize Washington on this question, but feared that increased Jewish immigration would arouse Arab hostility.

As in India, Britain simply lost control of events in Palestine. Britain's own military presence, alone costing around £40 million a year, and amounting to 10 per cent of Britain's entire armed forces, itself became the target for attacks by Jewish terrorist groups, most famously the bombing in July 1946 of King David's Hotel in Jerusalem, the headquarters of the British administration.[69] At the same time, any attempt to quell unrest would raise delicate political issues, notably the question of international reactions. Although this was becoming a major concern to London, and threatening at times to unleash an ugly anti-Semitic backlash in Britain, of paramount concern to Attlee's government in its handling of the Palestine problem was its wider implications for Anglo-Arab relations, and the importance of keeping the Arab world friendly to the West as an effective barrier to the spread of Soviet influence. In London's estimation, Arab goodwill was simply more desirable than the friendship of a future Jewish state, a view often believed to have been reinforced by the Foreign Office's traditionally pro-Arab leanings. Sensitivity to international Muslim opinion had wider, imperial, ramifications, explaining, to some extent, Britain's handling of the Indian problem, and its attempts to retain the goodwill of Jinnah's Muslim League. Furthermore, in Bevin's view, it was vital that the Palestine issue should not be allowed to endanger Britain's all-important relationship with the United States.

Although Britain vainly hoped, as in India, that a solution which could bridge the communal divide might yet be found, by introducing provincial autonomy for Arab and Jewish areas, as the prelude to later independence, it accepted pragmatically that it lacked the power to impose a solution on Palestine.[70] In February 1947, Bevin announced the government's decision to refer the entire Palestine problem to the United Nations, which retained ultimate responsibility for the territory. At this stage, Britain was gambling that the pro-Arab majority of UN members would engineer a settlement favourable to British interests.[71] Yet by abdicating responsibility for this question, and failing to make any recommendations to the UN, because of its concern not to offend either party, Britain was tacitly admitting that its own Palestine policy was bankrupt.

In September 1947, the UN Special Committee on Palestine (UNSCOP) reported in favour of partition, a suggestion approved by the General Assembly in November. Britain, unwilling to bear the responsibility for implementing a solution which neither local community accepted, and which Bevin was convinced would provoke a fresh Arab rebellion, decided to evacuate Palestine by August 1948.[72] In effect, Britain was recognizing that its presence in Palestine was no longer compatible with wider imperial strategy or the co-operation of Arab rulers on which British Middle Eastern policy was based.[73] More immediately, London was acknowledging that Palestine was no longer governable at a cost which Britain could bear. Britain's withdrawal in May 1948 was essentially an admission of failure. The declaration of the state of Israel was followed by an invasion by neighbouring Arab states. This first Arab–Israeli war incidentally demonstrated the hollow nature of Britain's previous security guarantees to its Arab partners. London's studied aloofness during the war infuriated both Arab and Israeli opinion, with lasting consequences for Britain's relations in the Middle East.[74] After 1948, Britain's problems in the region were aggravated by Arab resentment at Britain's responsibility for enabling Israel to come into existence.[75] The embittered atmosphere generated by Britain's role in the creation of Israel rendered Bevin's talk of winning local goodwill by promoting Middle Eastern development largely irrelevant, but rebuilding good relations with the Arab world would remain a priority in future years. Meanwhile, the debacle in Palestine, and continuing uncertainty over the Suez base, reinforced Britain's interest in developing a strategic presence in Libya, where a unified client state under King Idris was eventually cultivated.[76]

Late in the Labour government's life, a fresh nationalist challenge erupted, this time in Iran. In 1951, the Iranian government, which had long sought to increase the revenue it earned from the country's precious natural resources, nationalized Iran's predominantly British-owned oil refineries, valued at around £120 million, and obliged their British personnel to leave the huge complex at Abadan, posing a threat not only to Britain's commercial interests, but also to its prestige in the Middle East as a whole. This manifestation of Iranian nationalism was stimulated by the conclusion, in December 1950, of an unprecedented deal between the American oil conglomerate Aramco and the Saudi Arabian government, under which Saudi oil revenues were to be divided equally between the two, an arrangement which became the generally accepted model in the industry. While some hot-heads within the British Cabinet, led by Bevin's ill-qualified successor as Foreign Secretary, Herbert Morrison, leaned towards a show of force against Iran, Attlee and his more realistic colleagues, although smarting from the humiliation, judged that this was impossible, partly because Britain (without the Indian Army) lacked the necessary military capability, but above all because Washington was opposed to military intervention, and US opinion could not be flouted. As Attlee's government faced another general election, foreign affairs would briefly gain attention at the hustings, with pointed references being made to 'appeasement'. The Abadan crisis was another reversal for Britain, but it also served as a reminder that in the post-war world, nationalism had to be countered more subtly than in the past.[77] Ironically, there was relief in official circles that traditional, more robust, methods of upholding British interests seemed to have been outgrown. Events elsewhere in the Middle East only five years later would show this conclusion to be premature.[78]

By the end of Labour's period in office, the Middle Eastern policy constructed by Bevin, in which he based his vision of the region's relationship with Britain in part on the model of the Commonwealth, reinforced by ties of association and influence rather than by the crude projection of British power (an option which, in any case, was becoming less and less practicable), had been shattered. Having tried to forge these new relationships out of the congeries of arrangements which had represented Britain's traditional Middle Eastern presence, Bevin, and his successors, had to face the new disturbing realities of power in the region. First, Britain's crucial responsibility for Middle Eastern defence had in practice been eroded by the Cold War: the region's 'northern tier', comprising Greece, Turkey and Iran, had, of necessity, come under the mantle of American defence. In Palestine, Britain's policy had disintegrated amid humiliating retreat and the alienation of old allies. More worrying for the future was clear evidence, especially in Egypt and Iran, that Britain's traditional interests were being challenged by a new and potent spirit of nationalism.

Policy towards the colonial territories

For the extremely varied group of dependencies which were, technically, the responsibility of the Colonial Office, Attlee's government saw itself as being committed to an unprecedented worldwide experiment in 'nation-building', preparing the colonies for self-government on the lines set out in Oliver Stanley's watershed Commons speech in July 1943. This process was expected in most cases to be very gradual, and there was little sense of urgency among London's policy-makers. Britain was fortunate in that most colonies seemed, immediately after the war, to be politically quiescent, devoid of the kind of pressures which had forced the retreat from South Asia. It was considered important that colonies, once they became self-governing, should remain closely tied to Britain through membership of the enlarged Commonwealth. In a few cases, it was accepted, self-government was unlikely ever to be a realistic option. This was especially true in the case of territories which were so small as to be unlikely to achieve viable nationhood, or which were so important strategically that relinquishing them was inconceivable.[79] For the majority, however, Britain's aim was to create stable states, with democratic systems, to whom power could safely be transferred after what would probably be a slow process of political, economic and social development.[80] Of crucial significance would be the introduction of the electoral process, a key concession in Britain's hands, but one whose consequences could be alarmingly unpredictable.[81] For the time being, however, London remained confident that it could control this evolutionary process. Bearing in mind the experience of India, policy-makers hoped to avoid head-long confrontations with nationalism, where it existed or was nascent; rather, the aim was to manipulate nationalism instead of being manipulated by it. There was, at least in theory, a growing reluctance to retain colonies by the use of force, but, equally, there was no desire to impose independence on communities which were not considered 'ready' for it, as this might leave a 'dangerous vacuum' liable to be filled by less pliant strains of nationalism.[82] From Britain's point of view, if this long-term strategy succeeded, and friendly, well-prepared former colonies did join the Commonwealth, then not only would a 'powerful stabilizing influence' be added to international relations, but this would also be a measure of Britain's continuing strength in the world, not a sign of its weakness.[83]

1. The Empire mobilised: General Archibald Wavell, commander-in-chief of British forces in the Middle East, inspecting Indian troops serving in Egypt, early in the Second World War

2. Counterinsurgency in Malaya: a resettlement village constructed under the Briggs Plan, c. 1952

3. The Cyprus Emergency: a British aircraft, bombed by EOKA at Nicosia airport, March 1956

4. The Gold Coast general election, 1956. Before recording his vote, Dr Kwame Nkrumah has his thumb inked by a polling assistant

5. Defending Britain's post-Suez Middle Eastern foothold: a Scout car leaving the levy camp at
Dhala, Aden Protectorate, for a patrol, 1957

6. Labour-intensive development: land terracing in the Kiambu district of Kenya's Central Province, completed under the Swynnerton agricultural plan

7. Capital-intensive development: American visitors being shown the prestige Kariba Dam project in the Central African Federation, 1960

8. Negotiating decolonization: R.A. Butler, First Secretary of State with responsibility for Central African affairs, meets Kenneth Kaunda and other Northern Rhodesian nationalist leaders in Lusaka, January 1963.

One background factor of which policy-makers had to be aware was the existence of the United Nations, and the fact that many of its members took an interest in the status of the colonies. The UN served as a useful forum for colonialism's international critics: it was a source of embarrassment to Britain that these would soon be joined by independent India. A major concern for British ministers was to minimize UN interference in colonial affairs, to allow wartime talk of international supervision of the colonies to die a quiet death, and to forestall pressure, especially from the UN's Fourth Committee (which administered the UN Trusteeship system, the successor to the League of Nations Mandate system) to accelerate constitutional change in colonies which London considered were unready for self-government.[84]

Connected to this problem was the question of colonial rule as a Cold War issue, and Britain's fear of Communist influence among colonial populations. Although as early as 1946 Bevin was emphasizing the Soviet Union's hostility to Britain's imperial system, it was only in 1948, with the Cold War in plain view, that much was done, through propaganda campaigns, to pre-empt Communist infiltration of the colonies.[85] In this period, Communism was to make little headway: British Africa and most other colonies remained free of significant Communist activity. The major exception was Malaya, whose strategic and economic importance to Britain accounts for the lengths to which Britain went to defeat the Communist insurrection there after 1948.[86] Nevertheless, as Colonial Secretary James Griffiths warned in 1950, Britain faced an 'ideological battle' in the colonies.[87] An important theme in colonial policy, therefore, was to avoid, or remove, conditions favourable to the growth of Communism. Most concretely, this would embrace efforts to raise colonial living standards, but it also involved much more effective intelligence-gathering and policing, as well as attempts to win over the allegiances of local populations to a basically Western-orientated outlook, not only through propaganda, such as the development of broadcasting, but by encouraging a non-Communist institutional framework in trade unions, co-operatives and so on. Cementing these initiatives was a growing sensitivity to scope for charges of racial discrimination.[88] If Communism was a factor which the British government was increasingly alive to in its colonial policy, the Cold War nevertheless had welcome side-effects in softening American attitudes to colonialism. By 1950, the US government had concluded that British colonial rule was a useful bulwark against Communist expansion.[89]

Colonial economic policy and 'development'

In the period immediately after the war, economic policy towards the colonial empire was dictated by two major factors: a world situation of shortage of many basic requirements, especially food, and the problems confronting Britain in switching from a wartime to a peacetime economy. At an early stage, the colonies were warned that Britain would not be able to meet their demands for exports for some time, and that they should, if possible, seek to produce more goods for themselves. However, the worldwide shortage of many basic commodities did offer welcome new opportunities for colonial producers of exports such as cocoa.[90]

At an early stage, Attlee's government began to show an interest in the role the colonies might play in easing the situation of the metropolitan economy, and in helping to raise British living standards.[91] As Britain's own difficulties increased after 1947, this interest developed into a brief, but unprecedented fixation with drawing on colonial resources for Britain's benefit. This interest was widely shared among Attlee's colleagues. Bevin, most famously, was hypnotized by the mineral wealth of Africa, and the possibility it offered of achieving economic independence from the United States, and even of having the latter dependent on British colonial sources of key strategic materials.[92] Because of his belief in the empire as Britain's salvation, Bevin has been seen as a reluctant decolonizer.[93] He certainly hoped that the combined resources of Western Europe and the British and French colonies in Africa could be fused into a new economic bloc, 'Eurafrica', the core of a 'third force' strong enough to be on a par with the two 'superpowers'. Only the circumstances of devaluation in 1949, and France's growing preference for a European, not a colonial, solution, finally convinced Bevin that his dream was an illusion. Henceforth, he would devote his energies to securing the Atlantic Alliance.[94]

Meanwhile, Britain's acute shortage of dollars had important repercussions for colonial economic policy, which, as David Fieldhouse has remarked, became characterized by blatant 'neo-mercantilism'.[95] Above all, London sought to expand the colonies' output of commodities which could either save Britain from buying from dollar sources, or which could be sold on the open market for precious dollars. The stringent wartime regime of economic controls was either revived or extended, imposing strict limits on what the colonies were allowed to import, again particularly from the dollar area.[96] The purchase of major commodities by the British government, normally at fixed prices favourable to Britain, was a major feature of this period, as was a careful control of British investment in the colonies. The low prices paid to colonial producers also helped to contain colonial purchasing power, suppressing demand for manufactures and other goods which Britain reserved for sale in more lucrative foreign markets. Inevitably, dissatisfaction among colonial producers and consumers intensified. As members of the Sterling Area, the colonies were seen as playing a vital role in achieving economic recovery, to an extent greater than the area's independent members, who were not always so accommodating about curbing their own dollar spending. The colonies' resources were tapped into and used either to earn precious dollars, to be pooled in the Bank of England, or to supply Britain with dollar-saving imports. Malaya, for example, became particularly valuable, its tin and rubber exports earning $170 million during 1948 alone.[97] The major colonial dollar earners, Malaya and the Gold Coast, were prevented from using the dollars they earned to buy the goods they needed from outside the Sterling Area, even though Britain was at this time in no position to supply substitute goods. Forced to accumulate ever-growing sterling balances in London, the colonies were in effect supplying Britain with compulsory 'loans' at very low rates of interest.

The imperial government had begun to show an interest in mobilizing co-lonial resources before the onset of the convertibility crisis. But especially after the crisis of 1947, London sought to integrate metropolitan and colonial planning more effectively than hitherto.[98] A Colonial Primary Products Committee was created in May 1947 to review, commodity by commodity, the possibilities for expanded colonial production to help ease the balance of payments position. Similarly, an inter-departmental Colonial Development Working Party was established in Whitehall to investigate the allocation of the capital goods required for colonial development. In their wake, a Cabinet Committee on Colonial Development was formed. The aim of all this activity was to buttress, or regain, Britain's economic independence. In November 1947, the Chancellor, Sir Stafford Cripps, called for the tempo of African development to be increased 'out of all recognition', an attitude typical of the wildly unrealistic expectations current in government circles at this time.[99] Especially dramatic was the government's adoption of new machinery to promote expanded production of valuable commodities.[100] The Colonial Development Corporation, operative from 1948, was the implementation of an idea much discussed during the war to promote desirable development and economic diversification. Its novelty lay in the application of the British-style public corporation to the task of development. In practice, the CDC's early years were disappointing, and represented another failure for the Colonial Office. Even more disastrous was the ill-fated East African Groundnuts Scheme, a misguided attempt to promote the mechanized production of peanuts in Tanganyika, intended to help ease the persistent fats shortage. This, too, employed a public corporation. It rapidly became clear that the basic groundwork had been rushed, and that the implications of the scheme had not been properly considered. As a result, around £40 million of British public funds were spent to very little effect, and critics of public enterprise within Britain acquired a useful target for their bile.[101]

Although the British government at the time laid much stress on the mutu-ally beneficial consequences of these policies for Britain and the colonies, it is widely accepted by historians across the ideological spectrum that colonial economic policy during the later 1940s was exploitative, and that the interests of colonial populations were subordinated to those of Britain, a situation described by one historian as 'social imperialism'.[102]

This emphasis on expanded production beneficial to Britain and the rest of the Sterling Area had important repercussions for the wider policy of colonial development, which occupied so prominent a place in the colonial rhetoric of Attlee's government. Although much expanded development funding was made available by the coalition government in 1945, the reality of the years up to 1951 was that colonial expectations of progress with development were disappointed. There was no single British 'plan' for colonial development, rather each colonial government was expected to assemble its own programme reflecting local priorities, with little or no co-ordination between individual colonies. The basic problem, however, was that Britain could not, or would not, spare the materials necessary to implement the colonies' individual development plans. Essential commodities such as cement, for construction, and steel, for railways, were either needed for Britain's own post-war reconstruction, or for export to more lucrative markets. London had warned of these metropolitan constraints as early as September 1945, but Britain was slow to identify colonial requirements, and the Colonial Office found itself repeatedly outmanoeuvred in the machinery introduced by Whitehall to allocate scarce resources.[103] Access to the London loan markets was carefully controlled on the grounds that metropolitan needs took priority. Of the CD & W funds made available between 1946 and 1951, some £40.5 million were spent, amounting to rather less than 1 per cent of Britain's GDP, during a period when the colonies were obliged to 'lend', or tie up in London, around £250 million, representing 'disinvestment on the grand scale'.[104] Devaluation in 1949 could be seen as marking a turning point in development policy, underlining the problems confronting Britain in providing the funds for colonial development. Although new legislation in 1950 extended existing provision, the concurrent shortages associated with rearmament meant that the supply problem persisted. It was recognized in London that these continuing obstacles to the implementation of colonial development plans might have political consequences in the colonies, undermining local confidence in the constitutional progress which Britain was beginning to introduce, for example in West Africa, but this dilemma was not resolved during this period.[105] Ironically, the colonial state's commitment to development exposed it to more criticism than in the inter-war period, when its role had been negligible. As the state became increasingly interventionist in promoting 'development', its actions could be interpreted as those of an intrusive, even oppressive, external power. The 'Second Colonial Occupation' of the post-war years brought with it new personnel ('experts') and new methods liable to antagonize colonial opinion, resentful at interference and the degree of compulsion often associated with drives to expand production. More broadly, as colonialism emerged as an issue in the Cold War, so too did British sensitivity that Soviet criticism might focus on the hollow reality of development policy.[106]

Ever since the unveiling of the new colonial development policy in 1940, 'development' had never been intended to imply only economic development: rather, it was seen as a complex of complementary strategies designed to improve social conditions as well, paving the way for political development. In social terms, the emphasis was not only on improving health and educational provision, but also on cultivating an institutional infrastructure to reinforce the stability of colonial societies, with the encouragement of co-operative organizations, trade unions, and so on, an approach originally termed 'mass education', but later known as 'community development'. The common theme of these initiatives was that they were meant to promote an ethos of self-help, ultimately reducing the need for state action. Their additional function was to create a climate in which increased economic activity would be possible.[107]

Even more explicitly than in other manifestations of Britain's new commitment to overseas development, the Cold War was an important motive for Britain's promotion of the Colombo Plan, a six-year programme intended to stimulate economic and social development in the strategically sensitive Far East and South-East Asia, where the reality of Communist expansion was an ever-present reminder of the vulnerability of Western interests. The plan, which involved the provision of development funding by Britain and the wealthier members of the Commonwealth, later joined by the United States, was endorsed by Bevin, echoing his idea of aiding development in the Middle East. By 1950, Britain had contributed more than £100 million to the plan.[108]

The measures taken by Britain in the wake of the convertibility crisis did not mean that the colonies solved Britain's economic problems. However, colonial resources did assist in achieving metropolitan recovery. Exports from the colonies rose significantly, including exports destined for Britain: these were almost twice as high in 1948 as they had been in 1938. Crucially, the colonies, especially the Gold Coast and Malaya, were to become net dollar earners.[109] Yet, they were not allowed access to the wealth they themselves generated. Instead, under the operations of the Sterling Area, Britain bought the dollars they earned at fixed exchange rates, crediting the colonies' sterling balances in London with the appropriate sum. In effect, their earnings were being tied up in the Bank of England as low-interest loans to Britain, and could not be spent on development schemes.[110]

Malaya

During the war, reclaiming Britain's control of its colonies in South-East Asia had been a major priority, and the reoccupation of Malaya in 1945, although in itself enormously demanding for Britain, was a source of great satisfaction for London. Fortunately, the British had not had to reconquer the colony, and physical damage to the local economy had therefore been minimal. The two most important industries, rubber and tin production (which would become so important to the recovery of the Sterling Area) had not been ravaged by a retreating Japanese army, and could resume production relatively quickly.[111] During their enforced absence from the region, British planners had the opportunity to devise new policies for Malaya, intended to set the territory on a trajectory towards modernization, the aim being a centralized, administratively efficient, economically vibrant and militarily secure polity (in contrast to the diverse affair which had crumbled so ignominiously in 1942), prepared to embark on political reform resulting eventually in self-government. Here, as in other parts of the colonial empire, Britain sought to retain the initiative, strengthening its hold on the territory, controlling a process of orderly evolution, and anticipating the growth of nationalism before it might become unmanageable. Fortunately for Britain, Malay nationalism, when it became apparent and active, proved to be a beast of a markedly conservative temper, closer in spirit to that of Ceylon than of India.

The Malayan Union scheme, introduced in January 1946, was based on treaties negotiated by Sir Harold MacMichael, Britain's special representative, with the Malay sultans late in 1945. MacMichael's tactless manner had already antagonized these traditionally willing imperial collaborators.[112] Under the new

arrangements, the sultans would lose much of their traditional authority to a
governor (who would replace the pre-war High Commissioner). Although it
was meant to prepare Malaya for eventual self-government, the Union represented an unprecedented degree of direct rule by Britain and a centralized
administrative structure: in effect, Malaya was to be run as a 'typical' colony. Its
citizenship proposals were especially controversial, stoking Malay fears of an
eventual Chinese ascendancy. By extending citizenship rights to the non-Malay
majority, Britain hoped to divert local Chinese attention from the rival appeal
of Communism, and to create enhanced opportunities for Chinese entrepreneurial participation in the territory's economic development.[113]

The Union met immediate resistance from traditional Malay rulers, and
from their supporters in Britain, chiefly comprising old Malaya 'hands' from
the inter-war period. By May 1946, the sultans, who had pointedly boycotted
the installation of Sir Edward Gent as governor in April, had formed the
United Malays National Organization (UMNO) under the leadership of Dato
Onn. Although UMNO was a staunch defender of Malay interests, and so
opposed the Union, it was not irrevocably anti-British. Taken aback by the
unexpectedly vigorous mood of the sultans, anxious to appease UMNO, and
preoccupied with the deteriorating situation in India in summer 1947 and with
the disturbing situation in Indonesia, where the Dutch were struggling to
reassert colonial rule, London reversed its policy and abandoned the Union. In
its place came the Federation of Malaya, inaugurated in February 1948, a much
diluted version of the Union, in which the sultans substantially regained their
powers, and the Malays their political privileges, though within a much more
unified structure than had existed before 1939. The office of colonial governor
reverted to that of High Commissioner. Britain had to revise its hopes for a
multiracial citizenship code (although this remained, in theory, the goal of
British policy): for the time being, only a small proportion of the non-Malay
community gained political rights.[114] Although the new system preserved the
autonomy of the Malay states, albeit under a new federal central government,
Britain's core objective had been achieved in that the most important aspect of
the Union plan, a strong and financially stable central government, had been
safeguarded.[115] The Federation was seen in London as the basis of future self-
government for Malaya, but this was not thought to be imminent (before the
outbreak of the Emergency, even the leader of UMNO considered Malaya
unready for independence). The reversal of British policy denoted London's
need not only to defuse Malay hostility, but also to ensure Malay co-operation
in the event of unrest among other ethnic groups in the colony.[116] Ironically, in
reaffirming the foundations of Anglo-Malay collaboration, the British found
that they had only deepened communal tensions by alienating important
sections of the Chinese population.[117]

The onset of a serious, and largely unexpected, Communist insurrection in
June 1948, with the declaration of a state of emergency, posed a fundamental
challenge to Britain's goals for the gradual development of South-East Asia.
The insurrection, which began with the murder of three European planters and
their Chinese assistants, was portrayed as being inspired by forces in Moscow

or Beijing, but the local colonial authorities subsequently admitted that evidence for this claim was scant. Nor, in retrospect, should it have come as a surprise, given the extent of violence and labour unrest in the territory since the end of the war. But Malaya's strategic importance in the Cold War, as the cornerstone of British policy in the Far East, a 'front-line' state in the struggle to deflect a Communist challenge to Asia, coupled to its indispensability as a dollar-earner for the Sterling Area, hardened Britain's determination to suppress the Emergency. The Malayan Communist Party was proscribed, and troops and resources were devoted on an enormous scale to Malaya.[118] By April 1950, when Lt Gen. Sir Harold Briggs arrived in Malaya to become Director of Operations, Britain had committed 40,000 soldiers and 80,000 auxiliaries. Initially, however, the authorities were reluctant to employ tough counterinsurgency measures. They were anxious not to acquire too repressive a reputation, and they needed to avoid forcing the insurgents underground. Although constitutional development had temporarily to be suspended, the British remained committed to their strategy of 'nation-building' in Malaya. The case of Malaya undermines the argument that Britain simply 'caved in' before the onslaught of Asian nationalism after 1945: here was no evidence of retreat, planned or otherwise. Ironically, the Communist challenge in some ways eased Britain's task of promoting political evolution. The sultans, and the Malay population generally, shared Britain's concern to tackle Communism, and Malay nationalism saw this as the overriding goal. But, to defeat the insurrection, it was necessary for Britain to work closely with Malay politicians and to take steps to ensure the compliance and co-operation of the bulk of the population.[119] After the arrival of a new High Commissioner, Sir Henry Gurney, late in 1949, the authorities' aims focused on two major goals: to deny the insurgents aid from disaffected sections of the population, especially the landless squatters, and to form an association to compete with the Communists for the political allegiance of the Chinese population.[120] Before 1951, conditions seemed inappropriate for the holding of elections, as provided for in the 1948 federal constitution, but these remained a British aim.

Experience of the Emergency, rather like the earlier lessons of India, suggested that it might be more dangerous to retard, than to accelerate, political advance. This meant, as Britain's regional commissioner-general, Malcolm MacDonald, told South-East Asian governors in June 1950, that the original target of full self-government for Malaya 25 years hence, seemed to have been overtaken by events. Even while the military counterinsurgency campaign was under way, a broad strategy of political and social advance was being implemented by Britain.[121] A new approach was introduced after the British general election of February 1950, and Briggs' appointment as Director of Operations. The Briggs Plan involved a plan to relocate the squatters in 'New Villages', effectively isolating them from the insurgents, tighter co-ordination of the counterinsurgency strategy, together with a 'hearts and minds' campaign of measures designed to win local support.[122] Looking further ahead, it was fortunate for London that the Malays sought British assistance in resisting the emergence of the predominantly Chinese challenge to their own political supremacy: the Emergency underlined the essentially interdependent relationship of the British and the Malays.

Britain's African empire

With the demise of the Raj in India imminent, the centre of gravity in Britain's policy towards the dependent empire was increasingly to be found in Africa. Here, with the possible exception of the Gold Coast, and despite evidence of the local populations' dissatisfaction with colonial rule, often grounded in specific economic grievances, there seemed, during the 1940s, to be no widespread nationalist sentiment, on the scale that was so obviously sweeping Asia. British officials therefore remained confident about their ability to remain in control of the pace of change in the African colonies. Nevertheless, a desire to avoid in Africa the problems already experienced in India can be discerned in Whitehall's deliberations at this time.[123]

In the immediate post-war period, the Colonial Office was anxious to set out clear, coherent policy objectives, conscious that the inter-war years had been characterized by an 'aimlessness and drift' and that many serving officers were demoralized.[124] Indirect rule seemed to have outlived its usefulness: the times seemed to require meaningful African participation in government. Africans were now perceived as essential partners in the economic development process. This involved seeking a broader base of support for colonial rule than had ever obtained in India, with the encouragement of an educated middle class as co-operators, rather than the traditional chiefly allies. This new elite was to be given practical experience of democratic practices by participating in a new, efficient system of local government, as the Colonial Secretary, Arthur Creech Jones, outlined in February 1947. This experience would prepare the elite for an eventual role in the institutions of central government, as they, too, gradually became more democratic and representative of local populations.[125] This emphasis on local government demonstrated British officials' concern to distract the politically 'immature' African elite away from politics as such, and to give them a grounding in good administration. Implicit in the new policy was London's recognition that progress on these lines might have to be faster than local populations had been led to expect, especially in that the mass of the population was seen as a useful potential counterweight to the developing class of politicians, which might tend to further its own interests.[126] Britain's aim, as with the related development policy, was not only to demonstrate that colonial rule could be progressive, but also to prepare for an orderly transfer of power to stable, pro-British governments. These innovations were not, therefore, merely a response to a perceived nationalist challenge: rather they can be seen as an attempt to *anticipate* the growth of nationalism and as the first steps in creating a future 'informal' empire.[127]

The hallmark of the new approach was a much greater willingness to consult officials responsible for implementing policy at the local level. In contrast to what had appeared to be a strongly centralizing thrust in wartime styles of colonial administration, the emphasis by 1947 was towards a more flexible, devolved approach, restoring to some extent the initiative which colonial governments had enjoyed before 1939, with the Colonial Office's role being, theoretically, to offer advice.[128] In August 1947, a summer school was held in Cambridge to discuss the new policy of local government. This was followed in November by an unprecedented gathering of African colonial governors in London, intended to set out the Colonial Office's new thinking to the assembled governors. The preparations for this event revealed divergent views among senior officials, mirrored by varying responses from the governors, not all of whom were impressed by London's latest 'fads' or by the coherence of the new initiative (the Kenyan governor, for example, recorded that the Colonial Secretary had 'blathered a good deal').[129] Then, in September 1948, African administrators and 'unofficial' members of colonial legislatures met in London to hear the Colonial Office's new thinking.[130]

During spring 1947, preparations for the African Governors' Conference revealed key officials' ideas about the direction of Britain's African policies. It seemed that within a generation, a number of large colonies would become self-governing, within the Commonwealth (the term 'independent' was, significantly, not used). A basic assumption in the Colonial Office was that management of their own internal affairs, rather than a more fundamental breach with Britain, would satisfy African populations.[131]

Very revealing of contemporary attitudes was the report prepared in May 1947 by Andrew Cohen, the Colonial Office's Platonic philosopher-king, preparatory to the African Governors' Conference. Written for internal consumption, the report set out a plan for the staged evolution of the African colonies towards eventual self-government. Cohen began with the assumption that although colonialism was nearing the end of its life, if Britain could learn to anticipate local political developments, instead of simply reacting to them, colonial rule could be prolonged, to the benefit of both Britain and the colonies. Taking the earlier development of the Dominions as a model, Cohen believed that the existing colonial state could evolve into a Westminster-type political system. This would begin when each legislative council had an elected majority of 'unofficial' members, and the colonial government had devolved its administrative powers to individual departments, each headed by a British civil servant. Next, unofficial members of the Legislative Council might be appointed to the Executive Council, some of them being given responsibility for minor government departments. On particular issues, the governor could follow the advice of the majority of Executive Council members. Over time, the number of subjects 'reserved' in the hands of British officials would decline, and the Executive Council would gradually develop into a Cabinet, answerable to a fully elected legislature, though with the governor retaining the powers of a prime minister. The final stage in this process would be reached when the governor was able to transfer full power to a prime minister heading a Cabinet responsible for all areas of internal government, and accountable to a fully elected legislature. At this stage, full independence would be the logical outcome.[132]

In Cohen's view, the last two stages in this evolutionary model would take a long time to be achieved, because they would require essentially artificial colonial territories to develop a 'genuine' sense of unity and identity, and to produce authentic national leaders, serving communities schooled in democratic principles. As Cohen pointed out, policy would have to take account of the great regional diversity within Britain's African empire. Territories in East and Central Africa, for example, with their entrenched settler populations, would have to be treated differently to a relatively advanced, and predominantly African, colony such as the Gold Coast. Even in the latter, however, Cabinet government was unlikely to emerge in much less than a generation. Inherent in Cohen's approach was a deeply paternalistic outlook, a belief that Britain must remain in control of the process of colonial political evolution, and a conviction that only Britain could judge when African populations had 'proven' their fitness for self-government by subscribing unambiguously to the complex of values underpinning Western social democracy.[133] A further aspect of Cohen's report which merits emphasis is the fact that its proposals had, by definition, to remain confidential: it was essential that London should be able to conceal its hand, to withhold from aspiring colonial politicians the knowledge that Britain had already decided to reward them in the future with political power (or, as it has been put, the fact that they were in effect 'pushing at an open door'). The confidence enshrined in Cohen's report, the impression of ample time ahead to prepare for colonial self-government, is noteworthy because in less than three years, its prescriptions had been set aside: the pace of change at grass-roots level in Africa, especially West Africa, necessitated a radical reappraisal of British strategy and a telescoping of the leisurely timetable suggested by Cohen. As British policy-makers had already found before the war in India, and as they would be reminded throughout the course of decolonization, constitution-mongering in a cool, detached mood was a very different proposition from the implementation of those constitutions and entering the unpredictable waters of electoral politics.

The Gold Coast

Like many colonies in the immediate post-war period, the Gold Coast experienced social and economic strains, some of which had their origins in the war itself. Shortages of many imports, inflation, unemployment among demobilized soldiers, resentment at the low prices farmers received from state marketing boards, and at the measures taken by the colonial state to deal with a serious outbreak of swollen shoot disease which affected the territory's main export crop, cocoa, all combined to produce a mood of frustrated expectations and general dissatisfaction. Nevertheless, sustaining the reforming momentum initiated by the colony's liberal governor, Sir Alan Burns, since 1941, London had approved a new constitution for the Gold Coast in 1946. Not unlike the Malayan Union scheme, this was intended to integrate the colony's various regions more effectively and introduce greater representation for its population. Driven by the same modernizing impulse, and similarly holding out the prospect of accelerated economic development based upon widened local participation, the Burns Constitution had the important consequence of impressing upon the Gold Coast's small politically active urban elite that if their voices were to be heard in the country's developing organs of government, especially the expanded Legislative Council (in which *elected* 'unofficials' would, for the first time, form the majority), and if they were not to be eclipsed by the more conservative elites of the rural hinterland, it was necessary for them to participate in the new central institutions, and to organize politically to make that participation effective. These were the conditions in which the United Gold Coast Convention was born in 1947, representing the views of the colony's numerically small professional class. Far from being politically radical, the UGCC appeared intent to co-operate in working the new machinery approved by Britain. An important step, in keeping with London's gradualist vision, appeared to have been taken in the constitutional development of British Africa.

However, the apparent political calm of the Gold Coast was shattered in February 1948 by rioting in the capital, Accra, triggered when police fired on a demonstration by aggrieved ex-servicemen. The subsequent attacks on European-owned shops underlined the basically economic grievances of many of the rioters. Yet, coming when they did, at a time when Cold War tensions in Europe were deepening, the riots were interpreted by the newly installed colonial governor, Sir Gerald Creasy, as being Communist-inspired. Compared to the full-scale military campaigns then being waged by the French in Indo-China, and by the Dutch in Indonesia, the Accra Riots were a very minor affair. The scale of the local authorities' reaction can be explained partly in terms of their proximity to developments in India, and to contemporary developments in Europe. The colonial authorities declared a state of emergency and detained the leaders of the UGCC. A battalion was put in readiness to fly out to the Gold Coast from Gibraltar, and two ships were sent from the Cape. Although initial reactions to the Accra Riots assumed a Communist plot, in reality there was none: London had yet to learn to distinguish between Communism and nationalist grievances.[134]

To his credit, Creech Jones was unconvinced that the Gold Coast harboured a Communist conspiracy. He replaced the ailing Creasy with a new governor, Sir Charles Arden-Clarke (who had recent experience of combating insurgency in South-East Asia), and set up a commission of inquiry under Aiken Watson K.C. The Watson Commission reached the conclusion, embarrassing for London's policy-makers, that the 1946 Constitution, until then considered the most enlightened in British Africa, had been 'outmoded at birth', and recommended an accelerated route to self-government for the Gold Coast, involving an enlarged Legislative Council elected under a wider franchise, and the inclusion of Africans with executive responsibility in government.[135] Although the Watson Commission's findings were not substantively at odds with progressive thinking within the Colonial Office, what was radically different about them was the timescale envisaged for the introduction of fundamental changes, far in advance of what London had been contemplating. The British government nevertheless accepted this advice and established an all-African committee under Sir Henley Coussey to make specific recommendations on constitutional change. Even now, London was attempting to retain the initiative: the Coussey Committee was selected carefully so as to exclude unreliable African opinion, favouring instead 'moderate' and 'responsible' views. It was accepted that the recent past could not be ignored: instead, nationalism had to be accepted as a political fact of life if a more radical political challenge to British authority were to be averted. Meanwhile, Arden-Clarke set about reorganizing the colony's intelligence and security structures. In October 1949, the Coussey Committee proposed the creation of an entirely elected legislature, chosen indirectly by manhood suffrage, to which the Executive Council, including African ministers, would be responsible. At the same time, checks and balances were to be introduced to discourage local 'radicals'. For instance, age restrictions would limit the threat from younger election candidates, and a system of indirect voting in the rural areas was expected to advantage conservative groups. The British government accepted these recommendations, believing that it could control the situation in the colony.

Arden-Clarke's aim was to assist moderate African politicians in order to block the progress of more extreme tendencies. During 1949, the young UGCC organizer, Kwame Nkrumah, becoming impatient with his party's moderate leadership, had broken away to form his own, more radical, Convention People's Party, and was proving alarmingly adept at mobilizing the collective resentments of the so-called 'verandah boys', drawn from the Gold Coast's swelling population of educated, under-employed, and consequently frustrated youth. Adopting the techniques of earlier Indian nationalists, and sharing some of their charismatic qualities, Nkrumah embarked on a campaign of 'positive action' early in 1950, demanding 'self-government now'. Having introduced electoral politics, with all their uncertainties, the colonial authorities now sought to support their favoured candidates, the UGCC at the expense of Nkrumah (whom the governor dubbed 'our local Hitler'). Officials were inclined to believe UGCC claims that Nkrumah lacked a broad base of popular support, and still tended to see the rural heartland of the colony as politically quiescent. Yet it was Nkrumah's achievement to bring together disaffected Ashanti farmers and the Western-educated coastal, urban elite, together with the unemployed and dispossessed, in a transient, if effective, political alliance. A tough line was taken in response to the CPP's Positive Action campaign: Nkrumah and his senior colleagues were arrested and detained, and another state of emergency was declared.

A new constitution unveiled at the end of 1950 included safeguards designed to favour the moderate UGCC and penalize Nkrumah's 'radical' CPP. Ministerial reponsibility was only partly entrusted to African politicians, and among the members of the Executive Council, three were to be nominated officials (against eight elected unofficials). Pointedly, the unofficials in the council were to be headed not by a 'prime minister', but by a 'leader of government business', a small but significant distinction. Moreover, it was thought likely that the new electoral system would produce moderate, compliant, majorities. Nkrumah's CPP had initially condemned the new constitution, but once preparations for the Gold Coast's first general election got under way, the party worked assiduously to see that its supporters registered to vote and asserted their political rights. In this sense, ironically, the CPP was promoting the colonial government's policy of fostering a modern, democratic system. In the event, London's calculations misfired, and Nkrumah won a resounding victory, even though he had conducted his election campaign from his prison cell. He was released in February 1951 to take up his new duties as Leader of Government Business. Of particular importance was the fact that, leaving aside his necessarily forceful rhetoric, Nkrumah had quickly shown that he could play the game of constitutional development according to rules decided in London, and that he was willing, implicitly, to admit Britain's continuing control over that process. Before long, Arden-Clarke, who still retained considerable powers over justice and security, was reassessing Nkrumah and his ministers, who seemed agreeably 'competent and reasonable'. It was the governor who, aware of the political pressures on Nkrumah from his own supporters, urged London to maintain the momentum of constitutional progress. In summer 1951, Britain accepted that Nkrumah would soon be granted the coveted title of prime minister.

Developments in the Gold Coast had made a nonsense of Cohen's devolution timetable: responsible Cabinet government had arrived within two years, not the 20 Cohen had predicted, and before the basic preparations he had envisaged had been effected. Moreover, it was difficult to limit change to the Gold Coast: soon ministers in London accepted that similar political concessions would have to be granted to Nigeria, and a new constitution approved in 1950 gave African politicians an increased role both in central and in regional government, the latter being awarded greater autonomy in recognition of the colony's ethnic diversity.[136] Nigeria, too, had been set on the path towards eventual independence.

East and Central Africa were dealt with very differently. Here, although the broad goal of colonial policy was theoretically the same as in West Africa, namely self-government within the Commonwealth, British policy-makers faced a complicating factor absent in West Africa, the presence of a significant white settler population, and, in East Africa's case, a South Asian minority. London's response was to try to create conditions which would permit a gradual increase in African political involvement, leading eventually to rough equality in the political status of the various ethnic groups, or a multiracial 'partnership'. The key to stability, in London's eyes, was co-operation between the races, though it was tacitly assumed that the settlers would continue to enjoy a privileged position for the foreseeable future, lending their entrepreneurial flair to the region's economic 'development'. In contrast to the Gold Coast, there was no attraction in promoting 'nationalism', whether settler or African.[137]

In the post-war Colonial Office, especially under Arthur Creech Jones, there were misgivings about the way Kenya's settlers had been able, during the war, to consolidate their privileged position. However, there was equally reluctance to confront them, a course which it was feared might trigger a political crisis, at a time when Britain's economic circumstances required the uninterrupted production of East (and Central) African commodities, to which settler co-operation was considered essential. If 'partnership' was seen by London as a means both of reconciling settler and African interests, and of providing colonial rule with an acceptable appearance, settler opposition to African advancement (however limited) was soothed by the segregation of the electorate along communal lines.[138]

The economic potential ascribed by London to East Africa was matched by greatly expanded British interest in the region's strategic value. Facing growing challenges in other sensitive base areas, especially the Middle East, Attlee's government saw great possibilities for a major Kenyan base. In September 1947, with Britain still reeling from the convertibility crisis of the summer, work began on the new Mackinnon Road military complex, intended to serve both as a training camp and as a huge storage base. However, the practical problems of developing the Kenyan base, including providing it with an adequate transport infrastructure, proved as intractable as wider programmes of development in this period. Moreover, the Chiefs of Staff reconsidered their decision, and concluded that Kenya was, after all, too difficult to utilize and too remote from the Middle East, likely to be a 'hot' theatre in a future war.[139]

The post-war period saw an important reappraisal by London of its long-term policy towards Central Africa. Although the region's settlers had long shown interest in amalgamating Northern and Southern Rhodesia and Nyasaland, this had been resisted by the British government on the grounds that the three were still at very different stages of constitutional development. Concern at the possible growth of South African influence north of the Limpopo, and a desire to promote faster regional economic development, based especially on Northern Rhodesia's booming copper industry, led Attlee's government to consider a new federal structure, linking the three territories in an association strong enough to resist any encroachment from the south, though still under London's ultimate control.[140] Even otherwise 'liberal' policy-makers, such as Andrew Cohen in the Colonial Office, were willing to suppress their doubts about the fate of the African majority under a federal system dominated by white settlers. Faith was pinned in the scope for multiracialism to develop, implying a genuine partnership between the races in the region's development. Shortly before the Labour government's fall from power, a conference was held at Victoria Falls at which representatives of the several governments involved adopted the principle of federation. How African interests would be safeguarded in such an arrangement was a problem bequeathed to the returning Conservatives.

The problem of South Africa

Among the problems facing the Labour government in its policies towards Africa was the developing quandary of relations with South Africa, where a

hostile Nationalist government under Dr Malan took office in 1948, committed
to overtly racist policies. Malan replaced Field-Marshal Smuts, an ally of Britain
in both world wars and a staunch supporter of imperial defence. Although it
took time for the full extent of life under apartheid to become clear, British
ministers recoiled from its early symptoms. Nor could they ignore the likely
consequences on colonial opinion of being seen to co-operate with South
Africa. For its part, South Africa became alarmed at the direction of British
policy in Black Africa, fearing that the constitutional reforms initiated in West
Africa might be applied to colonies with settler populations, such as those in
Central Africa.[141]

Nevertheless, there were compelling reasons for continuing ties. Economically, South Africa was an important partner for Britain, which had a sizeable
stake in the former's mining and other industries. A member of the Sterling
Area, South Africa had provided Britain with an £80 million gold loan in
1948.[142] Strategically, too, South Africa was seen as an essential partner, a view
ironically reinforced by Pretoria's increasingly entrenched anti-Communism.
Britain's military chiefs were especially keen to secure South African co-
operation in the defence of the Middle East – the 'gateway to Africa' (a
concern sharpened by the outbreak of the Korean War in 1950) – and, more
generally, sought to involve the Union in a multilateral Western alliance. It was
for this reason that Britain offered to sell scarce military supplies to South
Africa, persuading the latter in 1950 to commit itself to Middle Eastern
defence.[143] Potentially a source of military manpower, South Africa more
immediately offered the naval base of Simonstown, considered vital by British
defence planners. Moreover, South Africa was a major source of the uranium
Britain required for its growing atomic programme, both civil and military.

Although Attlee's government was aware of the dangers of alienating colonial opinion by co-operating with South Africa, the latter's concern about
United Nations interference in colonies was shared by London. A further
problem was South Africa's ambition to absorb the UN Trust Territory, South
West Africa, which attracted international interest at the UN, and opposition
from countries such as India.[144] London acquiesced in Pretoria's claim to the
territory as the necessary price of securing South African co-operation in other
fields. Nevertheless, Britain was uncomfortably aware of the need to reconcile
its dependence, on Cold War grounds, on retaining South Africa within the
Commonwealth, with its overriding concern, also fuelled by Cold War considerations, to develop a genuinely multiracial Commonwealth. Because the loss
of South Africa, a 'founding member', might reduce the standing of the
Commonwealth, Attlee's government opted to work with Malan's regime as
closely as it could.[145] This, however, did not stop London seeking to set limits
to the spread of South African influence and policies further north: this was
the prime motive for creating the ill-fated Central African Federation in
1953.[146] Similarly, Britain continued to refuse to hand over the neighbouring
High Commission Territories, long coveted by Pretoria, to South Africa, in
view of their populations' reluctance to be absorbed. Nevertheless, concern to
appease the South African government influenced Britain's own policy towards

these territories. Most famously, in 1949, when the heir to the largest kingdom in Bechuanaland, Seretse Khama, married his English secretary, deference to outraged white South African sentiment led Britain to banish both Seretse and his uncle, an episode which ended only in 1956 when Seretse surrendered his claims to the throne.[147]

The years between 1945 and 1951 witnessed an important re-orientation in Britain's management of its imperial system. The government's experiences, perhaps especially in the Middle East and South Asia, had underlined the constraints on British power in the post-war world. The difficulties attaching to economic adjustment and recovery were accentuated by the increased global responsibilities which the maintenance of Britain's interests had seemed to require after 1945. Above all, and spilling over into every aspect of British overseas policy, was the importance of waging the Cold War successfully, a concern which, in Britain's case, could not be confined to selected regional commitments, but demanded a truly global role which was becoming more difficult to sustain given the paring of Britain's resources. Among the lessons derived from events since the end of the war was that it had become more difficult than ever for Britain to maintain rule over populations who would no longer accept it: indeed, even attempting to do so might be counter-productive, placing further strains on metropolitan resources and fomenting possibly insurmountable resistance. This did not mean that Britain had, by 1951, lost the will to preserve its overseas authority, least of all where crucial strategic or economic interests were at stake. But it did mean that calculations of national advantage would be more searching, and attempts to avoid confrontation would, where possible, continue. The experiences of Attlee's government reinforced London's commitment to the broad policy of promoting political development in the colonial empire, but developments in India, Egypt and, latterly, West Africa, had highlighted the need for London to seek to retain the initiative in managing nationalism, if necessary by making timely concessions in order to maintain ultimate control over the pace of political change. This could mean, as the Gold Coast had demonstrated, that timetables for constitutional advance drawn up in London might have to be discarded with almost indecent haste in the light of changing local circumstances. This fundamental concern to bolster British control over the processes subsequently termed decolonization would also be expressed in one of the hallmarks of British policy over the next decade, the quest for 'moderate' nationalist leaders, capable of blocking more threatening challenges from 'extremists' (as defined by London and its agents). If these things could be achieved, then the greatest prize of all might be realized: the maintenance of a close, cordial relationship with former dependencies, expressed in the expansion of the Commonwealth to include newly independent countries, and their orientation towards the West in the all-important global ideological struggle.

CHAPTER 4

CHANGE AND CONTROL UNDER CHURCHILL AND EDEN, 1951–57

At the beginning of the 1950s, Britain was still the world's third leading power, and would soon join the elite club of nuclear powers. In economic terms, it was still more powerful than either France or West Germany, soon to become Britain's rivals. Its range and extent of overseas commitments far outclassed those of any other European power, involving management of the British Commonwealth, the still sizeable colonial empire, and an 'informal' empire, centred especially on the Middle East. Increasingly, however, this system would come under strain, most worryingly in those parts of the world where Britain had vital interests. The new Conservative administration formed in 1951 by the veteran Winston Churchill attached great importance to maintaining Britain's world role. For Churchill himself, this involved a threefold strategy. The first objective was to hold together the Empire-Commonwealth, whose existence still formed the core of Britain's claims to great power status. Secondly, it was essential to maintain good relations with the English-speaking world, with the emphasis on preserving and consolidating the 'special relationship' with the United States, a task Churchill thought would be eased by the advent of the Eisenhower presidency in 1953. Finally, it was Britain's aim to encourage greater integration in Western Europe, without itself becoming entangled in that process (which might imply a reduction in Britain's distinctive status). The idea that these three policy goals could be depicted as three interlocking, and mutually dependent, circles was popularized by Churchill in the early 1950s: Britain's unique position was to have a role in all three, and its influence in each circle was thought to depend on its role in the other two. As the conclusion of this period would demonstrate unambiguously, it was the relationship with the United States which was crucial: although Britain was undoubtedly the junior power, its potential influence on Washington policy-makers was still significant, not only because Britain remained at the head of a global imperial system, but also because the United States had come to value the empire, and its resources, in a Cold War context. There was a danger, however, of over-estimating Britain's value as a partner, and its capacity to act independently of the United States, as Eden would discover late in 1956. It was in the defence field that Britain's dependence on Washington was most visible. On returning to power in 1951, Churchill hoped that the close wartime collaboration between Britain and the

US on nuclear matters might be resurrected; in this he was to be disappointed, and the most he extracted from Truman was an undertaking that the use of American bases in Britain during an emergency would be determined jointly by London and Washington, in the light of the circumstances.[1] In fact, by the early 1950s, Britain was entirely reliant on the American nuclear umbrella, but had no real influence over the use of US nuclear weapons.

Although maintaining Britain's global role would become increasingly difficult in the 1950s, the new Conservative government, like its Labour predecessor, did not question this fundamental objective. Like Attlee's government, those of Churchill and Eden would generally adopt a pragmatic approach, retreating from situations where British interests could not be defended satisfactorily, while holding on to the empire for its economic and strategic value. Yet, as the Global Strategy Paper of 1952 demonstrated, there was an inherent tension between the objectives of reducing Britain's overseas obligations on financial grounds, and maintaining them for what were still seen as vital reasons of prestige. As the Chiefs of Staff argued in October 1952, 'Our standard of living stems in large measure from our status as a great power and this depends to no small extent on the visible indication of our greatness, which our forces, particularly overseas, provide.'[2] The unfolding challenge was to find means of preserving Britain's global interests at a cost that was acceptable, given the significant reduction in the country's assets in the post-war world, and its accumulating economic problems. Not only was the economy growing more slowly than that of some important rivals, but also the balance of payments position remained difficult. The government found itself forced to continue a regime of austerity while trying to increase industrial production. In this, it met with some success, achieving an approximate balance of trade with the dollar area by 1952–53, despite the economic strains caused by rearmament and the Korean War. Moreover, it proved possible to avoid a further devaluation of the pound. Nevertheless, in this period, Britain faced unprecedented peacetime demands on its national wealth: in addition to the enormous burdens arising from defence spending (operating conscription, keeping forces in Europe and developing nuclear weapons, without US help), Britain was trying to manage the Sterling Area as a global financial system, and to find adequate investment for developing the Empire-Commonwealth.[3] While there were some successes, for example in domestic industrial investment, the relative decline of the British economy continued unabated during the early 1950s. To complicate Britain's balance of payments difficulties, the country's overseas competitors were not only becoming more economically powerful, but also supplanting Britain in some of its traditional export markets. Standing in the way of even and steady economic growth was the phenomenon of stop–go economic policies, in which expansion and restraint alternated in a frustrating manner.

One of the very first problems to be addressed by the new government was the balance of payments question. At this time, Britain's external deficit was growing by about £700 million a year, and the full effects of the rearmament programme were yet to be felt. The Chancellor, R.A. Butler, worried about the 'overloaded' economy, urged his colleagues to consider the existing scale of Britain's overseas commitments, and the country's capacity to meet them. As he pointed out, Britain had taken on considerably swollen responsibilities in the fields of defence and welfare, yet with a narrower wealth base than before the war. Given the extent of Britain's economic difficulties, hard questions would have to be asked about the feasibility of maintaining current high levels of overseas expenditure. Butler himself was pessimistic, foreseeing 'a continuing mountain range of difficulties'.[4] Yet any process of fundamental reappraisal would be difficult for a government which attached such importance to perceptions of British prestige.

As Churchill's Foreign Secretary, Eden set out a three-point summary of Britain's priorities. First among these was the defence of Western Europe, including participation in NATO; secondly, there were the various responsibilities arising from the imperial role, involving the need to defend interests in the Middle East, promote economic and social development in the colonies, and maintain a global system of military bases; finally, there were the assorted commitments stemming from any serious bid to be considered a major power, including effective membership of the United Nations, and playing a significant role in the Cold War. The need to be seen to be a major actor in the Cold War, preferably leading to victory in that struggle, was, along with a desire to maintain the empire as a major force in world affairs, central to British policy in the 1950s, as it had been under Attlee.[5] In Eden's view, there were strong reasons to avoid abandoning any of Britain's major commitments, not least because to do so might open doors to Soviet penetration, risk Britain's trading interests, and tarnish Britain's image in Washington as a major ally. For Eden, any of these consequences would be unthinkable, and so it was necessary to determine where Britain could safely reduce its overseas burdens, without jeopardizing any of its vital interests. One solution was to share as many of these burdens as possible with other countries, particularly the United States and other members of the Commonwealth. This would require a continuing American willingness to underwrite European security by stationing troops, and similar help in other parts of the world. If this strategy succeeded, it would enable Britain to devote its energies to defending its position in the Middle East, Asia and Africa. Clear assessments of the potential for economies in overseas spending were not easy to determine, however, as Eden was well aware. While it was increasingly obvious that Britain was trying to do too much with its limited resources, at a time when investment in the domestic economy was urgently needed, there were convincing reasons to avoid drastic cuts in overseas commitments. Defence spending seemed an obvious candidate, yet in the early 1950s Britain was not only committed to an ambitious rearmament programme, but it was also deploying troops on a large scale in Korea, Europe and the Middle East, while simultaneously tackling major insurgencies in Malaya and Kenya, soon to be joined by Cyprus.

Although the defence chiefs resorted to painting grim scenarios likely to arise from any spending cuts, defence remained a prime target for economies throughout this period. Some defenders of Britain's world role argued that its cost was justified by the potential economic returns it could bring, in promoting trade and so reinforcing full employment at home, and in safeguarding supplies essential to the country, such as oil (on which Britain was becoming increasingly dependent, as the coal industry headed for what seemed to be irremediable decline). The hard-pressed Chancellor, Butler, concerned about the resources available for social and industrial investment in Britain, repeatedly called for spending cuts, arguing that existing expenditure had been based on erroneous assumptions about the level of US aid and the likely extent of Britain's own economic recovery. The defence chiefs' predictable response was that the government must either find the money needed to maintain Britain's status, or risk losing that status (which they could safely assume no government would be willing to do).

Yet concern over defence spending persisted. Early in 1956, Butler's successor at the Treasury, Macmillan, observed: 'It is defence expenditure which has broken our backs ... The only way I can see by which we can restore the economy is by really getting down to the defence problem.'[6] Churchill's government had begun by cutting defence spending, yet even after the end of the Korean War, Britain was still spending more than twice on defence than its major European competitors, over 9 per cent of its gross domestic product by 1955. This high level was fuelled partly by new overseas entanglements, including the counterinsurgency campaign in Kenya. While NATO's existence seemed likely to reduce the threat of further Soviet incursions into Europe, this, it was feared, might lead Moscow to become more adventurous in investigating opportunities for expansion in the colonial territories; a Cold War success in Europe would offer little comfort to the West if this were immediately offset by failure in the developing world. In this context, it seemed sensible to bolster the colonies' own defence capability, which would have the additional benefit of taking the strain off the British Army. Yet, as the previous government had discovered, there were practical limits to the colonies' ability to contribute to their own, or to wider imperial, defence.

Ironically, with hindsight, the British government's enthusiasm for developing nuclear weapons was driven at least in part by a desire to economize. As the Global Strategy Paper of 1952 observed, only possession of an independent nuclear deterrent would guarantee that the United States would take British concerns seriously. Britain did successfully test its first atom bomb in 1952, but this was soon overshadowed by the development by both the Americans and the Soviets of enormously more powerful thermonuclear (hydrogen) weapons. Britain found itself obliged to respond in kind, if only, as the Cabinet agreed in 1954, to preserve its major power status, but also because it was still unsure of the reliability of the US nuclear umbrella. With a fleet of new, long-range V-bombers to deliver nuclear weapons, Britain became the world's third thermonuclear power in 1957. The increasing British reliance on a policy of nuclear deterrence had major consequences for traditional thinking on imperial defence. One of the major attractions of deterrence was its supposed cheapness, compared to maintaining a sizeable conventional capability, but this also cast doubts on the need for a far-flung system of military bases, essential to pre-nuclear defence policy, but now judged to be outmoded, a drain on metropolitan defence, and itself vulnerable to enemy action. Inevitably, such a major rethink of British strategic priorities would be controversial, not least among the service chiefs whose spending plans would accordingly have to be trimmed.

It was in an attempt to address these painful, but fundamental, questions that Eden, perhaps more willing than Churchill to tailor Britain's commitments more closely to the available resources, established a Policy Review Committee in June 1956, charged with finding acceptable ways of economizing on defence, currently accounting for around 10 per cent of government revenue, with Britain's commitment to the defence of Western Europe as part of NATO representing the largest single military burden. The Treasury (then headed by Macmillan), the Foreign Office and the Ministry of Defence together produced a report on 'The Future of the United Kingdom in World Affairs' which drew the increasingly obvious conclusion that Britain no longer had the resources to be considered a first-rank power on a par with the United States and the Soviet Union. More alarmingly, it suggested that Britain could be outstripped by nations such as China and Canada, each with vast, but as yet untapped, resources. Given these considerations, Britain's ambitions to remain a major world player would have to be based increasingly on its guardianship of the Sterling Area (since half the world's trade was still conducted in sterling), and on its possession of nuclear weapons.

Nevertheless, the current thrust of policies was untenable: Britain's post-war economy simply could not support the greatly enlarged responsibilities the country had taken on, and so priorities would have to be defined. Of these, defending sterling took precedence. It was recognized that since the war, Britain had been gambling dangerously in managing its currency without adequate reserves. Correcting this situation would require a paring of con-sumption of home, including cuts in social expenditure, and a reappraisal of responsibilities abroad. Britain's salvation, it was thought, might lie in thermo-nuclear weapons: the nuclear deterrent would enable Britain to cut its conventional defence spending in favour of subtler (and more economical) methods of fighting the Cold War, including political persuasion and propa-ganda. As Eden starkly summarized the position: 'We must now cut our coat according to our cloth. There is not much cloth.'[7] Defence spending in Europe seemed to be the obvious target, but this would require efforts to convince NATO allies that Britain was acting responsibly, even if this meant welfare cuts at home. In reality, ministers hoped to safeguard domestic social spending while at the same time transferring some of the defence burden to the Ameri-cans and Europeans.[8]

The British Commonwealth

In the eyes of the British government, the Commonwealth remained a corner-stone of Britain's global system of power and influence. It was axiomatic that as Britain's colonies in due course became independent, they should opt to join the Commonwealth. Here, again, there was clear continuity in British policy before and after 1951: the overall goal of colonial policy remained self-government *within the Commonwealth*. Ministers recognized this as a strategy to preserve British imperial influence employing new means. The alternative, allowing former colonies to drift away from British influence, was seen as a threat to Britain's international voice. Early in the new government's life, some members, including not only Churchill but also other 'imperially minded' figures such as Lords Salisbury and Swinton, feared that the addition of new members would inevitably alter the character of the Commonwealth. These misgivings had been strengthened by experience of decolonization in South Asia under Attlee's government, and especially India's embarrassing shift towards non-alignment and republicanism, even though for India, a continuing close relationship with Britain helped to counterbalance the interest being shown in Pakistan by the United States.[9]

In the early phase of the Churchill government, it was the prospect of the Sudan achieving independence which focused ministerial attention on the future development of the Commonwealth. A committee, including Swinton, Salisbury and the Colonial Secretary, Oliver Lyttelton, was created to study the question of Commonwealth membership. Salisbury voiced strong misgivings about the readiness of some colonies for entry to the organization, denying their political and national maturity. He felt that the entry of the Asian Dominions had fundamentally altered relations within the Commonwealth, eroding the confidence which had previously existed between members. These sentiments found resonance among some older Commonwealth members. The Australian prime minister, Robert Menzies, for example, was thought to be unruffled by the possibility of India's secession. Emphasizing the fundamental importance of common allegiance to the British Crown, and therefore disturbed by the diluting effects of republicanism, Menzies privately doubted whether the new Asian members would long maintain their membership. From Pretoria, too, came warnings from the British High Commissioner that Malan's Nationalist government would resist any proposal to include a Black African state in the Commonwealth.[10]

Faced with what they interpreted as a danger of disintegration and a loss of British control, some ministers became interested in the idea of creating different levels of Commonwealth membership. Swinton, nostalgic for the Commonwealth's traditional character, and anxious to retain South Africa as a member, was particularly keen to explore a category of 'junior' membership, under which Britain would remain responsible for defence and foreign relations.[11] Discussions on the possibility of a 'two-tier' Commonwealth, designed to preserve the special bonds of the more distinctively 'British' members, eventually concluded that the idea was unworkable: junior status would inevitably be resented by states to whom it was offered, as Governor Arden-Clarke reported from the Gold Coast in 1954, and might lead to their complete withdrawal.[12] The Cabinet Secretary, Sir Norman Brook, observed pragmatically that London would simply have to recognize that the Commonwealth was developing into a non-hierarchical, predominantly non-white organization. This did not, however, preclude Britain from maintaining especially close relations, particularly in the defence sphere, with certain members, as was already the case in practice. Since 1948, when London and Washington had agreed to share military intelligence, sensitive information had been passed to older Commonwealth members, but seldom to the newer South Asian members.[13] Although some ministers remained critical of the general thrust of colonial policy towards granting self-governing status, the Cabinet accepted Brook's recommendations at the end of 1954.

Meanwhile, the more practical concern of achieving greater Commonwealth cohesion in the defence field remained a British priority, as it had been under Attlee. When the ANZUS treaty was being negotiated, the Foreign Office and the Chiefs of Staff had warned that this might lead other countries to detect a dilution of the Special Relationship. Equally alarming was the possible implication that Malaya and Hong Kong, excluded from the treaty, were considered expendable in the event of a major Cold War crisis. In fact, it had been Australia, nervous about its own security within the Pacific region, rather than the United States, which had provided the momentum behind the ANZUS Pact.[14] By the early 1950s, the defence ties developed by various Commonwealth members had assumed a strikingly different character to that in existence before the Second World War. Just as Britain's own defence arrangements were centred on co-operation with the United States, so too Canada, Australia and New Zealand had become formally linked to Washington in this sphere.[15]

Until the mid-1950s, a common assumption among the governments of Britain, Australia and New Zealand was that, if another world war broke out, Australian and New Zealand forces would be sent to stiffen the defence of the crucial Middle Eastern zone, as had happened during the Second World War. This assumption had, however, to be revised in the face of the deteriorating situation in the Far East, with a full-blown war still raging in Korea, the Malayan Emergency and the crumbling French position in Indo-China. In 1953, Britain turned to Australia to add ground forces to the air support already being provided in Malaya.[16] By 1955, however, London had come to recognize that Australian and New Zealand priorities must inevitably focus on their own neighbourhood. In practical terms, this was expressed in the formation of the Commonwealth Strategic Reserve, based in Malaya, with British, Australian and New Zealand forces serving together.

The age of nuclear strategy gave the Commonwealth a fresh significance for Britain, which became dependent on Commonwealth co-operation in developing its nuclear weapons programme. When the Americans rejected British requests to use US weapons testing facilities in the Nevada desert, London looked to sparsely populated Commonwealth countries to provide test sites. A number of possible locations in Canada and Australia were considered before British planners eventually opted for the Monte Bello Islands off the northwest coast of Australia, where Britain's first atomic bomb was exploded in October 1952, arguably symbolizing British great power pretensions more effectively than any imperial role. After 1956, tests were conducted at Mural-

inga in the Australian outback. However, when, in 1954, Churchill's government decided that Britain must also develop the hydrogen bomb, it found
Menzies' government opposed to testing this awesome weapon on the Australian mainland. Similarly, when Eden approached the New Zealand government
in 1955 on using the Kermadec Islands, north-east of New Zealand, as a test
site, prime minister Holland demurred, largely because of the likely hostile
reaction of his own voters.[17] If understandably reluctant to be the testing
grounds for thermonuclear weapons, Commonwealth members were nevertheless willing to assist Britain in other ways. The prevailing doctrine of
'strategic dispersal', together with the possibility that large quantities of
electricity would be needed for a major Commonwealth atomic energy project,
seem to have been important factors in the Australian government's decision
to embark on the important Snowy Mountains hydro-electricity project.[18]

Another theme in Commonwealth relations surfacing during this period
was the question of migration between Commonwealth countries, particularly
immigration into Britain. Churchill personally called for a report on the
question of immigration from the colonies in 1952. Early on, this would
become a divisive issue within the British government. Some ministers, like
R.A. Butler, were instinctively liberal in their attitudes, while others foresaw
electoral difficulties if immigration went unchecked. Some stressed the economic advantages of immigration, at a time when some sectors of the economy
still faced labour shortages, while others gloomily predicted its implications for
an unprepared host community. For British colonial policy, immigration had an
important relevance. In the 1950s, Britain's aims in a number of colonial
territories hinged on the success of the 'multiracial' experiment, and fostering
good relations between diverse ethnic communities. It would be difficult for
the British government to claim good faith in this respect if, in connection with
colonial immigration into Britain, it tacitly accepted that the multiracial goal
was unachievable. As some observers commented, the prevailing attitude in
most colonies and Commonwealth countries was against the free flow of
migrants. There had long been antipathy, for example, in West Africa, towards
the entry of Lebanese entrepreneurs, giving rise after the war to a restrictive
immigration code. During the lifetime of the Churchill and Eden governments,
policy towards immigration into Britain remained unsettled. Ministers held
back from introducing legislation grounded in openly racial criteria, and
struggled to find a formula which, while limiting the entry of immigrants from
the West Indies, India and Pakistan, would not disadvantage those from older
parts of the Commonwealth. In effect, these difficult political questions were
simply evaded.[19]

The faltering imperial economy

As discussed previously, Britain's post-war economic policy-makers had
thought very much in imperial terms. After 1951, the Empire-Commonwealth
remained central to British economic calculations. It had been thought that the
Commonwealth and the Sterling Area would, taken together, give Britain an

unrivalled position in the world commodity trade, which in the years immediately after the Second World War, had been so buoyant. However, the peak in the fortunes of primary-producing countries, associated especially with the demand triggered by the Korean War and strategic stockpiling in the West, proved short-lived. As the Korean War declined into a tense cease-fire, world prices for many commodities slumped. The Conservative government was committed, perhaps on emotional as much as financial grounds, to Imperial Preference as a trading system valuable to Britain. Times were changing, however, and the system, devised in response to the world depression and reinforced by the effects of the Second World War, was beginning to lose its cohesion. Increasingly, independent members of the Commonwealth were looking beyond their traditional trading networks and seeking arrangements more advantageous to themselves, and, as the Korean War commodity boom dissipated after 1952, Commonwealth primary producers were keen, if possible, to diversify their economies to reduce their vulnerability to fluctuations in world commodity prices.[20]

By the mid-1950s, the independent members of the Sterling Area were more interested in pursuing their own economic development needs than in subordinating these to the needs of the area as a whole, although these long-term shifts in patterns of activity were not necessarily obvious to contemporaries.[21] One indicator of London's own recognition of changing needs came in 1954, when, encouraged by improvements in the Sterling Area's balance of payments position, the Cabinet considered a general relaxation of British import restrictions, even though this was bound to harm colonial exporters who had become accustomed to producing for the comparatively 'soft' metropolitan market.[22] As the 1950s progressed, it became increasingly clear that the composition of Britain's major export required wealthy, technologically advanced markets which few members of the imperial economic system could provide. By the same token, Sterling Area members were unwilling to consolidate their commercial ties with Britain (and with one another) at the expense of more profitable relationships with North America and Western Europe. By 1955–56, when Europe began to rival American and Commonwealth markets, a powerful argument emerged for a fundamental reorientation of the direction of British trade.[23] Ideally, Britain sought to maintain the benefits of its existing system of Imperial Preference while simultaneously expanding the scope for trade with the wealthier countries of Europe. This was the logic behind the scheme to construct a European Free Trade Area (EFTA), proposed by Macmillan and the president of the Board of Trade, Peter Thorneycroft, and intended to give Britain access to lucrative European markets *in addition to*, not instead of, traditional Commonwealth ones. At the same time, realists could see that Imperial Preference, while still a potent symbol for many British politicians, no longer enjoyed the economic rationale that it once had, nor could the arrangements and networks it enshrined offer a very convincing alternative to the rapidly expanding European market. Britain's traditional commercial partnerships had, after all, owed much to longstanding business connections, rather than to Imperial Preference as such, as the Board of Trade noted in

1956.[24] In the increasingly competitive commercial climate of the 1950s, as European rivals recovered, British exporters were also learning that traditionally 'soft' imperial markets could no longer be taken for granted. Shortcomings in the design, quality, price and speed of delivery of British goods were becoming a major cause for concern. It seemed, ironically, that the shielding effects of the imperial system, might, in the long term, have had an enervating effect on Britain's export sector.[25]

It was the unpalatable but unavoidable recognition that Commonwealth members no longer shared Britain's enthusiasm for Imperial Preference that dealt the system a fatal blow, dashing the hopes of ardent enthusiasts such as Leopold Amery. Some recently independent Sterling Area members, such as India, were unenthusiastic about arrangements which they regarded as being uncomfortably redolent of the colonial restrictions so recently cast off. At the Commonwealth Economic Conference of 1951, the Sterling Area members had committed themselves to a liberalized world trading and financial order.[26] The Conservative Party conference of 1954 marked this transition symbolically by acknowledging Britain's commitment to a fully free-trading system.[27]

The colonial economies

In the early 1950s, London still expected the colonial economies to perform the function of supplying Britain with raw materials, and of being earners of valuable dollars which could be pooled within the Sterling Area, at a time when the latter as a whole was in deficit with dollar countries. Certainly, there had been an increase in the proportion of trade Britain conducted with its colonial territories since the 1930s. By the mid-1950s, the colonies absorbed about 13 per cent of British exports, while Britain took about 10 per cent of its imports from the colonies.[28] Around a quarter of all colonial trade was conducted with Britain, making the colonies far more dependent on Britain than the latter was on them. Like its predecessor, the Conservative government was initially optimistic about the prospects for enhancing colonial productivity, and so of easing Britain's own economic situation even further. As in the late 1940s, however, the realities of colonial economic conditions, especially the continuing scarcity of money and equipment, stood in the way of any dramatic increase in the colonies' output.

Compounding this problem was the fact that the colonies were still unable to draw on their accumulated sterling balances to buy development goods, and that the metropolitan government continued to direct exports to more desirable markets. Originally seen by London as an important prop to sterling as a major world currency, the sterling balances were, by the early 1950s, coming to be seen as a liability which potentially detracted from international confidence in sterling, because they drew attention to Britain's swollen debt burden. Progressively, an argument in favour of relaxing control over the balances was that it was better to do this while the colonies were still under British control: after independence, former colonies might be less cautious in their spending.[29] After 1953, as the metropolitan economy began to emerge from its post-war period of acute dollar shortage, colonial dollar earnings were less important to Britain, and by 1955, with most of the sterling balances convertible, they had become a major source of instability, as they could be moved during a crisis.

Because colonial trade was still thought to be worth preserving, even expanding, the government remained keen to help colonial exporters, succeeding in 1955 in making the colonial territories exempt from the decision to bar further preference made by the General Agreement on Tariffs and Trade. On political grounds, too, it would be difficult for Britain to surrender its colonial trading privileges while France, the leading force in Europe, clung steadfastly to its colonial benefits. Nevertheless, important long-term shifts in Britain's economic relations with the colonial territories were becoming visible. Schenk has argued that by 1952, most colonies had removed their preferences favouring British manufactured goods. British exporters in colonial markets also found that their ability to compete with European rivals, in terms of price and quality, was declining.[30] Similarly, Feinstein has pointed out that by 1951, Britain was generally paying world market prices for the colonial produce it imported.[31] Shifts in imperial economic priorities were illustrated by the British government's interest in promoting the domestic production of synthetic rubber, inevitably damaging to the Malayan economy, and the encouragement of expanded imports of the synthetic product. This was part of the British government's central aim of sharpening the competitive edge of British industry by reducing costs, with the wider aim of stimulating exports to the dollar area. The resulting relaxation of import controls on synthetic rubber highlighted London's willingness to sacrifice colonial interests where these conflicted with those of the metropolitan economy.[32]

Colonial development

One of the central strands in British colonial policy remained the preparation of the colonies for ultimate self-government through sustained economic and social development. This policy, given concrete form during and after the Second World War, was an aspect of the broad bi-partisan political consensus within Britain. Nevertheless, it remained as nebulous and ambiguous as it had always been. The trend which had emerged after 1945, for London to hope that development projects could have the additional role of benefiting the Sterling Area as a whole, was still characteristic of the early 1950s. However, many of the difficulties in promoting development, experienced soon after the war, and seen most clearly in the ill-fated East African Groundnuts Scheme, had not been overcome. Soon after coming to power, the Conservatives demonstrated that they did not share their predecessors' enthusiasm for development under public auspices. Stressing the importance of genuinely commercial enterprise, the government finally disbanded the Overseas Food Corporation in 1954, and gave the Colonial Development Corporation a more stringent operating regime, though relations between Whitehall and the CDC's visionary chairman, Lord Reith, remained difficult. Development was still seen as embodying a wide range of economic and social activities, from prestige projects like the Volta River project in the Gold Coast, intended to provide hydro-electricity and so promote large-scale industrialization, to basic research into agriculture under tropical conditions.

As the 1950s progressed, it became increasingly clear that development was an inherently slow and difficult process, and that funding it adequately was a major long-term commitment. The Treasury, which had always had reservations about such an open-ended undertaking as CD & W, began to argue that aid to the colonies, and funding to the Sterling Area generally, was diverting much-needed finance from the metropolitan economy, especially the export industries, and even that colonial development (far from assisting Britain's own economic position) was aggravating the country's difficult economic situation in the early 1950s. As one official put it in 1952, it appeared that the 'whole conception of Commonwealth development as the solution to our difficulties is becoming something of a castle in the air'.[33] Sensing the growing pessimism of the Treasury, the Colonial Office, under Oliver Lyttelton, seized the initiative in 1953, seeking an extension of existing CD & W provision, due to expire in 1955. Lyttelton secured a further £115 million from the Treasury to cover the period 1955–60, arguing that the cost involved had to be measured against the potential long-term benefits to Britain. Nevertheless, under the Chancellorship of Harold Macmillan after 1955, Treasury criticism of spending on the colonies would resume. Against this background, it seemed unlikely that the major expected savings in public expenditure, to be derived from the switch to a strategy of nuclear deterrence, would produce much financial benefit for the dependent empire.

Ever since its wartime deliberations on post-war reconstruction, the Colonial Office had realized, perhaps more clearly than other interested parties, that metropolitan aid would never constitute more than a fraction of the capital required by a broad-ranging policy of colonial development, and that the major input would have to come from private sources. This had been stressed by Oliver Stanley in his keynote policy speech of 1943. Although such thinking had been partially eclipsed under Labour, it now received enthusiastic re-emphasis under the Conservatives. Oliver Lyttelton, as Colonial Secretary, was particularly keen to create a framework of conditions in the colonies attractive to private investors, and was prepared to consider more sympathetically than his predecessors the question of American investment in the colonies.[34] Attempts were made to revise taxation systems, but the fundamental problem remained that private investors simply found colonial development projects insufficiently attractive in terms of profitability, except where the production of minerals was concerned. Aggravating this problem was the fact that, as the 1950s progressed, the colonies' political future was becoming less certain, and there were growing doubts about the safeguards for external investors. This gave rise to calls, for example from the Crown Agents, for the British government to underwrite loans made to the colonies. London, however, felt that such a move would suggest a lack of metropolitan confidence in the regimes to which power was about to be transferred.

Ever since the wartime elaboration of colonial policy, it had been a key maxim that constitutional progress in the colonies would have to be preceded by the laying down of sound economic and social foundations. This belief had symbolized the unhurried approach to decolonization characteristic in British official circles as recently as the late 1940s. In reality, political advance in nearly all colonies far outstripped the rate of material progress. Typically, in the case of fast-moving West Africa, the Treasury resisted suggestions that something like the Colombo Plan should be devised for the region, arguing, to the distress of departments responsible for the Empire-Commonwealth, that colonies nearing self-government ought to become less dependent on metropolitan aid and turn to other sources, such as the International Monetary Fund. A similar attitude was displayed towards the advisability of the CDC undertaking projects in colonies nearing independence.[35] These difficulties and uncertainties surrounding development funding gave such projects as were undertaken a bias towards economic growth at the expense of social provision, very much at odds with the comprehensive development philosophy the Colonial Office had originally envisaged. Lyttelton, for example, urged colonial governments to focus their efforts on economic development which in turn might help to fund social services.

The problem of South Africa

Britain's relationship with South Africa in the early 1950s demonstrated the important part played by the Union in British policy calculations. South Africa was not only a senior member of the Commonwealth, taken into Britain's confidence far more readily than, say, India or Pakistan, one whose continuing membership of the Commonwealth was seen as important to the international standing of the group, but it was also a highly valuable trading partner. Moreover, close ties with South Africa were considered vital by Britain on strategic grounds. Especially in formulating its colonial and Commonwealth policies, Britain felt unable to ignore Pretoria's sensibilities. Although relations were inevitably less openly cordial after the Nationalist assumption of power in 1948, the British government's attitude remained broadly optimistic, and some Cabinet ministers actively sought a closer relationship. Nevertheless, the development of the apartheid regime seriously compromised this relationship. The northward migration of Afrikaner racial philosophy was considered especially dangerous, threatening to destabilize Britain's African interests, by fomenting racial unrest. Nor could Britain, if its claims to be an 'enlightened' colonial power were to be taken seriously, be seen to be too closely allied to a racist power, otherwise ties with African and Asian states would be endangered. London needed, therefore, to follow a course which balanced co-operation with South Africa and containment of the latter's disruptive potential.[36] In their shared concern to prevent South Africa complicating Britain's colonial policies north of the Limpopo, Attlee's and Churchill's governments revealed basically similar, if private, objectives. The Conservatives took up and developed Labour's scheme for a federation of the three Central African territories, to form a physical barrier to the spread of South African influence, favouring the region's white settler minority with disproportionate political power at the expense of the African majority. Similarly, London remained adamant that the High Commission Territories (Bechuanaland, Basutoland and Swaziland) should not be absorbed into the Union, despite the latter's long-standing ambitions in that direction.

Whatever its ethical and other misgivings about South Africa, Britain sought the Union's co-operation in the defence field, hoping in particular that the latter would contribute to defending the Middle East in a crisis. Although no less convinced of the strategic necessities posed by the Cold War than was Britain, South Africa tended to be preoccupied with its own internal security, and preferred to concentrate its military strength within its own borders. In contrast to Britain's hopes of constructing a Middle Eastern Defence Organization, South Africa suggested an African defence organization, through which the continent could be 'policed' by the Union and the colonial powers. Predictably, this notion received a cool response from Britain, where it was feared such an arrangement would not only be of limited practical value, but might evoke hostility from Britain's European allies and in the African colonies.[37]

One of the most important questions raised by relations with South Africa was that of the Simonstown naval base. On both sides, there seemed much to commend a deal under which Britain would transfer control of the base to South Africa, thereby saving money, while retaining the right to use it. Churchill, however, disliked this suggestion. Perhaps its chronological proximity to the Suez base agreement with Egypt smacked too much of a general abdication of British power. While both sides were anxious to achieve a settlement, each had its own ambitions: Britain sought to link the Simonstown question to a South African commitment to Middle Eastern defence, while South Africa linked the base to its proposals for an African defence organization. In the event, neither side was entirely satisfied with the eventual agreement, reached in 1955. Britain pledged to hold discussions with South Africa on defence matters, while South Africa undertook to form a military force which could be deployed outside the Union.[38]

The Middle East

At the beginning of the 1950s, Britain was still the major foreign power in the Middle East, and was determined to remain so. The region was vital to Britain on economic grounds, especially because of its oil, and on strategic grounds, because of its geographical location relative to the Soviet Union, and the continuing importance of the Suez Canal. Accordingly, Britain maintained an enormous military presence in the region. As well as operating the Suez base, it had airfields in Iraq, a major naval base at Aden, and essentially ran the Arab Legion in Jordan. A treaty concluded in 1953 with nominally independent Libya enabled Britain to maintain bases there. Middle Eastern defence requirements also explained Britain's continuing military interest in Malta and Cyprus. However, Britain's position would increasingly be challenged by the growth of Arab nationalism, not only because of its intrusive physical presence, but also because of its role in the creation of Israel.

Defending Britain's Middle Eastern position was therefore a major concern for the incoming Conservative government. Churchill was not alone among senior ministers in regarding it as essential to avoid surrendering vital interests. There was, however, a greater willingness to share the burdens of regional defence with the Americans, perhaps through a Middle Eastern Defence Organization, a strategy which appeared more achievable in the new climate of the Truman Doctrine. From the Foreign Office's point of view, it was necessary for Britain to look to diplomatic efforts, rather than military clout, to defend its Middle Eastern interests, and this would mean avoiding or minimizing the potential for friction.

The Suez base was a case in point. Enormously expensive to maintain, the base had itself become a major irritant in Anglo-Egyptian relations. A situation already strained by the Second World War had steadily become worse, and in October 1951, the 1936 Treaty (entitling Britain to maintain the Suez base for another 20 years) had been cancelled by the Egyptian government. Day-to-day operations in the base were becoming increasingly difficult for Britain, which felt that the Egyptian authorities strained few nerves to contain escalating anti-British violence. In January 1952, the situation deteriorated sharply, when British forces attempted to disarm the local auxiliary police, triggering extensive anti-Western riots in Cairo, and contributing to the military coup of July, among whose beneficiaries and key players was Colonel Gamal Abd al-Nasser. Nasser, part of that generation of Egyptian nationalists for whom British occupation had been an enduring humiliation, was instinctively opposed to foreign bases as symbolizing Western imperialism: British withdrawal from the Suez base became one of his principal aims.[39]

The Foreign Office's desire to defuse the situation and find a lasting and acceptable solution prompted Eden to seek a deal with Cairo on British withdrawal. Eden's preference was for an agreement under which the Suez Canal would come under international control, Egypt would sign up to a regional defence pact, and Britain would evacuate the Suez base, but with the right of return in an emergency. If Eden was, in this instance, trying to be the agent of pragmatic modernization of British policy, Churchill was unimpressed by the implied retreat, fearing that it might diminish Britain's imperial standing and create a precedent for the whole of Africa. He was only convinced when it was pointed out that the possibility of nuclear warfare made the Suez base a liability. In one respect at least, Churchill's predictions were not entirely without substance. As part of the wider process of mending fences with Egypt, Britain decided in 1953 to terminate its rule in the Sudan by 1956, in return for Cairo's abandonment of its claim to suzerainty over the entire Nile Valley. Thus it was the Sudan which would be the pioneer of British decolonization in sub-Saharan Africa. Although Britain sought to involve the United States in defending the Middle East, the Americans appeared to be more concerned about consolidating their own relations with the new regime, and pointedly (and in vain) waited for an invitation from the Egyptian government to discuss regional security.

Eventually, in October 1954, Britain and Egypt concluded an agreement on the evacuation of the Suez base, intended by Eden to demonstrate that London seriously proposed to treat Egypt as an equal.[40] Egypt was not, however, persuaded to join a regional defence organization. Under the terms of the agreement, British forces would be withdrawn within 20 months, but the Suez base would be maintained and Britain secured the right of return for a seven-year period. In retrospect, it is possible to see this episode as the first tangible acknowledgement by the new British government that a remodelling of Britain's overseas presence had become inevitable, although Churchill himself preferred to rationalize it not as a retreat but as a reorganization of military forces intended to safeguard Britain's Middle Eastern role.[41]

Having apparently resolved the Suez base question, Britain turned next to questions of regional defence, and in 1955 created the Baghdad Pact, formed around Turkey and Britain's most important ally in the region, Iraq. Pakistan and Iran subsequently joined the pact. The Americans regarded the pact with studied aloofness: to Secretary of State Dulles, the involvement of Iran was a needless provocation to the Soviet Union, and it seemed essential not to antagonize Nasser. London hoped that Egypt could be persuaded to join the pact with the promise of Western capital for the prestigious Aswan High Dam project. Ironically, the Baghdad Pact, which fell far short of the Middle Eastern Defence Organization to which Britain aspired, proved to be counter-productive. Fomenting tensions in the Middle East rather than ensuring stability, it was based on promises of military assistance to its members which Britain was in no position to fulfil. Since it was regarded as an attempt to divide the Arab world, and its core (Iraq) was his main regional rival, the pact alarmed Nasser, who had by now ousted his senior, Neguib, and this, together with continuing Israeli incursions, led Egypt to seek military aid from the Soviet bloc, fundamentally altering the regional balance of power. Henceforth Britain and Egypt would be locked in a competitive struggle for regional influence.[42]

When Britain reacted by attempting to enlarge the Baghdad Pact to include Jordan, London's Middle Eastern policy received a fresh set-back. Nasser responded to Britain's move by sponsoring demonstrations in the Jordanian capital, leading King Hussein to dismiss the British commander of the Arab Legion, General Glubb, in March 1956, throwing Britain's defence posture into confusion. Eden, who held Nasser responsible for this blow to British prestige, and who increasingly equated Nasser with a dictator such as Mussolini (comparisons to pre-war appeasement would become increasingly frequent) briefly contemplated reoccupying Suez. (London and Washington meanwhile plotted a coup in Syria to prevent its fusion with Egypt.) To the Foreign Office, in the summer of 1956, safeguarding Britain's Middle Eastern interests called for action in the political sphere, designed to win goodwill among the Arab world, rather than any crude show of military strength. Nevertheless, the British government resolved that Nasser must be removed from power: the nationalization of the Suez Canal by Egypt provided the perfect pretext.[43] The methods used by Britain to try to reassert its regional sway during the ensuing Suez Crisis owed much to the temperament, and shortcomings, of the ailing Eden.

The shape of colonial policy

As they returned to power in 1951, the Conservatives inherited a colonial policy which seemed both well established and largely uncontroversial, at least within metropolitan politics. The fundamental aim of the policy, as discussed above, was to prepare the colonial territories for ultimate self-government within the British Commonwealth. These preparations were to include laying the economic and social foundations on which constitutional reform and advance could be grafted. Not long after the general election, Lyttelton, partly seeking to reassure colonial public opinion, sought permission to declare that the broad thrust of policy would continue along these lines. Although this declaration was made, the new government, and that of Eden which followed, had its own distinctive views on the management of colonial affairs. While the course set by Attlee's government was to be followed, the Conservatives did not strain to step up the pace of change, and in important respects sought to moderate that change, applying brakes to a process which some ministers, including Churchill himself, felt had already gone too far, too quickly. A small, but revealing, linguistic detail which illustrates this point is the government's preference for the phrase 'full self-government' instead of 'independence' in the colonial context. Neither Churchill nor Eden was much interested in the details of colonial policy, unless issues of security were involved, and colonial affairs were not normally treated as a priority, but rather as one element in a group of global concerns, embracing diplomacy, strategy and economic interests. The latter would steadily increase in significance, as ministers grappled with the dilemma of maintaining Britain's international status (an unquestioned policy goal) at a cost which the country could reasonably afford. Wider global considerations, above all the Cold War background, also helped to shape colonial policy, most obviously in Malaya, but also in other situations.

The new government was perhaps the last in which imperially minded figures held sway. Foremost among them, possibly, was Churchill who, as late as 1954, talked of giving the Colonial Office an impressive new building at the heart of Westminster. Lyttelton himself, often regarded as a right-winger on colonial issues, was an enthusiastic supporter of the settler cause in Central Africa, and apt to adopt a tough stance in dealing with colonial dissent. His successor at the Colonial Office, Alan Lennox-Boyd, has acquired a similarly conservative reputation. The toughest line of all was taken by Lord Salisbury, Lord President of the Council between 1952 and 1957, who, having urged his colleagues to strengthen the powers of colonial governments to quell unrest, resigned over the proposed release from gaol of the Greek Cypriot leader, Archbishop Makarios, and thereafter remained a persistent thorn in Macmillan's side.

The government's broad approach to colonial policy has aptly been described as attempting to keep change 'within bounds'. In practice, this meant that, as far as possible, Britain should remain in control of developments in the colonies, limiting change where this was feasible rather than actively promoting it. As Macmillan commented in 1955, while Foreign Secretary, although it was established British policy to work towards self-government for the colonies, 'surely we ought not to make a fetish of this'.[44] Increasingly, however, London would come to realize that although the pace of innovation was sometimes uncomfortably brisk, the alternative, an attempt to delay reform, might be the more dangerous option. In the words of Sir Charles Jeffries, a senior Colonial Office official, writing in 1956:

> I think there is too much tendency to consider whether these places are 'ready' for Statehood. Of course they not, any more than the Gold Coast is 'ready' for independence, or than one's teenage daughter is 'ready' for the proverbial latch-key.[45]

Before this, the British government seems to have believed that it was genuinely in control of developments at the colonial level, and although the framework of policy was increasingly constrained by Britain's economic circumstances, by international opinion and by the political stirrings of the colonial populations themselves, there was no sense in Whitehall of a need fundamentally to reappraise colonial policy, nor was there yet any strong drive to calculate systematically just what benefits (or disadvantages) accrued to Britain from its possession of colonies.[46] Also in the early 1950s, London was confident that it could, if necessary, deploy its military resources to contain any serious challenge to its colonial authority, a confidence apparently borne out by its successes in Malaya and Kenya. Although the thrust of constitutional development remained broadly towards devolution, to the benefit of colonial elites approved of by Britain as being 'moderate', in situations where political challenges arose, Britain proved willing to reverse the trend, as in British Guiana in 1953, where an elected government under Cheddi Jagan was suspended because of its unpalatably radical complexion and plans to rein in the powers of foreign-owned enterprise.[47] Nevertheless, as the 1950s unfolded, there was a growing metropolitan distaste for confrontation in the colonial sphere. This probably had rather less to do with a shift in moral attitudes than with a pragmatic recognition that tough measures might be counter-productive, fuelling the fires of political opposition, while conciliation might buy time for Britain and greater freedom to manoeuvre, with the overriding aim of defending British interests. These interests were not yet being questioned seriously by decision-makers, but there was room for different opinions on how to safeguard them.[48]

More fundamentally, the government's aim was that Britain's wider global interests should not be endangered by the repercussions of colonial policy, for example, in efforts to appease colonial nationalism.[49] If self-government was the planned destiny for most colonies, some territories were viewed as being of such strategic value to Britain that continuing colonial rule was inevitable. The government still tended to see the colonies in positive terms, as being, on balance, economic assets to Britain, except in those cases where serious unrest, such as in Kenya, required costly military intervention.[50] Certainly, before the advent of Macmillan as prime minister, the British government was not actively seeking means of shedding its colonial responsibilities. While Churchill and Eden were prime ministers, no colony became independent. The Sudan, which became independent in 1956, had never been a colony as such: its acquisition and surrender were intimately linked to Britain's wider concerns in the Middle East. London was fortunate that in the years 1951–57, there was no devastating coincidence of disintegrative influences. The Cold War, although serious, was not undergoing one of its periodic escalations; the states of Western Europe had not quite yet revived to the extent that they posed a threat to the Anglo-American special relationship; unrest in the colonies still seemed of manageable proportions; and Britain's own economic position appeared to have eased perceptibly. In this period of relative tranquillity, it was tempting for British ministers to reassure themselves that they really were in control of the colonies and their development.[51]

An important area of continuity between the Labour and Conservative governments was concern about the future of territories which, by themselves, might not constitute viable nation states. The favoured solution was to bring such neighbouring territories together in order to enhance their political and economic prospects. This policy, which gave rise to a number of federations, was pursued with enthusiasm, even when local populations were clearly hostile to the idea, as was the case in the most important example, the Central African Federation (officially the 'Federation of Rhodesia and Nyasaland'), itself an indication of London's confidence in its ability to mould colonial polities at will. Other regions which were thought to be ripe for this federal treatment were East Africa and South-East Asia, while the Caribbean and South Arabia were other possible candidates. The federal option was hardly a novelty in imperial policy: Canada, Australia and, more painfully, South Africa, had all been earlier fruits of this centripetal thrust. It was ironic that while federal solutions were acceptable to Britain within the empire, they were shunned in the European context.

In keeping with its emphasis on maintaining control, the Conservative government proved willing to resort to force to counter threats to British authority. The Malayan Emergency had been bequeathed by Attlee's government, but its successor took a firm line, sending General Sir Gerald Templer to devise a new counterinsurgency campaign. Kenya, with the Mau Mau Emergency, an unfathomable challenge dismissed as 'barbarism', soon tied down 11 British infantry battalions in addition to many thousands of locally recruited 'auxiliaries'. In Uganda, the troublesome Kabaka of Buganda was sent into exile. In Cyprus, a vigorous anti-terrorist drive was mounted by Field-Marshal Harding. Colonial 'emergencies' could be a useful means of gaining time in which to attempt to cultivate 'moderates' and counteract the influence of 'extremists'.[52] Usually accompanied by propaganda campaigns aimed at undermining political opponents, they were, at least in the short term, generally successful from Britain's point of view, helped on occasion by the increasingly sophisticated nature of intelligence-gathering, inspired by Cold War anxieties.[53]

Successes in Malaya and Kenya tended only to reinforce Britain's belief in its ability to retain control. Nevertheless, progressive measures of devolution involved sometimes difficult decisions about when it was appropriate to hand over the 'reserved powers', especially over security and law and order, to local politicians, arguably a more meaningful measure of effective decolonization.[54] A more general feature of this period is that London's contribution to colonial policy-making inevitably declined as more and more power was transferred to territorial governments, making the early 1950s appear less dramatic and innovative than the years immediately after the war.

A desire to preserve control over constitutional developments in the colonies led Eden in 1955 to create a Cabinet Committee on Colonial Affairs, mainly because recent difficulties had not always been foreseen by ministers.[55] Shortly afterwards, the term 'independence' was dropped from the lexicon of colonial policy-making, in case its use was taken to imply an abrupt severing of ties with Britain, rather than the close post-colonial relationship envisaged by London.

Nationalism

The greatest single challenge to British colonial rule in this period was likely to come from the opposition of local colonial populations, a factor increasingly, if often inaccurately, described as 'nationalism'. To a great extent, the continuation of British colonial rule would depend upon London's success in harnessing this and responding to it successfully. The tight constraints within which the British government might strive to maintain control in its overseas possessions were privately recognized by the Cabinet Secretary, Sir Norman Brook, in 1954, when he told fellow senior officials that the rate of political devolution in the colonies was 'likely to be determined by the strength of nationalist feeling and the development of political consciousness within each territory'.[56] It would take time for ministers to grasp that they were increasingly being forced to respond to changes taking place in the colonies, and that their apparent control of the situation within each colonial territory might be diminishing. Within Whitehall, meanwhile, nationalism evoked different responses. The Foreign Office, for example, based largely on its experiences in the Middle East, was prone to see nationalism as a force which required firm handling when it threatened to affect British interests. The Foreign Secretary, Anthony Eden, thought that the pace of change in West Africa, for example, was precipitate. The Colonial Office, on the other hand, although criticized on occasions by the Foreign Office for its alleged lack of political judgement, was more inclined to see nationalism as a protean force which, with care, could be shaped into an acceptable, progressive and even co-operative influence. Indeed, one interpretation of Colonial Office policy after the war is that it was deliberately seeking to foster a sense of national identity in appropriate colonies as the basis of ultimate self-government.

Whitehall was also divided over the cost of maintaining colonial rule. While few denied the potential economic and other advantages to Britain of maintaining the colonial connection, not all departments relished the expense to Britain which this might involve. The Colonial Office, for which metropolitan expenditure on colonial development and welfare remained a foundation of policy, inevitably sought increased subventions from Britain. Departments involved in limiting colonial unrest, however, wanted more to be spent on security, while the Treasury, long sceptical about 'subsidizing' colonial living standards, was increasingly looking for ways of limiting its financial commitments to development aid.[57]

Whatever misgivings individual ministers may have harboured on the direction of change in the colonial territories, the Cabinet, accepting that it could not renege on established policy, usually acquiesced in measures of devolution proposed by the Colonial Office. Nevertheless, the government was anxious to avoid giving the impression that it was in retreat from its colonial responsibilities, or that it no longer had the stomach to be a colonial power. It is remarkable that even as late as 1954, when London attempted to predict which colonies would become independent during the next 20 years, its list of candidates was confined to the Gold Coast and Nigeria, the Central African Federation, a Malayan federation, and a still-to-be created West Indian federation. Up to 20 colonies were considered unsuitable for full independence, and were thought to be candidates only for internal self-government. In some cases, this reflected the colonies' strategic value to Britain; in others, it was a recognition that these particular polities were simply unviable. In May 1956, for instance, it was announced that Aden's strategic and economic importance precluded its independence.[58] Tiny, but strategically vital Malta was similarly not thought to be a contender, and was even briefly considered appropriate for administration as though it were a part of metropolitan Britain. Most famously, in 1954, the Colonial Office minister Henry Hopkinson was wrong-footed in the Commons, admitting that some colonies were so important to Britain that their independence was inconceivable.[59] He was referring in particular to the then still quiescent island of Cyprus, where British forces, eventually numbering 25,000, would soon become embroiled in a bitter counterinsurgency campaign, confronting Greek Cypriot fighters (EOKA) whose aim was not only independence from Britain, but *enosis*, or union, with mainland Greece. Although Britain found itself embroiled in a three-year struggle to contain terrorism, prompting growing unease at home about the acceptability of maintaining colonial rule by force, ministers were reluctant to make concessions to Greek Cypriot demands: having lost the Egyptian base, a stronghold in Cyprus seemed to be even more necessary; it was felt vital not to alienate Turkey, on whom Britain's calculations for Eastern Mediterranean defence largely depended; and, perhaps most importantly, Eden had no desire to be seen to vacillate over this question, especially as the 1954 Suez Agreement had triggered ripples of disquiet among imperial 'die-hards'. As Holland has commented, the early 1950s suggest a process of 'realistic adjustment' in British colonial policy-making. This involved a recognition that control of sizeable territorial units *per se* was not necessarily essential to British interests: in the age of air power and nuclear weapons, a much smaller number of critically important territories, an 'empire of points', seemed more relevant to changing British requirements, springboards for the rapid projection of British power.[60]

The reservations voiced by some in Whitehall about the rate of change in the colonial sphere were shared by a growing number of those officials at the territorial level charged with implementing policy, in other words those colonial administrators whose function was increasingly to enforce changes which would ultimately make most of them (literally) redundant. Successive colonial secretaries in the 1950s, especially Alan Lennox-Boyd, found themselves preoccupied with the fate of colonial civil servants whose long-term career prospects were being undermined by political devolution and the recruitment of local personnel. As had been the case immediately after the Second World War, officers' morale became a matter of concern in the early 1950s. Ironically, the size of the Colonial Service had grown dramatically since the war. In 1950, a total of 1,510 appointments had been made, compared with 551 in 1920, the best inter-war year, before depression and retrenchment had taken their toll.[61] Although recruitment increased by 50 per cent in the ten years after 1947, the number of resignations by disillusioned staff also grew, especially in those African territories where British officials found themselves working under local politicians. This prompted the Colonial Office to explore the possibility of a British Overseas Service which could hire out experienced personnel to newly independent countries in addition to administering the remaining colonies. The Treasury, under Macmillan and Butler, resisted what it saw as a potentially expensive means of defending the interests of serving and retired officials (Butler commenting sourly that it was not the Treasury's responsibility to underwrite officials 'whose general aptitudes are not suitable for most of the jobs at home'), but the change was finally introduced in 1954 with the creation of Her Majesty's Overseas Civil Service.[62] But the fact that a growing proportion of administrative jobs was being performed by local personnel led British policy-makers to fear for the future probity of public service structures in former colonies, a concern which heightened as independence drew nearer.

Malaya

At the heart of Britain's important interests in the Far East was South-East Asia, incorporating Singapore, the business and communications centre and naval base, and Malaya, important both strategically and economically as a supplier of key strategic commodities such as rubber and tin, whose value had increased because of the Korean War and the general Cold War background. The Conservatives inherited from Labour the Emergency which was still seen as a fundamental threat to Britain's interests, and which was estimated to be costing the British and Malayan governments up to £100 million a year between them by 1955.[63] Success in defeating the Communist insurrection was thought to be vital if the United States was to be convinced that Britain was 'pulling its weight' in the Cold War and was an ally worth helping. Still-fresh memories of the collapse in 1941–42, moreover, made abandonment of the territory unthinkable.

To deal with the Emergency in Malaya, one of the government's first measures was to despatch General Templer to the colony to co-ordinate the counterinsurgency campaign. Templer was given unprecedented powers, combining oversight of both civil and military affairs. Templer's appointment and early success in the areas of policing, intelligence and 'psychological warfare' are generally seen as marking a critical stage in Britain's handling of Malaya, representing a determination to achieve both a military and a political solution to the territory's problems, and during 1953 Malacca was declared the first area free of insurgent activity. However, Templer was able to build upon foundations laid before his arrival, notably the Briggs Plan, which aimed to 'win the hearts and minds' of the population, and was accompanied by measures to achieve greater local involvement in government and administration, and to promote economic and social development. Ironically, the economic boom associated with demand created by the Korean War gradually began to swing the balance of advantage away from the guerrillas and towards the Malayan government.[64]

Meanwhile, the continuing violence in the territory served to confirm the broad outline of British policy, highlighting the importance of collaboration between the British and the Malays, and of securing Chinese co-operation both in the counterinsurgency campaign and in the policy of 'nation-building', leading eventually to the calling of local elections. The British, confident that they were in control, had made it clear that before there could be major changes in Malaya's constitutional status, the territory would have to demonstrate that it could produce an authentic, multiracial political party. To co-operate in campaigning for local elections in 1952, UMNO and the Malay Chinese Association accordingly formed the Alliance, which was made formal early in 1953, and which the Malayan Indian Congress joined in the following year. The fact that, within the Alliance, Malaya's different ethnic communities remained distinct made the organization less than perfect in British eyes, and their tendency to dismiss it as an 'artificial' group, given cohesion largely by the Tunku Abdul Rahman's influence, was in some ways reminiscent of British attitudes towards the Indian National Congress in the 1930s. By September 1953, however, military success gave Templer the confidence to invite Alliance politicians into his Executive Council and to begin preparations for elections at the state and federal levels. From 1954 onwards, Abdul Rahman stepped up his demands for independence for a variety of reasons. Not only did the improved security situation make political activity feasible, but the Tunku was also under pressure from more radical elements within the Alliance. From the Malay point of view, there was also a strong incentive to secure the transfer of power before the Chinese community became more politically organized. Moreover, as in other colonies, the British in Malaya appeared to be willing to make concessions to Malay opinion.

Britain, for its part, felt under pressure of another sort. Circumstances in Malaya, and in Britain's other South-East Asian territories (Singapore, Sarawak, Brunei and North Borneo) could not realistically be isolated from broader developments in the region as a whole, notably the French struggle to reassert influence over the Indo-Chinese colonies, and the apparent strength of local variations of Communism. Instability in Indo-China was particularly worrying to Britain, but sympathy for France did not extend to a willingness to provide military assistance, despite US encouragement. London's reasoning was that Britain's military resources were already stretched to their limit. After 1954, when the French suffered their decisive defeat in Indo-China at Dien Bien Phu, Britain was left as the sole remaining colonial power in South-East Asia. It opted to play a leading role at the negotiations in Geneva (April–July 1954), at which Vietnam was divided, with the north coming under Communist government. Britain hoped that a peaceful, diplomatic solution had been found, but continuing uncertainty reinforced London's desire to construct a regional defence pact for South-East Asia, including Britain. This led eventually in 1955 to the creation of the South-East Asia Treaty Organization (SEATO). Several regional powers, most importantly India and Indonesia, were intent to avoid entanglement in such commitments, instead pursuing the policy of non-alignment, which bore fruit at the Bandung Conference, also in 1955, at which European colonialism was roundly condemned. Nevertheless, Britain's continuing ambition to construct a regional defence grouping centred on Malaya reflected not only the latter's growing strategic importance to Britain as independence loomed, but also London's concern to reinforce Britain's voice within the Western Alliance by orchestrating an Asian defence bloc outside Washington's immediate sphere of influence.[65]

Britain's South-East Asian concerns were not confined to the defence sphere. As early as 1956, the Policy Review Committee created by Eden had tried to find ways of reducing Britain's costly military burden in the Far East. As had been the case in the Middle East under Bevin, there was an enthusiasm for the potentially cheaper option of promoting economic and social development as a practical counterweight to the spread of Communist influence. For Britain, the most important example of this approach was the Colombo Plan, begun by Labour, but continued under Churchill. This, however, fell victim to Treasury demands for retrenchment, and like Britain's other Third World development initiatives, never received the level of funding it required to have much effect. There remained a tension between two strands of British policy: first, to prepare the ground for ultimate Malayan self-government; secondly, to safeguard Britain's key interests in the territory, particularly its desire to use Malaya as the core of its regional defence plans, involving shared Commonwealth responsibilities.

In July 1955, the Alliance won a landslide election victory, taking 51 out of 52 elected seats on the Federal Council, and Tunku Abdul Rahman became the territory's chief minister. This took London by surprise, and called into question Britain's policy of backing so-called 'moderates' since the formation of the Alliance. There was no alternative but acceptance of Abdul Rahman as the leader of an effective movement which was held together by the goal of independence and had demonstrated its multiracial character. The Alliance was not all the British had hoped for, but it seemed to be the best available partner to negotiate the transfer of power. Moreover, any attempt at stalling by

London might play into the hands of more extreme elements and endanger the Alliance. Early in 1956 a conference in London set out the basis for Malaya's independence in 1957, two years earlier than the Alliance's own target. The Colonial Office assured the Malayan delegates that the transfer of power would not be obstructed or delayed by Britain. It is important to point out that Malaya's independence was reached *before* Britain's principal goals had been achieved: the Emergency was not yet over (fighting would continue for another three years); the multiracial national identity which the British had sought to encourage did not yet exist; and Britain's ambition to weld Malaya into a larger political unit with Singapore and Borneo had still to be realized. Furthermore, the overriding British concern to secure Malay co-operation in the continuing counterinsurgency campaign made the authorities reluctant to tackle the thorny issue of converting the Malay sultans into committed constitutional rulers.[66] Nevertheless, London could be content that the transfer of power in Malaya's case represented no dramatic challenge to British interests: the country would continue to supply rubber and bank its earnings within the Sterling Area (even though natural rubber's importance was being challenged by the use of synthetic alternatives, particularly in the United States). And, through a defence treaty, Malaya would continue to offer Britain a major strategic foothold in South-East Asia.[67] Nevertheless, the rapid success of the Alliance had encouraged London to accelerate the transfer of power more quickly than had been planned, and in so doing to jettison some of its cherished preconditions for self-government. The introduction of electoral politics in the colonial context, had, once again, caught metropolitan policy-makers off-guard.

The Gold Coast

Among the colonial territories, the Gold Coast was to set the precedent for the Conservative government's approach to decolonization. For the Colonial Office, which saw few useful pointers in the British retreat from South Asia or Palestine, it was especially important that political change here should be managed successfully.[68] After 1951, responsibility for government was shared by British officials and African politicians, an arrangement reminiscent of the dyarchy operating in India between the wars. Both the Colonial Office and Nkrumah's CPP assumed that this would be a brief, transitional stage, leading to internal self-government, and ultimately to full independence within the Commonwealth. Of great symbolic importance was the award of the title of prime minister to Nkrumah in 1952. Oliver Lyttelton was less than enthusiastic about this gesture, and about the concomitant requirement for the colonial governor to consult Nkrumah on the selection of ministers. The British government understood this change to signify the fact that co-operative African politicians were being rewarded for their moderation, accepting the Colonial Office's view that withholding this elevation might encourage Gold Coast ministers to reassess the territory's vital role as a financial bulwark of the Sterling Area. From Accra, Arden-Clarke suggested that the momentum of devolution must continue in order to ensure that the Gold Coast was 'governed by consent'. This would involve handing over responsibility for financial matters, and possibly justice, to African ministers. Nevertheless, it is clear that London still sought to avoid a fundamental reordering of the balance of power in the territory. Lyttelton, who visited the territory in 1952, regarded the system being created in the Gold Coast as a 'stucco façade' and was keen to ensure that delicate topics such as intelligence and security remained in the hands of British officials. Control of the police was a particularly sensitive area, revealing British government fears that after independence, the police might be vulnerable to political interference.[69] Lyttelton was also adamant that before further major revision of the Gold Coast constitution, there would have to be 'proper consultation' with the population and the chiefs, and a general election. At this time, the governor of Nigeria, Sir John Macpherson, was voicing his concern about the impact devolution in the Gold Coast might have on his own territory. Nevertheless, in September 1953, it was agreed that the Gold Coast should, as the Accra government proposed, advance towards a single legislative chamber, with a Cabinet appointed on the advice of the prime minister, and reserve powers entrusted to the governor.[70]

Beneath the surface, however, political tensions were developing in the territory, undermining the claims of Nkrumah and the CPP to be broadly representative of the population. Ironically, it was economic growth, especially in the south, and the increased government expenditure which this made possible, which exposed fractures within Gold Coast politics. In the Ashanti region, there was growing resentment that profits accruing to the Cocoa Marketing Board, derived from Ashanti cocoa production, were being channelled into development projects elsewhere, particularly the south of the territory. Vocal elements of the northern population resented the low prices being paid for their cocoa. Many chiefs, too, felt excluded from the country's increasingly centralized political system, and called for a second chamber. Although the CPP won another election in 1954, in Ashanti the National Liberation Movement emerged, representing disgruntled cocoa farmers and chiefs in particular, and gaining some sympathy among the expatriate business community and the Conservative Party in Britain. The NLM was committed to a federal system, designed to prevent the CPP gaining control over the whole territory, but this posed a major challenge both to Nkrumah's ambitions and to London's plans. In July 1955, a constitutional committee, appointed by Nkrumah but shunned by the NLM, rejected the federal option but instead proposed the creation of regional councils. At the end of the year, a constitutional adviser appointed by the new Colonial Secretary, Alan Lennox-Boyd, recommended the establishment of regional assemblies, enjoying powers devolved by the central government.[71] Lennox-Boyd insisted that before a date could be set for the Gold Coast's independence, the CPP would have to demonstrate its popular support at the polls, and in July 1956, Nkrumah led his party to yet another election victory. While the still hostile NLM continued to demand partition of the territory, this option was overruled by London.

In the lead-up to Gold Coast independence, finally achieved early in 1957, there were growing signs of alarm among British officials in the territory about its readiness. The Commonwealth Relations Office, which would handle post-independence relations with what became Ghana (named after an ancient African empire, though not one contiguous with the Gold Coast), received troubling reports from its man on the spot. He pointed out that constitutional developments in recent years had not been matched by efforts to introduce sufficient numbers of trained Africans into the higher echelons of the civil service. Similarly, there were fears that in the boom economic conditions of the post-war period, the government had embarked on ambitious spending programmes which were jeopardized by the fall in cocoa revenue by the mid-1950s. It seemed that Britain might be obliged to provide substantial development aid to the new nation, if only to prevent it developing into an embarrassing critic of colonialism. Even more fundamentally, there were grave, if private, misgivings about the alleged corruption and undemocratic proclivities of African ministers, raising concern in London about the prospects for Ghana's post-independence stability. The Commonwealth Relations Secretary, Lord Home, observed at the beginning of 1957 that he was 'full of foreboding about the whole Gold Coast experiment', feelings shared by the new prime minister, Harold Macmillan.[72]

East and Central Africa: settler complications

If the Conservative government was resigned to the ultimate goal of self-government under majority rule in the West African colonies, there was no question in the early 1950s of applying the same formula to the ethnically diverse territories of East and Central Africa. Here, the existence of small, but vocal, settler populations, along with Asian communities, persuaded London to opt for a policy of multiracialism, based on shared power between the ethnic groups. While this had an agreeably progressive ring in the 1950s, on closer inspection it amounted to giving minority groups a strikingly disproportionate influence in political life, and specifically preserving the privileged position of the vastly outnumbered Europeans. The logic of this policy was that the long-term economic development of these territories depended primarily upon white settler enterprise, supplemented in some cases by the business skills of the Asian community. In time, a new African entrepreneurial class would emerge, identifying more with maintaining the existing economic and social structure than with the aspirations either of the growing urban working class or the landless rural poor. Pursuit of the multiracial goal comforted policy-makers in London that they remained in control of developments at the territorial level. Towards the end of 1955, Lennox-Boyd put forward proposals for 'systems of qualitative democracy' for these settler colonies. Under these proposals, the idea of universal suffrage was to be replaced by elaborate structures in which African political participation would be determined by economic and educational qualifications. The different ethnic groups, European, Asian and African, would be given separate electoral rolls (a device well established in British India, though with fateful consequences). This kind of deviation from standard definitions of democracy was bound to give rise to dissatisfaction within the affected territories, and to unease among metropolitan sympathizers, especially within the Labour Party, but the Cabinet's Colonial Policy Committee resolved to press ahead with the experiment, suggesting that London approached this question with what in retrospect would appear to have been a remarkable degree of confidence.

In the case of Kenya, colonial control had been rudely shaken by the Mau Mau episode, an outbreak of violence among the Kikuyu community during the later 1940s, which led to the declaration of a state of emergency in 1952. It soon became clear that the Kenyan authorities were unable to deal with the situation and needed outside assistance. This not only required expensive inputs of metropolitan military personnel, but revealed as a sham local settler pretensions to inherit exclusive authority over the territory (indeed Mau Mau had in part been triggered by the growing influence of the settlers themselves within the colonial state). The Emergency in Kenya, and its causes, were often difficult for European contemporaries to interpret. Rather than being merely an outburst of anti-colonial energy, Mau Mau was predominantly a phenomenon which affected Africans: by far the majority of the victims of violence were Kikuyu who were seen to be collaborating with, or benefiting from, colonial rule. Social disintegration under a variety of external pressures, rather than a spirit of nationalism, seemed to be its core.

Britain's experiences of counterinsurgency in Malaya inevitably coloured its response to the crisis in Kenya during the 1950s, and similar tactics were employed to deprive the Mau Mau fighters of grass-roots support. The extent of repression was high, and critical accounts of the treatment meted out to detainees began to circulate, providing ammunition for metropolitan critics of the Conservatives' African policies. This process would eventually culminate in 1959 in the horrifying revelations of brutality practised at the Hola detention camp, which would have major implications for the government's attitude to colonial policy. Meanwhile, the military operation was generally judged a success in official circles, even though its director, General Sir George Erskine, whose contempt for the settlers was notorious, was removed in 1955, possibly as a sop to white feelings.[73] As well as deploying a major military initiative, the British understood that long-term stability in the colony required reforms in the political and economic sphere. At the political level, the espousal of multiracialism was accompanied by a tough British attitude towards African political restlessness, and a determination to stifle the development of nationalism. The leading Kikuyu activist and President of the Kenya African Union, Jomo Kenyatta, whom the British claimed was a key instigator of Mau Mau violence, was given a seven-year prison sentence after what has come to be seen as a highly suspect trial. Political parties beyond the district level remained outlawed long after the insurgency had been contained. In this respect, British policy-makers demonstrated a remarkable degree of confidence in their ability to mould and control the local situation.[74] But the coercive aspect of suppressing unrest, involving the detention of some 80,000 alleged Mau Mau fighters by 1954, had, London realized, to be balanced with attempts to construct a stable basis for the colony's future development. This involved measures to expand representative government, in which Britain's aim was to encourage the settlers, in return for a larger role in the colonial state, to accept a degree of power-sharing with Kenya's Asian and African communities. Although multiracialism, not majority rule, remained the goal, Britain sought in particular to reward those Africans who had not demonstrated 'extremist' tendencies with constitutional concessions. As African representation gathered momentum, especially after the general election of 1957, so too did calls for ever larger representation for the majority of the population. Once again, the logic of introducing electoral politics was to create conditions which it would be increasingly difficult for Britain to control and political processes whose outcome it was hazardous to predict.[75]

Britain recognized that constitutional reform had to be reinforced with efforts to alleviate the fundamental economic and social problems which had made Mau Mau possible. The principal grievance fuelling Mau Mau had been the chronic land hunger of the Kikuyu, a problem developing since the inter-war period, and accentuated by African resentment that some of the colony's best farming land, the 'White Highlands', had been reserved for settlers.[76] In 1953, the governor of Kenya, Sir Philip Mitchell, secured the appointment of the East Africa Royal Commission to investigate the related questions of land and population, with a view to promoting higher African living standards. In its report, published in 1955, the commission advocated moves to encourage market-orientated farming based on security of tenure for African farmers, which would mean ending the settlers' traditional monopoly of Kenya's prime land. Significantly, these broad conclusions had been anticipated by the Kenyan government, which had unveiled its ambitious Swynnerton Plan, an attempt to create a class of African peasant entrepreneurs which would have a vested interest in political stability. Central to the success of the plan was the aim of enabling the Kikuyu to buy land. Recognizing the importance of practical conciliatory gestures to complement the continuing counterinsurgency campaign, London provided an initial grant of £5 million.[77]

One of the long-term ambitions London had been developing since the Second World War was to achieve closer integration of its East African territories in a federal arrangement, probably under the leadership of Kenya. Modest steps in this direction had been taken at the end of the war with the creation of the East African High Commission, but it was in the early 1950s that the idea began to have consequences for African politics in the region. In Uganda, the new governor, Sir Andrew Cohen, appointed in 1952, set about promoting constitutional reform, tackling the problem of democratizing the previously autocratic government of the Kingdom of Buganda. The coincidence of this with renewed talk of regional federation provoked African alarm that the region might come under effective white settler domination. When the ruler of Buganda demanded assurances that federation was not planned by London, and withheld his co-operation until he received them, he was summarily dismissed and exiled by Cohen, not being allowed to return to Uganda until 1955. For the remainder of the decade, Britain's primary aim in Uganda was to find a means of integrating Buganda into the larger territory.

It was the ambitious attempt to foster multiracialism in Central Africa which would rebound most seriously in the long term for Britain. Here, London had eventually opted not for the amalgamation of Northern and Southern Rhodesia, which local settlers had sought, but a federal structure to which was appended impoverished Nyasaland, and over which Britain retained considerable (if often unexercised) authority. The majority African population had been implacably opposed to the Federation since its inception. London's attitude was that Africans simply failed to understand what constituted the common good. As John Darwin has put it: 'With its telescope clapped firmly to its ear, London declared that opposition could be neither seen nor heard'.[78] African fears were not diminished by the inclusion of federal mechanisms supposed to safeguard majority rights, but were instead exacerbated as growing numbers of white immigrants arrived in the Federation, often bringing with them less accommodating racial attitudes than those of old Rhodesia hands. While the Federation certainly enjoyed economic success, fuelled by the wealth generated by its minerals and other commodities, and expressed in the building boom in its capital, Salisbury (Harare), the immediate benefits tended to accrue to the settlers rather than to the African majority. Reinforcing settler privilege was the 'colour bar' in the work place, which functioned to counteract the challenge of cheap African labour. The success of the federal idea hinged, ultimately, on settler willingness to share power with the majority population, a proposition which revealed the tensions between policy-makers in Britain and white politicians in the Federation. To complicate matters, key figures such as Lord Malvern, and his successor as federal prime minister, the bullish Roy Welensky, enjoyed a privileged relationship with elements of the Conservative Party's right wing. To the settlers, concerned about the pace of political reform elsewhere in British Africa (and impressed by the achievement of South Africa's whites), the Federation's obvious future was to achieve Dominion status, free of the remaining controls from London. Fearful that any delay might permit African nationalism to develop, and convinced of their own entitlement and qualifications to supervise the region's affairs (prejudices broadly shared in London), the settlers sought full self-government as rapidly as possible. An additional settler concern was to achieve independence while the Conservatives were still in office: a future Labour administration, it was feared, might not be so sympathetic to settler aspirations.

However, in 1956, the British government agreed that federal independence under white rule could not be contemplated, although a cosmetic adjustment of the Federation's status was permitted. London's reservations were informed less by sensitivity to African concerns than by a desire to avoid political complications at home or moves which might discredit the federal experiment (still being canvassed for East Africa, and under active consideration for other groups of dependent territories). The entire Central African situation was to be reviewed in 1960, but long before then, some British officials foresaw the possibility that settler politicians denied independence on their terms might resort to illegal methods to obtain their goal.

The international background to colonialism

The international dimension to British colonial rule, evident after 1945, became increasingly important in the 1950s, and was a significant constraint on policy formation and colonial practice. Most important of all, of course, was the Cold War, and the potential for colonialism to be seized upon by the Soviet bloc as a weapon with which to castigate the West generally. Intensified Cold War tensions, the emergence of colonial nationalism and the coalescing of a distinctive 'non-aligned' bloc of nations, themselves often former colonies, combined to make colonialism and its future a key theme in international relations during this period. The fact that Britain's first phase of decolonizing activity appeared to have ended in 1948 tended to place the British government in a defensive position, striving to maintain its claims to operate a benign, liberal colonial regime. With the declaration of several serious colonial 'emergencies', it became increasingly difficult to justify these claims. This problem was identified by a report accepted by the Cabinet late in 1953, which emphasized the practical consequences of anti-colonial criticism for British colonial rule and for its pattern of foreign relations generally.[79]

Especially awkward for London was the fact that among the most ardent critics of colonial rule, especially at the United Nations, was India. The Indian prime minister, Nehru, used the anniversary in 1953 of the Amritsar Massacre to pledge Indian support to Kenya's Mau Mau fighters. Nehru's stature in the developing world meant that his comments could not be ignored by the British government. Bowing to the Commonwealth Relations Office, whose concerns revolved around India's Commonwealth membership, and the fact that several British colonies (including Kenya) contained substantial Asian minorities, the government agreed to convey its dismay to New Delhi privately.[80]

India was not the only Commonwealth member to question the thrust of British colonial policy. As alluded to earlier, South Africa, too, was a potential critic, albeit for reasons different to India's. To some extent, Pretoria's anxieties were assuaged by the arrival of the Conservatives in 1951, but Malan's Nationalist government remained concerned about the implications of changes in Britain's African colonies. In 1951, for example, London felt it necessary to placate Malan over the pace of devolution in the Gold Coast. Imminent independence for the Sudan also seemed likely to strain the relationship with South Africa, which might block any Sudanese bid to join the Commonwealth. As often proved to be the case, the Colonial Office found itself isolated in Whitehall on the question of responding to South African opinion. More influential government departments, notably the Foreign Office, considered it vital to alleviate Pretoria's concerns about the future evolution of the Commonwealth. As it transpired, independent Sudan did not seek entry to the Commonwealth, and attention switched instead to how South Africa would react to the Gold Coast's imminent independence and candidacy for Commonwealth membership.[81]

For the governments of Churchill and Eden, as for that of Attlee, the scope for anti-colonial rhetoric and action at the United Nations was a source of continuing concern. From Britain's point of view, at least in the colonial sphere, the UN posed a fundamental challenge to British interests. It was a basic aim of British policy to avoid a situation in which the colonial powers would become accountable to the UN for their actions, as this would reinforce the position of hostile powers at the UN, and might give encouragement to critics of British rule within the colonies, either of which would undermine the gradualist approach to constitutional development favoured by Britain. For this reason, London adhered rigidly to the idea that colonial affairs were strictly a domestic British concern. In practice, however, British tactics were pragmatic, recognizing that the UN was in fact interested in colonial issues, and providing information to the UN's Trusteeship Council, while setting clear boundaries to British co-operation.[82] These tactics were generally successful during this period, and Britain was never forced to resort to the negative and humiliating measure of withdrawing from UN deliberations. Nevertheless, throughout this period, the number of former colonies joining the UN grew, swelling the ranks of the anti-colonial lobby, and it became more difficult for Britain to mobilize sufficient votes to deter unwelcome debates in the General Assembly. Even the support of longstanding Commonwealth partners could no longer be assumed by Britain. This was shown at the United Nations in 1954 over the question of inscribing an item on Cyprus, following intervention by the Greek government, impatient with the limited constitutional proposals being offered by London. Already under international pressure over this sensitive issue, the British government was dismayed to find Canada abstaining at the General Assembly. Australia offered reluctant support, but warned the Foreign Office that Britain's handling of the Cyprus problem was making it difficult to sustain this position.[83] After the Suez debacle in 1956, Britain's freedom of manoeuvre would be reduced, and its stance became increasingly defensive, precluding the kind of robust trumpeting of Britain's record and aims which the Foreign Office advocated. This was disappointing for ministers in London, who had hoped that Ghana's independence, coming soon after the Suez Crisis, would reflect well on British policy. More importantly, and ironically, Ghana would join India at the forefront of the anti-colonial lobby at the UN, if anything giving that grouping a fresh momentum, a trend which would continue as decolonization gathered pace in the early 1960s.

It was particularly important from Britain's point of view that the attention increasingly attaching to colonial issues in international politics did not harm Britain's wider network of external relationships and interests. Above all, Britain was keen to preserve and develop its special relationship with the United States. Washington's traditionally anti-colonial stance was therefore of major concern to London, and efforts increased during the early 1950s to bring the Americans around to seeing colonial affairs from Britain's point of view. Even if the US could not be converted to wholesale approval of British-style colonial rule, it could at least be encouraged to keep its criticism to a minimum, at least publicly. This was one major reason for Britain's grudging agreement to continue participating in discussions on the subject at the UN. During the early 1950s, bilateral discussions between British and US officials were conducted each year. At these, the Americans routinely reminded the British about their fundamental misgivings about colonialism, and their broad sympathy for colonial calls for independence At this time, the US Secretary of State, John Foster Dulles, was inclined to view colonial rule as an irrelevant distraction from the main task of achieving success in the Cold War; moreover, it seemed, by the mid-1950s, to be emerging as the key area for confrontation between East and West. The British line emphasized that Britain's position as a world power, and hence as a worthwhile ally in the Cold War, hinged on its success in maintaining the imperial system. A further argument deployed by London was that a hasty withdrawal from the colonial territories would create opportunities for Soviet bloc penetration of the developing world, given Moscow's growing interest in these regions after 1954.[84] Nevertheless, by 1956, Washington had become convinced that the development of colonial nationalism, and the prevailing international attitude, meant that the colonial era was drawing to a close, and that in these circumstances it was preferable that Britain should demonstrate its willingness to make concessions to 'friendly' (that is pro-Western) nationalists, and not risk unnecessary conflicts by seeking to prolong the life of colonial rule.

London's and Washington's divergent approaches were seen also in their respective attitudes towards the UN. Britain's determination to restrict the scope for UN interference in colonial matters contrasted with America's line, largely influenced by the desire to consolidate US relations with Third World countries, in part through the UN, still seen by US diplomats as a constructive force. While for this reason Washington continued to encourage the colonial powers to reassess their positions, it avoided embarrassing Britain by engaging in critical statements at the UN. The Americans tended to become impatient with the refusal of Britain and the other colonial powers to use the UN as a forum in which to defend their colonial records, and to shelter behind the somewhat sterile claim that colonialism was an internal, metropolitan concern. Nevertheless, London could generally rely on Washington's more important concern to preserve the alliance with Britain.[85]

Britain and Europe

During the early 1950s, there seemed to be no compelling reason for Britain to be drawn more closely into the affairs of continental Europe. The defence of Europe was, of course, a strategic priority, and was provided for by Britain's membership of NATO. For quite practical reasons, the British government was also sympathetic to moves within Western Europe to achieve a greater degree of economic and military integration: this would reduce the risk of conflict between France and Germany (who had already been to war three times within one lifetime), and equip Western Europe to resist Soviet expansion more effectively. London, however, saw no need to participate in the trend towards integration, through the European Coal and Steel Community and the proposed European Defence Community. Too close an attachment to Europe might, it was feared, undermine Britain's broader global aims, of maintaining the Anglo-American special relationship and the network of Commonwealth ties. In 1954, however, through the Paris accords, Britain did make an important concession to France, promising to station four divisions of British troops permanently in Germany, and in turn clearing the ground for West German rearmament and admission to NATO. This, it was hoped, would demonstrate the advantages of the Atlantic alliance over the more nebulous concept of 'supranationalism', which London had been keen to resist since the late 1940s. Although the continental commitment added to Britain's already considerable burdens, it was judged necessary in order to ward off any reappraisal by Washington of the US role in European defence.[86]

The British government's general position on Western European integration was therefore to encourage the development, without involving Britain directly in the process. Some ministers, however, did not believe that the question was closed, and accepted that Britain's position might have to be reassessed in the future, although in a way which would give Britain a greater voice in Europe while enabling it to preserve its system of imperial interests. As Harold Macmillan pointed out, a European *con*federation, in which Britain would take precedence, was preferable to a federation in which West Germany seemed bound to dominate. By 1956, with Churchill in retirement, the opportunity arose for those, like Macmillan and Selwyn Lloyd, who sought to achieve a closer, if conditional, alignment between Britain and Western Europe. This was prompted by the rapid economic recovery of Europe and the fact that Britain was already beginning to face stiff competition in its traditionally secure overseas markets from countries such as West Germany. Meeting this challenge, and making British export industries more competitive, not only in these markets but also in the increasingly attractive and expanding European market, seemed essential if Britain's own economic growth were to be safeguarded.

Those who thought along these lines would have to bide their time. When, in 1955, the six European countries most committed to integration met at Messina in Sicily to discuss their next moves towards creating a Common Market, Britain was invited to attend, but instead sent only an observer. A Whitehall working party created to examine the idea of greater integration revealed divided opinion. The Board of Trade was sympathetic, but the Treasury, the Bank of England and the Commonwealth Relations Office successfully argued the case that Britain had substantial economic interests outside Europe. The dangers of a protected bloc within Europe, and the implication of future political federation, were also emphasized as risks to be avoided. As Eden, who opposed federation, once put it to an official: 'What you've got to remember is that, if you looked at the post-bag of any English village and examined the letters coming in from abroad to the whole population, ninety per cent of them come from beyond Europe.'[87] More generally, a possibility suggested by ministerial exchanges during the mid-1950s is that counter-arguments to participation in Europe, especially the importance of defending wider Commonwealth interests, were a convenient pretext for avoiding something which the British government sought to avoid for other reasons.

Britain's response to the Messina Powers' proposals for a Common Market was Plan G, adopted by the Cabinet in October 1956, a scheme to create a European Free Trade Area, to comprise the Messina Six, Britain, and any other member of the Organization for European Economic Co-operation which chose to join. This would permit Britain to enjoy the advantages of increased commerce with Europe in manufactured goods while preserving the preferential trading system it had constructed with the Empire-Commonwealth. The emphasis within EFTA on manufactured goods was intended by Britain to protect the interests of Commonwealth primary producers. Even this alarmed some of those ministers particularly wedded to the Commonwealth relationship, notably Lord Salisbury. Nevertheless, discussions on creating EFTA began early in 1957. Continuing ministerial attachment to Imperial Preference was not so much based on any belief that the system in itself offered a viable alternative to greater economic association with Europe, but rather stemmed from the conviction that the advantages to Britain brought by the arrangements were, if limited, still worth having. More viscerally, Imperial Preference was still regarded as important in political terms, symbolizing Britain's overseas influence.[88]

Suez

The Suez Crisis of 1956 has often been depicted as a 'turning point' in the history of Britain's external relations and status as an imperial power. Certainly, the crisis illustrated forcefully the need for British governments to be aware of public opinion at home, which in turn may well have influenced the formulation of wider colonial policy. In July 1956, only weeks after the last British troops had evacuated the Suez base, Nasser nationalized the Suez Canal, in retaliation for British and American refusal to provide funding for the Aswan High Dam project. The British government publicly emphasized this event's economic ramifications, particularly the threat it posed to Britain's oil supplies. Privately, however, it was clear that London's objectives were, in the longer term, to ensure international control of the Canal, but in the short term, to use this opportunity to remove Nasser. This aim was grounded above all in London's preoccupation with British international prestige, and the threat Nasser posed to this, especially through his espousal of anti-British nationalist feeling, not only in the Middle East but in Africa too.[89]

One immediate consequence of the crisis was that the policy review recently initiated by Eden was put to one side, and the efforts of most members of the government were devoted instead to meeting what was treated as being a major challenge to Britain's standing as a great power. Early in the crisis, it seems, the government resolved to use military force, if necessary alone, even though the Foreign Office counselled that the era of gunboat diplomacy had passed. For Eden, the crisis had become the ultimate test: if Britain failed here, it would cease to be a world player.[90]

Eden displayed a far greater confidence than Churchill had that Britain could act independently of US opinion, stressing that Britain's interests in, and experience of, the Middle East were significantly greater than those of the United States. In this respect, he simply misjudged the wider context of international policy, and specifically misread the signals from Washington.[91] In the event, US attitudes would be decisive. The United States sought a diplomatic settlement of the crisis, and between August and October, Britain, the US and the Western powers ostensibly co-operated to find one. Meanwhile, Washington warned London not to try to coerce Egypt, though it had already colluded with Britain in Plan Omega, aimed at using covert political and economic measures to topple Nasser's regime. In September, President Eisenhower told Eden that he feared that an invasion of Egypt would lead the peoples of the Middle East to turn to Moscow for support, possibly bringing with them the Afro-Asian bloc of nations.

Nevertheless, British invasion planning proceeded and reservists were called up.[92] On 24 October, a secret agreement was reached between Britain, France and Israel, providing for an Israeli invasion of Egypt, to be followed by intervention by Britain and France to 'separate the combatants', occupy the Canal Zone and, it was hoped, remove Nasser. As David Reynolds has commented, this collusion with Israel in particular conflicted 'spectacularly' with Britain's longstanding quest for more secure relations with the Arab world, and underlines the aberrant nature of the whole episode and the extent to which the Foreign Office was temporarily marginalized in Whitehall.[93] Military operations began on 29 October with an Israeli attack, soon followed by British and French air raids on Egyptian airfields. Although the United States, the Soviet Union and the United Nations all called for an immediate cease-fire, the invasion went ahead, provoking condemnation both in Britain and abroad.

Political divisions soon emerged, undermining the resolve of Eden, who was seriously ill for much of the crisis. It was the reaction from Washington which was most serious, however. Having previously maintained a moderate position, the American government spoke out. Dulles, certainly no Anglophile, publicly attacked British 'colonialism', sentiments echoed by Eisenhower. But the rift in the Special Relationship had more practical and immediate consequences: on 6 November, the United States warned London that if a cease-fire did not follow immediately, it would withdraw support for a loan from the International Monetary Fund, essential to Britain in order to maintain sterling's position, as the invasion had triggered a run on the pound which cost the British reserves more than $300 million. With mounting economic pressure threatening the very existence of the Sterling Area, Britain had little option but to comply with US demands, and the withdrawal of its forces had been completed by 22 December. Shortly afterwards, Eden, his health broken and his reputation shattered, tendered his resignation.

The British government seems to have been genuinely surprised by international, especially US, reactions to the invasion of Egypt. Macmillan had evidently misinterpreted Eisenhower's position, or, perhaps, had deliberately given Eden a misleading account of his discussions with the president in September. The invasion was counter-productive, in that it not only strengthened Nasser's position within Egypt and as champion of the Arab world, and gave encouragement to anti-colonial movements around the world, but it also exposed serious strains within the Commonwealth, which, as the Cabinet Secretary observed, had become distinctly 'wobbly' during the crisis. Australia offered strong diplomatic support to Britain, along with New Zealand, but South Africa remained aloof. Among the Asian members, India's response was especially embarrassing to Britain, with prime minister Nehru condemning Eden's action publicly and siding with Egypt.[94] Canada, strongly committed to the UN, not a significant user of the Suez Canal, and alarmed at the consequences of Britain's actions for the Special Relationship and Commonwealth relations, was at the forefront of efforts at the UN to despatch a peace-keeping force. On pragmatic as well as ethical grounds, the Canadian government, which had assiduously sought to develop ties with the non-aligned countries, and had been drawn inexorably into closer defence ties with Washington, was appalled at Britain's behaviour.[95] To the dismay of the Commonwealth Relations Office in London, Eden had deliberately avoided consulting Commonwealth members, as might have been expected in such a crisis. Although 'senior' members were kept abreast of developments informally, there was no emergency meeting of Commonwealth prime ministers. Although no country actually left the Commonwealth over Suez, the crisis inevitably damaged the delicate Commonwealth relationship, and even raised fresh questions about the association's future.[96] India's robust criticism of Britain was seen by some as contrasting oddly with its relative indulgence towards the simultaneous Soviet occupation of Hungary. Most alarming, perhaps, was Soviet diplomatic intervention, which raised the prospect of military confrontation.

The Suez Crisis undoubtedly did great damage to Britain's standing as a world power, and Eden's successor, Macmillan, faced a formidable task in repairing British external relationships, above all with the Americans. For some commentators within Britain, Suez confirmed a growing suspicion that Washington's aim was to supplant Britain's traditional imperial role. At the UN, Britain, along with France and Israel, had been condemned and isolated in a humiliating manner. Suez represented an unambiguous failure to effect British aims, and to recover a lost position, simply by a show of strength: the underpinnings of that strength had been exposed as illusory. Nevertheless, Suez did not mark the abdication by Britain of its Middle Eastern role. The British military presence in Jordan, Iraq and Aden remained intact and was, for the time being, secure. The Baghdad Pact, engineered by Britain, was still in place, and British influence in the Persian Gulf remained. Anti-Western nationalism in the region had been stimulated, as would soon be demonstrated by the revolution in Iraq, the lynchpin in Britain's Middle Eastern system. Nevertheless, the extent of Britain's continuing confidence would soon be revealed by the unveiling of plans for the ambitious, if ultimately unworkable, South Arabian Federation. Further afield, Britain's East of Suez role was unaffected, and was to be enhanced early in 1957 by the conclusion of a defence treaty with independent Malaya. Even the strained Special Relationship would be restored with remarkable speed. There is little to suggest that the

Suez Crisis *in itself* caused Britain to accelerate its plans for decolonization, for example in Africa. Certainly, the Gold Coast became independent during 1957, but this was the outcome of a policy strand initiated by Attlee's government and well in hand before the crisis erupted. One practical consequence of the crisis, however, was to highlight the military value of Cyprus and to enhance Britain's desire to retain control of the island. However, the most important lesson arising from the Suez debacle was that never again could Britain allow itself to become so isolated and vulnerable as a result of its external policies. If the broad aims of Britain's global policy would remain unchanged, the methods used by London to secure them would in future require greater caution and flexibility, and an acute sensitivity to international, especially American, opinion.

CHAPTER 5

WINDS OF CHANGE, 1957–64

The years 1957 to 1964 undeniably mark an important phase in Britain's relationship with the wider world, which has been described as encompassing a major period of 'readjustment'. During these years, the vast majority of Britain's remaining colonial possessions became independent. Britain's traditional resistance to greater involvement in Europe appeared to undergo a sea-change as evidence gathered of the success of the new European Economic Community, culminating in Britain's abortive bid for entry in 1961. This move had been inspired, at least in part, by a concern to ensure that London's voice in Washington was not drowned out by those of its more successful European rivals. But any attempt to achieve greater involvement in Europe would inevitably raise questions about the nature and prospects of the Commonwealth. While British policy-makers remained committed to preserving a strong British relationship with all three circles, wider circumstances, among them the tense Cold War climate and a painful recognition of Britain's relative economic decline (and its implications for Britain's capacity to maintain the military resources required by a global role), demanded an increasingly ingenious response from the British government in its attempts to reconcile these fundamental goals in overseas policy.

Harold Macmillan, described by Harold Wilson as 'first in, first out' during Suez, succeeded Eden as prime minister in January 1957. It seems that an important factor in his selection was his acceptability to Washington, and the likelihood that he, rather than his rival Butler, was best qualified to heal the breach in the Special Relationship so painfully revealed during the autumn of 1956. Although he was not noted as an imperially minded minister, he inherited from Churchill a belief in Britain's unique world role as the point of intersection of the three great circles: the Commonwealth, the Atlantic alliance and Europe. This accounts for his interest in the expansion of the Commonwealth to include the existing colonial territories. An enlarged Commonwealth, so the reasoning went, would enhance Britain's relations with both the other circles.[1] As he explained to an audience in Singapore early in 1958, Britain might not be on a level with the superpowers, but it 'still chose to remain a great Power'. Although its authority might have diminished, it still had considerable influence in the world. In what was possibly a conscious echo of Churchill's wartime disclaimer, he reassured his audience that he had no intention of liquidating the British Empire.[2] Prior to becoming prime minister,

Macmillan had given little clear indication about his views on the colonies, even though he had served as a junior Colonial Office minister during the Second World War. There was enough, however, to suggest that his sympathies already lay more with colonial populations than with the pursuit of imperial interests as traditionally perceived. He had made radical suggestions on Kenya's future, for instance, proposing that white settler landowners should be bought out by the state and their lands redistributed among the African population, in order to ease their already serious land-hunger. As Chancellor of the Exchequer, he had been keen to cut expenditure on the colonies, bringing him into confrontation with the Colonial Office over the question of increased development aid. Like his immediate predecessors, Churchill and Eden, Macmillan seems generally to have lacked interest in the minutiae of colonial policy, being temperamentally better suited to the production of 'big ideas'. He tended to become involved directly in policy issues only when they impacted upon other major questions, such as international relations, or the government's standing in the country.

Initially, at least, his government's handling of colonial policy was cautious, and involved no startling initiatives. Both Ghana and Malaya became independent in 1957, in accordance with plans made before Suez. In keeping with his emphasis on rebuilding the Special Relationship, Macmillan met President Eisenhower twice during his first year in office, first in Bermuda in March 1957, and then in Washington in October. At these meetings, close ties were restored, described by Macmillan as constituting 'interdependence', with the two leaders committing themselves to co-ordinated policies in world affairs, for example in Asia and Africa, on the implicit understanding that Britain would never again attempt to mount a major overseas military operation of which the United States disapproved. At the Washington meeting, it was agreed that the most effective means of pre-empting Communist penetration in Africa was to transfer power to stable, friendly nationalist regimes, politically and economically aligned to the West. The Americans, like the British, were not convinced that most of colonial Africa was 'ready' for independence, but saw no realistic alternative strategy.[3] These exchanges prepared the ground for an attempt by London and Washington to examine the co-ordination of their policies towards Africa. From the British point of view, the advantage of co-operating with the Americans in this way was that it would create openings for London to influence US policy, and possibly to benefit from any increase in US investment in Africa.[4] The fundamental aim of both governments has been described as the creation of a new 'informal' empire in Africa, under joint Anglo-American auspices. However, one consequence of the rapid re-establishment of the Special Relationship was to deepen French anxieties about the motives of what was seen by Paris as an 'Anglo-Saxon' bloc: these misgivings would have important implications for Britain's subsequent bid to join an integrated Western Europe.

Although his immediate priority after Suez was to restore close ties with Washington, Macmillan also needed to mend fences with the members of the Commonwealth. Macmillan seems to have had a high opinion of the Commonwealth and its potential as a multiracial organization with a common heritage and outlook. This view, proved in hindsight to have been exaggerated, was strengthened by the highly successful (and reassuring) Commonwealth tour Macmillan made in 1957–58, the first by a serving prime minister. Macmillan subsequently became far more pessimistic. Developments in the South African apartheid state, in particular, seemed likely to tear the Commonwealth apart. Here, international outrage following the Sharpeville Massacre (March 1960), in which 67 African demonstrators were killed, highlighted not only the difficulties for Britain in defending its enormous financial stake in the country, but also the problems inherent in holding the Commonwealth together. Although opinion against South Africa was hardening, it still had friends within the Commonwealth, including the Australian prime minister, Sir Robert Menzies. Sharpeville seemed to demand some collective response, but, as Macmillan observed during the 1960 Commonwealth Prime Ministers' meeting, if the Commonwealth did nothing its credibility would be tarnished, while if it acted, it might drive South Africa out of the club, paving the way for a general disintegration, something over which he had no stomach to preside.[5]

Although not in itself a consequence of Suez, the government's reassessment of Britain's defence requirements, enshrined in the 1957 Defence White Paper, was important in shaping the framework of Macmillan's global policy. This fundamental review, driven above all by financial considerations and the desire to economize, switched resources from conventional to nuclear capability. The armed forces were to be cut from 690,000 to 375,000 by the end of 1962. This made possible the ending of conscription in 1960, but placed limits on Britain's ability to fight large-scale counterinsurgency campaigns, for example in the colonies.[6] The nuclear deterrent was to acquire an ever-growing political significance for Britain in the years immediately after Suez. It offered the prospect of a guaranteed hearing for London's views in Washington circles, in addition to insurance against challenges to British authority from smaller nations (as had just been experienced in the Middle East). Quite how 'useful' the British hydrogen bomb, first tested in 1957, would be was debatable: it would hardly be of much value in 'limited' conflicts, such as campaigns to overawe colonial resistance. But in terms of domestic politics, the deterrent arguably appealed to the disgruntled right wing of the Conservative Party, soothing the grievances of those alarmed at Britain's declining imperial status, and so possibly smoothing the path for decolonization.[7]

It was in the years after 1957 that some of the economic problems emerging in the early 1950s finally became inescapable. After 1959, especially, the situation became acute. Expectations of a significant increase in export earnings gave way to the reality of a large deficit in 1960, and in the following year a sterling crisis loomed. A pattern was developing characterized by stop–go economic activity, in which economic expansion tended to lead to a higher level of imports than of exports, which in turn put pressure on the value of sterling. The normal government response was to raise interest rates and attempt to cut consumer demand, in an effort to reduce imports, but this strategy threatened to introduce unwelcome recessionary effects, seen, for example, in the alarming increase in the level of unemployment after mid-1961.

Officially, at least, Britain still retained its faith in the Commonwealth as an important and valuable trading bloc. This commitment was restated at the Commonwealth Trade Conference in Montreal in 1958, at a time when almost half of Britain's exports to the Commonwealth enjoyed Imperial Preference. In practice, however, British trade with the Commonwealth had continued to decline during the 1950s. As a more liberal world trading order took shape, competition from other suppliers continued to erode Britain's share of Sterling Area markets. Whereas in 1950, over 47 per cent of Britain's exports had gone to Commonwealth destinations, by 1960 the figure was a little over 40 per cent. Imports from the Commonwealth shrank by a similar proportion in the same period. By the early 1960s, too, there were deepening doubts in Britain about the wisdom of exporting precious human capital, in the form of skilled and professional emigrants, to Commonwealth countries, simultaneously depriving the British economy of talent while adding to the competitive edge of its trading partners.[8] Although this was worrying, the full significance of these shifts did not become fully apparent until later in the 1960s (that is, *after* the most important decolonizing decisions had been made).

It was in the late 1950s that problems inherent in the operations of the Sterling Area became painfully apparent. Put simply, Britain's own balance of payments position was endangered whenever Sterling Area members faced trade deficits and drew on their sterling balances. This in turn endangered the value of sterling, and complicated the processes of domestic economic management. Despite this, an official investigation concluded in 1959 that the Sterling Area was still in Britain's best interests. This reflected the unshakeable conviction that London was, and must remain, a major international financial centre, the hub of a complex network of commercial and political relationships.[9] By 1962, Britain's foreign investment totalled £10,000 million, but increasingly this was seen as reducing the capital available for much-needed investment in Britain's own economy. The success of Britain's competitors, and the arguments for metropolitan modernization, raised questions about Britain's ability to remain a major world banker. A supplementary consideration was the way in which overseas commitments placed strain on Britain's reserves of foreign exchange. Complicating Britain's position was the fact that the City's business was becoming increasingly international in character. In 1958, the pound finally achieved *de jure* convertibility. Given that Britain's liabilities at this time stood at over £4,000 million (compared to reserves of around £700 million), convertibility inevitably placed more pressure on Britain's resources, at a time when earnings from so-called invisible exports were much smaller than they had been before the war. Whereas sterling had once been a leading world currency, it had, by the late 1950s declined in status to being a 'negotiated' currency, one which Britain had to *persuade* other countries to use in their transactions. Maintaining even this reduced status required strategies, including high interest rates, which were not necessarily in the interests of the domestic economy. Moreover, currency liberalization was expected to produce an increased demand from former colonies to draw on their sterling balances.[10]

The background of darkening economic horizons, and a continuing desire to obtain the best returns from the expenditure of dwindling resources, prompted an important initiative very early in Macmillan's prime ministerial career. In January 1957, Macmillan called on the Cabinet Colonial Policy Committee to determine which colonies might become self-governing in the near future, which ones would become eligible to join the Commonwealth, and what should be the fate of those ineligible for entry. Writing to the Lord President of the Committee, the 'die-hard' empire enthusiast Lord Salisbury, Macmillan said:

> I should like to see something like a profit and loss account for each of our colonial possessions, so that we may be better able to gauge whether, from the financial and economic point of view, we are likely to gain or lose by its departure. This would need, of course, to be weighed against the political and strategic considerations involved in each case.[11]

Much has been written about the significance of this move, and the extent to which it foreshadowed or represented a determination to shed Britain's colonial responsibilities. In the event, the results of this 'audit' of the colonial empire were hardly conclusive. The report of the Colonial Policy Committee suggested that Malaya, Nigeria, the West Indies (in a federation) and the Central African Federation were the territories most ready for independence. Rapid political change was also predicted for both East and West Africa. More than a dozen territories appeared to be candidates for self-government during the forthcoming ten years. On the financial cost of the colonies, the report observed that Britain was currently spending about £51 million a year on colonial development and related aid schemes. However, it warned against assuming that the net saving in the foreseeable future might be substantial, because the territories closest to independence were generally those least dependent on British aid. Moreover, in those cases where help from the metropolitan Exchequer was needed, for example in conducting the Malayan counterinsurgency campaign, strategic considerations might well outweigh purely financial ones. Nor would Britain save a great deal by withdrawing from other small territories which could not survive without outside assistance: if anything, this would smack of irresponsible behaviour on Britain's part. In addressing the economic aspects of decolonization, the report concluded that the arguments were 'evenly balanced', and that British economic interests were 'unlikely' in themselves to be 'decisive in determining whether or not a territory should become independent'. It recognized that while 'premature' independence might damage metropolitan interests, the economic dangers of delaying independence for territories ready for it would be 'far greater' than those of granting independence in an atmosphere of goodwill, as had existed in the cases of the Gold Coast and Malaya.[12] The economic advantages of colonial rule, to Britain, therefore no longer in themselves seemed to be an adequate reason for maintaining that rule. Broadly speaking, then, it appeared that it was safe to embark on decolonization without significantly jeopardizing British economic interests.

Any impression that Suez conclusively dealt a blow to British pretensions of a global role has to take account of the view, if anything strengthened after 1956, that Britain had a special part to play 'East of Suez'. The East of Suez mind-set was typified by Britain's continuing presence in Malaya after independence in 1957. In exchange for Malaya's continued membership of the Sterling Area, Britain provided Malaya's new rulers with the military aid they needed to counteract the country's internal guerrilla threat. These arrangements were highly acceptable to each side. In the same vein, although Singapore achieved self-governing status in 1957, London remained responsible for its defence and external relations, underlining Britain's determination to preserve the island as a major strategic base, and continuing hopes that a federation of its former colonies in South-East Asia might yet prove feasible.

East of Suez was no mere projection of the *amour propre* of a declining power: there were practical reasons for Britain's interest in this region. Britain, with a coal industry apparently on the verge of extinction, depended heavily on imported energy resources, and almost half its oil came from the Persian Gulf. Moreover, around a quarter of its exports were sold to countries bounded by the Indian Ocean and the Western Pacific.[13] Britain's military elite had similarly strong reasons to emphasize the importance of this region. All three services were trying to establish niches for their expertise in the wake of the uncertainties introduced not only by pressure to economize, but also by the ongoing strategic reappraisal of the mid-1950s. As late as 1962, the Chiefs of Staff, looking ahead to the forthcoming decade, argued that East of Suez would be Britain's most important global role. In practice, the financial savings expected to follow from the 1957 Defence White Paper were not achieved. The defence chiefs insisted that increased spending on nuclear weapons should not mean a significant reduction in expenditure on conventional defence. Late in 1957, it was decided that an effective East of Suez role called for the establishment of a strategic reserve in Kenya. Before long, an enormous military base there was being planned, involving considerable investment. Yet the thrust of colonial policy towards ever greater measures of political devolution, evident in Kenya's case by 1961, obliged the planners to switch their attention instead to Aden, where the British military presence had already quadrupled between 1957 and 1959, with the colony becoming home to Britain's Middle East Command. Here too, London would find its calculations complicated during the early-mid-1960s by escalating resistance to British rule.[14]

The Middle East

In the wake of Suez, there was initially no question of Britain abandoning its remaining Middle Eastern footholds. In his first Cabinet meeting as prime minister, Macmillan stressed the need for Britain to avoid giving any impression that it was in retreat from the region.[15] In some respects, there were some striking continuities in London's outlook before and after Suez. The conviction that Nasser represented the most serious threat to Britain's Middle Eastern interests was not dispelled, but in fact strengthened by the events of autumn

1956: containing this threat remained a cardinal policy goal. It was ironic that at a time when the 'three circles' model of Britain's global system held sway in Whitehall, Nasser himself adopted the concept, defining Egypt as being at the epicentre of the Arab, Islamic and African circles. One major shift in the context of British policy was the unveiling of the Eisenhower Doctrine in January 1957, which extended US activities overtly into the region, by offering military assistance and economic aid to countries threatened with aggression from any country under Communist influence. The implication of this was that British influence in the Middle East would inevitably be eclipsed by that of Washington. As officials recognized, it was impossible for Britain to compete in the region with the United States, especially in the provision of the investment sought by Middle Eastern countries. Instead, Britain would simply have to accept that it had become the junior partner in managing the West's interests in the region.[16] Nevertheless, the British government continued to believe that its expertise in Middle Eastern affairs far outclassed that of Washington.

British policy, as it evolved early in 1957, reflected the belief that defending Britain's vital strategic and economic interests in the Middle East from a hostile power (in this case the Soviet Union) did not necessitate British dominance in the entire region. What seemed essential, rather, was that Britain should retain its presence in Aden and the Gulf, ensuring the safety of essential communications routes. The best means of achieving this appeared to be to promote Anglo-US co-operation, although there was reluctance in Whitehall to surrender the longstanding British position in Iraq, not least because of its importance as a source of oil.[17] It came as a relief for Macmillan when he met Eisenhower at Bermuda in March 1957 to find that the president disclaimed any US intention of supplanting British influence, but instead suggested joint studies of Middle Eastern problems by London and Washington. One possibility, in London's view, was to try to secure US involvement in the Baghdad Pact, and to persuade Washington to take on part of the region's defence burden previously shouldered by Britain. To the Americans, however, this would be a dangerous strategy, risking the alienation of existing friends, especially Israel (which sought a US guarantee of its security) and Saudi Arabia. Eisenhower, partly from a desire to minimize US defence expenditure in the Middle East, repeatedly reassured London that he saw Britain as still being the paramount power in the region.

Developments during 1957 and 1958 clearly demonstrated that Britain still intended to take decisive steps when necessary to defend its stake in the Middle East. When, in 1957, Omani rebels, backed by Egypt and Saudi Arabia, attempted to oust their pro-British sultan, a successful British intervention was launched, symbolizing in Macmillan's eyes Britain's continuing capacity to play an independent world role. Because of its growing ties with Saudi Arabia, the United States was made uncomfortable by Britain's attitude. When a number of Arab states sought to raise the Oman problem at the United Nations, Washington remained aloof, to Macmillan's irritation. Nevertheless, the episode had shown that Britain could still mount operations on its own initiative, at least on a modest scale.

Compounding London's anxieties about Egyptian influence were developments in Iraq, in which Britain still had an enormous economic and strategic stake. When Britain entered the Baghdad Pact in 1955, its 1930 treaty with Iraq automatically lapsed. Eden had emphasized that the relationship between the two countries was now one of co-operation between equal partners. Nevertheless, all Britain's military requirements were met and Iraq's economy was still dominated by the Iraq Petroleum Company, in which Britain had a major share.

In February 1958, Egypt and Syria announced their fusion in the United Arab Republic. The pro-Western governments of Iraq and Jordan, alarmed by this manifestation of Nasserite radicalism, replied by creating the Arab Federation, and Iraq turned to Washington and London for economic help. Macmillan was willing to promise aid in the event of Iraq's oil pipeline being disrupted by hostilities with Syria. But he was uneasy at the enthusiasm of the Iraqi prime minister, Nuri Said, for Britain to relinquish its protectorate over oil-rich Kuwait, so that the latter could join the Arab Federation. Ever since Iraq's own independence, it had seen itself as the rightful heir to Ottoman suzerainty over Kuwait. Reinforcing this longstanding claim was Baghdad's desire to secure a port of its own on the Gulf and to deal with what was seen as a hot-bed of Nasserite and Communist propaganda.[18] Meanwhile, Nuri's domestic political problems were aggravated by his continuing depiction by radicals as a Western stooge.

The Iraqi Revolution of 14 July 1958, which swept away both the Hashemite monarchy and Nuri Said, Britain's closest ally in the region, was apparently a disaster for Britain's Middle Eastern interests. The coup, seen in London as a victory for Nasserite influence, precipitated a crisis which seemed to London to be potentially of even greater proportions than the events of Suez, and which has been seen as marking the end of Britain's effective imperial presence in the Middle East.[19] Since their treaty of 1930, Iraq's relations with Britain had given London continuing influence in the country, but local rulers had courted popular disapproval by appearing to be British puppets. The key to Iraq's significance was its rapidly growing oil wealth. The Iraq Petroleum Company, owned by a consortium of British, American and Western European interests, not only controlled oil production but set the level of royalties payable to the Iraqi government.[20] Fundamentally, the Iraqi Revolution laid bare the perils facing Britain in cultivating the most desirable collaborating elites to uphold its interests. London had, since Iraq's independence, come to rely on a highly conservative ruling class which, at least since the Second World War, was itself being challenged by socio-economic change and the emergence of new 'middling' interest groups. The fall of the Hashemite monarchy, and its supporters, spelled doom for British influence in the country.[21]

The reactions of neighbouring countries to the coup in Baghdad were predictably anxious. The regimes in both Lebanon and Jordan feared the growth of strident pan-Arab sentiment. Both countries quickly turned to Britain and the United States for assistance against a future military threat from Egypt,

Syria or Iraq. For Britain, Jordan's request was the most pressing problem. Although the kingdom had been independent since 1946, London continued to enjoy influence through advisers, development experts and others. Jordan's young king, Hussein, had to tread carefully because of domestic hostility to links with Britain. It was in response to this pro-Nasser opposition that he had expelled the British commander of the Arab Legion, Glubb, in March 1956. A radical government brought to power following elections in October that year not only sought closer ties with Egypt and the Communist world, but abrogated the Anglo-Jordanian Treaty in March 1957. Increasingly alarmed at the growth of Nasserite influence, domestically and externally, Hussein successfully defused a military coup in the same month, but turned to the United States for assistance. Soon, Washington would become Jordan's most significant Western patron.

The merger of Egypt and Syria, which brought the core of the movement for Arab unity uncomfortably close to Amman, inevitably alarmed Hussein, triggering his interest in a federation with Iraq, then still ruled by his Hashemite cousin, Faisal II. The Arab Federation, dismissed by pro-Nasser elements as a grouping of collaborators with imperialism, led to heightened rivalry in the region. Although Hussein, by now governing under martial law, clamped down severely on radical critics, sympathy for Nasser remained strong in Jordan. Following the Iraqi coup, Macmillan suspected that Hussein might seek Western help, and, anxious to avoid a repeat of Suez and determined to avoid action until assured of US approval, consulted Eisenhower. Fearing an imminent coup, Hussein formally requested British and American help two days after the coup in Baghdad, urging London to intervene militarily in Iraq. Macmillan's government, conscious of the pro-Nasser leanings of many Palestinian refugees in Jordan, however, was willing only to take limited steps, airlifting a total of 4,000 troops from Cyprus to secure the airfield in Amman and the royal palace. The crisis was interpreted by some in Whitehall as presenting an opportunity for joint British–US intervention, testifying to the recovery of the Special Relationship since Suez. Indeed, the crisis of July 1958 was in some sense a retrospective vindication of British ministers' fears of Nasser's generally destabilizing influence in the prelude to Suez. To have failed to provide assistance to Jordan when this was requested would have compromised British pretensions to be both a major power and a credible ally in the region. Moreover, there was the possibility that action over Jordan might help to restore some of the status Britain had lost at the time of Suez.[22] Above all, London was determined that the effects of the Iraqi Revolution should not be allowed to diminish Britain's remaining influence among conservative, pro-Western rulers in the Middle East. However, Washington, already preoccupied with a similar request for help from the Lebanese government, had advised that it would not join Britain in its Jordanian venture. Chiefly for economic reasons, furthermore, London and Washington told Hussein that they planned to recognize the new Iraqi regime of Brigadier Qassem.[23] Relieved that Qassem initially adopted a conciliatory stance, a meeting of the Baghdad Pact in London late in July decided to recognize the regime. The soothing of tensions in the region permitted the uneventful withdrawal of British and US troops during October and November. Although Britain's intervention threatened further to erode the legitimacy of the Amman regime, by highlighting its status as a Western client, growing rivalry between Iraq and Egypt for regional influence would eventually work in Jordan's (and Britain's) favour, with Nasser seeing the wisdom of softening his anti-Hussein rhetoric.[24]

The Jordanian crisis reinforced the central message of the Suez debacle, that not only had the United States succeeded Britain as the major Western power in the Middle East, but also that Britain could no longer mount independent action in the region without Washington's prior approval. Nevertheless, the episode revealed London's continuing determination to safeguard its regional interests. On a practical level, too, the operation had highlighted the value of Cyprus as a platform for limited operations in the Eastern Mediterranean.

As the immediate crisis of July 1958 receded, Britain sought ways of establishing good relations with the new regime in Iraq, partly in an effort to exploit the potential for fissures in Arab nationalism, and so isolate Egypt. At the same time, London could not ignore the possibility that Qassem would pose a threat to Britain's interests in Kuwait. An abortive attempt was made to secure US involvement in plans for the defence of the Gulf. From the middle of 1959 onwards, the Foreign Office even began to explore the possibility of fence-mending with Cairo. More immediately, Whitehall began to formulate plans for British military action to defend Kuwait.[25] The practical consequences of the Iraq coup for Britain were considerable. The federation between Iraq and Jordan was quickly dissolved, and Iraq ceased attending meetings of the Baghdad Pact, the centrepiece of Britain's regional planning, although it did not formally withdraw from the pact until March 1959. More ominously, Baghdad moved swiftly to establish relations with the Soviet Union and China, signalling the new regime's intention to pursue a foreign policy independent of British and Western pressure. On the question of the future of the oil industry, however, Qassem remained enigmatic: it seemed unwise in the early life of the regime to provoke an unnecessary confrontation with external interests, especially since the government drew some 70 per cent of its revenue from the operations of the Iraq Petroleum Company. In the event, the spectre of nationalization receded until the later 1960s.[26]

In June 1961 a fresh threat to British Middle Eastern interests arose when Iraq laid claim to sovereignty over Kuwait, fuelling anxiety that an Iraqi attack on the state might be imminent. By this time, Kuwait was the region's largest producer of oil, and the source of around 40 per cent of Britain's oil. Moreover, Kuwait had in turn invested substantial sums in the British economy. Arguably, Kuwait was Britain's single most important overseas economic interest. In the months preceding Iraq's claim, the ruler of Kuwait had been urging London to grant his emirate independence. Although an agreement was reached terminating Britain's protectorate, it was stipulated that Britain would aid Kuwait militarily if asked to do so. Ironically, this proved to be the trigger for Iraq's claim. To British policy-makers, Kuwait's independence raised the problem that even with a security guarantee from Britain, Kuwait might appear still more attractive to Iraq, and there were doubts in Whitehall over Britain's capacity to repel an entrenched Iraqi invasion force unaided, since the United States had signalled its unwillingness to participate in combined military planning. It was this concern, along with the fear that failure to protect Kuwait would damage British relations with the other Gulf emirates, that led to the large-scale deployment of British forces in Kuwait late in June, in an effort to pre-empt an Iraqi invasion.[27] Involving around 7,000 British troops, with another 3,000 in supporting roles, this was the largest mobilization of British forces in the Middle East in the post-Suez period. This operation, like the intervention in Jordan, highlighted the practical problem of transporting forces though other countries' air space and of keeping them supplied once in position. In this respect, it was fortunate for Britain that on this occasion no direct confrontation with Iraq ensued. As in the case of the Jordanian crisis, it was also deemed essential for London to secure US approval for the use of British force, along with an unambiguous request for intervention from Kuwait's ruler. Washington, concerned about the fate of a state in which there was a substantial US economic interest, was initially supportive of the British intervention, militarily, by offering naval back-up, and diplomatically, at the UN and by interceding on London's behalf with the Saudi government (with which Britain had no relations, owing to the disputed Saudi claim to Omani territory). Nevertheless, Kennedy's administration soon began to question the assumptions on which British action had been planned, especially the likelihood of an Iraqi attack.[28]

Ironically, Iraqi assertiveness was counter-productive within the Arab world, reinforcing the hostility of Nasser towards Qassem already inspired by Baghdad's vigorous suppression of domestic Nasserite opposition. For Nasser, Qassem was squarely to blame for the 'incredible' situation in which British 'imperialists' were once again in Kuwait (although, precisely because of the apparent Iraqi threat, he seemed to acknowledge the motives for Britain's response). Along with Saudi Arabia, Egypt was anxious to prevent Iraq's absorption of Kuwait. During the summer of 1961, support grew (encouraged by both London and Washington) for a local solution to a local problem, one which would obviate UN intervention. In July, Kuwait was admitted to the Arab League, making possible the replacement of British forces by an Arab League security force.

The entire Kuwait episode was important in concentrating minds in Whitehall both on the nature of Britain's interests in the Gulf, and on how best these might be defended. Generally judged a success, the operation was thought in London finally to have laid the ghost of Suez. The military had acquitted itself well, and incorporated the Kuwait experience into wider thinking on Britain's East of Suez role. As the 1962 Defence White Paper explained, it was in the Middle East and the Far East that developments were likely to demand growing British attention. However, British resources had been hard put to fulfil military commitments, and it had been shown that Britain would be unable to manage two simultaneous crises (this would have implications for

London's response to deteriorating conditions in Central Africa). In September 1961 the Cabinet Secretary, Sir Norman Brook, advised Macmillan that it was necessary to reconsider the traditional policy of attempting to meet Britain's oil requirements on the basis of deals with essentially autocratic rulers, underpinned by the promise of British military protection. The number of places in the world where foreign troops were tolerated was dwindling, yet Britain's current policy took 'no account of the rising tide of nationalism in these countries, and, so long as it forces us to support the Sheikhs and Rulers, we are bound to find ourselves, in the end, on the losing side'.[29] Underlining a theme which had already been raised in Whitehall in the early 1950s, the Kuwait crisis was a stark reminder that Britain could no longer hope to safeguard its Middle Eastern interests by using the methods of the nineteenth century.

In Southern Arabia and Aden, meanwhile, Britain's determination to maintain its existing presence was reinforced by the belief, at the heart of the East of Suez policy, that a secure Middle Eastern foothold was essential, preferably one beyond the orbit of Egyptian pan-Arabism. Southern Arabia seemed to fill this requirement, as its highly traditional society seemed to offer barren ground for the cultivation of modern nationalism. The local rulers of the protectorates neighbouring Aden, alarmed by the threat of incursions from Yemen, and by the uncertainties caused by the Iraqi coup, accepted the logic of some form of closer association. Accordingly, in 1959 the British constructed the Federation of South Arabia, to which Aden was subsequently added. Macmillan hoped that this arrangement would dissipate the threat of radicalism in the region.[30] However, the Federation, theoretically under British protection, was in practice soon undermined by a combination of revolutionary fervour in South Yemen and labour unrest in Aden, which erupted into nationalism and violence. In the meantime, this constitutional device was thought to provide Britain with a useful political counterweight in the region, one which might soothe backbench Conservative feeling at a time when the old colonial certainties were being swept away in Africa.[31]

Cyprus

In the aftermath of Suez, Macmillan also concluded that a new course was needed in relation to Cyprus, where British forces had been engaged in a bitter struggle with Greek terrorists since 1955. The available options seemed to be either to partition the island into separate Greek and Turkish zones, or to give it independence in its entirety, in return for which Britain would retain its military bases. Increasingly, however, the Cyprus problem was attracting international interest and, early in 1957, despite Britain's protests, the issue was debated by the United Nations. What emerged was a suggestion that NATO should be invited to mediate in this wrangle between three of its members. As a prelude to a settlement, and at the prompting of the Americans, the Greek Cypriot leader Archbishop Makarios was released from detention, a move which prompted an indignant reaction (and resignation) from Lord Salisbury. Makarios abandoned the aim of *enosis* with Greece and accepted the prospect of independence on Britain's terms, which in turn alienated the leader of EOKA, Grivas. During 1958, escalating communal violence on the island came at a time when the stability of the entire Eastern Mediterranean region was undermined by the effects of the Iraqi coup, which had shattered the Baghdad Pact, and the crises in both the Lebanon and Jordan. As a result, Turkey relaxed its stance and Washington became noticeably more sympathetic to Britain's aims in Cyprus, giving London diplomatic support at the United Nations. International pressure was mounting on both Greece and Turkey to find a compromise. In February 1959, an agreement was concluded between Makarios and the governments of Britain, Greece and Turkey, under which Cyprus would become an independent republic in 1960, and Britain would retain its important bases at Akrotiri and Dhekelia. An important factor persuading Makarios to accept independence and to give up the dream of union with Greece appears to have been the risk that the alternative would be the partition of Cyprus into Greek and Turkish zones. Since he was unable to accept this, a constitutional settlement in which each community would effectively be autonomous, and which was guaranteed by Britain, Greece and Turkey, appeared to be unavoidable.

The Cyprus Agreement reopened the question of whether such a small country (its population was only half a million) could become a full member of the Commonwealth. This broad issue was referred to the 1960 Commonwealth Prime Ministers' meeting. Meanwhile, Macmillan discussed the problem with Iain Macleod, the new Colonial Secretary, and with Home and Brook. Their conclusion was that although Makarios would hardly settle for anything less than full membership, if Cyprus did enter the Commonwealth, 'all the other tiddlers would demand this treatment'. In the event, the Whitehall study group suggested that it would not be consistent with Commonwealth values if smaller territories were denied entry.[32] On its independence, Cyprus accordingly joined the Commonwealth, setting a precedent for the future treatment of the West Indian islands.

In 1962, both Jamaica and Trinidad became independent, effectively sealing the fate of the short-lived Federation of the West Indies, created in 1958. It had been assumed by Britain that the ten territories comprising the Federation would become independent as a single unit which would be both viable politically and financially self-sufficient. Although a conference had been held at Montego Bay in 1947 to explore the possibility of a West Indian federation, it had been thought prudent to allow time for the idea to generate support in the region. During the 1950s, the federal option was confronted by the unexpectedly rapid advance of individual West Indian colonies towards self-government, and by the rate of economic development in both Jamaica and Trinidad and Tobago, which made their separate independence outside the Federation appear feasible. Local rivalries and wrangling over the Federation's financial arrangements were not overcome, and at the beginning of 1960 Macleod made it clear that he would not oppose Jamaica's independence. In September 1961, a referendum in Jamaica opted in favour of leaving the Federation. London accepted this verdict and, in view of the Cyprus precedent,

acknowledged Jamaica's right to separate independence, soon to be followed
by that of Trinidad, which feared that it would be expected to shoulder
financial responsibility for the rest of the Federation. Robbed of its two largest
components, the Federation was doomed, and was formally wound up in May
1962, paving the way for the independence of its components.[33]

The wind of change

In the story of British decolonization, 1959 is pivotal, a year of flux which
paved the way for the intense period of imperial retreat between 1960 and
1964, during which a total of 17 colonies, mostly in Africa, became independent. The speed with which this took place could not have been comprehended
by the official mind of the late 1950s, when many colonial territories were still
considered nowhere near ready for statehood. During 1959, Macmillan was
forced to pay increasing attention to colonial policy, and particularly to the
situation in Africa. For one thing, an election was looming in the autumn, and
the Labour Party was making political capital from some of the problems the
government was experiencing. The declaration of an emergency in Nyasaland
and the revelation in June of atrocities at the Hola detention camp in Kenya
also brought colonial issues into the metropolitan limelight in an intensely
embarrassing manner. Iain Macleod warned Macmillan in May that colonial
policy was the Conservative Party's biggest headache in trying to attract the
electoral middle ground. Arguably because of the broad consensus on economic questions and social policy, the handling of colonial affairs was the one
area on which the government appeared to be vulnerable.[34] Macmillan had to
tread carefully. Colonial policy was a difficult issue, prone to divide the
Conservative Cabinet, and Macmillan's growing desire to speed up decolonization was evidently not shared by Lennox-Boyd or Home, both of whom he
respected.[35] By mid-1959, Macmillan himself was predicting that problems in
Africa were likely to grow in importance. This troubled him because Africa was
one of the few world theatres in which the European powers still had some
direct influence. As he explained to the Foreign Secretary, Selwyn Lloyd, he did
not envisage any 'hasty shift' in policy, but he did think it was necessary to start
planning for the future.[36]

The British government's increased sensitivity over colonial questions was
accompanied by evidence of growing US interest in African affairs. In June
1959, at the request of the US Secretary of State, John Foster Dulles, Macmillan asked the Cabinet Africa Committee to oversee an official survey of the
situation in Africa, to suggest likely developments over the coming decade, and
how to safeguard Western interests in the continent. In the event, this study,
eventually presented as a report entitled 'Africa: the Next Ten Years', broadened to become a basis for British policy, an attempt to clarify Whitehall's own
thinking so as to enable it to retain greater freedom to manoeuvre in the face
of US pressure.[37] For at least one historian, the production of this report
marked the 'real' beginning of the 'wind of change', something which had only
been hinted at in the 'audit' early in 1957.[38]

The inter-departmental report emphasized the risk that the Soviet Union would be keen to encourage independence movements in Africa, vying with the Western bloc to sponsor each ex-colony. This posed a dilemma for Britain. While British reluctance to decolonize might lead African politicians to turn to Moscow (and perhaps, to Cairo), hasty decolonization might create successor states equally vulnerable to Soviet-bloc penetration. Officials concluded that the only effective means of curbing this encroachment would be to install pro-Western, independent regimes composed of co-operative nationalists.[39] The Africa Official Committee had, in its preliminary discussions, already agreed that decolonization was the key to ensuring the desirable objective of a pro-Western (or at least neutral) Africa.[40] The greatest threat to this delicate operation, as officials realized, was the risk of racial conflict, and here the Central African Federation presented the most serious danger. Here, the white settlers, reacting against political change in West Africa and alarmed at the spread of pan-African ideas, sponsored by Nkrumah in Ghana, were seeking independence for the Federation before it came under black majority rule. Already, there were fears in London that Southern Rhodesia, where the settlers were most entrenched, might seize independence unilaterally. With luck, the Federation might, in time, evolve into a genuinely multiracial society, a 'shock-absorber' between apartheid to the south and black nationalism to the north (the latter having been, to some extent, stimulated by the former). One of London's worst fears was that any use of force by the settlers to preserve their position might wreck Western relations with the rest of Africa.[41] It was therefore essential to resolve the problems posed by the settler presence in Central (and East) Africa, otherwise:

> Our past record of benevolent government will be forgotten and it will be the French and perhaps the Belgians who will be regarded by world opinion as the leaders, while we may be classed with the Portuguese as the obstacles to further advance.[42]

As the Colonial Office argued, Britain's overriding aim of maintaining good, close ties with former colonies, and colonies approaching independence, depended on securing and retaining African goodwill. This meant that the problem of resolving the divergent aims of African majorities and settler minorities in Kenya and Central Africa was urgent, not least because failure here might cost Britain the relationship it had managed to preserve in West Africa. London would, in effect, have to prove that it was not committed to propping up white supremacy.[43]

Some of these concerns had already been anticipated in Britain's handling of Nigeria, an instance of decolonization which bridged the official assumptions and preoccupations of the later 1950s and early 1960s. In Nigeria, itself an amalgamation of possessions formed in 1914, a federal constitution had been introduced in 1951, giving each of the territory's three regions its own assembly. It was seen as being to Britain's advantage that Nigerian politics evolved on broadly ethnic lines, giving London the opportunity to capitalize on mutual suspicions between the north and south, and to delay a conference on constitutional change which had been due in 1956. When the conference opened in London early in 1957, Nigerian delegates sought independence by 1959. Lennox-Boyd, temperamentally closer in sympathy to the conservative Muslim elites of the north than to the Westernized population of the south, feared that hasty political change might result in chaos, and possibly the north's secession. Nevertheless, he also recognized that local goodwill had to be preserved if Britain's commercial stake was to be safeguarded. Moreover, obstruction to reform might only serve to unite Nigerian opposition to British rule. Continuing discussions during 1958 revealed apprehension in Whitehall about the likely reaction of South Africa and other Commonwealth members to Nigerian independence, and about the need to secure guarantees over British defence facilities. In October 1958, the British government finally agreed that 1960 should be the target date for the territory's independence. The acceleration of Nigeria's progress to independence appears to have been due more to Britain's response to a growing international mood of hostility to colonialism, and to Cold War considerations, than to the strength of Nigerian nationalism *per se*.[44] As independent Ghana became the champion of pan-Africanism, and shed some of the democratic safeguards bequeathed by Britain, London began to see Kwame Nkrumah as a potential threat to British interests, or, as Lord Home put it in 1959, the 'Nasser' of Black Africa. For this reason, Britain came to see a united, friendly Nigeria as a valuable barrier to possible Ghanaian expansionism. Nevertheless, the strategic guarantees accepted by Britain in the prelude to Nigeria's independence fell short of what the Chiefs of Staff considered adequate; even these guarantees proved, in practice, to be flimsy, and the Federation to which London had attached such importance during the 1950s proved extremely difficult to manage.[45]

It was after his success in the October 1959 general election that Macmillan took decisive steps to alter the course and tempo of colonial policy. Although the broad direction of policy had been established even before Macmillan took office in 1957, it was he who made African decolonization a priority and recognized a growing need to accelerate it. In Macmillan's view, winding up formal colonial rule would not only reinforce Britain's claims to be an enlightened power, one attuned to new international attitudes and vigorous enough to respond to these constructively, but also create a much enlarged Commonwealth, equipped to fulfil a major role in the Cold War.[46] Believing that the Conservatives had only narrowly survived on this issue at the election, he personally took a much greater direct role in discussions than previously, and when he set up a Cabinet Africa Committee, comprising senior ministers, he himself took the chair.[47]

Most important of all, perhaps, was his appointment of Iain Macleod as Colonial Secretary in succession to Alan Lennox-Boyd. Macleod, a radical Tory by temperament, was personally committed to decolonization and keen to promote the political representation of Africans; he soon abandoned the painstaking, evolutionary approach to change until then nurtured by the Colonial Office, working at a brisk pace reminiscent of Mountbatten's style in India.[48] Reputedly not the easiest of colleagues, Macleod held the post of

Colonial Secretary for just two years, becoming Conservative Party chairman in October 1961. He once quipped that he intended to be the last Colonial Secretary.[49] During his tenure, five colonies became independent and steps were taken to prepare another six for majority rule, prompting the initially sympathetic Macmillan to conclude that Macleod had moved a little *too* far in the direction of accommodating African nationalism.[50] Against the background of the Algerian War, war in the Congo, growing racial tension in South Africa and the recent Central African emergency, Macleod was anxious to avoid a bloody confrontation in Africa. A practical, as well as moral, consideration informed this position: Britain did not have the resources to fight protracted colonial wars; moreover, the use of force to tackle nationalist resistance, even if this were practicable, would bring Britain into collision with hostile international opinion, and might even trigger intervention by the UN. Nor could it be assumed that public opinion in Britain would acquiesce in a coercive colonial policy. For Macleod, as for Macmillan, the purpose of decolonization was to preserve as much of Britain's overseas influence as possible, through arrangements acceptable to political elites in the colonies, designed to ensure successor states friendly to the West, not the Soviet bloc. Given the significance traditionally attached by commentators to Macleod's appointment, it is worth bearing in mind that it was balanced by that of the more cautious Duncan Sandys to the Commonwealth Relations Office, a move calculated by Macmillan to reassure Conservative traditionalists.[51]

By the beginning of November 1959, Macmillan had decided to make a visit to Africa. Among the factors influencing his decision were the criticism of government policy made by the former Conservative minister, Enoch Powell, and Macmillan's growing concern about his government's apparent failure to get its message across to the young. Added to these was Macmillan's awareness that the mood of African nationalism was intensifying, and his desire to assess the situation for himself. But it is clear from the views he minuted in December 1959 that he had come to see the white settlers, rather than the African majority, as the major problem facing Britain. Especially in the aftermath of the Devlin Report, which had made highly embarrassing comments on the authorities' handling of unrest in Nyasaland during the Emergency, he was determined to establish effective control over colonial policy, to retain the initiative, and not be dictated to by the settlers.[52]

All of these considerations persuaded him that he needed to act quickly and decisively. His African trip, during January and February 1960, embraced visits to Ghana, Nigeria, the Central African Federation and South Africa. While in West Africa, he assured local leaders of Britain's sympathy with African aspirations.[53] Better known, however, was his attempt while in the Federation, and especially in South Africa, to persuade white settlers to come to terms with the force of African nationalism. Most famously, in February 1960 he addressed the South African parliament in Cape Town, in what was the Union's 50th anniversary year. He talked of a 'wind of change' blowing across Africa, a spirit of nationalism, to which British, and, by implication, South African, policies must respond. He made a thinly veiled attack on South Africa's racial policies, distancing Britain from apartheid. Arguably, he had little to lose: later in the year, South Africa would vote to become a republic, requiring it to re-apply for Commonwealth membership. Among existing members, opposition to South Africa's continued membership grew, with Canada arguing that this would amount to tacit acceptance of apartheid, and candidates in waiting, such as Nigeria and Tanganyika, registering their disapproval. Against this climate, South Africa's own attitudes hardened, and in March 1961 Pretoria withdrew its application for Commonwealth membership. Long regarded as one of the definitive texts of British decolonization, the 'wind of change' speech was in fact an allusion to Stanley Baldwin's 1934 reference to the 'wind of nationalism and freedom blowing around the world'. To critics of the government's handling of colonial affairs, it was a capitulation, and was the direct inspiration in the formation of the Conservative Party's right-wing Monday Club.[54]

For Macmillan, international considerations were vital in shaping the new colonial policy. Given that the overall purpose of Macmillan's government was to preserve Britain's position as a great power, three factors had to be borne in mind. First, Britain could not ignore the precedents in African decolonization set by France and Belgium; secondly, the growth of a vocal bloc of Afro-Asian nations at the United Nations, increasingly the focus for public condemnation of colonialism, was likely to constrain the options for British policy-makers in the future; finally, and perhaps most important, was the need to maintain and develop the special relationship with the United States. Macmillan was person-ally haunted by France's experiences of confronting anti-colonial nationalism in Algeria, and was keen to avoid plunging Britain into similar, possibly unwin-nable, conflicts. He had, briefly, considered the possibility of greater consultation among the European colonial powers, designed to achieve greater co-ordination of their policies, and compensating to some extent for Britain's growing marginalization within Western Europe. Some half-hearted exchanges ensued but, as Lennox-Boyd drily commented, it was half a century too late for such initiatives.[55] The decision of de Gaulle, in 1958, to offer the French colonies autonomy within a new French Community, which led to the precipi-tate independence of a large group of new African states in 1960, inevitably caused agitation in Whitehall, which faced the embarrassing prospect of Britain seeming to be less liberal than France in its policies, and therefore felt under pressure to accelerate British plans. The Belgian decision to give independence to the Congo in 1960 was a similar goad to British action, especially once the new country was plunged into a fratricidal civil war over the secession of copper-rich Katanga Province, a conflict which Macmillan feared would draw in the two superpowers, creating the risk of wider international conflict at a time of deep Cold War tensions. Already by mid-1960, Macmillan was com-paring the Congo to the role Serbia had played in Europe in 1914.[56]

If the international background, involving the behaviour of other colonial powers, the attitudes of the UN and the broad context of the Cold War, provided a vital stimulus to the acceleration of British decolonization after 1959, there were inevitably some who felt that other policy objectives were being sacrificed in the process. As Sir Andrew Cohen (Britain's representative

on the UN Trusteeship Council, and one of the original architects of decolonization) commented in 1961, the emphasis on preventing the spread of
Communism into Africa was conflicting with the Colonial Office's long-
declared aim of preparing colonies for long-term viability after independence.[57]

In line with previous British attitudes, Macmillan's government sought to
avoid UN interference in colonial questions. Believing that anything else might
seem to be a tacit admission that Britain could not manage the process of
decolonization, London maintained its policy of minimum co-operation with
the UN, for example in supplying information on the colonies. Yet it was
becoming increasingly difficult to evade the UN's attention. An important
landmark was the General Assembly's adoption in 1960 of Resolution 1514,
supporting speedy independence for colonial peoples, and its establishment in
1961 of a Special Committee on Decolonization. Henceforward, it was clear
that anti-colonial pressure at the UN could not be resisted indefinitely: it was
increasingly necessary for Britain to stall, to buy time, as Macleod put it, to
enable Britain to take its remaining decisions on decolonization with as little
UN meddling as possible.[58]

Equally important in Macmillan's calculations were American attitudes.
Earlier in the 1950s, Washington had been inclined to view colonialism
pragmatically, suppressing its anti-colonial instincts and viewing colonial rule as
a useful barrier to the spread of Communism in the developing world. This had
caused the US government to fear that premature decolonization might create
opportunities for Soviet penetration. Increasingly evident in Washington's
calculations by the late 1950s, however, was a concern to reconcile the need to
maintain good relations with Western Europe with the need to adapt to the
emergence of Third World nationalism. In post-Suez Britain, there was a
lingering resentment in some quarters (which included Lennox-Boyd) at any
suggestion of US pressure to decolonize before adequate foundations had been
laid. There were still suspicions that Washington's primary motive was economic self-interest. Macmillan, like Churchill himself half-American, was less
troubled by US thinking, but he conceded that US misperceptions of Britain's
colonial policies stood in the way of close relations between London and
Washington. For this reason, he was keen to persuade the Americans that
British policy offered the best opportunity to keep Africa both stable and
within the Western orbit.[59] The arrival of the Kennedy administration in 1961
caused considerable alarm in London: the young president had long been
critical of colonial rule, and sought to forge a new relationship with the Third
World through increased development aid, an identification with the anti-
colonial struggle and US sponsorship of decolonization. Until reined in by the
Pentagon, concerned about its military links with Lisbon, he even offered
assistance to anti-Portuguese freedom fighters in Africa.

East and Central Africa

It was in East and Central Africa that the dramatic shift in British colonial
policy after 1959 was most evident. Amounting to a 'revolution' in policy-

making, the telescoping of constitutional change reflected London's growing belief that the alternative was the risk of a loss of control similar to that experienced in South Asia after 1945.[60] Here, the existence of settler populations precluded the kind of policies already pursued in relation to West Africa. The region also illustrated the fundamental problem confronting policy-makers in London, that the colonial territories could not always be treated individually, in isolation: rather, developments in one territory or country could influence expectations in its neighbours.

Early in 1959, a governors' conference was convened at Chequers to discuss East Africa's prospects, and the first attempt was made to predict tentative dates for independence for the region's three territories. While it was agreed that colonial rule could not continue here indefinitely, it did not seem that all three territories in the region could be treated similarly. Although Uganda and Tanganyika might be candidates for eventual African majority rule, perhaps by the late 1960s, the same could not be said of Kenya where, in London's view, time was needed to encourage the development of a moderate, non-racial political grouping. Lennox-Boyd stated in the Commons in April 1959 that he did not believe that Britain could withdraw from Kenya within a similar timescale. In this case, Macleod's intervention was to be both decisive and most obvious. By early 1960, it seemed that the timetables for political advance confidently drawn up in mid-1959 were already redundant.[61]

In East Africa, it was Tanganyika which led the way. Here, the settler population was relatively small. The territory was a UN Trust, and Britain was accountable to the UN for its administration. Since 1955, the UN had been calling for the creation of an African majority in the legislature. In April 1957, Tanganyika received a new constitution under which 30 of the Legislative Council's 67 members would be elected. Of these 30, ten would be allotted to each of the three principal ethnic groups in the territory. In the subsequent elections held in late 1958/early 1959, Julius Nyerere's Tanganyikan African National Union (TANU) won a resounding victory, taking nine of the African seats, while most of the successful European and Asian candidates were endorsed by TANU. This appeared to be a convincing rejection of the colonial government's aim of fostering multiracialism. Governor Sir Richard Turnbull responded in March 1959 by proposing a new Council of Ministers, in which the majority would still be officials, and the appointment of a committee to investigate further constitutional changes. In keeping with the broad thrust of the Chequers meeting, he expected an 'unofficial' majority to be achieved in or around 1965. Turnbull's fear was that too leisurely a process of reform, without major concessions to TANU, would undermine Nyerere's position, exposing him to threats from more 'extreme' rivals. The Colonial Office, in turn, feared that the governor would be led to propose much more rapid political advance than was currently being contemplated, which would upset London's long-term plans for the whole of East Africa. By May, Turnbull was warning London of the elected members' solidarity in calling for constitutional reform, and of TANU's trans-racial appeal. By bringing Nyerere into the government, following fresh elections and the creation of a slim 'unofficial' majority in the

Council of Ministers, he hoped to secure TANU's support for the colonial government's broad programme. Under Lennox-Boyd, however, the Colonial Office remained cautious, but it was extremely difficult for London to oppose quicker progress towards self-government for Tanganyika merely in order to pre-empt similar demands elsewhere in the region. On the other hand, granting significant concessions to Tanganyika would make it difficult to offer more modest proposals to Kenya.

In this respect, the appointment of Macleod in October 1959 helped to clear the policy impasse. Macleod, who met Nyerere during his East African trip late in 1959, had been impressed with the African leader. The new Colonial Secretary, free of his predecessor's inhibitions, resolved to press ahead with reforms in Tanganyika while determining to combine these with a major step forward on Kenya early in 1960.[62] Only weeks after assuming his new office, Macleod told his Cabinet colleagues that the Colonial Policy Committee had endorsed his plans for constitutional reforms in Tanganyika. These would give the territory a wider franchise and a government which, by 1960, would contain an African majority. Following fresh elections in 1960, Nyerere became chief minister, and followed an unobstructed path to full independence at the end of 1961. An important consideration in Colonial Office calculations had been a desire to prevent post-independence Tanganyika drifting towards a more authoritarian political system, and, by exchanging control for influence, to encourage Nyerere to work closely with Britain.[63]

In Uganda, the situation was more complex, because of the territory's marked regionalism, although it was spared the additional complication of a large white settler community. The fact that Uganda was primarily an 'African' state had been acknowledged by London since at least 1953. The chief obstacle to decolonization proved to be the determination of the Kingdom of Buganda to preserve its distinctive and privileged position within the territory. In 1959, direct democratic elections to the legislature had been proposed, but this had prompted resistance, and a refusal to co-operate, by the Baganda elite. Macleod broke this stalemate early in 1960 by announcing that elections would be held in 1961, to be followed by a constitutional conference on Uganda's future. Uganda's political elites were faced with the choice either of extending their appeal on a national basis, or becoming identified with much narrower regional interests. While the Uganda People's Congress, led by Milton Obote, emerged as the focus for nationalism, the conservative Baganda marked their disapproval of political centralization by shunning the elections held in March 1961, setting a dangerous precedent for the future. Macleod, however, insisted that Baganda regionalism would not be permitted to distract the broad thrust of policy, and in September 1961 the constitutional conference was attended by a Baganda delegation still hoping to achieve some sort of federal settlement.

The first elections had been held in 1958, and in 1961 elections based on universal suffrage were held, leading to the Executive Council coming under an African chief minister. In 1962, after full internal self-government had been achieved, fresh elections saw Milton Obote emerge as the political leader who would, later that year, take Uganda to full independence. Here, Britain pursued the aim of forcing the Kingdom of Buganda into a unitary state. After 1959, this was finally abandoned, and, as a compromise, a federal system was grafted on to Uganda, giving Buganda semi-autonomous status.

Of all the East African territories, Kenya would pose Britain the greatest difficulty because of its settler population. The most economically developed of Britain's East African territories, it was seen as the potential core of a future regional federation. Moreover, in the wake of Suez, the territory had become even more valuable in London's eyes as a key strategic base conveniently located for the defence of both the Middle East and the Indian Ocean. In Kenya, British policy had been to encourage the development of multiracial politics. This, along with the economic reforms embodied in the Swynnerton Plan, was intended to obstruct 'extreme' African elements seeking African majority rule on the basis of 'one man one vote' (OMOV). Meanwhile, African political movements were permitted only at a local level. London remained confident that its policy was not only right but the only course likely to avoid the disintegration of the territory. More generally, London was unwilling to modify its commitment to multiracialism in Kenya in case this jeopardized the prospects for its parallel ambitions for the development of Central Africa.[64] Late in 1957, Lennox-Boyd unveiled a new constitution for Kenya. Its aim was to increase African representation in the Legislative Council, leading eventually to parity with European representation, though with Europeans still occupying half the posts in government. Accompanying this change was the statement, which in retrospect betrayed a remarkable confidence, that there would be no further adjustments to the territory's political representation for the next ten years. Meanwhile, there was mounting evidence that Africans had become impatient with the promise of 'multiracialism', and in November 1958, all the African members of the legislature boycotted its sittings in support of their demand for majority rule. Crucially, London's approach before 1959 had failed to grasp that, in order to claim any kind of 'authentic' voice, Kenyan African politicians could co-operate in the multiracial experiment only if this was a temporary stage on the road to eventual majority rule.[65]

Early in 1959, Kenya was still technically in a state of emergency, and the African leader Jomo Kenyatta still languished in detention. It was in March that politically devastating revelations were made of the extent to which the colonial authorities' campaigns against Mau Mau had degenerated into brutality. Since the declaration of the Emergency, attempts had been made to 'rehabilitate' Mau Mau detainees. Faced with a growing number of unrepentant fighters, the authorities came under pressure to speed up this process. An 'unofficial policy' developed under which psychological pressure escalated all too easily into physical violence. On 3 March (ironically, the same day that an emergency was declared in Nyasaland), 11 detainees were beaten to death by their guards at Hola detention camp. When this became public knowledge, Labour MPs at Westminster were appalled, many Conservatives were shocked, and there were demands for an enquiry. The then Colonial Secretary, Lennox-Boyd, offered to resign, but this was rejected by the Cabinet. According to Macleod, it was this incident more than anything else which triggered the government's fundamental reappraisal of African policy.[66] Particularly embarrassing for the government was the condemnation of the Hola affair by the Conservative ex-minister, Enoch Powell, especially his damaging claim that standards of public conduct expected in Britain were being flouted in the African colonies.[67]

Earlier in 1959, considerably in advance of Macleod's arrival at the Colonial Office, there were already signs that important constitutional changes might come sooner rather than later. In April, while Lennox-Boyd was pondering the wisdom of making a public endorsement of the goal of eventual majority rule, a 'moderate' settler leader, Michael Blundell, formed a new political party, the New Kenya Group, committed to multiracialism, and enjoying support from the business community. From the colonial government's point of view, this made the NKG the ideal preferred candidate, and it seemed vital to do nothing to obstruct the development of a valuable counterweight to African nationalism. In the event, Lennox-Boyd's April 1959 statement suggested that a time could not yet be foreseen when colonial rule in Kenya could safely be ended. Meanwhile, a conference on Kenya's future was planned for 1960.[68] It was in preparation for this conference that the African members of the legislature succeeded, late in 1959, in temporarily setting aside their differences in order to present a common front in demanding both majority rule and the release of Jomo Kenyatta. For the Colonial Office, which had hoped that fractures among African nationalists would create openings for the NKG, this came as an unpleasant surprise.

Once the Mau Mau Emergency had been dealt with effectively, Britain arguably had much greater leverage over Kenya. Not only had the immediate threat to stability apparently been neutralized, but there had been gratifying developments among sections of the settler community. This group, whose size had trebled since 1945, had been diluted steadily by the entry of government officials and businessmen who lacked the strong sense of identification with the Kenyan soil displayed by their aristocratic and upper-middle class predecessors, and were quicker to learn the central lesson that Mau Mau had definitively exploded settler claims to control the colonial state. But London's policy-makers remained reluctant to impose radical change on the territory, partly because of the likely reactions in South Africa and Southern Rhodesia, but also because of the electoral consequences this might have at home, where settler leaders were well connected and maintained a vocal presence. After the October 1959 general election, this was a less dangerous problem for Macmillan, as the Conservative backbenches received an influx of younger MPs, less emotionally committed to symbols of empire than their predecessors.

Here again, Macleod's role was decisive. Having visited Kenya late in 1959, he ended the seven-year-old Emergency and at the Lancaster House Conference held at the beginning of 1960, called for the creation of an African elected majority in the Legislative Council, along with equal representation for Africans and non-Africans in the Executive Council, effectively abandoning London's earlier attempts to protect settler privileges and thereby arousing backbench Conservative fears that the 'kith and kin' were being betrayed. Terminating the Emergency may not have been an entirely disinterested gesture by London.

Since June 1959, Governor Baring of Kenya had been making a compelling case for this, along with a general amnesty, as a means of forestalling further embarrassing revelations of brutality towards detainees.[69] Nevertheless, the momentum initiated by Macleod culminated in Tanganyika, Uganda and Kenya becoming independent in 1961, 1962 and 1963 respectively, outcomes which had been inconceivable in 1959.[70] In the drive to appease African opinion, as Macleod told Macmillan in February 1960, the timescales for political change considered practicable in mid-1959 had simply been overtaken by events in East Africa, and, above all, in the Congo.[71] Nor did it seem feasible to withhold from Kenya the kind of political concessions already being proposed for neighbouring Tanganyika and Uganda: to do so would court hostile international comment and risk alienating 'co-operative' Africans. At the Lancaster House Conference, Macleod won African acceptance of a new constitution which promised to provide Africans with 33 out of the 65 elected seats in the legislature, based on a much expanded franchise. With the Colonial Office repeating the 1923 Devonshire formula that Kenya was, after all, a predominantly African country, a clear message was being sent to the territory's nationalist politicians: those who were willing and able to operate the new political system could, in time, expect to achieve their cherished goal of majority rule.

In addition to these elaborate constitutional manoeuvres, steps were being taken to reinforce Kenyan political stability within a more secure economic framework, designed to remove some of the more obvious sources of African (particularly Kikuyu) grievance which had originally helped to trigger Mau Mau. The British government found enough money to purchase around 186,000 acres of land in the prized White Highlands, for redistribution among African farmers, the aim being the fostering of a vigorous class of capitalist farmers. An important subsidiary aspect of this scheme was that it enabled those settler farmers unable to adapt to political change in the territory to move on without incurring great financial loss.

Nevertheless, until a late stage, British policy-makers clung to their hopes for multiracialism in Kenya. They saw in Blundell's New Kenya Group an ideal partner, and one which offered a middle way between African nationalism and settler intransigence. A new constitution, introduced in 1961, was meant to promote the growth of the New Kenya Group, and subsequently of the Kenyan African Democratic Union (KADU), with which the NKG merged. Two major African parties emerged, the Kenyan African National Union (KANU), composed chiefly of the Kikuyu and Luo and set on early independence, and KADU, representing many of the remaining African peoples of Kenya. In the 1961 elections, KANU received twice as many votes as KADU, but used the issue of Kenyatta's continuing detention to demonstrate its authentic nationalist credentials, and refused to take office until he had been released. This remained a deeply sensitive issue, Kenyatta having been described by the governor, Sir Patrick Renison, as recently as 1960 as a 'leader to darkness and death', and Macleod, sensitive to criticism from the right wing of his own party, refused to release him.[72]

KADU managed to form an interim coalition government with the support of the NKG, but having no wish to be outdone by KANU in its espousal of nationalist demands, it too began to campaign for Kenyatta's release. Following a fresh resignation threat by Macleod, this was eventually secured in August 1961, helping to calm a tense political climate, and Kenyatta shortly afterwards became a member of the Legislative Council. The pace of change in Kenya did not slacken after Macleod had been replaced in October 1961 by Reginald Maudling (who, perhaps to Macmillan's dismay, soon proved to be 'plus noir que les nègres'). New adjustments to the constitution were introduced in January 1962, which, by creating regional assemblies, were intended to benefit KADU, and prevent KANU achieving an unassailable political position. In April, encouraged by Britain, which sought to reduce possibly destabilizing tribal tensions, KANU and KADU formed a coalition, in which Kenyatta became minister for constitutional affairs and economic planning, to oversee the final stages of devolution by Britain. As in other earlier situations, the British found that once they had unleashed electoral politics, their outcome was difficult to predict. Kenyatta and KANU were simply more effective than their rivals in exploiting the new constitutional framework. Following another election in 1963, in which KANU secured a convincing majority, Kenyatta became prime minister and Kenya received full internal self-government, the prelude to independence in December 1963. This was a radically different outcome to the one London had fondly thought practicable just four years previously.[73] Yet this shift in British policy need not be seen as an abrupt decision to abdicate power in East Africa: rather, it may more accurately be depicted as an attempt by London to keep control, against the background of rapid local and international change, by offering concessions to groups who appeared willing and able to co-operate to safeguard fundamental British interests.[74]

In the short term, decolonization in Kenya had successfully resolved what had been seen as a difficult colonial problem, yet the 'safeguards' engineered by Britain in its retreat proved flimsy. The attempt to avoid a strongly centralized, Kikuyu-dominated state, did not long survive independence, and KANU emerged as not only the dominant, but eventually the only, party. Land redistribution, although initially successful, gave way to the re-selling of land to wealthier farmers, leaving agricultural labourers and squatters without land little better off than before Mau Mau. Finally the Asian community, the third putative component of London's projected multiracial Kenya, was left vulnerable to post-independence pressure for the Africanization of their interests, although those Kenyan Asians who at independence had opted to retain British citizenship theoretically had the right of entry into Britain.

The Central African Federation

In the phase of rapid decolonization ushered in by the 'wind of change', the most difficult problems confronting Britain emerged in Central Africa. Here, African opposition to the Federation of Rhodesia and Nyasaland, gathering pace since the latter's inception, gained momentum after 1957, when London had endorsed constitutional changes clearly intended to reinforce settler political privileges over the African majority, even though the local 'watchdog', the African Affairs Board, had objected to these. This not only cast doubts on the sincerity of the multiracial ideal, still being espoused by Britain, but inevitably fuelled African fears of becoming trapped permanently in a white-ruled, self-governing nation. These fears were expressed in increasingly effective political mobilization, drawing on Africans' experience of trade unionism, especially among mineworkers. An equally alarming signal of hardening settler attitudes came early in 1958 when the reform-minded prime minister of Southern Rhodesia, Garfield Todd, was ousted by his own United Federal Party. The reluctance of the federal authorities to share political power with the African majority was demonstrated early in 1958 when the federal prime minister, Sir Roy Welensky, denounced proposals for a slight increase in African representation in Northern Rhodesia, arguing that this would generate support for the (racist) Dominion Party. London, however, felt that it could not stand in the way of such modest reform, on the grounds that resistance might be counter-productive. Later in 1958, the Commonwealth Relations Secretary, Lord Home, identified the dilemma facing Britain as a result of the irreconcilable commitments it had entered into with respect to the Federation. On the one hand, Britain had, in the wake of the Gold Coast's independence in 1957, led Salisbury to believe that the Federation would achieve independence by 1960. On the other hand, the British government had promised in 1953 that the protected status of Northern Rhodesia and Nyasaland would not be rescinded without their populations' agreement. It was this second pledge which Home believed might have to be reinterpreted, in favour of the Federation.[75] London remained firmly committed to the federal experiment, and, in theory, to the goal of a multiracial 'partnership', a 'middle way' between the unacceptable extremes of African and settler nationalism. At this stage, however, Macmillan was apparently yet to be convinced that policy regarding the treatment of the African population required revision: his priority was to avoid action unacceptable to the federal government, which might endanger Britain's regional interests. Rather, London continued to pin its hopes on the very gradual extension of political rights to Africans who satisfied educational and property qualifications, a process which would eventually modify settler political dominance.

However, evidence of deep-seated African discontent began to surface before the end of 1958. In the middle of the year, the political activist Dr Hastings Banda, who had spent the years since 1953 living in Ghana, returned home to Nyasaland to assume the leadership of the Nyasaland African Congress and its anti-federal campaign. Disturbances erupted in the territory in October, prompting demands from local settlers for a general tightening of security. When fresh unrest gripped the territory in January 1959, the federal authorities began to consider the possibility of creating a pretext to remove Banda from Nyasaland. Intelligence gathered by the Federal Special Branch supposedly indicated that Banda's African National Congress was plotting an insurrection against the small European population. Accordingly, when violence again broke out in the territory, the Southern Rhodesian government declared an emergency, while shortly afterwards, Governor Armitage of Nyasaland, a veteran of the conflict in Cyprus, initiated Operation Sunrise, and the widespread detention of African political leaders, including Banda, and their supporters began.[76] Similarly tough measures were taken against African nationalists in Northern Rhodesia.

The declaration of a state of emergency, however, meant that there would have to be an official investigation. The resulting Devlin Report, which made embarrassing references to the 'police state' operating in Nyasaland during the emergency, and which Macmillan privately feared might bring down his government, made clear to London the risks of allowing local settlers to keep the initiative, and, along with the revelations of brutality at the Hola Camp in Kenya and France's abrupt decision to decolonize, seems to have convinced Macmillan of the need to establish clear British control over the situation in Central Africa. This led to the appointment of a review commission, chaired by the senior Conservative politician, Sir Walter Monckton.

For Welensky, the forthcoming review of the Federation's constitution seemed bound to result in a smooth progress towards self-government, without any fundamental redrawing of the existing electoral arrangements or challenge to white predominance. Continuing evidence of African opposition was dismissed by him as simple treason against a remarkable experiment which had patently brought material progress to all. Meanwhile, constructing the advisory commission on the constitution, and determining its frame of reference, proved no less controversial than the Federation itself. Welensky was adamant that any concession which allowed for the secession of components of the Federation was unacceptable. The British government appeared to endorse this view when it proposed that the commission ought to assume that the Federation was desirable, and should merely advise on any necessary modifications to its constitution. The Labour Party in turn found this constrained remit objectionable, and refused to participate in the commission.

Like Macleod, Macmillan became convinced that the survival of the Federation, whose uncertain political future was affecting local business confidence, depended on constitutional reform in Nyasaland.[77] While making a leisurely, sea-borne, progress home from South Africa early in 1960, Macmillan, responding to Macleod's advice (and fresh threats of resignation), agreed to the release of the obviously popular Banda from detention to give evidence to the Monckton Commission, which had arrived at Victoria Falls in February 1960. This move had enormous implications, effectively being an endorsement of Banda and his aims, and an implicit recognition that in the wake of the Devlin Report, the use of coercion against Nyasaland nationalists was no longer an option. Perhaps a true turning point in the history of decolonization, this has been seen as the moment at which the fate of the Central African Federation was decided.[78]

The Monckton Commission's report, delivered to Macmillan in September 1960, clearly reflected the extent of African hostility to the Federation. Most members of the Commission accepted that the Federation had an economic rationale, but believed it could not continue in its existing form. Stressing the importance of demonstrating that the multiracial ideal could be made to work in African conditions, they recommended measures designed to win African approval for the Federation, including equal representation in the Federal Assembly, as well as constitutional change at the territorial level aimed at creating African legislative majorities. The report also acknowledged that London retained the power to hear requests for secession by individual territories, and called on the government to state that it would do so. Although the Monckton Commission gave Macleod and Macmillan the justification they needed to push through constitutional reforms, its comments on secession had to some extent been anticipated by developments on the ground. A constitutional conference on Nyasaland had already met in London in July 1960, at which the territory's legislature had been given an African majority. Given that Banda was committed to secession, and that he seemed likely to do well in the elections scheduled for 1961, the prospects for federal cohesion were not promising. In a manner mirroring Britain's experience in East Africa, it would become evident that discussion of constitutional change in one territory could not be safely 'contained', but inevitably reverberated on the other two federal territories.

Banda was committed to Nyasaland's secession from the Federation, and in summer 1960, Nyasaland's legislature achieved an African majority. Elections in the following year brought Banda to power on a clearly secessionist platform. In November 1962, it was decided that Nyasaland would attain full internal self-government, and with it the right to secede. When fresh elections in 1963 confirmed Banda as prime minister, there could be little doubt as to the course he would choose.

For the Federation's prime minister, Sir Roy Welensky, the loss of Nyasaland would be unfortunate: unthinkable was that copper-rich Northern Rhodesia, the Federation's economic dynamo, should be lost as well. It was the future of this northern territory, and the review of its constitution announced by Macleod in October 1960, that brought Salisbury into growing conflict with London. Following Macmillan's trip to Africa in 1960, and his off-the-cuff comment that the populations of the northern territories would be given the chance to decide on their membership of the Federation, Welensky had developed suspicions that the British government might be prepared to see the Federation disintegrate if this were the price of appeasing African nationalism.[79] Relations were not improved by the abortive Federal Review Conference, which opened in London in December 1960, only to produce formal, set-piece position statements by the delegates, which inevitably provoked confrontation and a sterile adjournment, allowing separate initiatives to be produced on constitutional reform in Northern and Southern Rhodesia. At talks on the Northern Rhodesian constitution in January 1961, further stalemate emerged when settler leaders walked out, unable to agree with the British side on the kind of concessions which could 'safely' be offered to African nationalists. In February 1961, Macleod, who had concluded that

Kenneth Kaunda's United National Independence Party (UNIP) was the most sympathetic partner in reform, and who was committed to ultimate majority rule for the territory, proposed equal representation for Africans in the Northern Rhodesian legislature. This provoked a furious response from Welensky, who was determined to protect settler interests in the territory, and Salisbury mobilized troops, supposedly to deal with 'eventualities', but rumours abounded that a military coup was being contemplated by the federal authorities. Britain in turn responded by readying its forces in Kenya, but doubts surfaced about the willingness of some British officers to engage with their Rhodesian kith and kin. The Cabinet in London was bitterly divided over Northern Rhodesia, Macleod once again threatened to resign, and settler groups successfully exploited their contacts with the right wing of the Conservative Party (especially Lord Salisbury, who famously denounced Macleod for being 'too clever by half') and the Beaverbrook press, to put pressure on the government. Over 100 Westminster MPs signed an early-day motion, urging the government to abandon its plans for majority rule. During the entire process of decolonization, it was over the question of Northern Rhodesian constitutional reform early in 1961 that the Conservative Party came closest to splitting apart.[80] In June 1961, London responded to these various pressures with revised constitutional proposals, this time designed to secure a small settler majority. Perhaps predictably, violence erupted and further talk of reform was postponed. Coinciding with Britain's large-scale commitment of troops to Kuwait, the Northern Rhodesian disturbances were particularly worrying for London.[81]

Meanwhile, in self-governing Southern Rhodesia, where violence late in 1960 had demonstrated African anti-federal sentiment, prime minister Sir Edgar Whitehead was persuaded to introduce a marginally more liberal constitution, giving Africans greater, though still unequal, representation. Prior to this, in 1959, Whitehead had asked London to remove its remaining restrictions on full self-government for Southern Rhodesia. This was a delicate issue, as Home pointed out to the Cabinet Africa Committee. With the report of the Monckton Commission still pending, if Britain were to announce that it was giving up its residual powers to intervene in the territory's affairs, the African population might deduce that power was effectively being handed over to the white minority, and that this was London's intention for the entire Federation.[82]

Whitehead, who had responded to earlier unrest by introducing tough security measures, hoped to win enough African support, through a package of relatively liberal social policy measures, to enable him to negotiate full independence from Britain. These reforms, which included the prohibition of some aspects of racial discrimination and would involve repeal of the Land Apportionment Act (which gave white settlers a disproportionate share of the territory's most productive farm land), were part of a strategy to detach middle-class Africans from support for nationalism, and win their collaboration with 'liberal' settler elements. In the event, Whitehead's comparative liberalism failed to convince many enfranchised Africans (most of whom boycotted the

October 1962 elections, ironically helping to seal Whitehead's fate), while it infuriated white settlers, driving many of them towards the brand of 'populist nationalism' represented by the right-wing Rhodesian Front, led by Winston Field.

In February 1962, London unveiled its new constitution for Northern Rhodesia, this time along lines similar to those already established for Nyasaland, with the prospect of an African legislative majority following elections in October. With the precedent of the two northern territories before them, settlers in Southern Rhodesia increasingly argued that their independence, too, should be built upon the constitutional foundations devised early in 1961, even though these denied a political voice to the African majority. This remained the stumbling block in discussions between London and the territorial government in Salisbury.

Increasingly despairing of Central Africa and the domestic, African and international problems to which it exposed his government, Macmillan persuaded his loyal deputy, R.A. Butler (one of the handful of British ministers in whom Welensky still appeared to have some confidence) to accept the 'poisoned chalice' of responsibility for the Federation and what seemed inevitably to be its obsequies. Butler started from the premise that, while continuing political association between its components was unrealistic, some form of economic relationship might be possible. In the event, elections in both the Rhodesias in October 1962 brought to power governments openly opposed to continued membership of the Federation, to London's despair. There was little further point in withholding the right of individual territories to secede from the Federation (though it might be argued that the release of Banda in 1960 had made this outcome inevitable all along). Tacitly accepted in May, Banda's right to secede was confirmed in December 1962. In March of the following year, as expected, the new nationalist coalition government in Northern Rhodesia sought, and was given, the right to secede. Given that by then, Southern Rhodesia was being governed by politicians now intent on their own separate independence, there remained little to do but inter the Federation with whatever dignity was possible. A conference, held at Victoria Falls in summer 1963, divided up the Federation's assets among its three constituents, some observers noting with concern that the lion's share of the Federation's considerable military resources went to Southern Rhodesia, arguably equipping its government to take an increasingly intransigent line in its dealings with London. At the end of the year, the Federation, which had been created with such hopes in 1953, was formally terminated, representing yet another reversal for British policy. Northern Rhodesia and Nyasaland achieved independence in 1964, but given the extent of Southern Rhodesia's African opposition, there could be no question of this territory receiving independence on the terms of the constitution introduced in 1961. The Rhodesian problem remained unresolved by the time the Conservative government fell from power in 1964.

Europe

As discussed in the previous chapter, Britain's response to the Messina Powers' efforts to advance the cause of Western European integration had been proposals to form an alternative to the European Economic Community, namely the European Free Trade Association (EFTA). Although some observers, committed to the Common Market ideal, tended to see EFTA as a classic British 'spoiling tactic', the alternative view, promoted by Britain, was that true European integration could only be based on free trade, and that this was something which the Six would eventually discover for themselves. Meanwhile, EFTA appealed to British policy-makers because London, rather than Paris or Bonn, would be in the driving seat.[83] In November 1959, Britain, along with Denmark, Norway, Sweden, Austria, Switzerland and Portugal, signed an agreement in Stockholm under which they would form EFTA by July 1960. Meanwhile, a growing number of British manufacturers seemed to be won over to the EEC because of the protection it offered, especially after Imperial Preference had effectively been outlawed by the General Agreement on Tariffs and Trade.[84]

Historians sometimes speak of a 'revolution' in British foreign policy during the summer of 1960, during which the British government decisively turned its face towards Europe. Certainly, Macmillan chose this time to place pro-European ministers in key positions, including the Ministry of Agriculture, Fisheries and Food (MAFF) and the Commonwealth Relations Office. Edward Heath, a committed Europhile, was made responsible for European affairs. Early in his negotiations, Heath ascertained that the Six would not accept 'association' between Britain and the Common Market: instead, they insisted on full adherence to the Treaty of Rome.

During 1961, a number of missions were sent to Commonwealth countries to discuss British entry into Europe. Most Commonwealth leaders were surprisingly willing at least to wait and see if acceptable terms could be secured. This allowed Macmillan to reassure his own supporters that Commonwealth interests were being taken into consideration.[85] By the middle of 1961, London had won the acquiescence (if not much more) of both the Commonwealth and EFTA to begin negotiations on entry into the EEC.

Macmillan's motives during 1960 and 1961 were varied. Determined to create a distinctive international role for Britain, he had pursued the idea of a major East–West summit conference of the four powers. With Eisenhower's approval, a summit was arranged for May 1960, to be held in Paris. This disintegrated in acrimony when a US spy plane was shot down over the Soviet Union. Caught between the two superpowers, who were plunged into mutual recrimination, Britain's role appeared to be redundant, and its attempts at mediation futile. Macmillan was personally shaken by this abrupt reminder of the reality of Britain's diminished status, and this may have influenced his conclusion that Britain's future might have to lie in an integrated Western Europe, culminating in Britain's formal application, in July 1961, to join the EEC.[86] The timing of the shift in London's thinking on Europe may also partly explain the acceleration in Britain's decolonizing activity at this time. On the assumption that Britain would succeed in joining the EEC, it was important that Britain's standing should not be jeopardized by its becoming embroiled in a series of colonial conflicts.[87]

Another important background influence in London's conversion to support for entry into Europe was the theme, recurrent in the late 1950s and early 1960s, of the need to modernize Britain, and equip its economy to compete effectively in the world. Politically, as Macmillan recognized, this was an awkward subject. For a prime minister who had made much political capital as the kind of 'One-Nation' Tory who had not forgotten the impact of the inter-war Depression, or its effects in his north-east constituency, the economic discipline and deflationary climate which modernization might require were unacceptable. Macmillan's reluctance to impose unpalatable solutions led eventually to the resignation of his Treasury team early in 1958. Exposing Britain to the Common Market's competitive environment might, however, achieve the same ends, while softening the inevitable consequences, including unemployment, and so be less politically damaging to the government.[88] No longer able to shelter behind the Sterling Area, Britain's managers and workers would have to update both their practices and their general attitudes.

Understandably, within the EEC there were some who were inclined to question the depth of Britain's conversion to the ideal of integration, partly because London so obviously remained committed to a role beyond Europe. Here, in particular, the importance attached by Britain to an East of Suez presence was suggestive.[89]

In July 1961, Macmillan announced in the Commons that the British government was investigating whether acceptable terms for Britain's entry into the EEC could be found. In this sense, his position was cautious: he did not state explicitly that Britain should join the EEC. Nevertheless, he emphasized the risk of Britain becoming isolated, but also rejected the idea of federalism. His prime motive seems to have been that only by joining Europe could Britain be sure of reinforcing its special ties with the United States. Washington had been an enthusiastic supporter of the Common Market, and had made no attempt to disguise its indifference to EFTA. Moreover, the Kennedy administration had come to see British entry as a useful counterbalance to the influence of France and West Germany in Western Europe, and had been at pains to reassure Macmillan that joining the Common Market would, if anything, strengthen rather than dilute the bonds between London and Washington.[90] Macmillan's European bid can, therefore, be seen as an ambitious attempt to reconcile the objectives of closer ties with both Washington and Europe, without damaging the Commonwealth relationship.

Similarly, the British government's emphasis that membership of the EEC was not incompatible with Britain's Commonwealth links was, as John Darwin has put it, 'more than just an empty platitude'. On the contrary, it was based on the belief, at the heart of Churchill's world-view, and preserved by Macmillan, that the trick was to maintain a balance between Britain's roles in the 'three circles', and that these were interdependent and complementary.[91] Nevertheless, the whole question of British entry was a thorny issue in metropolitan politics. Not only were elements of the Conservative Party, backed by the Beaverbrook press, implacably opposed to any weakening of the Commonwealth nexus, but the Labour Opposition, under Hugh Gaitskell, argued that entering the EEC on the terms Macmillan seemed willing to accept would not only rob Britain of its independence, but destroy the Commonwealth too.[92]

Negotiations began in earnest in September 1961. By then, Heath was able to reveal the extent of the shift in British official thinking. London now claimed to accept the major elements of the Treaty of Rome, including a common external tariff, a common commercial policy and a common agricultural policy. Nevertheless, Britain was still seeking concessions reflecting its special requirements in relation to the Commonwealth, EFTA and British farmers, to cover a 'transitional' period, possibly lasting 15 years. By the summer of 1962, the situation seemed hopeful, with broad agreement having been reached on most Commonwealth food imports. Later that year, however, the discussions entered a more difficult phase concerning British agriculture, and the fact that the EEC was holding out for the adoption of its price support mechanisms. Even so, there was widespread optimism that these obstacles could, in time, be resolved.

In the event, British hopes were shattered in January 1963 when de Gaulle announced, at a press conference, that Britain was not qualified to enter the EEC because its interests were fundamentally extra-European, and in particular that it was too closely bound to the United States. To de Gaulle, who saw the EEC as a vehicle for the reassertion of French hegemony in Western Europe, Britain was little more than an American 'Trojan horse'. It appeared that longstanding French resentments might be bearing fruit, to Britain's disadvantage. On the day on which the abortive Suez campaign had been brought to a halt, the West German Chancellor, Konrad Adenauer, had allegedly observed to his aggrieved French counterpart, Guy Mollet, 'Europe will be your revenge.'[93] The implication that Britain's responsibilities in the wider world disqualified it from entry into Europe may, it has been suggested, have provided a further incentive to London to accelerate its remaining programme of decolonization.[94]

Losing an empire, finding a role?

Meanwhile, determining what Britain's world role was to be remained a sensitive issue for Macmillan's government. Late in 1962, the former US Secretary of State, Dean Acheson, commented that 'Great Britain has lost an Empire and has not yet found a role'. Significantly, this remark ruffled the feathers of members of the Conservative Party, some of whom had already been unsettled by the pace of decolonization and the apparent shift towards Europe. It was fortunate for Macmillan that he had not had to face simultaneous crises arising from his decolonizing policy. He was also, arguably, fortunate that right-wing dissent within his own party was blunted by the fact that Lord Salisbury, the obvious focus of dissent, had left the Cabinet in 1957 in disgust at the government's handling of the Cyprus question, robbing the right wing of a natural leader. Equally, the 'die-hard' vision of a white-run Commonwealth had been dealt a fatal blow in 1961 when South Africa was excluded, despite Macmillan's attempts at conciliation. This foreshadowed the Commonwealth's increasingly independent handling of the problem of apartheid, a policy which would in future years leave Britain isolated and condemned by its former friends. Given this shifting background, one area on which Macmillan could not afford to cede ground was Britain's claims to be a nuclear power. Practical political considerations stood in the way of any consideration of abandoning the nuclear deterrent: maintaining this, even though economic factors might have suggested otherwise, arguably helped to dissipate the misgivings some in Britain felt about the policy of decolonization. Britain's own dwindling resources, however, forced the cancellation of the Blue Streak project in February 1960, marking the end of Britain's bid to produce a home-grown surface-to-surface missile. Henceforward, Britain's growing dependence on US goodwill and co-operation in the nuclear field would become all too apparent. Crucially, in December 1962 at Nassau in the Bahamas, Macmillan extracted from Kennedy the promise that Britain could buy American Polaris missiles at a knock-down price. It is possible that Macmillan hinted darkly that if he failed to secure such a deal, he might be replaced by someone less agreeable to Washington.[95] Ironically, perhaps, the potential for cost savings inherent in decolonization, inevitably highlighted at a time of renewed balance of payments problems in the early 1960s, may have created a fresh bi-partisan consensus in favour of imperial retreat, approved by the right because it implied cuts in public expenditure, and by the left because it might free money for domestic social spending.[96]

Many of the policy decisions of the 1950s and early 1960s had been grounded in the belief (or hope) that decolonization need not mean the end of Britain's overseas influence, but rather the beginning of a new phase, in which Britain's global role would be buttressed, and in part defined, by its leadership of the Commonwealth. Yet as the Commonwealth expanded, its very nature inevitably changed. As one commentator has put it, ' "Commonwealth", which began as a synonym for Empire, came to signify its antithesis'.[97] In 1959, at Macmillan's request, officials had conducted a major study of Britain's antici-pated role in the world in the decade up to 1970. This revealed a clear divergence of thinking in Whitehall on the significance of the Commonwealth. Understandably, perhaps, the Commonwealth Relations Office emphasized the critical importance the association had in underpinning the special relationship between Britain and the United States, arguing that it was the Commonwealth connection which made Britain's role distinctive and its friendship desirable. The Foreign Office, predictably, was more circumspect: in its view, the Commonwealth, in contrast to ties with the United States and Western Europe, was not in itself a source of British power, though it might be a vehicle for the projection of such power as Britain still possessed.[98] By the early 1960s, when South Africa withdrew (in preference to being ignominiously expelled), the membership of the Commonwealth had grown to include six 'non-white' countries, making it very different from the predominantly white club of the period up to, and including the Second World War. As the Cabinet Secretary commented in 1962, its principal value was in keeping former dependencies orientated towards the West rather than the Communist bloc. Furthermore, if it became the basis of international co-operation as a genuinely multiracial organization, it might help to reduce racial friction and so help maintain world peace.[99] This did not, however, prevent irritation in official circles as the Commonwealth became more independently minded. As Macmillan privately observed to the Australian prime minister, Robert Menzies, early in 1962: 'I now shrink from any Commonwealth meeting because I know how troublesome it will be.'[100] However, because of his conviction that the ideological struggle 'really dominates everything', Macmillan remained clear that the multiracial Commonwealth had to be made to work.[101]

The ambition to transform the imperial system into a more acceptable network of 'informal' influence was also critically undermined by Britain's economic circumstances. The success of such an informal empire would hinge on Britain's capacity to remain the economic core of the Commonwealth, a role expected to be reinforced by continuing metropolitan financial assistance. One of the commitments undertaken by Britain at the 1958 Montreal Commonwealth Trade Conference was to provide increased overseas development aid. This indeed was done (British aid doubling between 1957 and 1960), but much of this aid was tied to the purchase of British goods, which limited the loans actually taken up. Moreover, although a new Department of Technical Co-operation was created in 1961 to assume the development functions of the contracting Colonial Office, the sums provided in aid remained tiny compared to the overall level of public expenditure, and represented a declining proportion of Britain's GNP.[102] For this reason, it is hardly surprising that London responded enthusiastically to signals from Washington that increased US development aid might become available, as a key strategy in the Cold War. It seems quite likely that British government calculations during the crucial phase of the 'wind of change' were influenced by the prospect of an 'informalized' empire in which the costs of keeping former colonies orientated to the West would be shared by Britain and the United States, but underpinning these calculations were what transpired to be over-optimistic assumptions about Britain's economic ability to shoulder its share of these responsibilities.[103]

Paradoxically, within Britain itself, the multiracial ideal, considered central to the Commonwealth's prospects for success, was coming under threat over the question of immigration. In 1962, the British government finally decided to adopt measures to control immigration from the Commonwealth into Britain. At the time, non-white immigrants were arriving at the rate of more than 130,000 per year, whereas in the early 1950s the annual figure had been less than 10,000. Ironically, given his previously liberal stance on this issue, these changes were associated with the Home Secretary, R.A. Butler. Since 1959 right-wing Conservative opinion at grass-roots level had been hardening on this question. By May 1961, Macmillan was becoming increasingly concerned about this. Ministers remained divided on the issue, which, to Macleod, was 'extremely distasteful'. Under the 1962 Act, a controversial new voucher system was introduced for immigrants (those from Ireland being exempted), giving preference to skilled applicants and those assured of employment. Inevitably, the impact on putative migrants in South Asia and the West Indies was considerable, intensifying anxieties that families would be prevented from joining relatives who had already settled in Britain.[104] As subsequent British governments would discover, these were questions whose significance would grow, and which would tap into popular sentiments which many in the political establishment found repugnant. In this way, the long-term consequences of managing a global imperial system would acquire a direct, and largely unanticipated, relevance to British society.

CHAPTER 6

IMPERIAL AFTERMATH

By the time the Labour Party returned to power under Harold Wilson in 1964, the greater part of Britain's decolonizing activity had been completed: all that remained for the new government to do was to continue the broad thrust of policy initiated by its predecessors. Wilson's government had no doubt about the need for Britain to maintain a global role. As Wilson told the Commons at the end of 1964, abandoning that role was simply inconceivable. In most respects, the techniques employed to maintain that role represented a fundamental continuity with policy under Macmillan and Home. A good example of this is the significance to London of good relations with Washington. The much-vaunted special relationship with the United States formed a key component in the new government's global thinking, and an important area of continuity with the previous government's handling of foreign affairs. A desire to develop Anglo-American links went further than Wilson's initial attempts to emulate the dynamism and charisma of the Kennedy administration. Significantly, Wilson's first overseas trip was to visit President Lyndon Johnson in Washington. The meeting was a success, with Wilson reassuring the Americans about his government's commitment to its overseas military obligations, and Johnson promising US support for sterling and diplomatic backing over Britain's residual colonial complication in Southern Rhodesia.[1] In the defence sphere, Wilson was equally determined to retain Britain's nuclear capability, even though this could no longer plausibly be described as independent, given its reliance on US-built delivery systems. Wilson succeeded temporarily in putting to one side the Labour Party's recent divisions over unilateralism in the interests of continuity in policy and of proving Labour's 'fitness to govern'. Of even more immediate importance was the government's willingness to maintain a relatively high level of spending on conventional defence, necessary to sustain existing commitments, especially the East of Suez role, to convince the United States that Britain remained a valuable and reliable ally, and to reassure the all-important 'middle ground' of the domestic electorate.

On entering office, Labour showed no great interest in a renewed application to join the EEC. At least on Labour's left, the Community tended to be seen as an unsavoury 'rich man's club'. Reinforcing this outlook, perhaps, was the rich vein of anti-German sentiment long a tradition in Labour circles, seen most clearly in the earlier posture of Ernest Bevin.[2] While in Opposition,

Labour had devoted considerable energy to portraying Britain's role in the Commonwealth as an *alternative* to membership of the EEC. To the Wilson government, Britain's presence in Europe took the concrete form of its military commitment: wider involvement seemed neither necessary nor particularly desirable before the mid-1960s. Yet even here, Britain was steadily being eclipsed by the resurgent West Germany, whose contribution to the defence of Central Europe, in terms of troop numbers, was five times greater than Britain's by 1964. This alone was a threat to Britain's claim to be the United States' most important European partner.[3]

One feature which distinguished the new government's general outlook from that of its predecessor was a greater enthusiasm for the Commonwealth, at least in the early phase of Wilson's period in office. Whereas many leading Tories had been dismayed by the diluting effects decolonization had had on traditional Commonwealth bonds, Labour viewed the association as being in tune with the strand of internationalism long evident in its own thinking. In its 1960 statement on overseas policy, the party had declared that 'The Commonwealth in its present form is the supreme example of an international organization which positively helps towards the development of a world society … The Labour Party therefore believes that Britain must put the Commonwealth before all other regional groupings.'[4] Wilson himself appears to have believed that the Commonwealth was still valuable to Britain in terms of trading and investment opportunities, and as an instrument which reinforced Britain's unique world role. Given the sympathy which the Labour Party in Opposition had often demonstrated for nationalist causes, especially in Africa, there appeared to be good reasons for optimism that the new government could cultivate friendly relations with many post-colonial regimes.

East of Suez under strain

In New Delhi in 1965, Wilson famously described Britain's 'natural frontiers' as lying on the Himalayas. There was more to this than mere rhetorical flourish. In practical terms, this translated into a determination to uphold the East of Suez commitment. This concept had been reinforced by the argument that a strong military presence in the region was necessary to safeguard Britain's commercial interests and investments, along with its supplies of oil and other raw materials. Yet the East of Suez shibboleth does not seem to have been subjected to rigorous analysis by those in Whitehall who upheld it. For example, Japan's regional economic success, not based on military power, was not apparently considered an instructive model by British policy-makers.[5] The government was aware that its actions were being monitored closely by the Chiefs of Staff, and had every reason to want to avoid the embarrassment likely to accompany any high-level resignations by service chiefs, which incautious retrenchment might trigger. Certainly, traditional East of Suez arguments were routinely, and often successfully, deployed by the Ministry of Defence in support of its claims for a sustained share of government revenue. A further bulwark of the policy was the approval of the US government for the East of

Suez role. What might once have appeared American tolerance for Britain's global aspirations had been transformed into positive US encouragement. By the time Wilson assumed office, it seemed that the East of Suez role was valued more highly by US policy-makers than Britain's contribution to NATO. Under both Kennedy and Johnson, Washington remained concerned that a British withdrawal would increase the risk of instability in the region. Particularly after the escalation of the Vietnam War, the Americans saw the East of Suez role as tangible evidence of Britain's willingness to share with Washington the ever-growing burden of responsibility for the security of the region bounded by the Indian Ocean. East of Suez therefore compensated partially for London's refusal to become embroiled directly in Vietnam. Although Washington continued to urge Britain not to abandon its East of Suez role, there is little evidence that, during the 1960s any more than previously, this gave London a countervailing leverage over US foreign policy. Nevertheless, it remains plausible to argue that in the mid-1960s, the United States was in effect subsidizing the British government to continue with policies which the latter was in any case keen to pursue.

The depth of Britain's commitment to an East of Suez role was clearly illustrated by London's response to the crisis in relations between Malaysia and its expansionist neighbour, Indonesia. As previously discussed, Malayan independence in 1957 did not see the abandonment by Britain of attempts to forge closer integration of South-East Asia. It had long sought to bring Malaya, Singapore and the Borneo territories into closer association, but Malayan independence and Singapore's achievement of 'statehood' in 1959 seemed to contradict this policy. Nevertheless, among Singapore's own anti-Communist political elite, the advantages of a merger with Malaya soon came to be seen as a safeguard of the new state's survival as a major commercial centre. Independence within a larger federation seemed to offer protection against Communist encroachment. When the Malayan ruler, Tunku Abdul Rahman, proposed a formal merger of Malaya, Singapore, Sarawak, North Borneo (Sabah) and Brunei in 1961, London had responded enthusiastically, seeing in this arrangement a means of promoting greater integration and settling the issue of the fate of Britain's remaining possessions in the region. The formal creation of Malaysia in 1963, from which Brunei decided to opt out (finally becoming independent in 1983), and Singapore seceded in 1965, was backed by British promises to defend the new association. Before long, a confrontation was triggered with Sukarno's Indonesia, which had its own territorial ambitions towards Borneo, but London was determined to honour its previous security guarantees to Malaysia. Between 1963 and 1966, British troops (reaching 50,000 at the height of the conflict), along with Malaysian and New Zealand detachments, were involved in a protracted campaign to protect the new federation from Indonesian expansionism.[6] A similar indicator of British concern about the strategic sensitivity of East Africa in relation to the Indian Ocean region had been evident in 1964, when London had been willing to mount interventions in Kenya, Uganda and Tanganyika, at the invitation of their governments, to help quell army mutinies.[7] This was tangible evidence that there had been no wholesale conversion in Whitehall to an exclusively, or even predominantly, Eurocentric outlook during decolonization: on the contrary, during the first half of the 1960s it was abundantly clear that British policy-makers were determined to preserve London's influence in Malaysia, and, by extension, in the entire East of Suez theatre.[8] Yet this determination to uphold security guarantees placed enormous strains on Britain's military capacity. Had another crisis arisen simultaneously elsewhere in the world, it is most unlikely that Britain would have been able to respond effectively. Moreover, the sheer cost of the Malaysia operation, and its adverse contribution to Britain's looming balance of payments problems, fed into a growing willingness in Whitehall to question how far the existing East of Suez commitment was still tenable.

In practical terms, the weakness of the East of Suez concept was that it necessitated a secure base somewhere on the rim of the Indian Ocean from which operations could be mounted. In the late 1950s, it had been thought that Kenya could fulfil this role, but that colony's rapid progress to decolonization had invalidated these assumptions, leading the planners to switch their attention to Aden, where large investments were made in developing adequate military facilities. Mounting unrest there, as a civil war spread from the interior to the coast, steadily made this base insecure. Increasingly, the viability of the East of Suez policy came to hinge on Britain's ability to maintain a large naval force in the Indian Ocean. Aircraft carriers, rather than land bases, seemed to be the solution, although Britain's fleet was expensive and ageing.

Retrenchment

Although much of Labour's appeal had rested with Wilson's image as a modernizer, committed to a revived Britain 'forged in the white heat' of a 'technological revolution', the economic realities were more prosaic, and the new government was to be dogged by financial problems. On assuming office, Labour inherited a balance of payments deficit of some £800 million, and for the next three years struggled to redress this problem without altering the value of sterling. Arguably, the sensible course would have been to devalue sterling immediately. However, sensitive to memories of Labour's devaluation in 1949, and even of the handling of the financial crisis in 1931, Wilson resisted this, fearing that it would smack of a 'Little England' mentality, at odds with the new government's internationalist aspirations.[9] Devaluation simply did not square with the government's continuing conception of Britain's role as being the core of a major economic bloc, and of London's importance as an international financial centre. Perhaps not unreasonably, the new government hoped that buoyant world trade would enable British economic growth to be maintained and even increased.

Nevertheless, by the time the government unveiled its hastily improvised National Plan late in 1965, designed to achieve a sustained period of growth, economic optimism was already turning to doubt and renewed perceptions of relative national decline. Stringency appeared to be the only option, particularly in cutting the escalating costs of Britain's defence and overseas commitments, but also affecting development aid, a keystone of any serious attempt to maintain 'informal' influence in former colonial territories. By 1964, British overseas aid had become heavily biased towards Commonwealth destinations (by 1968 the proportion was nearly 90 per cent). Wilson was keen to expand Britain's aid programme, creating a new Ministry of Overseas Development to co-ordinate these efforts, headed by a minister with Cabinet rank and overseen by that doyen of administrators, Sir Andrew Cohen. While some of the larger Commonwealth countries, such as India, succeeded in attracting aid from international agencies or countries like the United States, Britain's contribution was especially important to smaller, newer states, for example in Africa. Such assistance, of course, was not unconditional: by the late 1960s, over 40 per cent of Britain's bilateral aid was contractually tied to the purchase of British goods and services.[10]

Britain's economic condition also seemed to dictate controls on the flow of private capital out of the country, a drive to boost exports and curtailment of the cost burden of imports.[11] After 1965, British overseas investment effectively came to a 'shuddering halt', due both to voluntary agreements and exchange controls. Although government overseas spending levelled off, the days of sterling's role as a reserve currency were henceforth numbered.[12] By the time Britain eventually opted to devalue the pound, in November 1967, the British government's foreign debts were proportionately greater than those of any other country.

At the heart of Britain's difficulties in maintaining its prized world role was uncertainty about the country's ability to maintain its existing defence capacity in the light of these deepening financial problems. Denis Healey, Wilson's appointee as Minister of Defence, heading a newly streamlined and centralized defence structure in Whitehall, shared many of the traditional assumptions of his predecessors, for example on the importance of the East of Suez role. During a visit to Australia in 1966, Healey was at pains to stress that Britain had no intention of discarding its commitments. Nevertheless, he was well aware of the need to economize on defence spending, given the problem of inflation and the enormous inherited task of modernizing Britain's armed forces. Under the Conservatives, defence expenditure had reached 8.3 per cent of Britain's GNP; Healey, likening this burden to 'a runaway train', sought to reduce the figure to 6 per cent.[13]

The Defence White Paper of February 1965 acknowledged that instability in South-East Asia called for a strengthening of Britain's armed forces and explicitly repeated Britain's commitment to its security obligations. Healey argued that it would make no economic (or political) sense to abandon Aden, given the resources which had recently been devoted to it. But he made it clear that Britain would continue to keep defence expenditure under review, and wanted to explore the scope for a more equitable sharing of the defence burden.[14] In the April budget, the Treasury was able to insist that defence spending should be limited to £2,000 million, in itself a remarkable development in policy, the first time since the Second World War that such a ceiling had been imposed. Since the late 1950s, as the cost of defence technology escalated, there had been growing interest in developing weapons systems which could perform multiple roles. One example was the TSR-2 aircraft, designed to have both strike and reconnaissance functions, with a 1,000-mile operational range which would make it suitable for service East of Suez. However, wildly spiralling costs and unsatisfactory prospects led to the project's cancellation, expected to produce an immediate saving of around £300 million. To replace the TSR-2, Healey announced that 50 cheaper F-111 aircraft would be purchased from the United States.

In the last phase before the escalation of the Vietnam War would strain Anglo-American relations, Johnson seemed reassured by the new British government, and particularly by its continued espousal of the East of Suez role.[15] Once the situation in Vietnam deteriorated, and the US military presence increased sharply, London's initial attitude was supportive. Conveniently, however, Britain could use its position as co-chairman of the Geneva Conference on Indo-China to avoid becoming further entangled in Washington's policy. It was a source of strain in the Special Relationship that Britain refused to send even a token military force to assist in Vietnam (in 1966 Johnson famously told Wilson 'All I want is a battalion of the Black Watch'). Moreover, Britain's reluctance to become embroiled in the conflict contrasted sharply with the willingness of Australia and New Zealand to fulfil their alliance obligations. Wilson's proposal in 1965 for a Commonwealth peace mission to assist in a mediated settlement, probably a gesture to an increasingly restless Labour Party at home, was hardly calculated to secure an enthusiastic response from Washington (which remained suspicious of the non-aligned outlook of some Commonwealth members). Vietnam, and the Special Relationship, would become increasingly difficult issues for Wilson to manage, especially after the 1966 general election had expanded the numbers of left-wing critics on Labour's backbenches.

In the midst of deepening economic problems, Wilson's government restated its belief in the East of Suez role, even though this was becoming more difficult to fulfil, given the prolonged 'confrontation' with Indonesia and the stepping-up of anti-British terrorism in Aden.[16] Nevertheless, there was concern in Washington that Britain's growing economic difficulties might lead Wilson's government to shed its overseas defence commitments. As the US Secretary of State, Dean Rusk, urged London in May 1965: 'Don't pull out, Britain, because we can't do the job of world policeman alone.'[17] American anxiety intensified during 1965 when British officials privately intimated to their US counterparts that even the East of Suez role might have to be reappraised. Washington, in contrast, was seeking a firm British commitment to a military presence in the Indian Ocean and the Far East for at least a further decade.[18] The extent of mounting US anxiety is revealed by the provisions of a secret agreement reached in 1965 (whose existence Wilson subsequently denied) under which Washington promised to give continuing support for sterling provided Britain neither devalued the pound nor gave up its East of Suez commitments. The US administration also signalled that a failure to remain East of Suez would affect American willingness to buy British military equipment, which would have grave implications for Britain's balance of payments.[19] When Wilson visited Washington at the end of 1965, Britain's imminent annual defence review was inevitably the most pressing issue. While the American government sympathized with Britain's need to save foreign exchange, it argued that neither Britain nor the US could safely economize on defence, and described Britain's world role as vital. The complication for Wilson, however, was that his government had only accepted cuts in social spending during summer 1965 in exchange for a £100 million reduction in defence spending. Even then, Britain's role in NATO would escape largely unscathed, and the stated intention was to co-operate with the US in developing new bases in the Indian Ocean. Although the counterinsurgency campaign in Aden could not be conducted indefinitely, London was considering how Britain's foothold in the Persian Gulf could be strengthened.[20]

But it was Britain's wavering stance on the East of Suez role which became the most difficult theme in Anglo-American relations. Convinced that a permanent presence was no longer feasible, the British government believed it was now necessary to start planning for alternative arrangements for Far Eastern security, perhaps involving a sharing of responsibilities between Britain, the US, Australia and New Zealand. Ultimately, in London's view, it seemed sensible to surrender the major role in the Far East to the United States, allowing Britain to concentrate its dwindling resources in the Middle East and Africa. One controversial example of Britain's willingness to co-operate with the United States in the Indian Ocean came in 1965, when Britain created a new British Indian Ocean Territory, chiefly comprising the Chagos Archipelago, to enable joint British–US military bases to be constructed. Developing this key strategic outpost involved the removal of 2,000 civilians from the island of Diego Garcia to Mauritius.

In February 1966, in an attempt to rein in defence spending, Healey announced a package of economies which had important implications for the East of Suez role, as well as unveiling three new principles intended to guide strategic thinking. Henceforth, Britain would not embark on major military operations overseas unless it was acting with an ally; military assistance would not be made available unless the country affected could provide the necessary facilities; finally, there would be no attempt to cling on to defence facilities in an independent country against its will. The defence statement confirmed Britain's pledge to maintain a strong military presence in Germany. Although the decision to withdraw from Aden and the South Arabian Federation in 1967 or 1968 was repeated, it was declared that British forces would remain in Malaysia and Singapore. Particularly reassuring to Washington was London's confirmation that the order of 50 F-111 aircraft would stand, easing the United States' own balance of payments position and guaranteeing Britain's ability to perform a high-quality defence role.[21] However, the Royal Navy, the beneficiary of most of the increased defence spending since the 1957 Defence White Paper, saw a significant curtailing of its budget. Plans to build a new fleet of aircraft carriers were scrapped, and the existing fleet was to be decommissioned by the mid-1970s. This announcement led the navy minister and the First Sea Lord to resign.[22] The strong reactions to the treatment of the navy in 1966 were a reminder to Wilson of the political risks involved in tampering with a policy so entrenched, and so important to perceptions of British prestige, as East of Suez. Rather than risk further controversy, the government was careful to balance the measures it took in 1966 with assurances that Britain's presence in the Persian Gulf would be strengthened. Nevertheless, throughout 1966 the pressure to achieve further defence economies became progressively irresistible. At the end of the year the government, while renewing yet again its pledge to uphold the East of Suez commitment, considered halving Britain's military strength in the Far East, and cutting its forces in the Middle East by one-third.

Monitoring these developments was an increasingly anxious US administration, keen that Britain should maintain its East of Suez role. In advance of Wilson's next trip to Washington in summer 1966, some State Department officials argued that Britain had to be persuaded to abandon its claims to a global role, along with its 'independent' nuclear deterrent, and accept the logic of joining the EEC and playing an effective role in Europe. These were not new American preoccupations, but they were coming to have a new urgency. At the same time, there remained misgivings within the US government that if Britain did enter Europe, it would lose interest in some of its wider defence commitments, leaving Washington to shoulder these responsibilities.[23] As Britain's financial plight worsened during 1966, some of these fears appeared to be justified as the British government began to question the cost involved in the defence of Germany. Talk in Whitehall about removing troops from the British Army on the Rhine inevitably alarmed officials in the United States, where European defence was already a divisive issue.

This was the background against which critical decisions were taken on the future of Aden. Here, the manner of Britain's withdrawal, announced by London in November 1967, combined haste with humiliation. This important strategic centre, home to Britain's Middle East Headquarters since 1961, was simply proving to be ungovernable. At constitutional talks held in 1964, it seemed that independence by 1968 might be possible. Nevertheless, Britain remained remarkably optimistic that Aden, and the federation of which it was part, would remain closely tied to Britain through defence and financial agreements, and security guarantees from London. This strand of thinking was made irrelevant by Britain's financial predicament and by developments within the territory. Crucially, Britain proved unable to protect the emirs through whom it ruled.[24] This group arguably lost its local power base because it became too closely identified with Britain at a time when the dominant mood was anti-colonial and pan-Arab. A White Paper issued in February 1967 had declared that when Southern Arabia became independent, British forces would be withdrawn entirely. Amid unrest in the Cabinet at the continuing cost of the East of Suez role, efforts were made to accelerate the transfer of power in the Federation.

In July 1967, a supplementary Defence White Paper was introduced which revealed the impact Britain's straitened economic circumstances were at last having on traditional strategic thinking. The statement acknowledged that the full East of Suez commitment was no longer tenable, and provided a timetable for its scaling down. By 1971, British forces in Malaysia and Singapore were to be halved, and withdrawn completely by the mid-1970s. Aden was to be evacuated immediately, although a foothold in the Persian Gulf would be retained.

Given the importance attached to the region by Britain for so long, it was ironic that events in the Middle East should have precipitated the long-delayed realization of Britain's diminished power. The Six Day War of June 1967 between Israel and most of its Arab neighbours was accompanied not only by an orgy of financial speculation but also by the closure of the Suez Canal, which obliged Britain to buy more expensive oil from outside the Middle East, draining the country's dollar reserves. The Six Day War also represented the abrupt end of a period since the Suez Crisis during which Washington had been seeking to allow Britain's Middle Eastern role to be deflated painlessly. In a sobering reminder of the realities underpinning the Special Relationship, American policy during the conflict was made with little or no attempt to involve either Britain or the United States' other European partners.[25]

These developments finally, in November 1967, forced Britain's hand to take the decision which had so long been avoided by ministers, to devalue sterling from $2.80 to $2.40. This seismic failure of policy cost Britain's reserves around £1 billion. In its wake came a radical reappraisal of Britain's ability to maintain ambitious overseas commitments. It was devaluation more than anything else which revealed the hollowness of Britain's pretensions to a world role. One consequence of the operation was a radical reappraisal of Britain's prospects in Aden. In the second half of 1967, the National Liberation Front, formed in 1963, launched an insurrection which quickly brought down nearly all the Protectorate's traditional rulers, and which British forces could not contain. By September 1967, with the NLF in control of the whole area, the South Arabian Federation was clearly disintegrating, and there seemed little chance of Britain engineering an acceptable replacement. In November, as the last British troops withdrew, efforts were made to reassure the Gulf states that existing commitments to their defence would not be jeopardized. With alarming speed, Britain's ramshackle federal construction was swept aside and its place taken by the (Marxist) People's Democratic Republic of Yemen.[26]

By the beginning of 1968, it was becoming clear that devaluation had not had the intended effect of stabilizing sterling's value. Moreover, the operation had actually *increased* the overseas defence bill by around £50 million. To secure a loan from the International Monetary Fund, Britain would have to introduce substantial public spending cuts. As the Chancellor, Roy Jenkins, argued, a stable currency could only be achieved by a drastic reduction in Britain's overseas spending. Despite the strength of Jenkins' arguments, the Cabinet accepted his views by only a small majority. To the Johnson administration, increasingly beleaguered in Vietnam, retrenchment by Britain and withdrawal from East of Suez seemed the ultimate betrayal. Johnson personally warned Wilson that if London's plans went ahead, the United States could no longer regard Britain as a valuable ally in any major strategic theatre.[27] Nevertheless, what might long have seemed inevitable could no longer be postponed. In January 1968, with external pressures accumulating, Wilson addressed the Commons in terms which marked the effective end of Britain's global imperial system. Declaring that it was necessary for Britain to adjust to a realistic international role, one which its circumstances would permit, he announced the scrapping of the East of Suez role. Not only was the order for F-111 aircraft cancelled, depriving Britain's armed forces of the capacity to mount operations in the region, but the withdrawal of British forces was to be speeded up. By the end of 1971, Britain's military presence in Malaysia, Singapore and the Persian Gulf would be terminated (despite the assurances given to the latter only two months previously).[28] Once this had been completed, only the garrison in Hong Kong would remain.[29] As one Cabinet minister recalled, he and his colleagues had finally made the psychological leap which enabled them to break through the 'status barrier' which East of Suez had represented. The fact that support in Cabinet for the policy switch was not greater, even at this late stage, suggests that the eventual decision was shaped more by immediate, practical and insurmountable constraints than by any fundamental, heartfelt reappraisal of the East of Suez position. As the leading historian of the episode has commented: 'in the last resort the means determined the ends ... ultimately lack of resources rather than intellectual rejection ensured its abandonment'.[30]

The decision to withdraw, described by the former Foreign Secretary Patrick Gordon Walker as 'the most momentous shift in our foreign policy for a century and a half', came as a considerable shock to the rulers of the Persian Gulf, some of whom, concerned about the regional ambitions of their much larger neighbours, Iran and Saudi Arabia, offered to pay for continuing British protection (ironically, Saudi Arabia had also shown a willingness to subsidize a British military guarantee).[31] Bahrain and Qatar opted to take independence on the same model as Kuwait's, while five of the smaller sheikhdoms merged in 1971 to form the United Arab Emirates. Thus did Britain's informal Middle Eastern empire come to its conclusion, although British involvement in the Gulf was not yet over. Between 1970 and 1975, British forces played an important supporting role during the counterinsurgency campaign in Oman, whose sultan was threatened by a Marxist-inspired guerrilla war. London could not ignore the importance of Oman, given its commanding position as protector of the oil route through the Straits of Hormuz. Nevertheless, Britain's own financial problems, the army's growing commitments in Northern Ireland, and the likelihood of domestic political opposition precluded any full-scale military operation by Britain, which confined its efforts mainly to the provision of specialists and advisers.[32]

Significantly, when the Conservatives returned to power in 1970, they did not reverse their predecessors' decision to withdraw from the Gulf, even though attacks on Labour's policy of retreat had formed an element of their general election campaign. In 1971 it was announced that Britain's treaties with the Gulf states would become void by the end of the year. On withdrawal from Singapore, however, the Conservatives were more cautious, delaying full departure by concluding a deal with Malaysia, Singapore, Australia and New Zealand in 1971, providing for an ANZUK fleet to be stationed in Singapore and for an integrated air defence system to be developed for Malaysia. Nevertheless, when Labour returned to power in 1974, the withdrawal from Singapore resumed.

Europe

Having had its first application to join the EEC blocked by France, the British government left open the possibility of a second attempt. The arrival of a Labour government in 1964 seemed to make a fresh bid less imminent, given the substantial anti-European lobby within the Labour Party. For the party's left, the Commonwealth remained the core of a distinctive British foreign policy, while for the right, the Special Relationship was a greater source of comfort. On this, as on many other issues, Wilson's position seemed enigmatic: avoiding dissent within his party was an important influence on the formation of government policy. Notwithstanding his earlier ambivalence, Wilson appears by 1966 to have been convinced of the need at least to appear to be seeking EEC membership, 'provided essential British and Commonwealth interests are safeguarded'.[33] Whereas Britain's first application had involved considerable attention to the requirements of Commonwealth trading partners, this dimension was more muted during the negotiations which began in 1967. Even in the relatively short interval between Britain's two applications, the character of Commonwealth trade had continued to change, and for many members, the economic relationship with Britain had continued to decline in significance. Meanwhile, the apparently inexorable drift towards Europe also had important ramifications for British financial policy, undermining the government's determination to avoid devaluation if at all possible. Ministers committed to British membership of the EEC, including Roy Jenkins, had taken seriously the French government's advice during 1966 that devaluation would be a prerequisite for British entry.

When Britain made its second bid to enter the EEC in May 1967, in conditions significantly different to those which had applied in 1961, there was no great enthusiasm for the European option within the British government, rather a growing awareness that the 'globalist' strategy, involving leadership of the Sterling Area, the Special Relationship and the East of Suez role, was no longer a realistic alternative. By the winter of 1967–68, Washington's estimation of Britain's value as an ally had sunk to a new low: as the US ambassador to Britain commented privately, the Special Relationship was little more than 'sentimental terminology'.[34] In the event, de Gaulle repeated his veto on British membership, a blow felt all the more coming rapidly after the humiliation of devaluation. It was the resignation of de Gaulle in 1969, following his own domestic reversals during 1968, which made possible a fresh approach to European integration. De Gaulle's successor, Georges Pompidou, soon issued reassuring signals that he would not obstruct a new British application, provided London could demonstrate its commitment to Europe. The financial crisis of 1967–68 had compelled Wilson's government to focus its defence efforts more clearly on Britain's contribution to NATO forces in Western Europe, which had the additional result of underlining Britain's commitment to Europe generally, an important prerequisite to a successful bid to enter the Common Market. It fell to the Europhile Edward Heath to make a third, ultimately successful attempt, following his election in 1970.

Rhodesia

The most difficult legacy of empire bequeathed by the outgoing Conservatives, and one which the Labour government was unable to resolve, was the problem of Rhodesia. For many white settlers, it seemed that the dissolution of the Central African Federation had presented the opportunity for Southern Rhodesia to achieve independence on the same terms as its northern neighbours. Within the Rhodesian Front, impatience grew at Winston Field's failure to secure this. As attitudes hardened, Field was removed as leader in April 1964 and replaced by Ian Smith, who moved swiftly to suppress African opposition, banning both ZAPU and ZANU and imposing controls on the media, measures designed to reassure London that the problem of African opposition to the existing constitution had been neutralized. Smith failed, however, to convince the British government that African views were represented by an *indaba*, or conference, of chiefs, appointed by the government. Steeling himself for a possible confrontation, Smith placed a 'reliable' commander at the head of the army and called a general election. This demonstrated the extent of settler support for the Smith government's unwillingness to compromise, giving it the confidence to issue a unilateral declaration of independence (UDI) in November 1965, in effect a rebellion against British authority.

UDI, an outcome long thought possible in London, presented Wilson's government with a number of complications. Wilson himself emphasized the practical difficulties of military action by Britain against Smith, not least the likely cost (at a time when concern was mounting at the scale of the defence budget), but also the probability of hostile reactions from sympathetic sections of British society, including the army. Nor could London be confident that an acceptable government could be constructed to replace Smith's. Crucially, at an early stage, prior to UDI, Wilson publicly disavowed the idea of British military intervention, arguably strengthening Smith's bargaining position and resolve. Nevertheless, Britain remained adamant that Rhodesian independence was not negotiable until steps were taken to increase African political representation and to end racial discrimination, and until there was evidence of African acquiescence. Meanwhile, London imposed economic sanctions on Rhodesia, which Wilson famously claimed would begin to bite in weeks rather than months, but which before long were being effectively flouted.

The Rhodesian problem increasingly exposed the British government to criticism at home, from within the Commonwealth, and internationally. Domestically, the government faced criticism from the Conservative Party, among whose ranks there persisted considerable support for the Rhodesian rebels. Moreover, on diplomatic grounds, the problem was patently one from which Britain could not walk away: both the Commonwealth and the United States expected London to behave responsibly in handling this residual complication of African decolonization. In an attempt to break the deadlock, Wilson, who *inter alia* was concerned that the problem would provide a focus at home for opposition to his government, agreed to meet Smith in 1966, aboard HMS *Tiger*, and again in 1968, on HMS *Fearless*. However, Smith stood firm against demands for eventual majority rule and each meeting proved abortive. Sanctions failed to have much impact: with South African help, Rhodesia was able to circumvent the Royal Navy's blockade of the port of Beira, through which much of Rhodesia's oil had previously been imported. From 1966 onwards, African guerrilla units, belonging to the rival factions ZANU and ZAPU and with support from the Soviet Union and China, began to make raids into Rhodesian territory. After 1972, these would escalate into a full civil war which lasted 15 years.

Edward Heath's Conservative government, elected in 1970, introduced constitutional proposals which would, if implemented, have made majority rule an even more distant prospect than under the Wilson formula. This apparent retrograde step triggered strong misgivings both in Britain and in the Commonwealth. On the fundamental assumption that any settlement must pass the acid test of being acceptable to the African majority, Heath despatched a commission to Rhodesia headed by Lord Pearce. This initiative, effectively the last attempt by Britain to resolve Rhodesia's future through bilateral negotiation with Salisbury, revealed that the African population was overwhelmingly opposed to the gradualist vision of constitutional reform on the table.[35]

In the event, it was external factors, above all the regional implications for southern Africa of the Portuguese Revolution of 1974 (after which newly independent Angola and Mozambique became vital bases for guerrilla incursions into Rhodesia), and mounting pressure on Salisbury from South Africa and the United States, which forced Ian Smith's regime to broker some sort of political compromise. In 1978, the so-called 'Internal Settlement' was concluded between Smith and one wing of the African nationalist movement, under which Bishop Abel Muzorewa became prime minister in 1979, heading a government which appeared to enjoy substantial African support. Nevertheless, the rival nationalist faction, the Patriotic Front, rejected this compromise and continued the guerrilla war. Not until the end of 1979 was a compromise settlement reached, at Lancaster House in London, scene of so many previous 'transfers of power'. Under this agreement, Britain briefly resumed authority over Rhodesia while preparations were made for elections (won by Robert Mugabe's Patriotic Front), followed by independence in April 1980.

Outposts of empire

As previous chapters have attempted to note, one of the recurring themes in Britain's earlier handling of decolonization was the problem of dealing with states whose size or small population appeared to preclude them from any meaningful form of independence. Once the last sizeable territories had been shed, there remained some of those imperial 'points' which had once seemed likely to comprise the substance of a residual global network. In some of these, wider international complications stood in the way of a rapid transition to independence. Gibraltar, for example, whose strategic value to Britain seemed questionable following the jettisoning of the East of Suez role, could not easily be restored to Spanish sovereignty (vigorously claimed by Madrid) in the face of resolute hostility from its small but fiercely Anglophile population, whose views were made clear in a referendum held in 1967.

The Falkland Islands, largely unknown in the metropole except to school-boy philatelists, became the occasion of an extraordinary outpouring of post-imperial British indignation in 1982 when the military junta ruling neighbouring Argentina elected to reinforce its longstanding claims to sovereignty through forcible occupation. Prior to this, Britain had appeared relatively flexible on the future of the islands, suggesting to Buenos Aires in 1967 that the question was negotiable, while asserting that the interests of the islands' small population remained paramount. Few writers on imperial decline, accustomed to the muffled transitions of the 1960s and 1970s, could have anticipated the possi-bility of a large part of Britain's remaining navy being despatched to reclaim the islands. In retrospect, the episode underlined the dangers of assuming that the old imperial impulse had been extinguished, and served as a corrective to historiographical complacency, the tendency to stress the 'exceptionalism' in Britain's handling of imperial retreat, apparently so much more foresighted than that of the luckless continental colonial powers.

A certain wistfulness was evident in the mood in Britain surrounding the retrocession of Hong Kong to the People's Republic of China in 1997. Britain had dismissed the possibility of making the territory fully independent, fearing that this might prompt an invasion by Chinese forces (which Britain would be in no position to repel). Hong Kong, whose post-war development as one of the world's leading financial and commercial centres had been spectacular, proved to be as desirable in its existing form to the authorities in Beijing as it was to the British. Under an agreement concluded in 1984, China promised to respect Hong Kong's economic and social systems for 50 years after 1997. Symbolically, if not strictly accurately, the lowering of the Union Flag marked the end of Britain's imperial career.

The Commonwealth

Until the mid-1960s, membership of the Commonwealth was a token not only of constitutional independence, but also participation in what was in many respects still a privileged 'club'. The influence of the British official mind remained considerable, given that the Commonwealth was still effectively managed by the Commonwealth Relations Office and the Cabinet Office. Moreover, the Cabinet Secretary acted as Secretary-General of Commonwealth Prime Ministers' meetings.[36]

There was already a growing British willingness to introduce a greater de-gree of practical co-operation in Commonwealth affairs when, at the 1964 Prime Ministers' meeting, several members proposed the creation of a central 'clearing house' to enable joint projects to be co-ordinated more effectively. As the Cabinet Secretary, Burke Trend observed, it was better for Britain to go along with this initiative than to try to stifle it.[37] In 1965, the Commonwealth Secretariat was established, giving the organization a base in Marlborough House in London's Pall Mall (Queen Mary's former home), geographically as well as psychologically distinct from Whitehall.[38] Increasingly, the Common-wealth assumed the shape of a genuinely multilateral body, no longer merely an extension of British overseas policy, but a post-imperial association with a distinctive and autonomous sense of purpose, and with its own collectively 'owned' institutions and machinery. This in turn helped underline the value of continued membership, especially for those African former colonies troubled particularly by Britain's handling of the Rhodesia problem (following UDI, Tanzania and Ghana had to be persuaded not to leave the Commonwealth).[39] The promotion of development was a field in which the Commonwealth was increasingly active in the 1960s. According to one estimate, developing members received around 28 per cent of their total aid from fellow members of the Commonwealth. Certainly, some of the wealthier Commonwealth countries, including Canada and Australia, directed their development assis-tance towards other members of the association.[40]

As decolonization continued, so Commonwealth membership expanded, reaching 31 states by 1970. As the 1960s progressed, however, there was growing unease in Whitehall that an institution originally envisaged as being a buttress of Britain's world position was in practice becoming a threat to Britain's own freedom of action, readily voicing its disapproval of British foreign policy, and raising the humiliating spectre of British isolation. Com-monwealth members' criticism of Britain's apparent inability to resolve the Rhodesian question was felt particularly keenly by Wilson and his colleagues (who were themselves divided over the appropriate response to pursue). It is quite likely that Wilson's Commonwealth peace initiative on Vietnam, unveiled shortly before the 1965 Commonwealth Prime Ministers' conference, was intended not only to placate opinion on Labour's left, but also to ensure that the Vietnam problem would eclipse discussion of Rhodesia.[41] At the same time, metropolitan observers began to point to the dissonance between the Commonwealth's espousal of democracy and parliamentary government, at a time when many of its members were succumbing either to single party rule or military government.[42]

Compounding Commonwealth criticism of Britain's Rhodesian policy was the running sore of British relations with the apartheid regime in South Africa. Despite Labour's hostility, while in Opposition, to arms sales to South Africa, Wilson's government decided late in 1964 to proceed with the sale of military aircraft to Pretoria, fulfilling a contract inherited from the previous govern-ment, partly through reluctance to sacrifice the overseas earnings which would result.[43] A further consideration had been the concerns voiced by the defence establishment in Britain about the need to provide South Africa with the resources it required to fulfil its role in defending the strategically important Cape sea route, as provided for in the Simonstown Agreements of 1955. Wilson's government never entirely resolved the dilemma over arms sales to South Africa, and a Cabinet crisis was sparked late in 1967 over the possibility of lifting the export ban, as Pretoria had requested. While strategic and commercial self-interest might argue in favour of a relaxation, Britain was theoretically bound by the 1963 UN resolution banning arms supplies to South Africa. Although the Labour government eventually opted not to rescind its earlier ban, the problem resurfaced in July 1970 when the incoming Conservative government declared that it was reconsidering the question, arguing that Britain was bound by the terms of the Simonstown Agreements. Although this led to protests during the 1971 Commonwealth Heads of Government meeting in Singapore, especially from African members, Heath's government made it plain that they refused to allow the Commonwealth to dictate so sensitive an area as British defence policy.[44]

Further threats to Commonwealth integrity emerged when disputes erupted between its members, for example when India and Pakistan went to war in 1965 (a conflict temporarily resolved through Soviet, not British, mediation), or when civil war within one of its members evoked differing responses from other members, as happened when Nigeria was threatened by the secession of Biafra in 1967. In the latter case, Wilson's decision to support the federal government against the Biafrans, probably influenced by the fact that Britain imported one-tenth of its oil from Nigeria, exposed British policy to criticism at home and abroad. Yet another centrifugal force potentially threatening to Commonwealth cohesion was the growth of rival organizations, often composed of countries sharing broad regional concerns. The Association of South-East Asian Nations, formed in 1967 and including Malaysia and Singapore, was a case in point.[45]

As the Commonwealth became more independently minded and as its members increasingly pursued their own national or regional interests, London's conception of the association as a network or bloc operating in harmony with British interests, and reinforcing them, seemed progressively out of step with reality.

In 1971, at the Prime Ministers' meeting (called, for the first time, the Commonwealth Heads of Government meeting, or CHOGM) held in Singapore, the Commonwealth formally adopted the Commonwealth Declaration of Principles (the Singapore Declaration), enshrining the association's aims and values. Members committed themselves to the pursuit of peace, liberty and co-operation, and collectively set their faces against racism, colonialism and the increasingly manifest disparities in wealth throughout the world. In order to address the latter, members also created the Commonwealth Fund for Technical Co-operation.[46] Symptomatic of shifting attitudes in London was the fact that Edward Heath, not known for the depth of his interest in Commonwealth (especially African) concerns, had advised Queen Elizabeth II not to attend the Singapore meeting. It was feared that continuing irritation within the Commonwealth over Britain's Rhodesia policy, together with Britain's willingness to export arms to an increasingly ostracized South Africa, might create an embarrassing atmosphere, hardly helped by the eagerness of Heath's government to join the EEC and to restrict Commonwealth immigration.[47] The general attitude of the Conservative government towards the Commonwealth was made explicit in the 1971 statement which asserted that the Commonwealth simply could not offer Britain opportunities comparable to those anticipated from membership of the European Community: the eight-fold increase in British exports to Europe during the 1970s was only one of the more visible expressions of the fundamental shift in Britain's interests from being global to being regional in character.[48]

The economic underpinnings of the Commonwealth link, already under strain in the 1950s, continued to dwindle in the 1960s. Increasingly, members were opting to trade with countries outside the association. Britain itself was conducting a growing proportion of its trade with Western Europe: by 1967, British exports to the EEC countries had already overtaken exports to the Commonwealth.[49] By 1970, less than one-quarter of Britain's exports went to Commonwealth countries or South Africa, barely half the proportion of 20 years previously, while more than a third went to the United States and the European Community. Similarly, Commonwealth imports into Britain had shrunk to barely over 25 per cent, compared to 33 per cent from the United States and Western Europe. A similar story emerges in the field of investment: in 1970, some 62 per cent of Britain's overseas investment was in countries *outside* the Sterling Area. By the time Britain finally entered the EEC in 1973, although the shift in metropolitan priorities hit some Commonwealth members hard, notably New Zealand, most had long been cultivating other economic ties. Especially noticeable was the change in Britain's economic relationship with recently independent territories, and the shift from the 'open economy' characteristic of the colonial era to the closed economy made possible by decolonization. In many post-independence regimes, expatriate firms experienced reduced freedom of action and a climate of economic nationalism, expressed in expanded government regulation. The assertion of economic independence, to reinforce political sovereignty, took the forms of a reluctance to maintain large currency balances in London, a drive to achieve economic diversification through import-substituting manufacturing, and a mood of suspicion towards foreign enterprises, such as large multinational companies, often seen as the agents of 'neo-colonialism'. Many former colonies opted for a statist model of development, and so built on the foundations of government regulation put in place by the late colonial state. The British imperial system as a network of economic relationships therefore came to an end at some imperceptible point between devaluation in 1967, when sterling lost its role as a major world reserve currency, followed by the winding up of the Sterling Area in 1972, in the wake of the collapse of the Bretton Woods system of fixed exchange rates, and 1973, when entry into the EEC broadcast the unambiguous message that Britain saw its future as lying within the European, not the wider, global sphere.[50]

Migration from Britain to the Commonwealth remained an option, and many in the 1960s took advantage of the heavily subsidized assisted passages to Australia. Not all found the transition easy, and a significant proportion of migrants opted to return to Britain. More generally, a quiet and very gradual transformation occurred in the Old Commonwealth countries over immigration policy. Beginning with Canada in 1962, and followed by Australia in 1973 and New Zealand in 1987, the Dominions modified the discriminatory practices they had operated for so long. The fact that this broadly coincided with an intensification of Britain's own discriminatory immigration policies was another irony in the story of the Commonwealth's evolution. The free movement of all empire subjects into Britain, safeguarded under the 1948 Nationality Act, had been challenged first by the 1962 Commonwealth Immigrants Act, which penalized those who lacked British passports, and then by more stringent controls introduced in 1968. In 1971 the Immigration Act erased the legal distinction between Commonwealth and foreign immigrants, marking the end of a cornerstone of traditional conceptions of the cohesion of the imperial system.[51]

The Commonwealth remains as one of the most curious legacies of Britain's long management of a global imperial system. Although its members broadly subscribe to shared aims and values, it is an entirely voluntary association and has no written constitution: indeed, the absence of binding definitions of the Commonwealth nexus may in part explain why the association has managed to survive in the face of so many centrifugal tendencies since the waves of decolonization in the 1940s and early 1960s. It is not in any sense a military alliance. While some of its members are involved in regional defence pacts, others have continued to aspire to non-alignment. Yet despite their different interests, its members clearly believe that something is to be gained from maintaining a forum for mutual co-operation and consultation, one cemented above all by the commitment to multiracialism. An index of the association's success is the growing interest in membership being shown by some countries, such as Mozambique, which have had no tradition of association with Britain. Similarly, the return of South Africa to the fold after the collapse of apartheid has arguably given the Commonwealth a new potential for authority and cohesion, for so long undermined by Britain's attitude to the problem. As a vehicle for international discussion and co-operation, with a highly diverse membership, whose constituents can gather on equal and informal terms, the Commonwealth is, quite simply, unique.

CONCLUSION

The inter-war imperial system depended on a uniquely favourable set of circumstances, which may have disguised the real impact of the First World War on British power. Specifically, it required the absence of any major external threat, in the form of another major war, and the maintenance of internal political stability within the system's components. In the first respect, Britain was fortunate that for so long, no external threat emerged. The fact that the European powers were preoccupied with post-war reconstruction and recovery, and that the United States and the Soviet Union were largely absorbed in their own internal affairs, left Britain in a position of apparent strength as a leading actor on the international stage. With its combined imperial resources, Britain could plausibly be regarded as the world's only 'superpower' during this period. This position could survive only as long as potential threats remained dormant. By the late 1930s, these were once again apparent in the form of 'aggressor' nations, Germany, Italy and Japan, all of which had imperial ambitions of their own. The revival of this external threat highlighted the perennial problem of defending a genuinely global network of British interests, at a time when economic conditions dictated financial restraint and retrenchment: the larger the empire became in geographical extent, the more effort had to be devoted to defending it. Although throughout this period, the idea that the empire was a source of strength remained a remarkably persistent one in British circles, much depended on that system not being tested again too severely by a major international conflict.

As it had done in the past, the inter-war empire displayed a striking facility to adapt to change. Potential threats to the system's cohesion, in the form of centrifugal trends, were apparently dissipated or defused with success. Above all, Britain's imperial managers had demonstrated that through pragmatic responses to nationalism, the 'crisis' of the years immediately after 1918 could be overcome. The Dominions were awarded effective independence, limited concessions were made to Indian political aspirations, and in the Middle East the substitution of informal influence for direct control seemed to have succeeded. By a process of tactical adjustment, and the deployment of new techniques of management, Britain generally avoided costly and unwelcome confrontations with hostile political forces within the empire, and sought, where possible, to maintain the substance of imperial power, while being willing to sacrifice some of its overt forms.

The Second World War abruptly shattered this interlude: it fundamentally altered the pattern of international relations, forced Britain to devise new means of tapping into imperial resources, thus straining the often delicate pre-war relationship between Britain and the components of the empire and unleashing energies later expressed in anti-colonial political movements, and crucially weakened the British economy.

While the overall significance of the Second World War in the story of imperial disengagement seems indisputable, there is a need for care in interpreting its precise consequences. In the short term, at least, the war did not signal the end of Britain's imperial ambitions. On the contrary, for at least a decade after 1945, the empire seemed vital to Britain. Economically, it offered a means of securing metropolitan recovery. Trade with the empire helped to keep Britain's often precarious balance of payments close to equilibrium, while management of the Sterling Area helped to keep London in a strong position as a major international financial centre and contributed an important segment of Britain's invisible earnings. In economic terms, during the war and until the mid-1950s, the imperial system was more important to Britain than it had ever been before. In political terms, too, the war reinforced an established British conviction that the maintenance of the imperial system was the key to preserving Britain's status as a great power, with the ability to protect and project its own independent interests, and so to strengthen its increasingly important alliance with the United States. The post-war revival of Britain's imperial impetus was exemplified by the central role occupied by 'development' in British thinking. The 'Second Colonial Occupation' involved not only the export of British expertise, but depended in part on the identification, or nurturing, of new collaborative elites, willing to participate in the development project, which was supposed to benefit both metropole and periphery. Yet as the late colonial state became more ambitious, as it interfered with growing regularity in the economic practices of colonial populations, so it exposed itself to criticism, and the scope for friction between governors and governed increased. The widening of political participation, the necessary corollary of economic and social development, was a process which, once initiated, could prove alarmingly difficult to control. In short, paradoxically, the post-war acquisition by Britain of a new sense of colonial purpose, a mission to 'modernize' the colonial territories, carried with it the seeds of eventual colonial disintegration. By fundamentally altering the nature of colonial rule, which in turn helped to create new local conditions, the British made their own task of government far more difficult and complex than it had been before 1939.

As a growing number of studies testify, Britain's disengagement from empire cannot be comprehended unless proper consideration is given to wider developments in international politics, and particularly to the Cold War context in which it unfolded. Ideological rivalry between the superpowers arguably worked to Britain's advantage, at least for the first decade after the Second World War, if not beyond. Although it required from Britain a very high level of defence spending (often twice the proportion spent by its closest economic competitors), the Cold War served, especially during the 1950s, to make the

United States broadly sympathetic to Britain's imperial system, as a buttress to Britain's own strength and effectiveness as an ally, and as a useful barrier to the spread of Communist influence in the developing world. American security guarantees, especially in Western Europe, effectively freed Britain to concentrate its attention and resources on maintaining the imperial system. On to traditional problems of imperial defence, then, was grafted a new strategic framework, designed to contain the perceived threat of Soviet expansion. This British commitment to contributing to Western defence had its advantages and its drawbacks. On the favourable side, it eventually secured for Britain the kind of defensive alliance which had continually proved elusive between the wars: Britain was arguably far more secure than it had been during the 'Twenty Years' Peace'. However, defence spending, especially attempts to keep abreast of post-war developments in military technology, stretched metropolitan resources to the limit, probably diverting much-needed investment from domestic economic regeneration comparable to that witnessed in Western Europe in the post-war decades. The requirements of global strategy could, of course, also be counter-productive and impose constraints on Britain's freedom of action. In an attempt to resolve existing defence problems, fresh difficulties might be generated. A classic case would be the military presence in Egypt, originally central to plans to defend Britain's Far Eastern interests, but increasingly in the post-war years a source of friction in Anglo-Egyptian relations, leaving the Suez base vulnerable to local nationalist hostility. The implications of high British defence spending would be seen once again in the early 1950s, when massive rearmament became an index of Britain's commitment to retaining great power status, and of its willingness to play the role of the United States' most reliable and well-equipped partner in waging the Cold War, despite the resulting adverse effects on the metropolitan economy.

In return for American acquiescence in the continuation of the British imperial system, Britain was obliged to refashion the style and purpose of colonial rule, to embrace a new commitment to the modernization of colonial rule and the development of its colonies, bringing forward constitutional change and leading ultimately to the creation of democratic institutions. This process of redefining the relationship between Britain and its dependent empire as a new 'partnership', initiated by the wartime need to appease American criticism of Britain's colonial record, was given a fresh relevance by the Cold War and the overriding concern, shared by Britain and the US, to keep colonial populations broadly sympathetic to Western political aims. The Special Relationship, inevitably an unequal one, was itself strengthened by the Cold War, but it was potentially awkward for both parties. London, for instance, with one eye on domestic public opinion, was keen to disguise the true extent of its dependence on US assistance, and was concerned that its ties with Washington might erode Britain's capacity to conduct a genuinely independent foreign policy. The US government, while generally reluctant to create complications for its closest ally, had no wish to be closely associated with support for British colonialism, particularly once the Cold War threatened to spread beyond Europe to other regions of the world. Nevertheless, US support was substantial and essential to

Britain: in addition to the help it had provided in the period immediately after 1945 (the post-war loan and Marshall Aid), Washington continued to provide an indirect subsidy to Britain's imperial system both through its support for sterling and through its role in NATO. This underlined the critical importance of Whitehall planners remaining attuned to American policy objectives, a lesson reinforced by the disastrous experience of Suez in 1956. While there was always scope for divergence in the aims of the two countries, for example over recognizing Communist China, over the future of Indo-China, or over the Congo Crisis, and while there remained in some sections of Whitehall a lingering resentment at US power and influence, at a higher level in the British decision-making structure there was a pragmatic recognition of the need to keep British policy in step with that of Washington, a tendency only strengthened by the elevation of Macmillan in 1957.

Although, by the later 1950s, Washington was keen that Britain should speed up the process of decolonization (to prevent the developing world from falling prey to Soviet or Chinese penetration), it was also inclined to accept British warnings about the risks inherent in 'hasty' decolonization under the 'wrong' conditions. This accounts for US willingness to support Britain, for example at the United Nations, over London's handling of residual colonial complications, especially Rhodesia. What ensured a generally harmonious Anglo-American relationship during the episode of imperial retreat was the fact that London and Washington shared a fundamental belief in the importance of keeping former colonies definitely aligned to the Western bloc. The absence of US pressure on Britain to surrender its imperial system is seen nowhere more clearly than in Washington's sustained encouragement towards Britain to maintain an East of Suez role, even after the point where it had become obvious to London that this was a luxury which the straitened metropolitan economy could no longer support, even with generous American subventions.

In addition to American opinion, British policy-makers were influenced by a concern to pre-empt criticism from the United Nations, which by the later 1950s was becoming an important mouthpiece of anti-colonial sentiment. Although Britain had long treated UN interest in overseas dependencies with a suspicion bordering on obstructionism, this essentially negative posture was becoming more difficult to maintain as the UN itself expanded to include many former colonies, and as the Soviet bloc seized upon UN machinery as a means of embarrassing its ideological foes. Nor could Britain be entirely dismissive of the sentiments of the growing non-aligned group of nations, many of whom were also Commonwealth members. A further international dimension, which generated unanticipated pressure on London for an acceleration of Britain's decolonizing efforts, was the behaviour of France and Belgium in bringing forward their own withdrawal from Africa. Anxious not to be cast in the same category as the less 'liberal' colonial powers, such as Portugal, Britain felt under considerable pressure by 1960 to compress its own timetables for colonial independence.

To Britain's policy-makers, it seemed that the fundamental changes wrought by the Second World War required a new approach to managing the imperial system. What they embarked on in the next 20 or so years was a remarkably ambitious experiment, an attempt to substitute informal association with Britain for formal rule, transforming the dependent empire into a component of a new multiracial Commonwealth under British leadership. Their underlying intention was not to abandon the patterns which had constituted the traditional imperial system, but rather to preserve British global influence and give Britain's claims to be a world power a new framework and lease of life. In this respect, it must be borne in mind that for British policy-makers, the formal control of a substantial territorial empire was not necessarily the benchmark of Britain's global power. Colonial rule had only ever been one among several means through which British imperial interests had been manifested, and it was not self-evidently the most important. Informal control, which, in theory was relatively inexpensive and considerably more flexible, was, arguably, a far more attractive strategy.

Despite the reminiscences of many politicians and administrators who participated in the process, British decolonization cannot plausibly be described as being either the result of clear-sighted British planning, or under British control. The actual sequence of events during, for example, the 'wind of change', was generally very different from what London had envisaged in the late 1940s or even the later 1950s. Timetables for constitutional change, once drawn up in a mood of confidence and optimism, were abandoned with remarkable speed. Long-term colonial policy goals, for instance the concepts of multiracialism and federation, deemed appropriate in highly varied settings, disintegrated in the face of unexpectedly rapid change on the ground and in response to the international political climate. However, well into the 1950s, and even on the eve of the withdrawal from Africa, British officials did display an almost astonishing confidence in their own ability to shape the long-term development of the colonial territories. The enthusiasm shown for federal structures, drawing on a device with a long imperial pedigree, is one example of a policy which implied a reassertion, not a diminution, of British control. British officials were particularly keen to retain control over the timing of individual instances of decolonization for as long as possible, and regarded this as a key bargaining counter in their negotiations with nationalist leaders. However, this aim had to be balanced against the equally important aim of transferring power to the most co-operative of the available elites, before their popularity was outstripped by more radical groups, and before these often flimsy political coalitions began to unravel. Co-operative groups had to be 'rewarded' by the British if their popular support were to be safeguarded and their legitimacy maintained. This, in turn, might lead to the telescoping of previously made British plans to offer more gradual stages of constitutional reform. Similarly, as the case of East Africa demonstrates, it was difficult to withhold from one territory concessions already offered to one of its neighbours: individual instances of decolonization could seldom be treated in isolation, but rather were liable to have regional and even wider reverberations. Perhaps the most that can be claimed is that in the majority of colonial situations, though certainly not all, Britain managed to retain the initiative in policy-making, or the appearance of control, just long enough to secure the 'transfer of power' to acceptable elites, and to be able to withdraw leaving what seemed at the time to be the foundations of continuity and 'good government', and continuing ties with Britain.

Britain's evolving relationship with the various 'nationalist' (perhaps, more accurately, 'independence') movements it encountered is a further theme which must be addressed here. The extent and significance of such movements varied enormously among the territories of the dependent empire and the 'informal' empire. The trigger of this political activity, however, was often the expansion of British intervention, either during the war, or in its aftermath, in order to secure basic imperial interests. Wartime mobilization and post-war development combined to create conditions of British 'overrule' which provided openings for local activists. As it had done between the wars, Britain responded pragmatically to colonial resistance in the decades after 1945. Although it was usually unwilling to succumb to what it perceived as 'extremism', it was prepared to offer concessions to political groups identified as being 'moderate'. In practice, decolonization, especially in its later stages, revealed that the former could be repackaged as the latter with disconcerting speed. Unruffled transfers of power called for a certain expediency on London's part in overlooking what had once been considered irredeemable shortcomings in political opponents. The dynamics of anti-colonial resistance could embody contradictory elements. Movements had to be sufficiently confrontational to be taken seriously by the British and so win concessions, yet as many quickly learned, a willingness to co-operate with the British might secure still more concessions. Conversely, movements had to remain sufficiently radical to retain the allegiance of their supporters and pre-empt the growth of rival groups. With few exceptions, groups eschewing violence were likely to receive a more sympathetic hearing from Britain. Leaving aside the inflated rhetoric of contemporary exchanges, Britain generally enjoyed a fundamental advantage in its dealings with colonial opponents, the fact that the majority of nationalist leaders were willing to play the political game according to London's rules in order to secure self-government. Moreover, most identified themselves, or aligned themselves, at least in the short term, with Britain and the West, and therefore represented no fundamental challenge to British interests. Once again, Britain appeared remarkably confident about its ability to manipulate colonial nationalism, and to steer its development along 'acceptable' lines. In certain situations, a desire to modernize colonial territories into centralized, efficient polities led Britain actively to encourage the sense of cohesion which might stem from a 'national' consciousness.

In those instances where colonial political mobilization was translated into actual resistance to British rule, Britain attempted after 1945, as it had done in India between the wars, to combine a policy of concession (designed to encourage moderates) with coercion (in order to contain extremists). But when overriding imperial interests were at stake, even if these were relatively short term, Britain was willing to resort to a more overt use of force, as in India during the Second World War, or subsequently in Malaya, Kenya and elsewhere. Even when full-scale counterinsurgency operations were mounted, the military effort was matched, wherever possible, with a political response, designed to woo moderate opinion. Although Britain had been successful in a number of cases during the 1950s in containing local challenges to its rule, there was a growing apprehension in London that similar confrontations might be encountered in the future. By the early 1960s, this concern was reinforced by the evidence of French reversals and the domestic and international instability these generated. Prolonging formal colonial rule on the basis of force would be a dangerous strategy against the background of an intensifying and spreading Cold War. Moreover, given the sustained attempts to trim Britain's conventional military strength, there was good reason to question whether Britain would be in any position to mount successful campaigns of colonial 'pacification', even if political and wider diplomatic considerations permitted this, which seemed increasingly unlikely. Therefore, it is perhaps reasonable to argue that it was generally not the physical strength of colonial resistance which accounts for the speed and timing of British withdrawal, but rather a desire to forestall confrontations which might be insurmountable, or surmountable only at costs Britain had become unwilling to bear. In this respect, it was particularly important from London's point of view to avoid becoming embroiled in *simultaneous* colonial crises, as efforts to contain these would increasingly be beyond Britain's resources.

If the outcome of decolonization was generally not what Britain had hoped for, in that, on the whole, London failed to preserve close relations with its former colonies into the post-colonial era, British calculations during the process were characterized by a consistent aim: to maintain British influence, both commercial and political. This aim was enshrined in the agreements normally negotiated by Britain at the time of independence, to protect British economic and strategic interests, and through former colonies' willingness to join the Commonwealth. It was, above all perhaps, the attempt to replace formal control with 'informal influence' which revealed the extent to which British power had declined since the Second World War. To be successful, this strategy would require strong economic underpinnings, enabling Britain to consolidate its commercial ties, provide aid and offer attractive defence packages. In the event, Britain's capacity, especially in the provision of aid, was simply overtaken by the United States and international agencies. Moreover, understandably, many newly independent countries were keen, if possible, to assert their sovereignty in diplomatic terms and to avoid binding strategic and other commitments.

The Commonwealth is another crucial factor in understanding Britain's approach to decolonization. Its existence, and its capacity for expansion, promised to make decolonization a process of transition, rather than a radical rupture in Britain's relations with its colonies. It was of enormous importance to Britain's self-perception as a major world player that the relationship with the Dominions, which had proven itself in two world wars, could be built upon after 1945 and adapted to new purposes. The absorption of India and Pakistan offered the possibility of creating a genuinely multiracial grouping, a factor of growing significance against the backdrop of the Cold War, during which the equation of colonialism with racism became increasingly difficult for Britain to refute. Ultimately, Britain's ambitions proved to be over-optimistic. As had been the case before the Second World War, there was a tendency in British government circles to overestimate both the community of interests among Commonwealth members, and members' willingness to subordinate their own interests to those of Britain. Nevertheless, Britain's handling of decolonization was, arguably, made easier by the availability of a pre-existing model for political devolution within the empire, namely the important inter-war developments in Britain's relationship with the Dominions. To those managing the transitions involved in decolonization, it could plausibly be maintained that after the Second World War, Britain was simply applying to the dependent empire (albeit at an accelerated rate) a constitutional formula which had already proved to be successful. This ability to emphasize that imperial relations were shifting to another plane, and were not being abruptly broken, softened the metropolitan political impact of decolonization, cushioning what might otherwise have been a far more disruptive episode.

Britain's experience of decolonization has traditionally been seen as relatively trouble-free, at least in comparison to France's handling of imperial disengagement. While there is a danger in minimizing the importance of Britain's numerous colonial 'emergencies', and of underestimating the potential for greater violence during the latter phase of colonial rule, Britain was certainly fortunate in that it faced nothing to compare with Dien Bien Phu or the Algerian War. As has been seen, British policy-makers were well aware of the problems encountered by the French and sought to avoid similar quagmires. In this respect, they were generally successful. Arguably, one advantage they enjoyed was that British colonial policy had been more flexible than France's, and was more amenable to the kind of pragmatic adjustments required by changing post-war circumstances. Much was made of the relatively smooth British handling of decolonization. The very speed with which its final major phase was completed meant that most of the process had been completed before the various problems surrounding post-colonial political and economic structures became visible. The notion that Britain was bequeathing democratic institutions (as it had done previously in India) was a source of satisfaction within Britain, even though it is now clear that contemporaries, both in Whitehall and at the periphery, sometimes harboured deep (private) misgivings about the prospects for post-independence stability. Nevertheless, the appearance of stability and continuity at the time of the transfer of power was important in reassuring metropolitan opinion: had decolonization during the 1960s been more protracted, and had it become apparent sooner that post-colonial regimes might be transient, the later sequence of withdrawal might well have been complicated. In this respect, and again in contrast to French experiences, decolonization apparently had very little direct impact on domestic British politics. For most of the period discussed here, there appears to have been a broad political consensus on the central aims of imperial policy. Although criticism of government policy from the Labour Opposition increased from the late 1950s, this never threatened to produce a fundamental rift, still less a political crisis. With the exception of Suez, which was, in most respects, *sui generis*, and despite the lobbying efforts of settlers and their supporters, imperial retreat never became a major political issue within Britain. The one related theme which did threaten to complicate Britain's post-imperial politics was immigration, and even this generated a good deal of cross-party distaste for the attitudes of parts of the electorate.

The relative calm characteristic of British politics during this episode was, of course, far from accidental. In terms of its presentation to the British public, and to the political elite, the process of imperial disengagement was managed with extreme care, especially by Macmillan but also by his predecessors (with the exception of Eden) and successors. Charged with supervising what could have been interpreted as a process of retreat, symbolizing the reality of Britain's relative decline, successive governments emphasized the themes of controlled adjustment and qualified change, the celebration of past achievements, fundamental continuity of purpose and the identification of new opportunities to reinforce Britain's world role. It is hardly surprising, then, that the people of Britain have been so slow to embrace a dispassionate or rounded view of their imperial past.

NOTES

Introduction

[1] R.F. Holland, *European Decolonization 1918–1981. An Introductory Survey* (Basingstoke: Macmillan, 1985), pp 1–33.

[2] J. Gallagher and R. Robinson, 'The imperialism of free trade', *Economic History Review*, 2nd ser., 6/1 (1953), pp 1–15.

[3] R. Robinson, 'Non-European foundations of European imperialism: Sketch for a theory of collaboration', in R. Owen and B. Sutcliffe (eds), *Studies in the Theory of Imperialism* (London: Longman, 1972).

[4] Andrew Porter, *European Imperialism*, 1860–1914 (Basingstoke: Macmillan, 1994).

Chapter 1: The imperial system between the wars

[1] A. Clayton, '"Deceptive might": Imperial defence and security, 1900–1968', in J.M. Brown and Wm Roger Louis (eds), *The Oxford History of the British Empire, Vol IV: The Twentieth Century* (Oxford: Oxford University Press, 1999), p 282; A. Clayton, *The British Empire as a Superpower, 1919–39* (London: Macmillan 1986).

[2] Clayton: *OHBE IV*, pp 281–2.

[3] S.R. Ashton and S.E. Stockwell (eds), *British Documents on the End of Empire, Series A, Vol 1: Imperial Policy and Colonial Practice, 1925–1945* (London: HMSO, 1996), p xciv n18.

[4] W. David McIntyre, 'Australia, New Zealand, and the Pacific Islands', *OHBE IV*, p 673.

[5] Ashton and Stockwell: *British Documents on the End of Empire*, p xxxiii.

[6] Clayton: *OHBE IV*, p 284.

[7] *Ibid.*, p 283.

[8] Ashton and Stockwell: *British Documents on the End of Empire*, p xxxiv.

[9] B.R. Tomlinson, *The Political Economy of the Raj, 1914–47: The Economics of Decolonization in India* (London: Macmillan, 1979) pp 114–17.

[10] N. Owen, 'Critics of empire in Britain', *OHBE IV*, p 192.

[11] Clayton: *OHBE IV*, p 290; D.E. Omissi, *Air Power and Colonial Control. The Royal Air Force 1919–1939* (Manchester: Manchester University Press, 1990).

[12] Ashton and Stockwell: *British Documents on the End of Empire*, p xxxiv.

[13] W. David McIntyre, 'The strange death of Dominion status', in R.D. King and R. Kilson (eds), *The Statecraft of British Imperialism: Essays in Honour of Wm. Roger Louis* (London: Frank Cass, 1999), p 195.

[14] A.B. Keith (ed), *Speeches and Documents on the British Dominions 1918–1931: From Self-Government to National Sovereignty* (London: Oxford University Press, 1962), p 318.

[15] J. Darwin, 'Imperialism in decline? Tendencies in British imperial policy between the wars', *Historical Journal* 23/3 (1980), p 662.

[16] J. Darwin, 'A third British empire? The Dominion idea in imperial politics', *OHBE IV*, p 69.

17 S. Constantine (ed), *Emigrants and Empire: British Settlement in the Dominions between the Wars* (Manchester: Manchester University Press, 1990).

18 Darwin: *OHBE IV*, pp 72–3.

19 Darwin: *OHBE IV*, p 86; J.M. Mackenzie, '"In touch with the infinite": The BBC and the empire, 1923–53', in J.M. Mackenzie (ed), *Imperialism and Popular Culture* (Manchester: Manchester University Press, 1986), pp 165–91.

20 Ashton and Stockwell: *British Documents on the End of Empire*, p lxii.

21 D.K. Fieldhouse, 'The metropolitan economics of empire', *OHBE IV*, p 101.

22 Fieldhouse: *OHBE IV*, pp 111–12; P.J. Cain and A.G. Hopkins, *British Imperialism, vol II: Crisis and Deconstruction 1914–1990* (Harlow: Longman, 1993), p 85.

23 Ashton and Stockwell: *British Documents on the End of Empire*, p lxiii.

24 R.F. Holland, 'The end of an imperial economy: Anglo-Canadian disengagement in the 1930s', *Journal of Imperial and Commonwealth History* 2 (1983), pp 159–75.

25 I.M. Drummond, *Imperial Economic Policy 1917–1939: Studies in Expansion and Protection* (Toronto: University of Toronto Press, 1974), pp 29–32.

26 P. Clavin, *The Failure of Economic Diplomacy. Britain, Germany, France and the United States, 1931–36* (Basingstoke: Macmillan, 1996), pp 117–41.

27 D. Meredith, 'The British government and colonial economic policy 1919–1939', *Economic History Review*, 2nd ser., 28/3 (1975), pp 484–99.

28 Ashton and Stockwell: *British Documents on the End of Empire*, p lxiv.

29 Cain and Hopkins: *British Imperialism*, vol II, pp 76–83.

30 Fieldhouse: *OHBE IV*, p 97.

31 P.J. Cain and A.G. Hopkins, 'Afterword: The theory and practice of British imperialism', in R.E. Dumett (ed), *Gentlemanly Capitalism and British Imperialism. The New Debate on Empire* (Harlow: Longman, 1999), pp 210–11.

32 Ashton and Stockwell: *British Documents on the End of Empire*, p lxiii; S. Constantine, '"Bringing the empire alive": The Empire Marketing Board and imperial propaganda, 1926–33', in J.M. Mackenzie (ed), *Imperialism and Popular Culture* (Manchester: Manchester University Press, 1986), pp 192–231.

33 Constantine (ed): *Emigrants and Empire*.

34 Darwin: 'Imperialism in decline?', p 674.

35 J.M. Brown, 'India', *OHBE IV*, p 432.

36 Wm Roger Louis, 'Introduction', *OHBE IV*, p 33.

37 *Ibid.*

38 S. Ball, *Baldwin and the Conservative Party: The Crisis of 1929–31* (New Haven: Yale University Press, 1988), p 115.

39 Ashton and Stockwell: *British Documents on the End of Empire*, p xlvi.

40 R.J. Moore, 'India in the 1940s', in R.W. Winks (ed), *The Oxford History of the British Empire, Vol V: Historiography*, p 233.

41 J. Darwin, 'Decolonization and the end of empire', *OHBE V*, p 545.

42 Darwin: 'Imperialism in decline?', p 677.

43 M. Misrah, *Business, Race and Politics in British India, c.1860–1960* (Oxford: Oxford University Press, 1999), chs 5 and 7; M. Misrah, 'Gentlemanly capitalism and the Raj: British policy in India between the wars', in Dumett (ed): *Gentlemanly Capitalism and British Imperialism*, pp 169–70.

44 D.E. Omissi, *The Sepoy and the Raj: The Indian Army, 1860–1940* (Basingstoke: Macmillan, 1994).

45 Brown: *OHBE IV*, p 439; Clayton: *OHBE IV*, p 285.

46 Brown: *OHBE IV*, p 440.

47 Louis: *OHBE IV*, p 33.

48 Brown: *OHBE IV*, p 430.

49 F. Robinson, 'The British empire and the Muslim world', *OHBE IV*, pp 410–11.

[50] Ashton and Stockwell: *British Documents on the End of Empire*, p xlvi.

[51] G. Balfour-Paul, 'Britain's informal empire in the Middle East', *OHBE IV*, p 503.

[52] G.H. Bennett, *British Foreign Policy during the Curzon Period, 1919–24* (Basingstoke: Macmillan, 1995).

[53] K. Jeffery, *The British Army and the Crisis of Empire, 1918–22* (Manchester: Manchester University Press, 1984).

[54] J. Darwin, 'An undeclared empire: The British in the Middle East, 1918–39', in R.D. King and R. Kilson (eds), *The Statecraft of British Imperialism: Essays in Honour of Wm. Roger Louis* (London: Frank Cass, 1999), p 169.

[55] P. Sluglett, 'Formal and informal empire in the Middle East', *OHBE V*, pp 425–6.

[56] Louis: *OHBE IV*, p 33.

[57] Darwin: 'An undeclared empire', p 166.

[58] Balfour-Paul: *OHBE IV*, p 504.

[59] Darwin: 'Imperialism in decline?', p 668.

[60] Jeffery: *The British Army*, p 141; J. Darwin, *Britain, Egypt and the Middle East. Imperial Policy in the Aftermath of War 1918–1922* (London: Macmillan, 1981).

[61] Sluglett: *OHBE V*, p 431.

[62] R. Holland, *The Pursuit of Greatness. Britain and the World Role, 1900–1970* (London: Fontana, 1991), pp 119–20.

[63] Darwin: 'An undeclared empire', pp 170–1.

[64] *Ibid.*, p 169.

[65] Clayton: *OHBE IV*, pp 292–3.

[66] Darwin: 'An undeclared empire', p 172.

[67] J. Darwin, *Britain and Decolonisation. The Retreat from Empire in the Post-War World* (Basingstoke: Macmillan, 1988), pp 28–9.

[68] Darwin: *OHBE V*, p 545.

[69] Ashton and Stockwell: *British Documents on the End of Empire*, p xxvii.

[70] *Ibid.*

[71] *Ibid.*, p lx.

[72] J.W. Cell, 'Colonial rule', *OHBE IV*, p 235; Ashton and Stockwell: *British Documents on the End of Empire*, p xlviii.

[73] Ashton and Stockwell: *British Documents on the End of Empire*, p xlviii.

[74] Cell: *OHBE IV*, p 235.

[75] T. Falola, 'British imperialism: Roger Louis and the West African case', in King and Kilson (eds): *The Statecraft of British Imperialism*, p 132.

[76] Ashton and Stockwell: *British Documents on the End of Empire*, p l.

[77] *Ibid.*, p li.

[78] *Ibid.*

[79] *Ibid.*, p lxi.

[80] S. Constantine, *The Making of British Colonial Development Policy 1914–1940* (London: Frank Cass, 1984).

[81] H. Johnson, 'The British Caribbean from demobilization to constitutional decolonization', *OHBE IV*, p 609; H. Johnson, 'The West Indies and the conversion of the British official classes to the development idea', *Journal of Commonwealth and Comparative Politics* 15/1 (1977), pp 55–75.

[82] W.M. Macmillan, *Warning from the West Indies: A Tract for Africa and the Empire* (London: Faber and Faber, 1936).

[83] Ashton and Stockwell: *British Documents on the End of Empire*, p lxvii.

[84] *Ibid.*, p lxviii.

[85] H. Kuklick, *The Savage Within. The Social History of British Anthropology, 1885–1945* (Cambridge: Cambridge University Press, 1991), p 207.

[86] Ashton and Stockwell: *British Documents on the End of Empire*, p lxxvii.

[87] *Ibid.*, pp lxxviii–lxxix.

[88] *Ibid.*, p lxxxv.

[89] *Ibid.*, p lxxxvii; M. Nicholson, *The TUC Overseas. The Roots of Policy* (London: Allen & Unwin, 1986), pp 176–253.

[90] Ashton and Stockwell: *British Documents on the End of Empire*, p xxviii.

[91] Clayton: *OHBE IV*, p 284.

[92] Ashton and Stockwell: *British Documents on the End of Empire*, p xciv n22.

[93] *Ibid.*, pp xxxiv–xxxv.

[94] *Ibid.*, p xciv n25.

[95] Clayton: *OHBE IV*, p 286.

[96] Ashton and Stockwell: *British Documents on the End of Empire*, p xxx.

[97] R. Ovendale, 'The Empire-Commonwealth and the two world wars', *OHBE V*, p 357.

[98] Ashton and Stockwell: *British Documents on the End of Empire*, p xxxv; A.J. Crozier, *Appeasement and Germany's Last Bid for Colonies* (London: Macmillan, 1988).

[99] M.J. Cohen, 'British Strategy in the Middle East in the wake of the Abyssinian Crisis, 1936–39', in M.J. Cohen and M. Kolinsky (eds), *Britain and the Middle East in the 1930s. Security Problems, 1935–39* (Basingstoke: Macmillan, 1992), p 21.

[100] Ashton and Stockwell: *British Documents on the End of Empire*, p xxxv.

[101] *Ibid.*, p xciv n26.

[102] *Ibid.*, p xxxvi.

[103] Clayton: *OHBE IV*, p 282.

[104] D. Mackenzie, 'Canada, the North Atlantic triangle, and the empire', *OHBE IV*, p 586.

[105] D. Reynolds, *Britannia Overruled. British Policy and World Power in the Twentieth Century* (Harlow: Longman, 1991), p 131.

[106] Ashton and Stockwell: *British Documents on the End of Empire*, p xxxvi.

[107] *Ibid.*, pp xxxvi–xxxvii.

[108] *Ibid.*, pp xciv–xcv n28.

[109] Cited in Reynolds *Britannia Overruled*, p 130.

Chapter 2: The impact of the Second World War

[1] K. Jeffery, 'The Second World War', in J.M. Brown and Wm Roger Louis (eds), *The Oxford History of the British Empire, Vol IV: The Twentieth Century* (Oxford: Oxford University Press, 1999), pp 306–7.

[2] J. Darwin, *Britain and Decolonisation. The Retreat from Empire in the Post-War World* (Basingstoke: Macmillan, 1988), p 24.

[3] S.R. Ashton and S.E. Stockwell (eds), *British Documents on the End of Empire, Series A, Vol 1: Imperial Policy and Colonial Practice, 1925–1945* (London: HMSO, 1996), p xxxvii.

[4] *Ibid.*

[5] M. Cowen and N. Westcott, 'British imperial economic policy during the war', in D. Killingray and R. Rathbone (eds), *Africa and the Second World War* (London: Macmillan, 1986), pp 20–67.

[6] Jeffery: *OHBE IV*, p 312; J. Gallagher, *The Decline, Revival and Fall of the British Empire. The Ford Lectures and Other Essays*, edited by Anil Seal (Cambridge: Cambridge University Press, 1982).

[7] B.R. Tomlinson, *The Political Economy of the Raj, 1914–1947: The Economics of Decolonization in India* (London: Macmillan, 1979), pp 92–100.

[8] PRO: CO 822/111/46705, telegram to African governors, 21 March 1942.

[9] Ashton and Stockwell: *British Documents on the End of Empire*, p lxxxix.

[10] Quoted in D.E. Moggridge, 'From war to peace – the sterling balances', *The Banker*, CXXII/558 (August 1972), pp 1032–5.

[11] L.J. Butler, *Industrialisation and the British Colonial State: West Africa, 1939–1951* (London: Frank Cass, 1997).

[12] D.K. Fieldhouse, 'War and the origins of the Gold Coast Marketing Board, 1939–40', in M. Twaddle (ed), *Imperialism, the State and the Third World* (London: British Academic Press, 1992), pp 153–82.

[13] D.K. Fieldhouse, 'The metropolitan economics of empire', *OHBE IV*, p 92.

[14] J.M. Lee, '"Forward thinking" and war: the Colonial Office during the 1940s', *JICH* 6/1 (1977), pp 64–79.

[15] Jeffery: *OHBE IV*, pp 323–4; A. Jackson, *Botswana 1939–1945. An African Country at War* (Oxford: Clarendon Press, 1999).

[16] Ashton and Stockwell: *British Documents on the End of Empire*, pp xc–xci.

[17] J.M. Lee and M. Petter, *The Colonial Office, War, and Development Policy. Organisation and the Planning of a Metropolitan Initiative, 1939–1945* (London: Maurice Temple Smith, 1982), pp 115–43.

[18] S. Constantine, *The Making of British Colonial Development Policy 1914–1940* (London: Frank Cass, 1984).

[19] M. Havinden and D. Meredith, *Colonialism and Development. Britain and Its Tropical Colonies, 1850–1960* (London: Routledge, 1993).

[20] A.J. Stockwell (ed), *British Documents on the End of Empire, Series B, Vol 3: Malaya* (London: HMSO, 1995).

[21] Darwin: *Britain and Decolonisation*, p 45.

[22] Jeffery: *OHBE IV*, pp 310, 320.

[23] M. Gowing, *Britain and Atomic Energy, 1939–1945* (London: Macmillan, 1964).

[24] J. Darwin, 'A third British empire? The Dominion idea in imperial politics', *OHBE IV*, p 84.

[25] D. Mackenzie, 'Canada, the North Atlantic triangle, and the empire', *OHBE IV*, pp 587–88.

[26] Jeffery: *OHBE IV*, p 317.

[27] Ashton and Stockwell: *British Documents on the End of Empire*, pp lv–lvi.

[28] J. Darwin, 'An undeclared empire: The British in the Middle East, 1918–39', in R.D. King and R. Kilson (eds), *The Statecraft of British Imperialism: Essays in Honour of Wm. Roger Louis* (London: Frank Cass, 1999), p 176 n59.

[29] Jeffery: *OHBE IV*, p 318.

[30] G. Balfour-Paul, 'Britain's informal empire in the Middle East', *OHBE IV*, p 504.

[31] Darwin: *Britain and Decolonisation*, p 42.

[32] *Ibid.*, p 55.

[33] PRO: CAB 66/65, WP(45)256, 13 April 1945.

[34] Ashton and Stockwell: *British Documents on the End of Empire*, p xliii.

[35] *Ibid.*, pp xliii–xliv.

[36] R.J. Moore, *Churchill, Cripps, and India 1939–1945* (Oxford: Clarendon Press, 1979).

[37] W. David McIntyre, 'The strange death of Dominion status', in King and Kilson (eds): *The Statecraft of British Imperialism*, p 197.

[38] J.M. Brown, 'India', *OHBE IV*, p 436.

[39] J.W. Cell, 'The Indian and African freedom struggles: some comparisons', in King and Kilson (eds): *The Statecraft of British Imperialism*, pp 116–17.

[40] R.J. Moore, 'India in the 1940s', in R.W. Winks (ed), *The Oxford History of the British Empire, Vol V: Historiography*, p 237.

[41] Jeffery: *OHBE IV*, p 324.

[42] Ashton and Stockwell: *British Documents on the End of Empire*, p xxxix.

[43] Wm Roger Louis, *Imperialism at Bay. The United States and the Decolonization of the British Empire, 1941–1945* (Oxford: Oxford University Press, 1977).

[44] Ashton and Stockwell: *British Documents on the End of Empire*, p xxxix.

[45] *Ibid.*

[46] J. Tomlinson, *Public Policy and the Economy since 1900* (Oxford: Clarendon Press, 1990), pp 172–202.

[47] M.W. Kirby, *The Decline of British Economic Power since 1870* (London: George Allen & Unwin, 1981), pp 94–5; L.S. Pressnell, *External Economic Policy since the War, Vol I: The Post-War Financial Settlement* (London: HMSO, 1986), ch 8; R. Gardner, *Sterling–Dollar Diplomacy* (rev. ed., New York: Oxford University Press, 1969), pp 154–5.

[48] Ashton and Stockwell: *British Documents on the End of Empire*, p xl.

[49] *Ibid.*

[50] *Ibid.*

[51] *Ibid.*, p xli.

[52] *Ibid.*; A.N. Porter and A.J. Stockwell, *British Imperial Policy and Decolonization 1938–1964, Vol I: 1938–51* (Basingstoke: Macmillan, 1987), pp 28–9.

[53] Ashton and Stockwell: *British Documents on the End of Empire*, p xlii.

[54] Darwin: *Britain and Decolonisation*, p 43.

[55] *Ibid.*, p 41.

[56] J.E. Flint, '"Managing nationalism": The Colonial Office and Nnamdi Azikiwe, 1932–43', in King and Kilson (eds): *The Statecraft of British Imperialism*, p 152.

[57] *Hansard*, 5th ser., 391, cols 48–69, 13 July 1943.

[58] Gallagher: *The Decline, Revival and Fall of the British Empire*, pp 142–3.

[59] Lee and Petter: *The Colonial Office*, pp 147–99.

[60] H. Johnson, 'The Anglo-American Caribbean Commission and the extension of American influence in the British Caribbean, 1942–1945', *Journal of Commonwealth and Comparative Politics* 22 (1984), pp 180–203.

[61] PRO: CO 852/588/2, memorandum, 12 August 1943.

[62] Butler: *Industrialisation and the British Colonial State*, p 171; Sir C. Jeffries, *Whitehall and the Colonial Service: An Administrative Memoir, 1939–1956* (London: Athlone Press, 1972).

[63] Lee and Petter: *The Colonial Office*, pp 202–5.

[64] PRO: CAB 66/57, WP(44)643, memorandum by Stanley, 15 November 1944.

[65] Jeffery: *OHBE IV*, p 321.

[66] K.M. de Silva (ed), *British Documents on the End of Empire, Series B, Vol 2: Sri Lanka Part I: The Second World War and the Soulbury Commission 1939–1945* (London: The Stationery Office, 1997).

[67] Wm Roger Louis, 'Introduction', *OHBE IV*, p 34; S.R. Ashton, 'Ceylon', *OHBE IV*, p 460.

[68] J. Flint, 'Planned decolonization and its failure in British Africa', *African Affairs* 82/328 (July 1983), pp 389–411; C. Sanger, *Malcolm MacDonald. Bringing an End to Empire* (Liverpool: Liverpool University Press, 1995), pp 146–9.

[69] J.W. Cell, *Hailey: A Study in British Imperialism, 1872–1969* (Cambridge: Cambridge University Press, 1992), pp 254–65.

[70] Ashton and Stockwell: *British Documents on the End of Empire*, p liii.

[71] R. Rathbone (ed), *British Documents on the End of Empire, Series B, Vol I: Ghana Part I* (London: HMSO, 1995).

[72] PRO: CO 554/132/33727, 'Constitutional development in West Africa', June/July 1943.

[73] Flint: '"Managing nationalism"', p 155.

[74] R. Robinson, 'British imperialism: The Colonial Office and the settler in East-Central Africa, 1919–63', in E. Serra and C. Seton-Watson (eds), *Italia e Inghilterra nell'eta dell imperialismo* (Milan: Franco Angeli, 1990), pp 195–212.

[75] PRO: CO 967/57/46709, 'A federal solution for East Africa', July 1942.

[76] M. Chanock, *Unconsummated Union: Britain, Rhodesia and South Africa, 1900–1945* (Manchester: Manchester University Press, 1977).

[77] Ashton and Stockwell: *British Documents on the End of Empire*, pp lvi–lvii.

78 *Ibid.*, p lviii.
79 Porter and Stockwell, *British Imperial Policy I*, pp 37–8.
80 N. Tarling, 'The British Empire in South-East Asia', *OHBE V*, p 412.
81 A.J. Stockwell, 'Imperialism and nationalism in South-East Asia', *OHBE IV*, p 477.
82 M. Nicholson, *The TUC Overseas. The Roots of Policy* (London: Allen & Unwin, 1986).
83 Kirby: *The Decline of British Economic Power*, pp 83–4.
84 Louis: *OHBE IV*, p 331.
85 J.M. Keynes, 'Overseas financial policy in Stage III', circulated to War Cabinet, 15 May 1945, in D. Moggridge (ed), *The Collected Writings of John Maynard Keynes, Vol XXIV: Activities 1944–46: The Transition to Peace* (London: Macmillan, 1979), pp 256–95.
86 Ashton and Stockwell: *British Documents on the End of Empire*, p lxxii; A.E. Hinds, 'Imperial policy and colonial sterling balances 1943–56', *Journal of Imperial and Commonwealth History* 19/1 (1991), pp 24–44.
87 Jeffery: *OHBE IV*, p 327.

Chapter 3: Attlee and post-war adjustments, 1945–51

1 R. Hyam (ed), *British Documents on the End of Empire, Series A, Vol 2: The Labour Government and the End of Empire 1945–1951* (London: HMSO, 1992), p xxiii.
2 J. Darwin, *Britain and Decolonisation. The Retreat from Empire in the Post-War World* (Basingstoke: Macmillan, 1988), p 69.
3 Hyam: *British Documents on the End of Empire*, pp xlii–xliii.
4 *Ibid.*, p xliii; A. Cairncross, *Years of Recovery. British Economic Policy 1945–51* (London: Methuen, 1985), pp 123–30.
5 Hyam: *British Documents on the End of Empire*, p lvii.
6 *Ibid.*, p xliii.
7 D. Reynolds, *Britannia Overruled. British Policy and World Power in the Twentieth Century* (Harlow: Longman, 1991), p 179.
8 *Ibid.*, pp 162–3.
9 *Ibid.*, pp 168–9, 173.
10 Hyam: *British Documents on the End of Empire*, p lix.
11 *Ibid.*, p xliii.
12 Reynolds: *Britannia Overruled*, p 179.
13 Hyam: *British Documents on the End of Empire*, p xliv.
14 *Ibid.*
15 Reynolds: *Britannia Overruled*, p 180.
16 Hyam: *British Documents on the End of Empire*, p xliv.
17 *Ibid.*, pp lxviii, xxiv–xxv.
18 *Ibid.*, p lxix; A. Inder Singh, 'Keeping India in the Commonwealth', *Journal of Contemporary History* 20 (1985), pp 469–81.
19 N. Mansergh, *The Commonwealth Experience* (London: Macmillan, 1982), pp ii, 158.
20 Darwin: *Britain and Decolonisation*, p 153.
21 *Ibid.*, p 150.
22 Hyam: *British Documents on the End of Empire*, p lxviii.
23 A.J. Stockwell, *British Documents on the End of Empire, Series B, Vol 3: Malaya* (London: HMSO, 1995), p lxxix.
24 W. David McIntyre, 'Commonwealth legacy', in J.M. Brown and Wm Roger Louis (eds), *The Oxford History of the British Empire, Vol IV: The Twentieth Century* (Oxford: Oxford University Press, 1999), p 696.
25 S. Constantine, 'Waving goodbye? Australia, assisted passages, and the Empire and Commonwealth Settlement Acts, 1945–72', *JICH* 26/2 (1998), pp 176–95.
26 Hyam: *British Documents on the End of Empire*, p lix.

27 W. David McIntyre, *Background to the ANZUS Pact: Policy-Making, Strategy and Diplomacy, 1945–55* (London: Macmillan, 1995).

28 Hyam: *British Documents on the End of Empire*, pp lix–lx; D. Devereux, 'Britain, the Commonwealth, and the defence of the Middle East, 1948–56', *Journal of Contemporary History* 24 (1989), pp 327–45. See also R. Ovendale, *The English-Speaking Alliance: Britain, the United States, the Dominions and the Cold War, 1945–1951* (London: Allen & Unwin, 1985), pp 231–3;. PRO CAB 21/1786, minutes of meeting of Commonwealth Defence Ministers, June 1951.

29 Hyam: *British Documents on the End of Empire*, p lx.

30 *Ibid.*, p liii.

31 Reynolds: *Britannia Overruled*, p 187.

32 Hyam: *British Documents on the End of Empire*, pp lxx–lxxi.

33 Reynolds: *Britannia Overruled*, p 192.

34 Hyam: *British Documents on the End of Empire*, p lxxi; Reynolds: *Britannia Overruled*, p 181.

35 Reynolds: *Britannia Overruled*, pp 176–7; J. Darwin, *The End of the British Empire. The Historical Debate* (Oxford: Basil Blackwell, 1991), pp 61–7.

36 J.W. Young, *Britain, France and the Unity of Europe, 1945–1951* (Leicester: Leicester University Press, 1984), p 127.

37 Hyam: *British Documents on the End of Empire*, p lxxi.

38 Reynolds: *Britannia Overruled*, p 195.

39 J. Darwin, 'British decolonization since 1945: A pattern or a puzzle?', *JICH* 12/2 (1984), pp 187–209.

40 Hyam: *British Documents on the End of Empire*, p xxv; T. Burridge, *Clement Attlee: A Political Biography* (London: Jonathan Cape, 1985).

41 R.J. Moore, *Escape from Empire. The Attlee Government and the Indian Problem* (Oxford: Clarendon Press, 1983).

42 Reynolds: *Britannia Overruled*, p 165.

43 H. Tinker, 'The contraction of empire in Asia, 1945–48: The military dimension', *JICH* 16/2 (1988), pp 218–33.

44 Hyam: *British Documents on the End of Empire*, pp lvii–lviii; B.R. Tomlinson, *The Political Economy of the Raj, 1914–47: The Economics of Decolonization in India* (London: Macmillan, 1979), p 147; R. Aldrich and M. Coleman, 'Britain and the strategic air offensive against the Soviet Union: The question of South Asian air bases', *History* 242 (1989), pp 400–26.

45 Reynolds: *Britannia Overruled*, p 165; N. Mansergh *et al* (eds), *Constitutional Relations between Britain and India: The Transfer of Power, 1942–1947, Vol IX: The Fixing of a Time Limit*, p 41, Wavell to Sec of State for India, 11 November 1946.

46 Hyam: *British Documents on the End of Empire*, p xxv.

47 Tinker: 'The contraction of empire in Asia', p 224.

48 Darwin: *Britain and Decolonisation*, p 92.

49 PRO: CAB 128/8, (46) 108, Confidential annex, 31 December 1946, cited in Wm Roger Louis, 'Introduction', *OHBE IV*, p 328.

50 Hyam: *British Documents on the End of Empire*, p xxv; Reynolds: *Britannia Overruled*, p 168.

51 N. Mansergh and P. Moon (eds), *Constitutional Relations between Britain and India: The Transfer of Power, 1942–47, Vol X: Mountbatten Viceroyalty, Formulation of a Plan*, p 329.

52 Reynolds: *Britannia Overruled*, p 168.

53 P. Darby, *British Defence Policy East of Suez, 1947–1968* (London: Oxford University Press, 1973), pp 10–31.

54 Hyam: *British Documents on the End of Empire*, p xxvi.

55 PRO: CAB 128/9, 44(47), 6 May 1947, cited in Darwin: *Britain and Decolonisation*, p 105.

56 S.R. Ashton, 'Ceylon', *OHBE IV*, pp 463–4.

57 R.B. Smith, 'Some contrasts between Burma and Malaya in British policy in South-East Asia, 1942–6', in R.B. Smith and A.J. Stockwell (eds), *British Policy and the Transfer of Power*

in Asia: Documentary Perspectives (London: School of Oriental and African Studies, University of London, 1988), pp 46–8, 68–72.

58 P.W.T. Kingston, *Britain and the Politics of Modernization in the Middle East, 1945–1958* (Cambridge: Cambridge University Press, 1996).

59 Hyam: *British Documents on the End of Empire*, pp xxviii, xlviii; Reynolds: *Britannia Overruled*, p 190.

60 Reynolds: *Britannia Overruled*, p 190.

61 M.J. Cohen and M. Kolinsky (eds), *Demise of the British Empire in the Middle East: Britain's Response to Nationalist Movements 1943–1955* (London: Frank Cass, 1998).

62 PRO: CAB 131/4, DO(47)23, memorandum by Chiefs of Staff, 7 March 1947.

63 Hyam: *British Documents on the End of Empire*, p lv.

64 J. Kent, 'Informal empire and the defence of the Middle East 1945–56', in R. Bridges (ed), *Imperialism, Decolonization and Africa. Studies Presented to John Hargreaves* (Basingstoke: Macmillan, 2000), pp 114–52.

65 Hyam: *British Documents on the End of Empire*, p lviii.

66 *Ibid.*

67 Wm Roger Louis, *The British Empire in the Middle East 1945–1951. Arab Nationalism, The United States, and Postwar Imperialism* (Oxford: Clarendon Press, 1984), pp 9–10.

68 Hyam: *British Documents on the End of Empire*, p xxviii.

69 Reynolds: *Britannia Overruled*, p 166.

70 Hyam: *British Documents on the End of Empire*, p xxvi.

71 M.J. Cohen, *Palestine and the Great Powers, 1945–1948* (Princeton, New Jersey: Princeton University Press, 1982), p 392.

72 Hyam: *British Documents on the End of Empire*, pp xxvi–xxviii.

73 PRO: CAB 129/21, CP(47)259, memorandum by Foreign Secretary.

74 R. Holland, *The Pursuit of Greatness. Britain and the World Role, 1900–1970* (London: Fontana, 1991), p 224.

75 Hyam: *British Documents on the End of Empire*, p lviii.

76 Darwin: 'British decolonization since 1945'.

77 Hyam: *British Documents on the End of Empire*, p xxviii; Louis: *The British Empire in the Middle East*, pp 666, 688.

78 R. Hyam, 'Africa and the Labour government, 1945–1951', *JICH* 16/3 (1988), p 158.

79 Hyam: *British Documents on the End of Empire*, pp xxix, xxxv.

80 *Ibid.*, pp xxiv–xxv.

81 R.F. Holland, 'The imperial factor in British strategies from Attlee to Macmillan, 1945–63', *JICH* 12/2 (1984), pp 165–85.

82 Hyam: 'Africa and the Labour government', p 153.

83 Hyam: *British Documents on the End of Empire*, p xxv.

84 *Ibid.*, pp xxiv, lv.

85 *Ibid.*, p lii; S.L. Carruthers, *Winning Hearts and Minds. British Governments, the Media and Colonial Counter-Insurgency 1944–1960* (Leicester: Leicester University Press, 1995), pp 1–24.

86 Hyam: *British Documents on the End of Empire*, p liii.

87 *Ibid.*, p lii.

88 *Ibid.*, pp liii–liv.

89 *Ibid.*, p li.

90 *Ibid.*, p xlii.

91 A.E. Hinds, 'Sterling and imperial policy, 1945–51', *JICH* 15/2 (1987), pp 148–64.

92 Hyam: *British Documents on the End of Empire*, p l.

93 *Ibid.*, p xlix.

94 *Ibid.*, p li.

[95] D.K. Fieldhouse, 'The Labour government and the Empire-Commonwealth, 1945–1951', in R. Ovendale (ed), *The Foreign Policy of the British Labour Governments 1945–1951* (Leicester: Leicester University Press, 1984), pp 83–120.

[96] Hyam: *British Documents on the End of Empire*, p xliv.

[97] A.J. Stockwell, 'British imperial policy and decolonization in Malaya, 1942–52', *JICH* 13/1 (1984), pp 68–87.

[98] Hyam: *British Documents on the End of Empire*, p xlii.

[99] PRO: CO 852/1003/3, speech, 12 November 1947.

[100] Hyam: *British Documents on the End of Empire*, p xlv.

[101] *Ibid.*, pp xlvi–xlvii; L.J. Butler, 'Reconstruction, development and the entrepreneurial state: The British colonial model, 1939–51', *Contemporary British History* 13/4 (Winter 1999), pp 29–55.

[102] Fieldhouse: 'The Labour governments and the Empire-Commonwealth' p 99; P.S. Gupta, 'Imperialism and the Labour government of 1945–51', in J.M. Winter (ed), *The Working Class in Modern British History* (Cambridge: Cambridge University Press, 1983).

[103] Hyam: *British Documents on the End of Empire*, p xlii.

[104] Fieldhouse: 'The Labour governments and the Empire-Commonwealth', p 98.

[105] Hyam: *British Documents on the End of Empire*, p xlviii.

[106] Reynolds: *Britannia Overruled*, p 188. On the concept of the 'Second Colonial Occupation', see 'Introduction', in D.A. Low and A. Smith (eds), *History of East Africa*, vol III (Oxford: Oxford University Press, 1976).

[107] Hyam: *British Documents on the End of Empire*, pp lxi–lxii.

[108] *Ibid.*, pp xlviii–xlix.

[109] *Ibid.*, p xlv.

[110] Reynolds: *Britannia Overruled*, p 188; Hinds: 'Sterling and imperial policy'.

[111] A.J. Stockwell, 'Southeast Asia in war and peace: The end of European colonial empires', in N. Tarling (ed), *The Cambridge History of Southeast Asia, Vol Two: The Nineteenth and Twentieth Centuries* (Cambridge: Cambridge University Press, 1996), pp 355–6.

[112] Stockwell: *British Documents on the End of Empire*, p lviii.

[113] Darwin: *Britain and Decolonisation*, p 109.

[114] Hyam: *British Documents on the End of Empire*, p xxxviii.

[115] Stockwell: 'British imperial policy'.

[116] Stockwell: *British Documents on the End of Empire*, p lxi.

[117] A.J. Stockwell, 'Imperialism and nationalism in South-East Asia', *OHBE IV*, p 485.

[118] Hyam: *British Documents on the End of Empire*, p xxiv.

[119] *Ibid.*, p xxvii.

[120] Stockwell: *British Documents on the End of Empire*, p lxvii.

[121] Hyam: *British Documents on the End of Empire*, p xxvii.

[122] Carruthers: *Winning Hearts and Minds*, pp 90–5.

[123] Hyam: *British Documents on the End of Empire*, pp xxix–xxx.

[124] PRO: CO 847/25/47234, memorandum by G.B. Cartland, 'Native administration policy', 1946; R.D. Pearce, 'Morale in the Colonial Service in Nigeria during the Second World War', *JICH* 11/2 (1983), pp 175–96.

[125] Hyam: *British Documents on the End of Empire*, p xxx; R.D. Pearce, *The Turning Point in Africa. British Colonial Policy 1938–1948* (London: Frank Cass, 1982), pp 162–84.

[126] Hyam: *British Documents on the End of Empire*, pp xxx–xxxi.

[127] Pearce: *The Turning Point in Africa*, pp 162–84.

[128] Hyam: *British Documents on the End of Empire*, p xxxi.

[129] *Ibid.*, p xxxiii.

[130] *Ibid.*, p xxx.

[131] *Ibid.*, p xxxv.

[132] Fieldhouse: 'The Labour governments and the Empire-Commonwealth', pp 106–10.

133 *Ibid.*

134 Hyam: *British Documents on the End of Empire*, p lii.

135 R. Rathbone (ed), *British Documents on the End of Empire, Series B, Vol I: Ghana Part I* (London: HMSO, 1995), pp xliv–xlv.

136 Hyam: *British Documents on the End of Empire*, p 155, citing PRO CAB 128/17, CM 30(50)6, 11 May 1950.

137 Hyam: *British Documents on the End of Empire*, p xxxvii.

138 Hyam: 'Africa and the Labour government', p 156.

139 *Ibid.*, pp 159–61.

140 Darwin: 'British decolonization since 1945'.

141 Hyam: *British Documents on the End of Empire*, p lxv.

142 *Ibid.*

143 G. Berridge, 'Britain, South Africa and African defence, 1949–55', in M. Dockrill and J.W. Young (eds), *British Foreign Policy, 1945–1956* (Basingstoke: Macmillan, 1989), pp 101–25; G.R. Berridge and J.E. Spence, 'South Africa and the Simonstown Agreements', in J.W. Young (ed), *The Foreign Policy of Churchill's Peacetime Administration 1951–1955* (Leicester: Leicester University Press, 1988).

144 Hyam: *British Documents on the End of Empire*, p lxv.

145 *Ibid.*, pp lxiv–lxv; Ovendale: *The English-Speaking Alliance*, ch 9.

146 Hyam: *British Documents on the End of Empire*, p xxxvi; R. Hyam, 'The geopolitical origins of the Central African Federation: Britain, Rhodesia and South Africa, 1948–1953', *Historical Journal* 30/1 (1987), pp 145–72.

147 S. Marks, 'Southern Africa', *OHBE IV*, pp 567–8.

Chapter 4: Change and control under Churchill and Eden, 1951–57

1 D. Reynolds, *Britannia Overruled. British Policy and World Power in the Twentieth Century* (Harlow: Longman, 1991), p 181.

2 J. Kent, 'Informal empire and the defence of the Middle East 1945–56', in R. Bridges (ed), *Imperialism, Decolonization and Africa. Studies Presented to John Hargreaves* (Basingstoke: Macmillan, 2000), pp 133–4.

3 Reynolds: *Britannia Overruled*, p 198.

4 D. Goldsworthy (ed), *British Documents on the End of Empire, Series A, Vol 3: The Conservative Government and the End of Empire 1951–1957* (London: HMSO, 1994).

5 J. Kent, 'The Egyptian base and the defence of the Middle East, 1945–54', *JICH* 21/3 (1993), pp 45–65.

6 Reynolds: *Britannia Overruled*, p 210.

7 Goldsworthy: *British Documents on the End of Empire*, p xxix.

8 *Ibid.*

9 R.F. Holland, 'The imperial factor in British strategies from Attlee to Macmillan, 1945–63', *JICH* 12/2 (1984), p 173.

10 W. David McIntyre, 'The admission of small states to the Commonwealth', *JICH* 24/2 (1996), pp 256–7.

11 Goldsworthy: *British Documents on the End of Empire*, p l.

12 W. David McIntyre, *British Decolonization, 1946–1997. When, Why and How Did the British Empire Fall?* (Basingstoke: Macmillan, 1998), p 40.

13 Goldsworthy: *British Documents on the End of Empire*, pp li, lxvi n47.

14 *Ibid.*, p lxv n14.

15 J. Darwin, *Britain and Decolonisation. The Retreat from Empire in the Post-War World* (Basingstoke: Macmillan, 1988), p 149.

16 Goldsworthy: *British Documents on the End of Empire*, p lxv n18.

[17] J. Crawford, '"A political H-bomb": New Zealand and the British thermonuclear weapon tests of 1957–58', *JICH* 26/1 (1998), pp 131–4.

[18] *Ibid.*, p 130.

[19] S. Brooke, 'The Conservative Party, immigration and national identity, 1948–1968', in M. Francis and I. Zweiniger-Bargielowska (eds), *The Conservatives and British Society, 1880–1990* (Cardiff: University of Wales Press, 1996), pp 147–70.

[20] C.R. Schenk, 'The Sterling Area and British policy alternatives in the 1950s', *Contemporary Record* 6/2 (1992), p 280.

[21] R. Holland, *The Pursuit of Greatness. Britain and the World Role, 1900–1970* (London: Fontana, 1991), pp 260–1.

[22] N.J. White, *Decolonisation. The British Experience since 1945* (Harlow: Addison Wesley Longman, 1999), p 27.

[23] Goldsworthy: *British Documents on the End of Empire*, p lvi.

[24] C.R. Schenk, 'Decolonization and European economic integration: The free trade area negotiations, 1956–58', *JICH* 24/3 (1996), pp 445–7.

[25] Schenk: 'Decolonization and European economic integration', pp 445–6; D.K. Fieldhouse, 'The metropolitan economics of empire', in J.M. Brown and Wm Roger Louis (eds), *The Oxford History of the British Empire, Vol IV: The Twentieth Century* (Oxford: Oxford University Press, 1999), pp 107–8.

[26] Schenk: 'The Sterling Area', pp 276–7.

[27] C.H. Feinstein, 'The end of empire and the golden age', in P. Clarke and C. Trebilcock (eds), *Understanding Decline. Perceptions and Realities of British Economic Performance* (Cambridge: Cambridge University Press, 1997), pp 227–8.

[28] T. Hopkins, 'Macmillan's audit of empire, 1957', in Clarke and Trebilcock: *Understanding Decline*, p 248 fn 49.

[29] Goldsworthy: *British Documents on the End of Empire*, p lvi.

[30] Schenk: 'Decolonization and European economic integration', p 450.

[31] Feinstein: 'The end of empire', p 224.

[32] N. White, 'Gentlemanly capitalism and empire in the twentieth century: The forgotten case of Malaya, 1914–1965', in R.E. Dumett (ed), *Gentlemanly Capitalism and British Imperialism. The New Debate on Empire* (Harlow: Addison Wesley Longman, 1999), pp 192–3.

[33] A.N. Porter and A.J. Stockwell, *British Imperial Policy and Decolonization 1938–64, Vol 2: 1952–64* (Basingstoke: Macmillan, 1989), pp 176–7.

[34] Goldsworthy: *British Documents on the End of Empire*, pp xxxvii, lvii–lviii.

[35] *Ibid.*, pp lviii–lix.

[36] R. Hyam, 'The parting of the ways: Britain and South Africa's departure from the Commonwealth, 1951–61', *JICH* 26/2 (1998), p 158.

[37] Goldsworthy: *British Documents on the End of Empire*, p xxxviii.

[38] *Ibid.*

[39] M. Mason, '"The decisive volley": The Battle of Ismaelia and the decline of British influence in Egypt, January–July 1952', *JICH* 19/1 (1991), pp 45–64.

[40] Roger Louis, 'The tragedy of the Anglo-Egyptian settlement of 1954', in Wm Roger Louis and R. Owen (eds), *Suez 1956: The Crisis and its Consequences* (Oxford: Clarendon Press, 1989), pp 43–72.

[41] Goldsworthy: *British Documents on the End of Empire*, pp 101–2.

[42] Reynolds: *Britannia Overruled*, pp 192, 203.

[43] *Ibid.*, pp 203–4.

[44] P. Murphy, *Alan Lennox-Boyd. A Biography* (London: I.B. Tauris, 1999), p 192.

[45] Quoted in D. Goldsworthy, 'Keeping change within bounds: Aspects of colonial policy during the Churchill and Eden governments, 1951–57', *JICH* 18/1 (1990), p 92.

[46] Goldsworthy: *British Documents on the End of Empire*, p lii.

47 H. Johnson, 'The British Caribbean from demobilization to constitutional decolonization', *OHBE IV*, p 618.

48 Goldsworthy: *British Documents on the End of Empire*, p liii.

49 Goldsworthy: 'Keeping change within bounds', p 85.

50 Goldsworthy: *British Documents on the End of Empire*, p xlv.

51 Goldsworthy: 'Keeping change within bounds', p 103.

52 F. Furedi, *Colonial Wars and the Politics of Third World Nationalism* (London: I.B. Tauris, 1994).

53 D. Killingray and D.M. Anderson, 'An orderly retreat? Policing the end of empire', in D.M. Anderson and D. Killingray (eds), *Policing and Decolonization. Politics, Nationalism, and the Police, 1917–65* (Manchester: Manchester University Press 1992), p 5.

54 Goldsworthy: *British Documents on the End of Empire*, p xlviii.

55 Goldsworthy: 'Keeping change within bounds', pp 84–5.

56 Quoted in D.A. Low, 'The contraction of England: An inaugural lecture, 1984', in his *Eclipse of Empire* (Cambridge: Cambridge University Press, 1991), p 10.

57 Goldsworthy: *British Documents on the End of Empire*, p xlvii.

58 Holland: *The Pursuit of Greatness*, p 266.

59 Goldsworthy: 'Keeping change within bounds', p 100.

60 Holland: *The Pursuit of Greatness*, pp 261–2.

61 Sir Ralph Furse, *Aucuparius. Recollections of a Recruiting Officer* (London: Oxford University Press, 1962), Appendix I.

62 Goldsworthy: *British Documents on the End of Empire*, pp li–lii; Goldsworthy: 'Keeping change within bounds', p 86.

63 A.J. Stockwell, 'Imperialism and nationalism in South-East Asia', *OHBE IV*, p 486.

64 R. Stubbs, *Hearts and Minds in Guerrilla Warfare: The Malayan Emergency 1948–1960* (Singapore: Oxford University Press, 1989).

65 A.J. Stockwell, 'British imperial strategy and decolonization in South-East Asia, 1947–1957', in D.K. Bassett and V.T. King (eds), *Britain in South-East Asia*, Occasional Paper 13 (Hull: Centre for South-East Asian Studies, University of Hull, 1986), p 88.

66 S.C. Smith, *British Relations with the Malay Rulers from Decentralization to Malayan Independence 1930–1957* (Kuala Lumpur: Oxford University Press, 1995).

67 A.J. Stockwell (ed), *British Documents on the End of Empire, Series B, Vol 3: Malaya* (London: HMSO, 1995), pp lxxix–lxxx.

68 Goldsworthy: 'Keeping change within bounds', p 88.

69 Goldsworthy: *British Documents on the End of Empire*, p xlviii.

70 R. Rathbone (ed), *British Documents on the End of Empire, Series B, Vol 1: Ghana* (London: HMSO, 1992), pp lix–lx.

71 *Ibid.*, p lxii.

72 *Ibid.*, p lxviii; Goldsworthy: *British Documents on the End of Empire*, pp liii–liv.

73 Murphy (1999), p 154.

74 N. Owen, 'Decolonisation and postwar consensus', in H. Jones and M. Kandiah (eds), *The Myth of Consensus. New Views on British History, 1945–64* (Basingstoke: Macmillan, 1996), pp 168–9.

75 K. Kyle, *The Politics of the Independence of Kenya* (Basingstoke: Macmillan, 1999).

76 T. Kanogo, *Squatters and the Roots of Mau Mau 1905–63* (London: James Currey, 1987); D.W. Throup, *Economic and Social Origins of Mau Mau 1945–53* (London: James Currey, 1987).

77 B. Berman, *Control and Crisis in Colonial Kenya. The Dialectic of Domination* (London: James Currey, 1990), pp 111, 369–71, 387–8.

78 J. Darwin, 'British decolonization since 1945: A pattern or a puzzle?', *JICH* 12/2 (1984), p 190.

[79] D. Goldsworthy, 'Britain and the international critics of British colonialism, 1951–56', *Journal of Commonwealth and Comparative Politics* 29 (1991), pp 1–3.

[80] Goldsworthy: *British Documents on the End of Empire*, pp xlii–xliii.

[81] *Ibid.*, pp xliii–xliv.

[82] *Ibid.*, p xliv; Goldsworthy: 'Britain and the international critics', pp 4–5.

[83] R. Holland, *Britain and the Revolt in Cyprus 1954–1959* (Oxford: Clarendon Press, 1998), p 42.

[84] Goldsworthy: *British Documents on the End of Empire*, p xl; Goldsworthy: 'Britain and the international critics', p 13.

[85] Goldsworthy: *British Documents on the End of Empire*, p xli.

[86] *Ibid.*, p xxx; Reynolds: *Britannia Overruled*, pp 196–7.

[87] Quoted in Holland: *The Pursuit of Greatness*, p 255.

[88] Schenk: 'Decolonization and European economic integration', p 446.

[89] Reynolds: *Britannia Overruled*, p 204; Holland: *The Pursuit of Greatness*, p 272.

[90] Goldsworthy: *British Documents on the End of Empire*, pp xxxiii–xxxiv.

[91] Reynolds: *Britannia Overruled*, p 204; Goldsworthy: 'Keeping change within bounds', p 103.

[92] Goldsworthy: *British Documents on the End of Empire*, p xxxiv; Reynolds: *Britannia Overruled*, p 204.

[93] Reynolds: *Britannia Overruled*, p 206.

[94] Louis and Owen: *Suez 1956: The Crisis and its Consequences*, pp 173–88.

[95] D. Mackenzie, 'Canada, the North Atlantic triangle, and the empire', *OHBE IV*, p 593.

[96] Reynolds: *Britannia Overruled*, p 205; McIntyre: 'The admission of small states to the Commonwealth', p 259; Louis and Owen: *Suez 1956: The Crisis and its Consequences*, pp 257–318.

Chapter 5: Winds of change, 1957–64

[1] P.E. Hemming, 'Macmillan and the end of the British Empire in Africa', in R. Aldous and S. Lee (eds), *Harold Macmillan and Britain's World Role* (Basingstoke: Macmillan, 1996), p 101.

[2] W. David McIntyre, *British Decolonization, 1946–1997. When, Why and How Did the British Empire Fall?* (Basingstoke: Macmillan, 1998), p 46.

[3] Wm Roger Louis and R. Robinson, 'The imperialism of decolonization', *JICH* 22/3 (1994), pp 462–511.

[4] *Ibid.*

[5] A. Horne, *Macmillan 1957–1986* (London: Macmillan, 1989), p 204.

[6] R. Holland, *The Pursuit of Greatness. Britain and the World Role, 1900–1970* (London: Fontana, 1991), p 179; D. Reynolds, *Britannia Overruled. British Policy and World Power in the Twentieth Century* (Harlow: Longman, 1991), p 211.

[7] Holland: *The Pursuit of Greatness*, pp 281–2.

[8] S. Constantine, 'Waving goodbye? Australia, assisted passages, and the Empire and Commonwealth Settlement Acts, 1945–72', *JICH* 26/2 (1998), pp 176–96.

[9] J. Darwin, *Britain and Decolonisation. The Retreat from Empire in the Post-War World* (Basingstoke: Macmillan, 1988), pp 237–9.

[10] T. Hopkins, 'Macmillan's audit of empire, 1957', in P. Clarke and C. Trebilcock (eds), *Understanding Decline. Perceptions and Realities of British Economic Performance* (Cambridge: Cambridge University Press, 1997), p 255.

[11] PRO: CAB/134/1555, 28 January 1957.

[12] Hopkins: 'Macmillan's audit of empire', pp 249–50.

[13] Reynolds: *Britannia Overruled*, pp 225–6.

[14] Holland: *The Pursuit of Greatness*, pp 292–4.

[15] PRO: CAB 128/30 pt 2, CM4(57), 9 January 1957.

16 R. Ovendale, *Britain, the United States and the Transfer of Power in the Middle East, 1945–1962* (Leicester: Leicester University Press, 1996), pp 192–4.

17 Ovendale: *Britain, the United States and the Transfer of Power*, p 183.

18 M. Joyce, 'Preserving the sheikhdom: London, Washington, Iraq and Kuwait, 1958–61', *Middle Eastern Studies* 31/2 (1995), pp 281–92.

19 Wm R. Louis, 'Harold Macmillan and the Middle East Crisis of 1958' (Elie Kedourie Memorial Lecture), *Proceedings of the British Academy*, 94 (1996) *Lectures and Memoirs*, pp 207–28.

20 R.A. Fernea and Wm Roger Louis (eds), *The Iraqi Revolution of 1958. The Old Social Classes Revisited* (London: I.B. Tauris, 1991).

21 M. Eppel, 'Degrees of accommodation with Britain: The decline of British influence and the ruling elite in Iraq', in M. Cohen and M. Kolinsky (eds), *Demise of the British Empire in the Middle East: Britain's Responses to Nationalist Movements 1943–1955* (London: Frank Cass, 1998), p 196.

22 N.J. Ashton, 'A microcosm of decline: British loss of nerve and military intervention in Jordan and Kuwait, 1958 and 1961', *Historical Journal* 40/4 (1997), pp 1069–83.

23 L. Tal, 'Britain and the Jordan Crisis of 1958', *Middle Eastern Studies* 31/1 (1995), pp 39–57.

24 Ashton: 'A microcosm of decline', p 1082.

25 *Ibid.*, pp 1072–3.

26 M. Farouk-Sluglett and P. Sluglett, *Iraq since 1958. From Revolution to Dictatorship* (London: KPI, 1987), pp 50, 100.

27 Ashton: 'A microcosm of decline', p 1073.

28 N. Ashton, 'Britain and the Kuwaiti Crisis, 1961', *Diplomacy and Statecraft* 9/1 (1998), pp 163–81.

29 PRO: PREM 11/3430, Brook to Macmillan, 13 September 1961, cited in Ovendale: *Britain, the United States and the Transfer of Power*, p 235.

30 P. Murphy, *Alan Lennox-Boyd. A Biography* (London: I.B. Tauris, 1999), p 194.

31 Holland: *The Pursuit of Greatness*, pp 294–5.

32 McIntyre: *British Decolonization, 1946–1997*, p 53.

33 *Ibid.*, p 54.

34 R. Ovendale, 'Macmillan and the wind of change in Africa, 1957–60', *Historical Journal* 38/2 (1995), pp 455–77.

35 J. Turner, *Macmillan* (Harlow: Longman, 1994), p 199.

36 PRO: PREM 11/2587, Macmillan to Lloyd, 2 July 1959.

37 Ovendale: 'Macmillan and the wind of change', p 463.

38 *Ibid.*, p 477.

39 Louis and Robinson: 'The imperialism of decolonization', p 487.

40 Ovendale: 'Macmillan and the wind of change', p 463.

41 Louis and Robinson: 'The imperialism of decolonization', p 489.

42 Cabinet Africa (Official) Committee report, 'Africa: The Next Ten Years' (May 1959), quoted in Ovendale: 'Macmillan and the wind of change', p 469.

43 Louis and Robinson: 'The imperialism of decolonization', p 488.

44 Wm Roger Louis, 'The dissolution of the British Empire', in Judith M. Brown and Wm Roger Louis (eds), *The Oxford History of the British Empire, Vol IV: The Twentieth Century* (Oxford: Oxford University Press, 1999), p 350.

45 Louis: 'The dissolution of the British Empire', *OHBE IV*, p 349.

46 Hemming: 'Macmillan and the end of the British Empire in Africa', p 101.

47 Horne: *Macmillan 1957–1986*, 183, citing Macmillan to Norman Brook, 1 November 1959.

48 Wm Roger Louis, 'Introduction', *OHBE IV*, p 30.

49 R. Shepherd, *Iain Macleod: A Biography* (London: Hutchinson, 1994).

50 Louis: 'The dissolution of the British Empire', *OHBE IV*, p 351.

51 J. Ramsden, *The Winds of Change: Macmillan to Heath 1957–1975* (Harlow: Longman, 1996), p 147.

52 PRO: PREM 11/3075, minute, 28 December 1959; Holland: *The Pursuit of Greatness*, p 299.

53 Louis and Robinson: 'The imperialism of decolonization', p 489.

54 Ramsden: *The Winds of Change*, pp 5–6.

55 Hemming: 'Macmillan and the end of the British Empire in Africa', p 112.

56 H. Macmillan, *Pointing the Way, 1959–1961* (London: Macmillan, 1972), citing diary entry for 4 July 1960, p 264.

57 R. Hyam, 'The primacy of geopolitics: The dynamics of British imperial policy, 1763–1963', in R.D. King and R. Kilson (eds), *The Statecraft of British Imperialism: Essays in Honour of Wm. Roger Louis* (London: Frank Cass, 1999), p 45.

58 PRO: CO 936/681, Macleod to Poynton, 10 August 1961, cited in Hemming: 'Macmillan and the end of the British Empire in Africa', p 113. See also E. Luard, *A History of the United Nations, Vol 2: The Age of Decolonization, 1955–1965* (London: Macmillan, 1989), pp 175–97.

59 Hemming: 'Macmillan and the end of the British Empire in Africa', p 114.

60 J. Darwin, 'Decolonization and the end of empire', in Robin W. Winks (ed), *The Oxford History of the British Empire, Vol V: Historiography* (Oxford: Oxford University Press, 1999), p 545.

61 Louis and Robinson: 'The imperialism of decolonization', pp 489–90.

62 Murphy: *Alan Lennox-Boyd*, pp 228–32.

63 Louis: 'The dissolution of the British Empire', *OHBE IV*, p 352.

64 Darwin: *Britain and Decolonisation*, pp 188–9.

65 J.D. Hargreaves, *Decolonization in Africa* (2nd ed., Harlow: Longman, 1996), p 178.

66 Ovendale: 'Macmillan and the wind of change', p 471.

67 Murphy: *Alan Lennox-Boyd*, pp 220–1.

68 *Ibid.*, pp 226–7.

69 *Ibid.*, pp 222–3.

70 Louis: 'The dissolution of the British Empire', *OHBE IV*, p 351.

71 PRO: PREM 11/3030, Macleod to Macmillan, 8 February 1960, cited in Louis and Robinson: 'The imperialism of decolonization', pp 489–90.

72 K. Kyle, *The Politics of the Independence of Kenya* (Basingstoke: Macmillan, 1999), pp 113–15, 130.

73 J. Darwin, 'British decolonization since 1945: A pattern or a puzzle?', *JICH* 12/2 (1984), p 204.

74 Murphy: *Alan Lennox-Boyd*, p 232.

75 *Ibid.*, p 184.

76 C. Baker, *State of Emergency: Crisis in Central Africa, Nyasaland 1959–1960* (London: I.B. Tauris, 1997); J. Darwin, 'The Central African Emergency, 1959', *JICH* 21/3 (1993), pp 217–34.

77 Ovendale: 'Macmillan and the wind of change', p 476.

78 Holland: *The Pursuit of Greatness*, p 299.

79 Louis and Robinson: 'The imperialism of decolonization', p 489.

80 P. Murphy, *Party Politics and Decolonization. The Conservative Party and British Colonial Policy in Tropical Africa 1951–1964* (Oxford: Clarendon Press, 1995), pp 184–90.

81 Darwin: 'British decolonization since 1945', pp 204–5.

82 Ovendale: 'Macmillan and the wind of change', p 474.

83 Holland: *The Pursuit of Greatness*, p 286.

84 *Ibid.*, p 289.

85 Turner: *Macmillan*, pp 218–19.

86 Holland: *The Pursuit of Greatness*, pp 285–6.

87 Darwin: *Britain and Decolonisation*, p 235.

88 Holland: *The Pursuit of Greatness*, p 290.
89 *Ibid.*, p 291.
90 Reynolds: *Britannia Overruled*, p 220.
91 Darwin: 'British decolonization since 1945', p 234.
92 Reynolds: *Britannia Overruled*, p 231.
93 M. Vaïsse, 'Post-Suez France', in Wm Roger Louis and R. Owen (eds), *Suez 1956: The Crisis and its Consequences* (Oxford: Clarendon Press, 1989), pp 335–40.
94 R.F. Holland, 'The imperial factor in British strategies from Attlee to Macmillan, 1945–63', *JICH* 12/2 (1984), p 182; Hargreaves: *Decolonization in Africa*, pp 186–7.
95 Holland: *The Pursuit of Greatness*, p 311.
96 Holland: 'The imperial factor in British strategies', p 181.
97 W. David McIntyre, 'Commonwealth legacy', *OHBE IV*, p 693.
98 R. Hyam, 'Bureaucracy and "Trusteeship" in the colonial empire', *OHBE IV*, p 262.
99 Hyam: *OHBE IV*, p 263.
100 McIntyre: 'Commonwealth legacy', *OHBE IV*, p 698.
101 R. Hyam: 'The primacy of geopolitics', pp 27–52.
102 Hopkins: 'Macmillan's audit of empire', p 255.
103 Louis and Robinson: 'The imperialism of decolonization'.
104 J.D.B. Miller, *Survey of Commonwealth Affairs. Problems of Expansion and Attrition 1953–1969* (London: Oxford University Press, 1974), pp 341–4.

Chapter 6: Imperial aftermath

1 J. Pickering, *Britain's Withdrawal from East of Suez. The Politics of Retrenchment* (Basingstoke: Macmillan, 1998), p 148.
2 R. Holland, *The Pursuit of Greatness. Britain and the World Role, 1900–1970* (London: Fontana, 1991), p 322.
3 D. Reynolds, *Britannia Overruled. British Policy and World Power in the Twentieth Century* (Harlow: Longman, 1991), p 239.
4 Quoted in P. Catterall, 'Foreign and Commonwealth policy in opposition: The Labour Party', in W. Kaiser and G. Staerck (eds), *British Foreign Policy, 1955–64: Contracting Options* (Basingstoke: Macmillan, 1999), p 94.
5 M. Dockrill, *British Defence since 1945* (Oxford: Basil Blackwell, 1988), pp 86–7.
6 A. Clayton, '"Deceptive might": Imperial defence and security, 1900–1968', in J.M. Brown and Wm Roger Louis (eds), *The Oxford History of the British Empire, Vol IV: The Twentieth Century* (Oxford: Oxford University Press, 1999), p 303; J.D.B. Miller, *Survey of Commonwealth Affairs. Problems of Expansion and Attrition 1953–1969* (London: Oxford University Press, 1974), pp 82–98.
7 J.D. Hargreaves, *Decolonization in Africa* (2nd ed., Harlow: Longman, 1996), p 213.
8 N. White, 'Gentlemanly capitalism and empire in the twentieth century: The forgotten case of Malaya, 1914–1965', in R.E. Dumett (ed), *Gentlemanly Capitalism and British Imperialism. The New Debate on Empire* (Harlow: Longman, 1999), p 194.
9 Holland: *The Pursuit of Greatness*, pp 318–19.
10 Miller: *Survey of Commonwealth Affairs*, pp 302–5.
11 J. Darwin, *Britain and Decolonisation The Retreat from Empire in the Post-War World* (Basingstoke: Macmillan, 1988), pp 241–2.
12 J. Darwin, 'A third British empire? The Dominion idea in British politics', *OHBE IV*, p 85.
13 Dockrill: *British Defence since 1945*, pp 88–9.
14 D.B. Kunz, '"Somewhat mixed up together": Anglo-American defence and financial policy during the 1960s', in R.D. King and R. Kilson (eds), *The Statecraft of British Imperialism: Essays in Honour of Wm. Roger Louis* (London: Frank Cass, 1999), pp 214–15.

15 Holland: *The Pursuit of Greatness*, p 324.

16 Darwin: *Britain and Decolonisation*, p 287.

17 Kunz: '"Somewhat mixed up together"', p 215.

18 *Ibid.*, pp 217–18.

19 P. Darby, *British Defence Policy East of Suez 1947–1968* (London: Oxford University Press, 1973), p 296.

20 Kunz: '"Somewhat mixed up together"', p 219.

21 *Ibid.*, p 220.

22 Holland: *The Pursuit of Greatness*, p 330.

23 Kunz: '"Somewhat mixed up together"', p 223.

24 W. David McIntyre, *British Decolonization, 1946–1997. When, Why and How Did the British Empire Fall?* (Basingstoke: Macmillan, 1998), p 64.

25 Holland: *The Pursuit of Greatness*, p 332.

26 S.C. Smith, 'Rulers and residents: British relations with the Aden Protectorate, 1937–59', *Middle Eastern Studies* 31/3 (1995), pp 509–23.

27 Pickering: *Britain's Withdrawal from East of Suez*, pp 170–3.

28 Holland: *The Pursuit of Greatness*, pp 332–3.

29 Kunz: '"Somewhat mixed up together"', pp 227–8.

30 Darby: *British Defence Policy*, p 334.

31 P. Sluglett, 'Formal and informal empire in the Middle East', in Robin W. Winks (ed), *The Oxford History of the British Empire, Vol V: Historiography* (Oxford: Oxford University Press, 1999), p 434.

32 J. Pimlott, 'The British Army: the Dhofar campaign, 1970–1975', in I.F.W. Beckett and J. Pimlott (eds), *Armed Forces and Modern Counter-Insurgency* (London: Croom Helm, 1985), pp 16–45.

33 S. George, *An Awkward Partner. Britain in the European Community* (Oxford: Oxford University Press, 1990), p 37.

34 C.J. Bartlett, *'The Special Relationship' A Political History of Anglo-American Relations since 1945* (Harlow: Longman, 1992), p 118.

35 Darwin: *Britain and Decolonisation*, pp 318–19.

36 W. David McIntyre, 'Commonwealth legacy', *OHBE IV*, p 693.

37 W.D. McIntyre, 'Britain and the creation of the Commonwealth Secretariat', *JICH* 28/1 (2000), p 135.

38 McIntyre 'Commonwealth legacy', *OHBE IV*, p 693; McIntyre: *British Decolonization*, p 65.

39 McIntyre: *British Decolonization*, p 122; F. Madden and J. Darwin (eds), *Select Documents on the Constitutional History of the British Empire and Commonwealth, Vol VI: The Dominions and India since 1900* (Westport, Connecticut: Greenwood, 1993), p 5.

40 Miller: *Survey of Commonwealth Affairs*, p 305.

41 C. Wrigley, 'Now you see it, now you don't: Harold Wilson and Labour's foreign policy 1964–70', in R. Coopey, S. Fielding and N. Tiratsoo (eds), *The Wilson Governments 1964–1970* (London: Pinter, 1993), pp 123–35.

42 Madden and Darwin: *Select Documents*, p 5.

43 Wrigley: 'Now you see it, now you don't', pp 123–35.

44 Miller: *Survey of Commonwealth Affairs*, pp 164–5.

45 McIntyre: *British Decolonization*, p 123.

46 McIntyre, 'Commonwealth Legacy', *OHBE IV*, pp 698–9.

47 McIntyre: *British Decolonization*, p 68.

48 Darwin: *Britain and Decolonisation*, p 324.

49 McIntyre: *British Decolonization*, p 85.

50 B.R. Tomlinson, 'Imperialism and after: The economy of the empire on the periphery', *OHBE IV*, p 358; P.J. Cain and A.G. Hopkins, *British Imperialism, vol II: Crisis and Deconstruction 1914–1990* (Harlow: Longman, 1993), p 285.

[51] Wm Roger Louis, 'Introduction', *OHBE IV*, pp 14–15.

CHRONOLOGY

1919	League of Nations Mandates system created
	Government of India Act
	Amritsar Massacre
	Egyptian uprising
	Ten-Year Rule adopted in British defence policy
1920	San Remo Conference allocates Mandates
	Rebellion in Mesopotamia
	Gandhi's first non-co-operation campaign
1921	Anglo-Irish Treaty
1922	Lugard's *The Dual Mandate* published
	Chanak Crisis
	Allenby Declaration on Egypt
	Empire Settlement Act
1923	Southern Rhodesia becomes self-governing
	Devonshire Declaration on Kenya
1924	Planning for Singapore base begins
1925	Indirect rule introduced in Tanganyika
1926	Imperial Conference defines Dominion status
1928	Simon Commission on Indian constitution
1929	Colonial Development Act
	Irwin Declaration on Dominion status for India
1930	Passfield White Paper on Palestine
	Gandhi's civil disobedience campaign
	Round Table Conference on India (London)
1931	Statute of Westminster
	Gandhi–Irwin talks
	Round Table Conference on India
1932	Ottawa Conference introduces Imperial Preference
	Anglo-Iraqi Treaty
	Gandhi resumes civil disobedience campaign, is gaoled
1934	Disturbances break out in West Indies
1935	Government of India Act
	Strike on Northern Rhodesian Copperbelt
1936	Anglo-Egyptian Treaty
	Arab Revolt in Palestine

1937	Congress successes in Indian elections
1938	Singapore naval base opens
	Lord Hailey's *African Survey* published
	Malcolm MacDonald becomes Colonial Secretary
	West India Royal Commission appointed
1939	White Paper on Palestine
	Bledisloe Commission reports on Central Africa
	Introduction of bulk-purchasing in colonies
	Carlton House meeting on colonial policy
1940	Colonial Development and Welfare Act
	Muslim League passes Lahore Resolution on Pakistan
	Churchill becomes prime minister
	Fabian Colonial Bureau established
	Strikes on Northern Rhodesian Copperbelt
	'August Offer' on Indian Dominion status
	Congress provincial governments in India resign
	US–Canadian Ogdensburg Agreement
1941	Hailey Report on *Native Administration and Political Development*
	Atlantic Charter
	Hyde Park Agreement between Canada and US
	Britain and USSR occupy Iran
	Japanese attack on Pearl Harbor
	Britain declares war on Japan
	Japanese capture Hong Kong
1942	Fall of Burma, Singapore and Malaya
	Cripps Mission to India
	'Quit India' movement
	Anglo-American Caribbean Commission established
	Washington proposes Anglo-American statement on colonial policy
	Constitutional reform in Nigeria, Gold Coast, Sierra Leone
1943	Bengal famine
	Commitment to self-government for Ceylon
	US proposal for an International Trusteeship administration
	Oliver Stanley's speech on colonial self-government
1944	New constitution in Jamaica awards internal self-government
1945	Colonial Development and Welfare Act
	Yalta Conference agrees role of UN Trusteeship Council
	Clement Attlee becomes prime minister
	Negotiations on India's future begin
	East African High Commission created
	Anti-British terrorism resumes in Palestine
	Arab League established
	Soulbury Commission Report on Ceylon published
	Fifth Pan-African Congress held in Manchester
	West India Royal Commission Report published

1946	Malayan Union scheme unveiled
	United Malays National Organization created
	US loan ($3.75 billion) to Britain
	Canadian loan ($1.25 billion) to Britain
	Anglo-American Committee of Inquiry on Palestine
	Cabinet Mission to India
	Jinnah launches 'Direct Action' in India
	Bomb attack on King David Hotel, Jerusalem
	Transjordan becomes independent
	New constitutions in Gold Coast, Nigeria, Gambia, Malaya
	Arthur Creech Jones appointed Colonial Secretary
1947	Federation of Malaya inaugurated
	Sterling crisis
	Britain announces withdrawal from Palestine
	UN Special Committee on Palestine proposes partition
	India and Pakistan independent
	Colonial Office issues Local Government despatch
	United Gold Coast Convention formed
	Montego Bay Conference on West Indian closer association
	Overseas Resources Development Act
	African Governors' Conference (London)
1948	Marshall Plan comes into effect
	British Nationality Act
	Ireland leaves Commonwealth
	National Party forms South African government
	British withdrawal from Palestine
	Accra Riots
	Last British troops leave India
	Ceylon independent
	Burma independent
	Emergency declared in Malaya
1949	Devaluation of the pound
	North Atlantic Treaty Organization established
	Ireland becomes a republic
	Convention People's Party established in Gold Coast
	India becomes republic within Commonwealth
	People's Republic of China established
	Newfoundland enters Canadian Confederation
1950	Colombo Conference of Commonwealth Ministers
	Korean War begins
	British rearmament programme
	James Griffiths appointed Colonial Secretary
1951	Churchill becomes prime minister
	Oliver Lyttelton appointed Colonial Secretary
	Anglo-Iranian Oil Company nationalized
	Egypt abrogates 1936 treaty with Britain

Libya independent
ANZUS Pact
CPP wins Gold Coast elections; Nkrumah becomes Leader of Government Business

1952   British atomic tests
Empire Settlement Act renewed
Military coup in Egypt
Mau Mau rebellion in Kenya; state of emergency declared
Nkrumah becomes prime minister in Gold Coast

1953   Central African Federation (Federation of Rhodesia and Nyasaland) inaugurated
British Guiana's constitution suspended
Jomo Kenyatta tried in Kenya
Mussadiq overthrown in Iran

1954   Nasser gains power in Egypt
Anglo-Egyptian Agreement
Alan Lennox-Boyd appointed Colonial Secretary
Gold Coast elections lead to formation of all-African government
Federal constitution in Nigeria

1955   Anthony Eden becomes prime minister
Baghdad Pact formed
Egyptian arms deal with Czechoslovakia
EOKA begins terrorist campaign in Cyprus
Report of East Africa Royal Commission published
South-East Asia Treaty Organization formed
Australia and New Zealand announce role in Commonwealth Far Eastern Strategic Reserve
Bandung Conference launches non-aligned movement

1956   Sudan independent
Suez Canal nationalized
Suez Crisis
Plan G adopted by Cabinet
Malayan independence talks

1957   Harold Macmillan becomes prime minister
Macmillan begins tour of Commonwealth
Eisenhower Doctrine unveiled
Gold Coast independent
Malaya independent
Anglo-Malayan Defence Agreement
Defence White Paper
North American Air Defence Agreement
Eastern and Western Nigeria become self-governing
New constitutions in Tanganyika and Kenya
London approves constitutional revisions in Central African Federation

1958	Sterling becomes fully convertible
	Revolution in Iraq
	British intervention in Jordan
	Commonwealth Trade Conference (Montreal)
1959	Conservatives re-elected
	Chequers conference on future of East Africa
	Iain Macleod appointed Colonial Secretary
	Emergency declared in Central Africa
	Devlin Report on Nyasaland Emergency
	New Kenya Group formed
	Hola Camp atrocities in Kenya
	International agreement on future of Cyprus
	Singapore becomes internally self-governing
1960	Nigeria independent
	Cyprus independent
	European Free Trade Association created
	Lancaster House Conference on Kenya
	Congo Crisis begins
	Macmillan's 'wind of change' speech
	Monckton Commission presents report
	Sharpeville Massacre in South Africa
	Malayan Emergency ends
	UN adopts Resolution 1514 on colonial independence
	(Central African) Federal Review Conference (London)
1961	First British application to join EEC
	Discussions on Northern Rhodesian constitution
	Sierra Leone independent
	Tanganyika independent
	Kuwait crisis
	Reginald Maudling appointed Colonial Secretary
	South Africa leaves Commonwealth
1962	Commonwealth Immigrants Act
	Duncan Sandys appointed Colonial Secretary
	Uganda independent
	Winston Field wins Southern Rhodesian elections
	Jamaica independent
	Trinidad and Tobago independent
	Federation of the West Indies dissolved
	Macmillan meets Kennedy at Nassau
1963	De Gaulle vetoes Britain's EEC application
	Sir Alec Douglas-Home becomes prime minister
	Kenya independent
	Zanzibar independent
	Central African Federation dissolved
	Nigeria becomes republic

	Federation of Malaysia inaugurated
1964	Harold Wilson becomes prime minister
	Insurgency in Aden escalates
	Nyasaland independent
	Northern Rhodesia independent
	Malta independent
1965	Commonwealth Secretariat established in London
	Gambia independent
	Singapore secedes from Malaysia
	Unilateral Declaration of Independence by (Southern) Rhodesia
1966	Harold Wilson re-elected
	Controversial Defence White Paper
	Military coup in Nigeria
	Botswana independent
	Lesotho independent
	Guyana independent
	Barbados independent
1967	Arab–Israeli ('Six Day') War
	Devaluation of the pound
	De Gaulle's second veto on British membership of EEC
	South Arabian Federation collapses
	Britain evacuates Aden
	Civil war in Nigeria
1968	British decision to withdraw forces from 'East of Suez'
	Britain announces withdrawal from Persian Gulf by end of 1971
	Commonwealth Immigrants Act
	Mauritius independent
	Swaziland independent
	Nauru independent
1970	Edward Heath becomes prime minister
	Britain assists Oman in Dhofar campaign
	Nigerian civil war ends
	Fiji independent
1971	Immigration Act
	Commonwealth Declaration of Principles adopted
1972	Formal end of Sterling Area
	Commonwealth Settlement Act expires
	Pakistan leaves Commonwealth
1973	Britain enters European Economic Community

MAPS

224

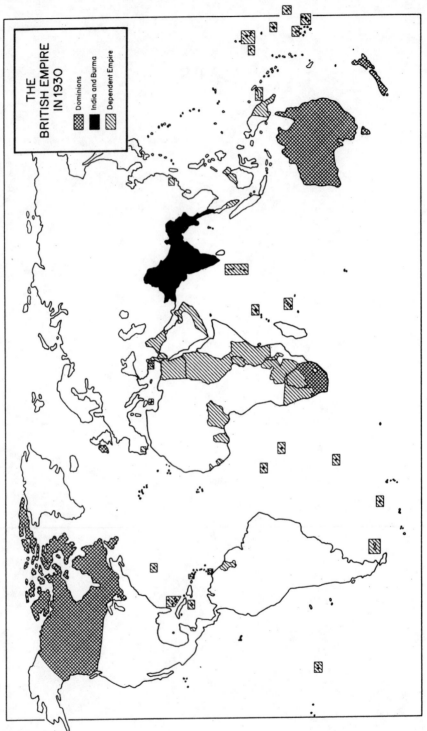

THE
BRITISH EMPIRE
IN 1930

Dominions

India and Burma

Dependent Empire

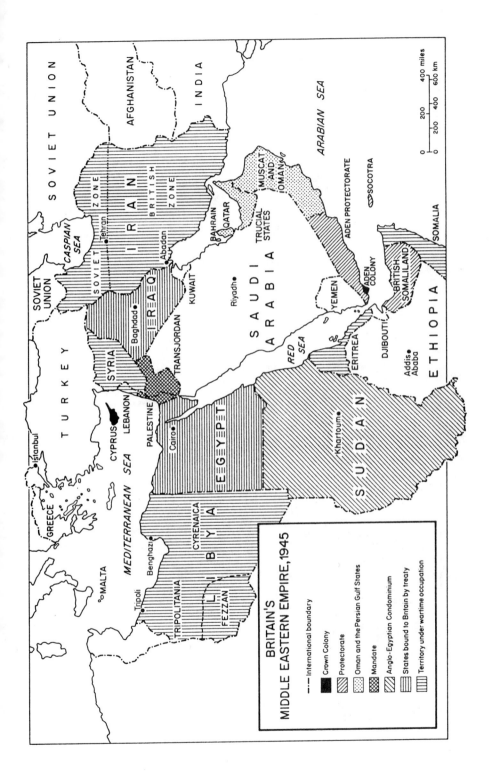

BRITAIN'S
MIDDLE EASTERN EMPIRE, 1945

- - - International boundary
Crown Colony
Protectorate
Oman and the Persian Gulf States
Mandate
Anglo-Egyptian Condominium
States bound to Britain by treaty
Territory under wartime occupation

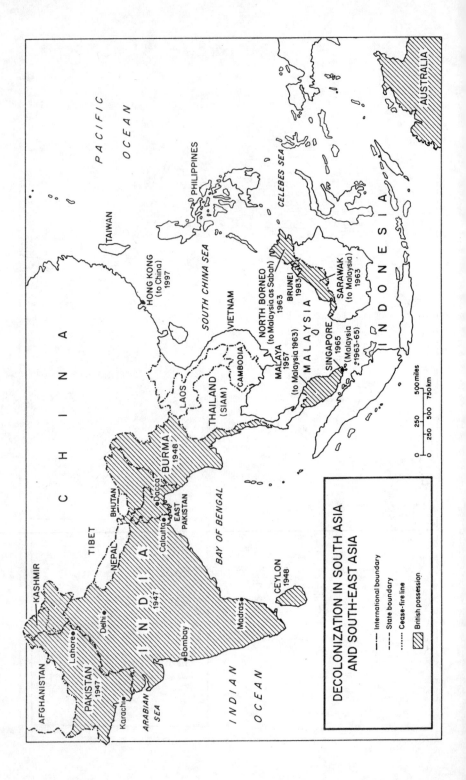

DECOLONIZATION IN SOUTH ASIA
AND SOUTH-EAST ASIA

--- International boundary
--- State boundary
...... Cease-fire line
▨ British possession

AUSTRALIA

INDONESIA

PACIFIC

OCEAN

PHILIPPINES

TAIWAN

HONG KONG
(to China)
1997

CELEBES SEA

NORTH BORNEO
(to Malaysia as Sabah)
1963

BRUNEI
1983

SARAWAK
(to Malaysia)
1963

SOUTH CHINA SEA

VIETNAM

MALAYA
1957
(to Malaysia 1963)

SINGAPORE
1965
(Malaysia
1963–65)

M A L A Y S I A

LAOS

CAMBODIA

THAILAND
(SIAM)

CHINA

TIBET

KASHMIR

NEPAL

BHUTAN

BURMA
1948

EAST
PAKISTAN

Dacca

Calcutta

BAY OF BENGAL

CEYLON
1948

AFGHANISTAN

PAKISTAN
1947

Lahore

Delhi

I N D I A
1947

Karachi

Bombay

Madras

ARABIAN
SEA

INDIAN

OCEAN

0   250   500 miles
0 250 500 750 km

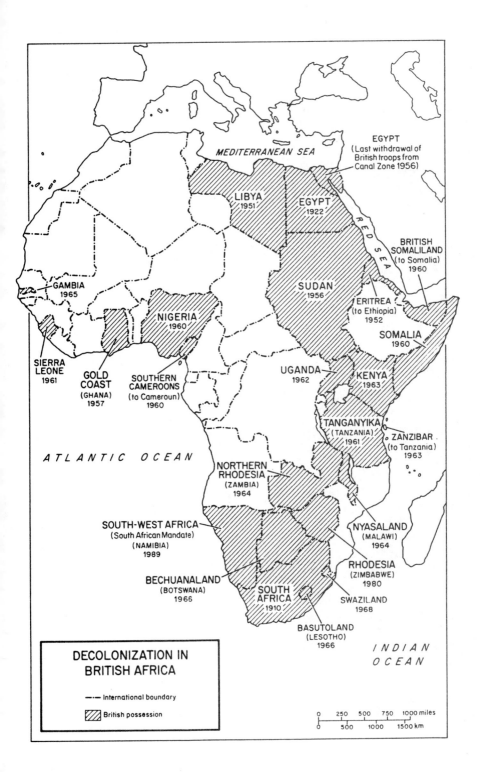

MEDITERRANEAN SEA

EGYPT
(Last withdrawal of
British troops from
Canal Zone 1956)

LIBYA
1951

EGYPT
1922

RED SEA

BRITISH
SOMALILAND
(to Somalia)
1960

GAMBIA
1965

SUDAN
1956

ERITREA
(to Ethiopia)
1952

NIGERIA
1960

SOMALIA
1960

SIERRA
LEONE
1961

GOLD
COAST
(GHANA)
1957

SOUTHERN
CAMEROONS
(to Cameroun)
1960

UGANDA
1962

KENYA
1963

ATLANTIC OCEAN

TANGANYIKA
(TANZANIA)
1961

ZANZIBAR
(to Tanzania)
1963

NORTHERN
RHODESIA
(ZAMBIA)
1964

SOUTH-WEST AFRICA
(South African Mandate)
(NAMIBIA)
1989

NYASALAND
(MALAWI)
1964

RHODESIA
(ZIMBABWE)
1980

BECHUANALAND
(BOTSWANA)
1966

SOUTH
AFRICA
1910

SWAZILAND
1968

BASUTOLAND
(LESOTHO)
1966

INDIAN
OCEAN

DECOLONIZATION IN
BRITISH AFRICA

—·— International boundary

British possession

| 0 | 250 | 500 | 750 | 1000 miles |
| 0 | 500 | 1000 | 1500 km | |

FURTHER READING

The literature on the contraction of the British Empire is now extensive. What follows is a small selection of the most helpful available studies, intended to be read in conjunction with the notes to each chapter. Important general surveys include J. Darwin, *Britain and Decolonisation. The Retreat from Empire in the Post-War World* (Basingstoke: Macmillan, 1988) and the same author's *The End of the British Empire. The Historical Debate* (Oxford: Basil Blackwell, 1991), R.F. Holland, *European Decolonization 1918–1981. An Introductory Survey* (London: Macmillan, 1985) and *The Pursuit of Greatness. Britain and the World Role, 1900–1970* (London: Fontana, 1991) and D. Reynolds, *Britannia Overruled. British Policy and World Power in the Twentieth Century* (Harlow: Longman, 1991). Also useful are M. Kahler, *Decolonization in Britain and France* (Princeton, New Jersey: Princeton University Press, 1984) and P. Darby, *Three Faces of Imperialism. British and American Approaches to Asia and Africa 1870–1970* (New Haven and London: Yale University Press, 1987). Recent short introductions include the concise but masterly synthesis by N.J. White, *Decolonisation. The British Experience since 1945* (Harlow: Addison Wesley Longman, 1999) and W. David McIntyre, *British Decolonization, 1946–1997. When, Why and How Did the British Empire Fall?* (Basingstoke: Macmillan, 1998), which challenges recent fashions by placing the Commonwealth at the centre of the debate. The volumes of the new *Oxford History of the British Empire* (editor-in-chief, Wm Roger Louis, Oxford: Oxford University Press, 1999) are indispensable, especially *Vol IV: The Twentieth Century*, edited by Judith M. Brown and *Vol V: Historiography*, edited by Robin W. Winks.

Important collections of essays include the seminal work by J. Gallagher, *The Decline, Revival and Fall of the British Empire. The Ford Lectures and Other Essays*, edited by Anil Seal (Cambridge: Cambridge University Press, 1982), D.A. Low, *Eclipse of Empire* (Cambridge: Cambridge University Press, 1991), W.H. Morris-Jones and G. Fischer (eds), *Decolonization and After: The British and French Experience* (London: Frank Cass, 1980) and R.F. Holland and G. Rizvi (eds), *Perspectives on Imperialism and Decolonization. Essays in Honour of A.F. Madden* (London: Frank Cass, 1984).

Important theoretical contributions include R.E. Robinson, 'The non-European foundations of European imperialism', in R. Owen and B. Sutcliffe (eds), *Studies in the Theory of Imperialism* (Harlow: Longman, 1972) and the same author's 'Imperial theory and the question of imperialism after empire', *JICH*

12/2 (1984) and 'The excentric theory of imperialism, with or without empire', in W.J. Mommsen and J. Osterhammel (eds), *Imperialism and After: Continuities and Discontinuities* (London: German Historical Institute, 1986). A briefer, but equally suggestive study is J. Osterhammel's *Colonialism. A Theoretical Overview* (Princeton, New Jersey: Markus Wiener Publishers, 1997).

J. Darwin, 'What was the late colonial state?', *Itinerario* XXIII/3–4 (1999) addresses the problem of the increasingly complex nature of late colonialism, and the implications of the assumption by colonial authorities of new and challenging roles. The composition, training and outlook of those officials charged with administering the dependent empire are the subject of A.H.M. Kirk-Greene, *Britain's Imperial Administrators, 1858–1966* (Basingstoke: Macmillan, 2000), while Sir C. Jeffries, *Whitehall and the Colonial Service: An Administrative Memoir, 1939–1956* (London: Athlone Press, 1972) provides the insights of a senior official into the context of British decolonization.

A.N. Porter (ed), *Atlas of British Overseas Expansion* (London: Routledge, 1991) contains an unusually varied collection of relevant maps, with accompanying text. A useful compendium of chronologies, glossaries and biographies is provided by M.E. Chamberlain, *The Longman Companion to European Decolonisation in the Twentieth Century* (Harlow: Addison Wesley Longman, 1998).

There is an extensive amount of published documentary material dealing with Britain's changing imperial circumstances. Leading the way is N. Mansergh and P. Moon (eds), *Constitutional Relations between Britain and India: The Transfer of Power* (12 vols, London: HMSO, 1970–83), which is complemented by H. Tinker (ed), *Burma: The Struggle for Independence, 1944–1948* (2 vols, London: HMSO, 1983 and 1984). Similarly useful are F. Madden and J. Darwin (eds), *Select Documents on the Constitutional History of the British Empire and Commonwealth, Vol VI: The Dominions and India since 1900* (Westport, Connecticut: Greenwood, 1993) and *Vol VII: The Dependent Empire. Colonies, Protectorates, and Mandates 1900–1948* (Westport, Connecticut: Greenwood, 1994). A.N. Porter and A.J. Stockwell (eds), *British Imperial Policy and Decolonization 1938–64* (2 vols, Basingstoke: Macmillan, 1987 and 1989) provides a judicious selection of British government documents dealing with colonial policy, together with a series of substantial introductory chapters. More comprehensive collections can be found in the series *British Documents on the End of Empire*, produced under the auspices of the Institute of Commonwealth Studies, University of London, and published by first HMSO and then The Stationery Office. Each volume contains an introductory essay which is in itself a substantial piece of research. Series A consists of general volumes on the policies of particular British governments, and Series B comprises country volumes, such as those covering Malaya and Ghana.

The importance of the Commonwealth in the evolution of Britain's imperial system is the subject of N. Mansergh, *The Commonwealth Experience, Vol II: From British to Multi-Racial Commonwealth* (London: Macmillan, 1982), D. Judd and P. Slinn, *The Evolution of the Modern Commonwealth, 1902–80* (London: Macmillan, 1982), W. David McIntyre, *The Commonwealth of Nations: Origins and*

Impact, 1869–1971 (Minneapolis: University of Minnesota Press, 1977) and *The Significance of the Commonwealth, 1965–1990* (Basingstoke: Macmillan, 1991).

For the domestic political context of policy-making, two older, but still valuable studies are D. Goldsworthy, *Colonial Issues in British Politics 1945–1961. From 'Colonial Development' to 'Wind of Change'* (Oxford: Oxford University Press, 1971) and P.S. Gupta, *Imperialism and the British Labour Movement 1914–1964* (London: Macmillan, 1975). These can now be supplemented with J.G. Darwin, 'The fear of falling: British politics and imperial decline', *Transactions of the Royal Historical Society*, Fifth Series, 36 (1986), N. Owen, 'Decolonisation and postwar consensus', in H. Jones and M. Kandiah (eds), *The Myth of Consensus. New Views on British History, 1945–64* (Basingstoke: Macmillan, 1996), P. Murphy, *Party Politics and Decolonization. The Conservative Party and British Colonial Policy in Tropical Africa 1951–1964* (Oxford: Clarendon Press, 1995) and S. Howe, *Anticolonialism in British Politics: The Left and the End of Empire, 1918–1964* (Oxford: Clarendon Press, 1993).

Studies of Britain's changing economic circumstances during this period include M.W. Kirby, *The Decline of British Economic Power since 1870* (London: George Allen & Unwin, 1981), J. Tomlinson, *Public Policy and the Economy since 1900* (Oxford: Clarendon Press, 1990) and A. Cairncross, *The British Economy since 1945. Economic Policy and Performance, 1945–1995* (2nd ed., Oxford: Basil Blackwell, 1995). R. Floud and D. McCloskey (eds), *The Economic History of Britain since 1700, Vol 3: 1939–1992* (2nd ed., Cambridge: Cambridge University Press, 1994) contains several relevant chapters. P.J. Cain and A.G. Hopkins, *British Imperialism, Vol II: Crisis and Deconstruction 1914–1990* (Harlow: Longman, 1993) is an important reassessment of the metropolitan basis of British imperial expansion. The implications of Cain and Hopkins' thesis of 'Gentlemanly capitalism' for wider imperial historiography are discussed in the valuable collection of essays, R.E. Dumett (ed), *Gentlemanly Capitalism and British Imperialism. The New Debate on Empire* (Harlow: Addison Wesley Longman, 1999).

For an overview of the overseas economic impact of imperialism, see D.K. Fieldhouse, *The West and the Third World* (Oxford: Basil Blackwell, 1999). Essential reading on the Indian economy under British rule is B.R. Tomlinson, *The Political Economy of the Raj, 1914–47: The Economics of Decolonization in India* (London: Macmillan, 1979), which can be supplemented with the same author's *The New Cambridge History of India, III 3: The Economy of Modern India 1860–1970* (Cambridge: Cambridge University Press, 1993).

British colonial development policy is examined in D.J. Morgan, *The Official History of Colonial Development* (5 vols, London: Macmillan, 1980) and the more digestible M. Havinden and D. Meredith, *Colonialism and Development. Britain and its Tropical Colonies, 1850–1960* (London: Routledge, 1993). A very detailed comparative discussion of the late colonial state's attempts to regulate labour as part of the wider development initiative is provided by F. Cooper, *Decolonization and African Society. The Labor Question in French and British Africa* (Cambridge: Cambridge University Press, 1996).

Important studies addressing the role of British business in decolonization include R.L. Tignor, *Capitalism and Nationalism at the End of Empire. State and*

Business in Decolonizing Egypt, Nigeria, and Kenya, 1945–1963 (Princeton, New Jersey: Princeton University Press, 1998), N.J. White, *Business, Government, and the End of Empire. Malaya, 1942–1957* (Kuala Lumpur: Oxford University Press, 1996), M. Misrah, *Business, Race and Politics in British India, c.1860–1960* (Oxford: Oxford University Press, 1999) and S. Stockwell, *The Business of Decolonization: British Business Strategies in the Gold Coast* (Oxford: Oxford University Press, 2000). A detailed study of the responses of one major expatriate firm to decolonization is provided by D.K. Fieldhouse, *Merchant Capital and Economic Development: The United Africa Company, 1929–1989* (Oxford: Clarendon Press, 1994). An overview is provided by N.J. White, 'Business, government, and decolonization in the twentieth century', *Economic History Review*, 2nd ser., 53/3 (2000).

The evolving context of British defence policy is explored in M. Howard, *The Continental Commitment: The Dilemma of British Defence Policy in the Era of the Two World Wars: The Ford Lectures in the University of Oxford 1971* (London: Maurice Temple Smith, 1972), M. Dockrill, *British Defence since 1945* (Oxford: Basil Blackwell, 1988), R. Ovendale (ed), *British Defence Policy since 1945* (Manchester: Manchester University Press, 1994) and P. Darby, *British Defence Policy East of Suez, 1947–68* (Oxford: Oxford University Press, 1973). The security implications of attempting to maintain imperial rule are the subject of R. Holland (ed), *Emergencies and Disorders in the European Empires after 1945* (London: Frank Cass, 1994), T.R. Mockaitis, *British Counter-Insurgency, 1919–60* (London: Macmillan, 1990) and D.M. Anderson and D. Killingray (eds), *Policing and Decolonization: Nationalism, Politics and the Police, 1917–65* (Manchester: Manchester University Press, 1992). The increasingly important function of propaganda is discussed in S.L. Carruthers, *Winning Hearts and Minds. British Governments, the Media and Colonial Counter-Insurgency 1944–1960* (Leicester: Leicester University Press, 1995).

General regional surveys of decolonization are patchy. Africa has been best served, with studies such as J.D. Hargreaves, *Decolonization in Africa* (2nd ed., Harlow: Addison Wesley Longman, 1996), P. Gifford and Wm Roger Louis (eds), *The Transfer of Power in Africa. Decolonization, 1940–1960* (New Haven and London: Yale University Press, 1982) and the sequel volume *Decolonization and African Independence: The Transfers of Power, 1960–1980* (New Haven and London: Yale University Press, 1988). Useful articles include J. Flint, 'Planned decolonization and its failure in British Africa', *African Affairs* 82 (1983) and R.E. Robinson, 'The moral disarmament of African empire, 1919–1947', *JICH* 7/1 (1979). On India, J.M. Brown, *Modern India. The Origins of an Asian Democracy* (Oxford: Oxford University Press, 1985), A. Inder Singh, *The Origins of the Partition of India 1936–1947* (New Delhi: Oxford University Press, 1987) and D.A. Low, 'India and Britain: the climactic years 1917–1947', in the author's edited collection *Eclipse of Empire* (Cambridge: Cambridge University Press, 1991) offer lucid introductions to what is a major historiographical theme in its own right. For the Middle East, see M. Cohen and M. Kolinsky (eds), *Demise of the British Empire in the Middle East. Britain's Responses to Nationalist Movements, 1943–55* (London: Frank Cass, 1998). The historiographical neglect of the

West Indies, which reflected the low priority attached to the region by the British government, has been corrected with the publication of S.R. Ashton and D. Killingray (eds), *British Documents on the End of Empire, Series B, Vol 6: The West Indies* (London: The Stationery Office, 1999). N. Tarling, *The Fall of Imperial Britain in South-East Asia* (Singapore: Oxford University Press, 1993) offers a number of useful essays together covering a long chronological period.

Chapter 1: The imperial system between the wars

J. Darwin, 'Imperialism in decline? Tendencies in British imperial policy between the wars', *Historical Journal* 23/3 (1980) provides an important reassessment of British aims and their outcome, while K. Jeffery, *The British Army and the Crisis of Empire, 1918–22* (Manchester: Manchester University Press, 1984) examines the turbulence of the immediate post-war years. Useful overviews of the imperial system are R.F. Holland, *Britain and the Commonwealth Alliance, 1918–1939* (London: Macmillan, 1981), A. Clayton, *The British Empire as a Superpower, 1919–39* (Basingstoke: Macmillan, 1986) and S.R. Ashton and S.E. Stockwell (eds), *British Documents on the End of Empire, Series A, Vol 1: Imperial Policy and Colonial Practice, 1925–1945* (London: HMSO, 1996). Despite its age, K. Robinson's *The Dilemmas of Trusteeship: Aspects of British Colonial Policy between the Wars* (London: Oxford University Press, 1965) remains an invaluable guide. Developments in the Middle East are the subject of J. Darwin, *Britain, Egypt and the Middle East. Imperial Policy in the Aftermath of War 1918–1922* (London: Macmillan, 1981), the same author's 'An undeclared empire: The British in the Middle East, 1918–39', in R.D. King and R. Kilson (eds), *The Statecraft of British Imperialism: Essays in Honour of Wm. Roger Louis* (London: Frank Cass, 1999) and M. Cohen and M. Kolinsky (eds), *Britain and the Middle East in the 1930s: Security Problems, 1935–39* (New York: St Martin's Press, 1992). Important studies of India include R.J. Moore, *The Crisis of Indian Unity, 1917–1940* (Oxford: Clarendon Press, 1974) and B.R. Tomlinson, *The Indian National Congress and the Raj, 1929–1942: The Penultimate Phase* (Cambridge: Cambridge University Press, 1976). The shifting economic context is discussed in I.M. Drummond, *Imperial Economic Policy 1917–1939. Studies in Expansion and Protection* (Toronto: University of Toronto Press, 1974), T. Rooth, *British Protectionism and the International Economy* (Cambridge: Cambridge University Press, 1992) and D. Meredith, 'The British government and colonial economic policy, 1919–1939', *Economic History Review*, 2nd ser., 28/3 (1975). S. Constantine, *The Making of British Colonial Development Policy, 1914–1940* (London: Frank Cass, 1984) offers a detailed study of the evolution of a new British policy commitment.

The appeal of emigration from Britain is discussed in S. Constantine (ed), *Emigrants and Empire: British Settlement in the Dominions between the Wars* (Manchester: Manchester University Press, 1990) and K. Fedorowich, *Unfit for Heroes: Reconstruction and Soldier Resettlement in the Empire between the Wars* (Manchester: Manchester University Press, 1995). Some of the intellectual, cultural and administrative assumptions shaping imperial policy are explored in A.

Roberts, 'The imperial mind', in A. Roberts (ed), *The Colonial Moment in Africa. Essays on the Movement of Minds and Materials, 1900–1940* (Cambridge: Cambridge University Press, 1990).

Chapter 2: The impact of the Second World War

N. Mansergh, *Survey of British Commonwealth Affairs: Problems of Wartime Co-operation and Post-War Change, 1939–1952* (London: Oxford University Press, 1958) remains a valuable overview, although subsequent archival research has inevitably challenged some of its assumptions. The importance of US attitudes is discussed in detail in Wm Roger Louis, *Imperialism at Bay. The United States and the Decolonization of the British Empire, 1941–1945* (Oxford: Clarendon Press, 1977). J.M. Lee, ' "Forward thinking" and war: the Colonial Office during the 1940s', *JICH* 6/1 (1977) and J.M. Lee and M. Petter, *The Colonial Office, War, and Development Policy. Organisation and the Planning of a Metropolitan Initiative, 1939–1945* (London: Maurice Temple Smith, 1982) examine administrative priorities and policy-making, while J.W. Cell, *Hailey: A Study in British Imperialism 1872–1969* (Cambridge: Cambridge University Press, 1992) is an authoritative study of a major influence on official thinking. The imperial war economy is examined in M. Cowen and N. Westcott, 'British imperial economic policy during the war', in D. Killingray and R. Rathbone (eds), *Africa and the Second World War* (London: Macmillan, 1986), which contains a number of important essays. Detailed studies of wartime policy towards India include A. Inder Singh, *The Origins of the Partition of India, 1936–1947* (New Delhi: Oxford University Press, 1987), R.J. Moore, *Churchill, Cripps and India, 1939–1945* (Oxford: Clarendon Press, 1979) and N. Owen, 'War and Britain's political crisis in India', in H. Jones and B. Brivati (eds), *What Difference Did the War Make?* (Leicester: Leicester University Press, 1993), while African policy is assessed by R.D. Pearce, *The Turning Point in Africa: British Colonial Policy, 1938–1948* (London: Frank Cass, 1982), J. Flint, 'Planned decolonization and its failure in British Africa', *African Affairs* 82/838 (July 1983) and N.J. Westcott, 'Closer union and the future of East Africa, 1939–1948', *JICH* 10/1 (1981). On the Middle East, in addition to those books already cited, M.J. Cohen, *Palestine: Retreat from the Mandate: The Making of British Policy, 1936–45* (London: Elek, 1978) discusses a deepening problem.

Chapter 3: Attlee and post-war adjustments, 1945–51

R. Hyam, *British Documents on the End of Empire, Series A, Vol 2: The Labour Government and the End of Empire, 1945–51* (London: HMSO, 1992) offers an excellent overview, while shorter surveys are provided by D.K. Fieldhouse, 'The Labour government and the Empire-Commonwealth, 1945–51', in R. Ovendale (ed), *The Foreign Policy of the British Labour Government, 1945–51* (Leicester: Leicester University Press, 1984) and P.S. Gupta, 'Imperialism and the Labour government of 1945–51', in J.M. Winter (ed), *The Working Class in Modern British History* (Cambridge: Cambridge University Press, 1983). The increasingly important international context is examined in Wm Roger Louis, 'American anti-colonialism and the dissolution of the British Empire', *International Affairs* 61 (1985), J. Kent, *British Imperial Strategy and the Origins of the Cold War, 1944–49* (Leicester: Leicester University Press, 1993) and the same author's 'The British Empire and the origins of the Cold War, 1944–49', in A. Deighton (ed), *Britain and the First Cold War* (Basingstoke: Macmillan, 1990) and R. Ovendale, *The English-Speaking Alliance: Britain, the United States, the Dominions and the Cold War, 1945–51*. A.E. Hinds, 'Sterling and imperial policy, 1945–51' *JICH* 15/2 (1987) assesses the post-war economic significance of empire, which is also partly the subject of L.J. Butler, *Industrialisation and the British Colonial State. West Africa, 1939–1951* (London: Frank Cass, 1997).

On Indian independence, an authoritative account is provided by R.J. Moore, *Escape from Empire. The Attlee Government and the Indian Problem* (Oxford: Clarendon Press, 1983) and the same author's *Making the New Commonwealth* (Oxford: Clarendon Press, 1987). Developments in the Middle East are covered comprehensively in Wm Roger Louis, *The British Empire in the Middle East 1945–1951. Arab Nationalism, the United States, and Postwar Imperialism* (Oxford: Clarendon Press, 1984), while R. Ovendale, *Britain, the United States, and the End of the Palestine Mandate, 1942–1948* (London: Royal Historical Society, 1989), J. Kent, 'The Egyptian base and the defence of the Middle East, 1945–54', *JICH* 21/3 (1993) and the same author's *British Documents on the End of Empire, Series B, Vol 4: Egypt and the Defence of the Middle East Part I: 1945–1949* (London: The Stationery Office, 1998) deal with specific themes in the region. Post-war developments in African policy are discussed in R.D. Pearce, *The Turning Point in Africa*, R. Hyam, 'Africa and the Labour government, 1945–1951', *JICH* 16/3 (1988) and the same author's 'The geopolitical origins of the Central African Federation: Britain, Rhodesia and South Africa, 1948–1953', *Historical Journal* 30/1 (1987). On Malaya, A.J. Stockwell, 'British Imperial Policy and Decolonization in Malaya, 1942–52', *JICH* 13/1 (1984) and S.C. Smith, *British Relations with the Malay Rulers from Decentralization to Malayan Independence, 1930–1957* (Kuala Lumpur: Oxford University Press, 1995) are especially useful.

Chapter 4: Change and control under Churchill and Eden, 1951–57

D. Goldsworthy (ed), *British Documents on the End of Empire, Series A, Vol 3: The Conservative Government and the End of Empire 1951–57* (London: HMSO, 1994) is an extremely valuable study of a period which has previously escaped detailed attention, with a briefer survey provided by the same author's 'Keeping change within bounds: aspects of colonial policy during the Churchill and Eden governments, 1951–57', *JICH* 18/1 (1990). An older, but still useful study is J.D.B. Miller, *Survey of Commonwealth Affairs: Problems of Expansion and Attrition, 1953–1969* (London: Oxford University Press, 1974). D. Goldsworthy, 'Britain and the international critics of colonialism, 1951–56', *Journal of Commonwealth and Comparative Politics* 29 (1991) examines the diplomatic context of British policy. P. Murphy, *Alan Lennox-Boyd. A Biography* (London: I.B. Tauris, 1999) provides an important study of a figure hitherto neglected in accounts of decolonization. Essential reading for Britain's two most important colonial territories are A.J. Stockwell, *British Documents on the End of Empire, Series B, Vol 3: Malaya* (London: HMSO, 1993) and R. Rathbone (ed), *British Documents on the End of Empire, Series B, Vol 1: Ghana* (London: HMSO, 1992). Britain's handling of the Cyprus question is authoritatively covered in R. Holland, *Britain and the Revolt in Cyprus 1954–1959* (Oxford: Clarendon Press, 1998). Britain's long-term plans in the Middle East are dealt with in P.W. Kingston, *Britain and the Politics of Modernization in the Middle East, 1945–1958* (Cambridge: Cambridge University Press, 1996), while R.L. Jasse, 'The Baghdad Pact: Cold War or colonialism?', *Middle Eastern Studies* 27 (1991) reassesses an important British regional initiative.

On Suez, the most useful introduction, which contains a selection of documents, is A. Gorst and L. Johnman, *The Suez Crisis* (London: Routledge, 1997), while more detailed discussion is provided by Wm Roger Louis and R. Owen (eds), *Suez 1956: The Crisis and its Consequences* (Oxford: Clarendon Press, 1989), W. Scott Lucas, *Divided We Stand: Britain, the US and the Suez Crisis* (London: Hodder and Stoughton, 1991) and D. Carlton, *Britain and the Suez Crisis* (Oxford: Basil Blackwell, 1988).

Important revisionist studies of the economic background are C.R. Schenk, *Britain and the Sterling Area: from Devaluation to Convertibility in the 1950s* (London: Routledge, 1994) and the same author's 'The Sterling Area and British policy alternatives in the 1950s', *Contemporary Record* 6/2 (1992).

Chapter 5: Winds of change, 1957–64

British policy in the Middle East in the aftermath of Suez is discussed in R. Ovendale, *Britain, the United States and the Transfer of Power in the Middle East, 1945–1962* (Leicester: Leicester University Press, 1996) and G. Balfour-Paul, *The End of Empire in the Middle East: Britain's Relinquishment of Power in Her Last Three Arab Dependencies* (Cambridge: Cambridge University Press, 1991). Wm Roger Louis and R. Robinson, 'The imperialism of decolonization', *JICH* 22/3 (1994) is an important contribution to the debate on the purposes of decolonization and the substitution of informal influence for political control. On the shift in colonial policy associated with Macmillan, R. Ovendale, 'Macmillan and the wind of change in Africa, 1957–60', *Historical Journal* 38/2 (1995), P.E. Hemming, 'Macmillan and the end of the British Empire in Africa', in R. Aldous and S. Lee (eds), *Harold Macmillan and Britain's World Role* (Basingstoke: Macmillan, 1996) and T. Hopkins, 'Macmillan's audit of empire, 1957', in P. Clarke and C. Trebilcock (eds), *Understanding Decline: Perceptions and Realities of British Economic Performance* (Cambridge: Cambridge University Press, 1997) are particularly valuable. Studies of specific African developments include K. Kyle, *The Politics of the Independence of Kenya* (Basingstoke: Macmillan, 1999), J. Darwin, 'The Central African Emergency, 1959', *JICH* 21/3 (1993), C. Baker, *State of Emergency: Crisis in Central Africa, Nyasaland, 1959–1960* (London: I.B. Tauris, 1997) and L.J. Butler, 'Britain, the United States and the demise of the Central

African Federation, 1959–1963', *JICH* 28/3 (2000). A. James, *Britain and the Congo Crisis 1960–63* (Basingstoke: Macmillan, 1996) is the first detailed discussion of Britain's response to developments in the Congo.

Studies of the Commonwealth's significance to decolonization include R. Hyam, 'Winds of change: The Empire and Commonwealth', in W. Kaiser and G. Staerck (eds), *British Foreign Policy, 1955–1964: Contracting Options* (London: Macmillan, 1999) and the same author's 'The parting of the ways: Britain and South Africa's departure from the Commonwealth, 1951–61', JICH 26/2 (1998), while L.J. Butler, 'Winds of change: Britain, Europe and the Commonwealth, 1959–61', in B. Brivati and H. Jones (eds), *From Reconstruction to Integration: Britain and Europe since 1945* (Leicester: Leicester University Press, 1993) attempts to relate Britain's first bid to join the EEC to wider, and complementary, Commonwealth and Atlanticist considerations. W. David McIntyre, 'The admission of small states to the Commonwealth', *JICH* 24/2 (1996) deals with a problem arising from accelerating decolonization.

Chapter 6: Imperial aftermath

In view of the 30-year rule applying to the release of British government records, archival research into the period since the early 1960s is still in its infancy. However, a number of useful studies have appeared, including C. Wrigley, 'Now you see it, now you don't: Harold Wilson and Labour's foreign policy, 1964–70', in R. Coopey, S. Fielding and N. Tiratsoo (eds), *The Wilson Governments, 1964–1970* (London: Pinter, 1993) and D.B. Kunz, ' "Somewhat mixed up together': Anglo-American defence and financial policy during the 1960s', in R.D. King and R. Kilson (eds), *The Statecraft of British Imperialism: Essays in Honour of Wm. Roger Louis* (London: Frank Cass, 1999), which also includes K.O. Morgan's essay, 'Imperialists at bay: British Labour and decolonization'. The evolution of the Commonwealth is discussed in W. David McIntyre's 'Britain and the creation of the Commonwealth Secretariat', *JICH* 28/1 (2000) and 'Commonwealth legacy', in *OHBE IV*. The same author's *British Decolonization, 1946–1997*, already cited, takes the discussion further chronologically than most general accounts. A number of older studies, already referred to, remain required reading for this later period. Among them are J.D.B. Miller, *Survey of Commonwealth Affairs* (1974) and P. Darby, *British Defence Policy East of Suez, 1947–68* (1973).

INDEX